25 xmas
tree

Plt 137

YOU COME TOO

YOU COME TOO

My Journey with
ROBERT FROST

Lesley Lee Francis

UNIVERSITY OF VIRGINIA PRESS
Charlottesville & London

University of Virginia Press
© 2015 by Lesley Lee Francis
All rights reserved
Printed in the United States of America on acid-free paper

First published 2015

9 8 7 6 5 4 3 2 1

Library of Congress Cataloging-in-Publication Data
Francis, Lesley Lee, 1931–
  You come too: my journey with Robert Frost / Lesley Lee Francis.
    pages   cm
  Includes bibliographical references and index.
  ISBN 978-0-8139-3745-8 (cloth : acid-free paper)—ISBN 978-0-8139-3746-5
(e-book)
  1. Frost, Robert, 1874–1963—Family. 2. Francis, Lesley Lee, 1931– 3. Poets,
American—20th century—Biography. 4. Frost family. 5. American poetry—
History and criticism. I. Title.
  PS3511.R94Z6529 2015
  811'.52—dc23
  [B]   2015000675

Cover photo: Robert Frost with Lesley Lee (*left*) and Elinor ca. 1941–42

To "the children"
(theirs and mine)

Contents

Illustration galleries follow pages 56 and 142.

Foreword • JAY PARINI

Lesley Lee Francis is the granddaughter of Robert Frost, arguably America's finest—and certainly its favorite—poet. She has spent a good deal of time and scholarly energy over the past decades with projects that involve her grandfather, digging into her family history and its unique relationship not only with Frost but with the art of poetry itself. Building on her previous book on her grandfather, *Robert Frost: An Adventure in Poetry, 1900–1918*, she gives readers a fresh sense of what it might have been like to grow up in the presence of this gifted if complex man who possessed a deep knowledge of the art of poetry, which he communicated to his children during their childhood years.

In *You Come Too*, Francis brings to a kind of conclusion her work of a lifetime, looking closely at the relationship between Frost and her highly gifted mother. It's an intimate book that brings us eerily close to the man who wrote dozens of poems that have become classics of American literature. With an admirable patience, Francis sinks into the life of her grandfather, viewing it in the context of the poetry in ways that illumine the work—as well as the life—in unexpected ways, showing the degree to which good biographical criticism can enhance our understanding of a body of work.

To some extent, this is a book of recollections, structured in roughly chronological fashion, a shadow biography in which the author brings into play a wealth of family portraits and occasions centering on key junctures in her grandfather's life from his time in Derry, New Hampshire, with a young family in tow through the formative years in England (about which Francis has written importantly in her first book on Frost) and beyond. We encounter Frost at work in his teaching and farming lives, and within his family—an aspect of his life that has never gotten enough attention. Francis writes that her book is an effort "to add to the public's understanding of the 'length and breadth' *and* the depth of this man as I knew him: as a husband, as a father, and as a man."

Francis offers loving evocations of the man as well as the poet, saying: "The grandfather I knew was the man in the poems: a brilliant mind dedicated to the creation of revolutionary poetry; a great craftsman able to handle the intricacies of meter as well as the dramatic nuances of synecdo-che, ambiguity, irony, and a sharp wit." But there is no easy idealization of Frost here; indeed, his granddaughter takes into account the many tones and complexities of the personality: "He had overcome swings of mood and despondency through self-mockery and self-deprecation, accompanied by a clear understanding of his place in the world of metaphor and the imag-ination, of what he called 'education by poetry,' that extended to younger poets, his students, and to members of his own family."

Needless to say, this picture of Frost serves as a contrast to the one put forward by some biographers, such as Lawrance Thompson, who wrote an infamous three-volume biography of Frost in the late 1960s and early 1970s that put a harsh spin on the man behind the poems, regarding him as a career-driven "monster," to use Thompson's own term. Many Frost scholars, myself included, have worked diligently to alter this perception, and I'm glad to say that this volume by Lesley Lee Francis adds further evidence to the still-evolving portrait of Frost as a generous poet, mentor of younger writers and students, and father.

One saw the unique approach to her grandfather—his life and work—developing in her previous book on Frost, with its distinctive combination of memoir and criticism. In *Robert Frost: An Adventure in Poetry, 1900–1918,* her focus was on the dynamics that evolved in a family beginning on the farm in Derry up to the time of its return from England, during the First World War, to Franconia. It became clear in that volume that Frost was preoccupied with his children: a point that Francis made abundantly clear as well as palpable in that book. Now she develops this line through the rest of the poet's lifetime and beyond with further detail, amplifying what was there already but not seen in full.

One lovely aspect of the new volume is her wonder at the rediscovery of her grandfather's poetry, an impression that comes through in passage after passage, as when she writes: "Whenever I read—with my adult students or alone—the beautiful poem 'Iris by Night,' my voice cracks when we come to the lines 'And then we were vouchsafed the miracle / That never yet to other two befell / And I alone of us has lived to tell.'" She adds: "My grandfather was right: 'No tears in the writer, no tears in the reader.'"

Throughout this study, Francis makes use of her grandfather's brilliantly written and compelling letters, such as those to Susan Hayes Ward, an early editor and correspondent. One has seen many of these letters before, in var-ious editions, but Francis has an eye for the right quotation, and one gets a fine sense here of Frost's clear-eyed and unswerving ambition, his growing awareness of his own poetic powers, and his obvious delight in the evolution of his own language and thought. One also gets a sense of Frost's productive involvement with other poets, such as Amy Lowell. Francis writes: "Sparring over their differing uses of humor, dialect, and regional peculiarities in their verse, RF and Amy shared a 'little weakness for dramatic tones.' 'I go so far,' RF wrote Amy, 'as to say that there is no poetry of any kind that is not made up of dramatic tones.'" Lowell's response took a similar tack. "It is strange," she wrote back to him, "I come to feel that the dramatic is the great interest in poetry." It's in such passages that literary drama of this book unfolds.

Readers will discover a good deal of interesting material about the author's mother, Lesley Frost, and the role she played in her father's life and vice versa, as in this passage:

> Once back in America, and having finished high school in Amherst, Massachusetts, Lesley entered Wellesley College in the fall of 1917. Her talent for interpreting her early experiences through the prism of her poetic, somewhat romanticized imagination is evidenced in a series of compositions written for her freshman English class. In one, she recalls being seasick: "I came up on deck early in the morning to try to overcome the first attack of sea-sickness by breathing and swallowing the strong wind and rain that were sweeping across the ship."

One can, it seems, learn a great deal about the poet by coming to terms with his daughter's imagination of her father.

The book has a fulcrum, that crucial year of 1938. Everything changed in Frost's life at that point, with the death of Elinor, his beloved wife and Francis's grandmother. "When Elinor collapsed," she explains, "Mother accused her father of bringing on her mother's heart failure by having insisted upon living upstairs where he would not hear the children running above him. In an emotional state, she tried and succeeded in keeping her father from Elinor's bedside until it was too late." In such moments, one feels close to the white-hot center of the Frost family.

In the later parts of this book, Francis writes insightfully on Frost's intellectual life, including his interest in Mexico, Central America, and other ancient civilizations. And the description of Frost in Brazil on tour at the behest of the U.S. government is full of fresh and interesting material, as in this passage:

> While RF, who spoke no Portuguese, delighted in meeting the press and through a translator managed to convey his infectious, if somewhat sardonic, sense of humor, the same was not true of his co-delegate, William Faulkner. According to press accounts brought home by my mother, Faulk-

ner was seldom seen and ran shy of reporters. On one occasion, interviewed in his hotel room, he walked over—a martini glass in hand—to the window overlooking downtown São Paulo, and exclaimed, "*My* how Chicago has changed!" He left the Congress early in order to attend his daughter's wedding back in the States.

There is another fascinating section here about Frost's late trip to England to be honored with a doctorate at Oxford University. Francis writes: "Personal highlights were the meeting with W. H. Auden and E. M. Forster while at Oxford. Back in London, RF and I accompanied the then poet laureate, C. Day Lewis, to Hyde Park to watch the sheep dog trials with border collies like Gillie herding the sheep into corrals on whistled commands from their shepherds." One gets a fine sense here of the rich life that Frost was able to live well into old age.

The journey that Lesley Lee Francis took with her grandfather (literally and figuratively) was deeply personal. "As I draw this account to a close," she writes near the end, "with its passing back and forth between those accounts drawn from memory and those retrieved from research, and while I realize that the two approaches are, in many ways, inseparable, I must hasten to warn my readers of the obvious conclusion: that the man and the poet are one." It's something to bear in mind as we read, and—I predict—those in love with the poetry of Robert Frost will find themselves enchanted, illumined, and grateful to the author for undertaking this journey.

Many of you will recall the events of January 1961 and the inauguration of John F. Kennedy to the presidency of the United States. He and his secretary of the interior, Stewart Udall, had invited Robert Frost to recite "The Gift Outright" during the ceremony. With a few other family members, I participated in this storm-driven and icy occasion—actually, a blizzard of no small proportions. It proved to be only one of a number of highly publicized affairs that we experienced before the death of both men.

Last year we celebrated the hundredth anniversary of the publication in London of RF's first two volumes, *A Boy's Will* (1913) and *North of Boston* (1914). With the recent publication of his *Notebooks* and, this year, the long-overdue publication of the first of what promises to be some four volumes of his *Letters*, we have another opportunity to assess the legacy of our great American poet. A poem I wrote years ago treats the inevitable compartmentalization of a beloved life: "It wasn't until he was dead, buried, and memorialized / That I could measure the full length and breadth of the man. / I was too close." Although the poem is not explicitly about RF, it is certainly applicable to what happened after my grandfather's death in 1963.

My experience adds to the public's understanding of the "length and breadth" *and* the depth of this man as I knew him: as a husband, as a father, and as a man. Evident throughout are the strength and loving support critical to the emergence and recognition of RF, the poet, accorded him by many friends—including a number of strong, independent women. He came to share with others, besides his extraordinary gifts of poetic imagination and craft, his many shifts of mood from despair to exhilaration: they would come to know him over a long life devoted to both family and the poetic imagination. He *did* lodge in our collective memories a few poems difficult to dislodge. There is no favorite poem, but I hope you can experience and enjoy the extraordinary balance and lyrical power in poems like "After Apple-Picking" and "Stopping by Woods on a Snowy Evening," or simply the "sheer morning gladness at the brim" of others.

For me—and I hope for you—listening to certain chamber music; holding and reading a cherished book; contemplating a great Renaissance or Baroque painting or sculpture; repeating from memory a favorite poem are among the private, intimate experiences that touch the soul, that soothe the spirit. My grandfather wanted the best of poets—Chaucer, Henley, Keats, Hardy, and others (a group that probably would include, today, the likes of Heaney and Wilbur)—to be appreciated aesthetically, extending the power of poetry and metaphor as far as it may take us as a people. For each of us, the journey is different—a road taken, many roads not taken—but I hope we can share the goal.

• • •

I grew up in a small family: my mother, Lesley Frost, and my sister, Elinor Frost Francis. Named Lesley Lee Francis after my mother, I was known in the family as Lee. My grandfather, Robert Lee Frost (whose namesake was General Lee, a middle name the poet soon dropped), we called "RF"—although to his face I always said hello to "Grandfather." My father, J. Dwight Francis, had left before I was born; we met briefly at the time I entered college; as a consequence, he and his parents were seldom in touch with us.

My early life, you will learn from this book, was an adventure with Mother: whether in Rockford, Illinois; Mexico; Washington, D.C.; Putney, Vermont; or Madrid, Spain, my sister and I were never without excitement or out of touch with books and the literary life. Certainly, I was aware of the prominence of Robert Frost the poet from a young age, but our visits to my grandparents' various homes, which often included my uncle Carol and his family, and my cousin Robin, were family affairs. My focus at the time was on my studies and getting used to frequent changes of location. At Radcliffe College, it was modern European history; at the University of Miami and Duke University, it was Romance languages that led to the Ph.D.

Only when Mother returned from South America—where she had accompanied her father to the World Congress of Writers in São Paulo—bringing me her notes and clippings was I inspired to research and publish my first article on my grandfather, "The Majesty of Stones upon Stones." Thus I was led on a journey that has continued unabated.

In the search for adventure in poetry, Mother reminded us children of the shifting pendulum or two strong alternating currents between physical action and contemplation, enhanced by the poetic world of the imagination. And I would recall the closing lines from my grandfather's poem "Two Tramps in Mud Time" in which he urges us to join "as our two eyes make one in sight" both vocation and avocation, love and need. My vocation had become that of a professor of Spanish language, history, and literature; helping to run an academic program in Spain; serving for more than twenty years on the professional staff of the American Association of

University Professors (AAUP); raising—as a single parent—my three daughters; becoming an age-group Top Ten in U.S. Masters Swimming. But Robert Frost soon became both a love and avocation, one that I could indulge alongside my other interests, in teaching, writing, and lecturing.

I was raised among women. It wasn't part of a plan, just happenstance. Three of my grandparents' four surviving children were girls; Mother became the dominant figure in her generation; my sister, Elinor, and I knew only a single-parent household, and I, similarly divorced, saw to adulthood my three daughters. Mother struggled financially in significant measure—not because of a lack of talent or work ethic—but because she was born a woman in a man's world.

My grandfather, having emerged into the world of poetry in England and America, found himself no less surrounded by women. Women often were instrumental as editors or simply poetry enthusiasts. A few, such as Amy Lowell, Elizabeth Bishop, Eleanor Farjeon, and Marianne Moore, were successful poets. Seen through the prism of poetry and its power, the world of Robert Frost reflected that power.

If you read my grandfather's love poems—including "West Running Brook," "The Master Speed," and "The Silken Tent"—you will sense the concept expressed in his wife's epitaph: "wing to wing and oar to oar." You will not find here in these relationships a dominance of sexual attraction, lust, or overpowering jealousy. These raw emotions of course exist in RF's poems, but it is the sense of balance, of equality of tension and understanding that underpin the aesthetic ideal of love.

Departing from the annotated scholarly work or textbook, I envision these lives as part of a metaphorical umbrella encompassing personal experience and scholarly revelations. By elevating the internalized spirit of the poems (by RF as by others), filtered through the extraordinary adventures in poetry of my mother, as well as my own interactions within our family, I incorporate my scholarly work into a broader instrument. Unlike my earlier book on Frost—*Robert Frost: An Adventure in Poetry, 1900–1918*—I present here an interactive personal/academic memoir in which my academic research—spanning many years and some fourteen published articles, book reviews, and the like—is an important part of the "journey." Conceived as a seamless entity, moving freely between two separate ways of assimilation—personal experience and research, action and contemplation—the content is nourished equally by the scholarly efforts and quality time with the subject. The enjoyment of poetry, sometimes romanticized, sometimes not—life taken poetically and philosophically—remains fundamental.

Within this context—of "education by poetry"—I pursue several themes:

the dominance of RF's poetry and its transmittal to me through the "poetic" adventures of my mother. Important, too, is the at-home education of the children and the development of their writing and artistic skills; the role of my mother, frequently dismissed or misunderstood by biographers, informs the whole; no less important is a closer look at RF's understanding of women, reached through a life with women (mother, sister, wife and daughters, granddaughters, and women dedicated to the arts in general or to poetry in particular), a life full of tragedies, assimilated philosophically in a Jamesian tradition and expressed in his poems—above all, the poems.

The themes that inspired me, while enjoyed in the company of others engaged in the ambitions of poetry, are an expression of my single, often lonely, journey in and through poetry. Riding on their own emotion, the poems—by RF and others—are the connective tissues that raise us above the daily frustrations, disappointments, even tragedies that can shape our lives. The poetic image, which comes and goes in making form out of chaos, creates the momentary stay against confusion. As the poet discusses in his essay "Education by Poetry," the spirit immersed in the material finds fact-based expression derived from certain core beliefs: "the self-belief, the love-belief, and the art-belief," in themselves closely related to the God-belief. Taking the art of autobiography in a different direction, not as a goal but as the natural association of the disparate threads of the past gathered figuratively through the art of poetry, the result is my personal take on the life of my grandfather and on the particular lives that helped me to understand.

I · BEFORE 1938

$\mathcal{L}$OOKING BACK, can we say we know much about our grandparents or parents: the road they chose or that was chosen for them; whether the choices were in fact made on limited understanding of the broader context of their lives; what emotions, ambitions, inspirations moved them along? And there was always the road *not* taken! I believe we hunger in retrospect for an opportunity to clarify somehow the vision we have of their lives and in so doing give deeper meaning to our own. We long for that lost opportunity to ask what now seem obvious questions.

In more recent reassessments of my grandfather's life and work—by Jay Parini, William Pritchard, Richard Poirier, and others, in the notebooks, prose, letters, many surfacing only now, and, perhaps one day in the plethora of tapes—I think we are making progress in appreciating the wonders of what is most important of all: the poetry itself, in which the man rests his case. Just let the man speak for himself!

The grandfather I knew was the man in the poems: a brilliant mind dedicated to the creation of revolutionary poetry; a great craftsman able to handle the intricacies of meter as well as the dramatic nuances of synecdoche, ambiguity, irony, and a sharp wit. He had overcome swings of mood and despondency through self-mockery and self-deprecation, accompanied by a clear understanding of his place in the world of metaphor and the imagination, which extended to younger poets, his students, and to members of his own family. He was a *good man*—with only average human failings: easily discouraged as an artist and overly sensitive to perceived or real slights; he was a *good husband* to an intelligent, dedicated woman who provided intimate and responsive support to his Muse, and whom he loved unconditionally; he was a *good father and grandfather*, struggling to understand and encourage his often troubled children and to provide critical financial aid to all of them, including my mother.

The Derry Years

It would be difficult to overstate the importance of the Derry years not only in the development of the poet's idiom but also in the formation of a close-knit family. At the time of their move to the Derry Farm, their firstborn Elliott had died and my mother, Lesley Frost, was born. They were a family of three in 1900; by 1905 they were a family of six: Robert, Elinor, Lesley, Carol, Irma, and Marjorie.

The years spent on the Derry Farm in New Hampshire, farming and writing, then teaching and writing, would establish the foundation and provide the confidence for RF to move forward as a poet. He would find time to write in England and Franconia, as well, but it would be here in Derry that the children's at-home schooling and shared family experience would create a lifetime attachment. The acquisition and restoration of the farm by the State of New Hampshire many years later, assisted by the vivid and detailed recollection of my mother, has enabled us better to understand what the Frost family enjoyed during the Derry years, 1900–1911.

The strong family attachment to life on the Derry Farm brought to life for me the story of my grandfather and his family. Directly and through my mother's journals and notebooks, I was drawn into the family dynamics of this and subsequent periods of our lives together.

We have, then, a young, aspiring poet searching for recognition, no less committed as an anxious husband and father. I was drawn less to the biographical data than to what RF liked to call "education by poetry," or efforts to develop the world of the imagination by metaphor and synecdoche and to convey his often moral, often humorous, message, projecting a strength of mind and spirit capable of overcoming the many challenges.

Once graduated from Lawrence High School, and having spent only a few weeks at Dartmouth College, RF realized the need of a career independent of his poetic aspirations. While impatiently waiting for Elinor to complete her studies at St. Lawrence University in Canton, New York, he took over some of his mother's classes at the old Methuen, Massachusetts, Second Grammar School, restoring order among a number of unruly students in the eighth grade. (Only recently, class rosters and attendance sheets signed by RF in Methuen in 1892 were discovered and publicized.) Having moved his mother and sister, Jeanie, with whom he was living, to Salem, New Hampshire, RF continued his teaching at Belle's elementary school, with Elinor assisting when she could. Besides teaching, RF took a number of odd jobs at the Lawrence cotton mills and as a reporter for the *Daily American* and *Sentinel*. Meanwhile, in 1895, Elinor graduated from St. Lawrence University and was visiting her sister Leona White Harvey, a portrait painter, for the summer, when RF finally persuaded her to marry him in a ceremony conducted by a Swedenborgian pastor. Their first son, Elliott, was born the following year, in Lawrence, where the family had moved and where RF and Elinor continued to teach in his mother's school.

Further pressured to resume his studies, RF took and passed for a second time the comprehensive entrance exams at Harvard University, in Latin, Greek, French, ancient history, English, and physical sciences. Despite high honors and a scholarship, as well as a part-time teaching position in a North Cambridge night school, family exigencies forced him, in his second year at Harvard, to abandon his studies and return to Salem, to help his mother through what proved to be terminal cancer. Doctors also warned RF that his overcommitment to teaching and studying had weakened his lungs and advised against continuing in Cambridge. Following the birth of his daughter Lesley, in April 1899, RF returned home to Lawrence.

With support from his grandfather, William P. Frost Sr., a manager in the Arlington Cotton Mill, he decided to take up poultry farming, renting a farm and barn in Methuen and purchasing eggs for incubation. Reaching an understanding with his Grandfather Frost, shortly before his death in 1901, RF agreed to provide his family a source of income as a farmer in return for a promise to give him the twenty years he needed to fulfill his ambition as a poet. Fortunately, RF's grandfather had provided him a home and source of income as a farmer by purchasing the Derry Homestead in nearby New Hampshire. The gift provided a five-hundred-dollar monthly annuity for ten years; its terms passed full ownership to RF in 1911. On thirty acres two miles from Derry Village, the "Magoon property" consisted of a relatively new and spacious house surrounded by an apple orchard and a variety of peach, pear, and quince trees. The Frosts would soon identify with the many trees (maple, oak, beech, and birch), the Hyla and West-Running brooks, the pastures, paths, and stone walls.

The timing of the Frost family's move to the farm coincided with a rash of family problems. The couple's firstborn child, Elliott, almost four years old, died suddenly from an undiagnosed fever: cholera is often mentioned. Robert suffered chest pains and Elinor, never strong physically, succumbed to a deep sadness, briefly entering a sanatorium. When it became apparent that RF's mother, Belle, was dying of cancer, she was moved to a nursing home. Elinor's sister and father were both ill, as well. In the meantime, RF's sister, Jeanie, a graduate of the University of Michigan and a schoolteacher, was increasingly disturbed, creating additional pressure for the family. Belle died in 1900, Grandfather Frost the following year.

In those critical years, home was with Elinor and the children on the Derry Farm. It was here that RF developed his poetic idiom, only hinted at in earlier poems such as "My Butterfly: An Elegy": "The gray grass is scarce dappled with the snow; / Its two banks have not shut upon the river," lines RF singled out as a sign of things to come. Or evoked in the line, "sheer morning gladness at the brim," from "The Tuft of Flowers," suggesting an approach to life's wonders, a philosophy he later embraced that does not measure consequences.

In the unstructured and free environment of the Derry Farm, RF was able to store away unconsciously the mass of material and images needed for his developing idiom: by talks/walking, farming, botanizing, helping raise his and Elinor's children at home, always with the same emphasis on both writing and reading aloud. Papa and Mama, as they were called by their children, shared a central role in their at-home education, to which my mother alludes in the preface to her Derry journals (later published in facsimile as *New Hampshire's Child*):

> It was to Mama we returned with full accounts of our adventures, adventures encountered on our own and out walking with Papa. The house was her castle, her province, and she *was* home. . . . By the time we had divided up the day, even the time of year, there was very little time left over to worry about. . . . Reading (by the age of four) and being read aloud to (until the age of fifteen), I unconsciously heard the warp and woof of literature being woven into an indestructible fabric, its meaning always heightened by the two beloved voices going on and on into the night as a book was passed from hand to hand. We children could linger to listen until we were sleepy, however late.

Life on the Derry Farm was relaxed and varied. While there was little money for the extras we take for granted today, by contemporary standards the Frosts enjoyed a happy and healthy existence. Besides cultivating a garden and orchard and mowing the pastures, they tended to the farm animals.

While RF gradually abandoned poultry farming and farming in general in favor of teaching, he retained a detailed understanding of the business. As with other observations amassed over the years at Derry, the imagination of the poet translated the experience into fine poetry. We find the farmer John Hall in "The Housekeeper," and Charlemagne Bricault in "A Blue Ribbon at Amesbury," and, of course, these poultry farmers are featured in the delightful, witty essays that appeared in the poultry journals while RF was still on the Derry Farm.

Finding himself responsible for four young children—Lesley, born in 1899, the year before the move to Derry, with Carol, Irma, and Marjorie arriving in quick succession—and despite the annuity from RF's grandfather, RF needed additional income. With help from William E. Wolcott, pastor of the First Congregational Church in Lawrence, and Charles Merriam, minister of the local Presbyterian church, RF secured a teaching position at nearby Pinkerton Academy, first part-time and then full-time.

On one occasion, when the Reverend Merriam asked him to recite "The Tuft of Flowers" (and later his Civil War poem "The Lost Faith"), shyness forced RF to ask the Reverend to read it for him as he sat nearby. But by the fall of 1906, once among admiring students and a supportive administration at Pinkerton Academy, he overcame his shyness and threw himself into the rigors of a faculty appointment, teaching five English classes, while tutoring in Latin, history, and geometry. Considered an unconventional, somewhat dreamy teacher, he was praised by most colleagues and by the principal. Popular with his classes, he was invited to coach the Debating Club and to join his students in athletics and on picnic outings; students often visited at his home with his family, where Elinor played the role of the demure hostess. RF's interest in dramatic dialogue found full expression when he directed his students to put on plays at frequent intervals: Shakespeare's *A Midsummer Night's Dream*, Marlowe's *Doctor Faustus*, Sheridan's *The Rivals*, and two plays by Yeats, *The Land of Heart's Desire* and *Cathleen ni Houlihan*, the latter two daringly modern.

But RF pushed himself too far, walking in bad weather each way the two miles to and from class. His health failed; it would take two months' convalescence in the spring of 1907 to recover from life-threatening pneumonia. Elinor, meanwhile, overtaxed herself, gave birth to their sixth child, Elinor Bettina, who died several days later and was buried in the Lawrence cemetery by the Reverend Wolcott. Overwhelmed, RF and Elinor concluded that change was essential to the family's survival.

Robert Frost and the Child

The poet's peculiar approach to the young reader, with its invitation to enter the world of the imagination and intuition, of free association and metaphor, where the natural spirit of literature could be awakened, is fundamental to our understanding of his work.

Since RF came from a family of teachers, it is of no surprise that he ended up as a teacher himself. From his earliest moments in San Francisco, tutored at his mother's knee, so to speak, the urge to teach became so ingrained that even when he tried to walk away, he always returned to the classroom.

As teachers and as parents, Robert and Elinor were preoccupied throughout their lives with the education of their children. Having taught in a North Cambridge night school while at Harvard and assisted his mother in her school at Salem, New Hampshire, RF would go on to teach at the Pinkerton Academy in Derry and the Plymouth Normal School before taking his family to England. Although he described himself as "imperfectly academic," once RF returned to the United States in 1915, his association with academia would be uninterrupted. He liked to say, "I am a teacher; I like to be understood."

When, in 1959, not long before his death in 1963, RF put together a selection of his poems for young readers, he took the title *You Come Too* from "The Pasture" and dedicated the volume to his mother, Belle Moodie Frost, "Who knew as a teacher that no poetry was good for children that wasn't equally good for their elders." The English edition, with a touching foreword by Eleanor Farjeon, carries the same dedication and purpose. Frost chose from among his poems a variety he deemed accessible to the young reader, a young reader treated as an adult, without condescension or patronizing attitude.

In 2000, the Cyder Press published *As Told to a Child: Stories from the Derry Notebooks,* a collaborative production of eighteen stories by Frost with illustrations by his children from the *Bouquet,* a private literary magazine created by the Frost children and their friends in England. The limited edition shows us visually the imaginative world of the Frost family as it was shared between parents and children in New Hampshire and Gloucestershire on the eve of World War I. It is clear, from this and other collaborative efforts that it was his young audience, at home and in the schools, that helped shape his early verse.

As teachers, RF and Elinor sought to convey to the children the intangible concepts of justice, mercy, truth, and love through their readings, but no less through their direct observations: on leisurely walks, identifying the birds and their songs, gathering checkerberries, hunting for orchids, identifying ferns and other flora and fauna. My mother recalled enjoying long walks with her father talking about a wide variety of topics: what is "generally" true, astronomy, dreams, make-believe, fairies and goblins, inventing word games. And she shared her father's excitement and heightened receptiveness to their surroundings: a pasture with groves of pine, maple, or chestnut trees; swinging birches; sitting on stone walls; chatting for hours with friends in town; or following Papa's lead in dealing with her fears— of the cold nights, the dark cellar, sudden movements of animals in the woods, the sound of gunfire, or too much snow, too fast, from a snowstorm coming on.

From letters and other biographical materials, and consistent with my mother's and my own interactions with him, we know that RF cared a great deal about his family. He also cared about the development of young people outside the immediate family. In his poem "What Fifty Said," he noted: "When I was young my teachers were the old. / . . . / I went to school to age to learn the past./Now I am old my teachers are the young./.../I go to school to youth to learn the future."

RF understood the need for dramatic accent and catchiness in verse. The expression is embedded in the lines; certain poems, like haphazard knowledge, stick to you like burrs in the field. He didn't need to tell you, the public, how to read the lines because it's in you. You've all been raised on Mother Goose. The first two stanzas of "Lines Written in Dejection on the Eve of Great Success" are suggestive:

> I once had a cow that jumped over the moon,
> Not on to the moon but over.
> I don't know what made her so lunar a loon;
> All she'd been having was clover.
>
> That was back in the days of my godmother Goose,
> But though we are goosier now,
> And all tanked up with mineral juice,
> We haven't caught up with my cow.

In a conversation with Cleanth Brooks and Robert Penn Warren, he is more explicit about throwing the public "back on their Mother Goose . . . with the play of ideas in it; how deep the Mother Goose is." He recites his own humorously perverted version of "Pussy cat, pussy cat, where have you been?/I've been to London to see the Queen./Pussy cat, pussy cat, what did you there?/I frightened a little mouse under the chair." And that's very deep; it draws you in—the "little insights," the play; in these lines the idea that "you could stay right at home and see it all"—and be a regionalist.

In his teaching methods—or lack of them—with his many students as in verse, RF expressed his ideas on education. In his poem "Build Soil," he explores the problem of a laid-on education in stifling the world of the imagination:

> Keep off each other and keep each other off.
>
> . . . .
> We're too unseparate out among each other—
> With goods to sell and notions to impart.
>
> . . . .
> We congregate embracing from distrust
> As much as love, and too close in to strike
> And be so very striking. Steal away
> The song says, Steal away and stay away.
> Don't join too many gangs. Join few if any.

Join the United States and join the family—
But not much in between unless a college.

Like the French Canadian Baptiste in "The Ax-Helve," he knew that

    . . . the lines of a good helve
    Were native to the grain before the knife
    Expressed them, and its curves were no false curves
    Put on it from without. . . .

He emphasized the need of "reading for pleasure" in "families where the word improvement is never heard." It is preferable, he said, "not to have children remember you as having taught them anything in particular. May they remember you as an old friend. That is what it is to have been right with them in their good moments."

During the years the four Frost children were growing up on the farm at Derry, their parents acted on the belief that reading and being read to were essential to their education. Through their readings, writings, and direct observations, the children were exposed to the clarifying concepts of justice, fidelity, love, and courage, not as lessons imposed by their parents, but as discovery, as experience, as an organic part of the adventure of living.

My grandfather spoke often and publicly about his concern for the quality of education, especially in the high schools. His hope was to elevate and honor teachers through the establishment of endowed chairs in the schools. I was pleased recently to discover online one of many obituaries following RF's death, carried in the January 30, 1963, *New York Times:* "The Frost family suggested that instead of flowers contributions may be made to a Robert Frost fund to establish special chairs for high school teachers. A number of such chairs have already been created in the poet's name, and the project was one in which he was deeply interested. Contributions should be sent to Mr. Frost's publisher, A. C. Edwards of Holt, Rinehart & Winston, 383 Madison Avenue, New York 17, N.Y." Imagine my dismay when efforts failed to track down this fund at Henry Holt & Company, of which Al Edwards served as president and who later served as RF's executor. I came up empty-handed; no record appears to exist. Presented there was an educational concept well worth pursuing. There is no question that a strong high school curriculum is critical to producing students able to benefit from a liberal arts education in college and to go on to other achievements as adults.

Because of their at-home schooling, the Frost children were excused from school in Derry Village. My mother recalls that she was taught the alphabet on a typewriter, and by the age of three was writing, phonetically but legibly, on the machine. By five, I was writing longhand, also legibly, though highly misspelled. . . . My mother taught the organized subjects, reading (the phonetic method), writing (then known as penmanship), geography, spelling. My father took on botany and astronomy. They both went over our stories for criticism, though it was my mother who scanned them first for spelling and grammar. . . . Reading was most important.

Robert and Elinor understood the shaping power of the imagination as an educative force for good. They encouraged reliance on intuition, on the direct observation of human nature no less than of their natural surroundings. They believed that the freedom of association, the trusting view of life, and freshness of response that reduces the distance between reader and writer are strongest in the child. "I think young people have insight," RF would write:

They have a flash here and a flash there. It is like stars coming out in the sky in the early evening. They have flashes of light. They have that sort of thing which belongs to youth. It is later in the dark of life that you see forms, constellations. And it is the constellations that are philosophy. It is like forcing a too early mathematics on a child, to bring him to philosophy too young. We have system and we have plan all too soon now. You know too well and have convictions too well by the time you are forty. The flashing is done, the coming out of the stars. It is all constellations.

Shortly after I drew attention to this quote in my article "Robert Frost and the Child," I heard from friend and poet Richard Wilbur and his wife, Charlee: "We are delighted to see that you continue to tell people of RF's early times with his children. . . . I had not encountered your grandfather's delightful words about the flashes that young people see, and the constellations they may come to see."

My mother's journals and her recollections from this period shed light on the intense interaction and shared family experience. She would recall, for example, how her somewhat anxious dwelling upon fairies and goblins, and the use of her little "stories" to overcome real or imagined fears on the farm, were strongly stimulated by her father and his Celtic roots: he liked to read aloud from books of fairy tales or from his own stories for and about his children. In fact, Mother spoke often of her fears and her father's attempts to allay them. On one occasion, he placed coins on a stump down the road at night and gave one to each child who went in the dark to recover it. She experienced nightmares then as later, at times confusing her dreams for real happenings, as she apparently did with the oft-cited "revolver incident" in which her father threatened violence to either himself or her mother with a gun. She later realized this was probably one of her nightmares. After all, a gun for security and hunting were commonplace in rural New England at the time.

Besides providing a view of the farm that parallels the children's journals, RF's little prose stories for and about his own children reflect the poet's developing poetic idiom. Jotted down casually to amuse the children—perhaps, also, to allay their fears on a cold winter's night—the stories represent a view of life that contrasts sharply with the often grim themes of the *North of Boston* blank verse narratives. Always the poet, RF worked through these stories to catch the tones, strategies, and expressions of living speech: colloquial double negatives, hesitations, what he came to call "the sound of sense." Mimetic mastery and a rich, unsentimental frankness add to the stories' expressiveness and intimacy of detail. The humorous, yet psychologically true, depictions of family situations—with a woodchuck, a squirrel, a monkey, a cow, and even a lion and a rhinoceros—capture our imagination. These are personalized tales in which the children and the animals appear as characters, and, as one reviewer points out, they have the feel of the prose poem and the "implicit presence of the poet's *actual* voice."

In the Derry journals, in RF's made-up stories for his children, and in his verses, we see how one consequence of the persistent concern for the children's education was the enrichment of his own creative genius. As many as thirty of RF's poems coincide with specific topics or incidents treated in my mother's daily compositions. The topics undoubtedly were those discussed during their walks and evening gatherings; the fact that Elinor and Robert read and commented on each journal entry certainly reinforced these mutual associations.

"The Last Word of a Bluebird," included in the *You Come Too* selection, is also from the Derry notebooks. Originally entitled "The Message the Crow Gave me for Lesley one Morning Lately when I went to the Well," the poem was written for and about my mother (growing up, I thought it had been written for me); her father wanted to reduce her anxiety by having the crow send her a reassuring message. Long after he had written them, RF added "as told to a child" to this and another early poem, "Locked Out." The subtitle would become the title of the English edition of his little stories with the children's illustrations.

In "Maple," another poem Frost included in the *You Come Too* selection, we find the names of all four children:

What was it about her name? Its strangeness lay
In having too much meaning. Other names,
As Lesley, Carol, Irma, Marjorie,
Signified nothing. . . .

 .   .   .   .

Better a meaningless name, I should say,
As leaving more to nature and happy chance.

 .   .   .   .

Name children some names and see what you do.

Independent of their biographical significance, apart from a philosophical application of his ideas on education to his own children, it becomes increasingly clear that RF's verses carry in them a literary reflection, a metaphoric translation of the power of innocence the poet celebrated.

Raised near the Golden Gate, Robert "was one of the children told / Some of the blowing dust was gold." And some of his poems, like "In a Vale," with its "misty fen" and "maidens pale," retain the childlike sense of wonder, others the wonder of love. *A Boy's Will*, the title of his first volume of poems, was a tribute to Longfellow, who, in "My Lost Youth," wrote: "A boy's will is the wind's will, / And the thoughts of youth are long, long thoughts." When *A Boy's Will* appeared in London in 1913, the table of contents included a gloss for many of the poems. For "Asking for Roses" (later dropped from the *Collected Poems*), it read, "[He is no dissenter] from the ritualism of youth which is make-believe."

RF moved away from the make-believe in the dramatic narratives of *North of Boston*. But the "imagination thing," the metaphor, the unforced natural thought, were the building blocks of the poet's nature and of his poetry. His mother before him, his wife, Elinor, and his children were imbued with the romantic spontaneity and suspension of disbelief of their early readings.

The accessibility of RF's poems to children and his writing for them were tendencies that led to their inclusion in his poems in varied and telling ways. Given his preoccupation with children and their upbringing, the fact that he taught child development at the Plymouth Normal School, using as text William James's *Principles of Psychology*, and that a number of his poems were published in *Youth's Companion* before 1912, it is not surprising that children appear as a leitmotif in his work.

Besides the two poems mentioned earlier, "Locked Out" and "The Last Word of a Bluebird," subtitled "as told to a child," other poems delve philosophically into the wonder years, often in an adult and challenging con-

text. In "The Black Cottage," for example, he addresses the power of innocence as a "force that would at last prevail" and the reluctance to change
the Creed, causing heartache similar to that of a child missing an "unsaid
Good-night." And again, in "Directive," he describes

> Some shattered dishes underneath a pine,
> The playthings in the playhouse of the children.
> Weep for what little things could make them glad.

He found evidence of the innocence "in the bubbling of children," a common, recurring force in his poems. In "Storm Fear," he writes: "I count our
strength,/Two and a child," and in "The Fear," he defends a child being
out so late: "Every child should have the memory/Of at least one long-
after-bedtime walk." "A Girl's Garden" is a perceptive tribute to a young
girl, suggestive of his own daughter who planted a garden at the Derry
Farm. In another poem, "In the Home Stretch," he describes the encroaching woods "waiting to steal a step on us whenever/We drop our eyes or turn
to other things,/As in the game 'Ten-step' the children play." When "The
Bonfire" appeared in Louis Untermeyer's *Seven Arts*, its assertion "War is
for everyone, for children too" was taken as a radical comment on current
events, much to RF's dismay. "The Runaway"—a favorite in my household—
by inference is about a youngster frightened by a sudden snowstorm:

> "I think the little fellow's afraid of the snow.
> He isn't winter-broken. It isn't play
> With the little fellow at all. He's running away.
> I doubt if even his mother could tell him, 'Sakes,
> It's only weather.' He'd think she didn't know!
> Where is his mother? He can't be out alone."
>
> . . . .
>
> "Whoever it is that leaves him out so late,
> When other creatures have gone to stall and bin,
> Ought to be told to come and take him in."

"Gathering Leaves" reminds us of our children's familiar pastime in the fall
of the year; yet the poem—like many others—conveys its metaphorical message, extending, I believe, to his own collected poem, as he does in "After
Apple-Picking."

RF, who could travel the spectrum of mood and emotion, explores the
darker side of life in "Home Burial" and "'Out, Out—,'" where, in the face of
a child's sudden and violent death, life must go on.

The wonder of unexpected discovery in my grandfather's poems touches me even now. "The Exposed Nest," for example, included in his *You Come Too* selection, makes my point for me. Drawn in by the simplest of human (albeit humane) experiences—the shared experience of trying to save a bird's nest from destruction—the reader awakens to the broader and deeper philosophical considerations of the human condition: the desire to spare exposure to "too much world at once," a common Frost theme; a likely negative outcome to the best-intended acts of kindness; the forgetfulness brought on by turning "to other things." While moral ambiguities persist, the poet and his daughter "saw the risk . . . in doing good, / but dared not spare to do the best we could / Though harm should come of it." Father and daughter "could not wait to learn" if their meddling might make the mother more afraid. Above all, the poem conveys the pride and compassion of a father concerned with protecting a child from life's cruelties.

This example illustrates not only the poet's sensitive observation of natural phenomena but a deep parental anxiety and psychological realism that explain and awaken the heart to the artist's impassioned humanity. *You Come Too,* he beckons. Invited into the unpredictable world of the imagination, of metaphor and the free association of ideas, young and old readers alike may share the underlying sentiments with the open intuition of a child. It is the overriding power of innocence these poems poignantly explore.

The English Years

In retrospect, RF would summarize the importance for poetry of those years on the Derry Farm: "I might say the core of all my writing was probably the five free years [before he started teaching at Pinkerton Academy] I had there on the farm down the road from Derry Village toward Lawrence. The only thing we had plenty of was time and seclusion. I couldn't have figured in advance. I hadn't that kind of foresight. But it turned out right as a doctor's prescription" (RF to Robert Chase, March 4, 1952). He might have added that many of the poems he would write in England were, in fact, drawn from impressions made on him at the Derry Farm and the homesickness he felt for his family's life there.

When the principal of Pinkerton Academy, Ernest Silver, left Derry to head the Plymouth Normal School in the fall of 1911, RF agreed to follow with his family. He soon found himself overburdened with teaching subjects unrelated to literature. Also, the living arrangement, as guests in the new principal's home, was causing friction: Frost children running in every direction; a kitchen in disarray night and day.

By the following spring, RF and Elinor agreed it was time to move away from the distractions of teaching, either by joining two of his students from Pinkerton Academy who had married and moved to Vancouver to write (his preference) or going to England (Elinor's choice). With the family assembled in Silver's kitchen, the toss of a coin came up England. In the decision to pull up stakes and cross the Atlantic, Elinor could now share with Robert and their children "a life that goes rather poetically," the excitement of returning to the land of Palgrave's *Golden Treasury*, and the prospect of living under thatch. Once in England, nostalgia for New England held sway. RF had sold his farm behind him—burning his bridges, so to speak—and leaving him with "the ache of memory" expressed prophetically in his uncollected poem "On the Sale of My Farm" (1911):

> Well away and be it so,
> To the stranger let them go.
> Even cheerfully I yield
> Pasture or chard, mowing-field,
> Yea and wish him all the gain
> I acquired of them in vain.
> Yea and I can yield him house,
> Barn, and shed, with rat and mouse
> To dispute possession of.
> These I can unlearn to love.
> Since I cannot help it? Good!
> Only be it understood,
> It shall be no trespassing
> If I come again some spring
> In the grey disguise of years,
> Seeking ache of memory here.

The pattern begun on the Derry Farm of writing and teaching, teaching and writing, would change upon reaching a decision at the Plymouth Normal School in favor of writing only, choosing to live cheaply from the sale of the farm. Plans for departure in the summer of 1912 moved along quickly.

Leaving Plymouth, my mother, Lesley, had turned thirteen, Carol ten, Irma nine, and Marjorie seven. In her Derry notebook, under the heading "Different Feelings," Lesley wrote: "Excited! If we children were not ex[c]ited the last week or two before we left 'The Cottage, No. 8 Highland Avenue, Plymouth, N.H.' I don't know who ever gets excited. It seemed all like a dream." Nothing suggests the children were aware of their father's determination to be a published poet. "It became increasingly clear," my mother would recall years later, that "all that had been contemplated was fresh scenery, peace to write, the excitement of change."

Knowing no one in England, the Frost family of six left Plymouth on short notice, sailed out of Boston in August 1912 on the SS *Parisian* for Glasgow, taking the train to London. With advice from a randomly chosen bobby, they found inexpensive lodging in the nearby town of Beaconsfield; at the train station, a realtor coincidentally named Frost helped them locate the bungalow.

Once settled in Beaconsfield, outside London, the Frost children put together a 120-page notebook they presented to their parents: on the cover they wrote, "An Important Year by Four Children, Dedicated to Papa & Mamma." (This and other papers, including the surviving issues of the *Bouquet*, from that period were in my mother's possession when she died, and I subsequently gave them to the University of Virginia Special Collections.) Besides the excitement of travel and adventure, the sense of an imminent transformation in their lives permeates its pages: seasickness, seagulls, the desolate coast of Ireland, Glasgow Harbor, a train ride across the purple hills of heather to the London metropolis, and on to the London suburb of Beaconsfield. There their shared excitement would find expression in the gathering together of a few poems into two small manuscripts (lyric and narrative), typed by my mother on the Blickensderfer typewriter brought with them from America. Taking the poems to the London publisher David Nutt, RF was offered a contract for his first two volumes, *A Boy's Will* and *North of Boston*. While it is only a guess why he chose David Nutt, we do know he greatly admired William Ernest Henley, whose first book, *A Book of Verses,* was published by David Nutt in 1888, containing the oft-quoted RF favorite "Invictus" (a title added later):

> It matters not how strait the gate,
>> How charged with punishments the scroll,
> I am the master of my fate:
>> I am the captain of my soul.

The widowed daughter-in-law of David Nutt, the original owner of the publishing house, personally accepted the poems for publication. Madame Nutt, who dressed entirely in black, was a strong French woman—but also self-destructive and bitter. Her autobiography, *A Woman of Today,* was being published at the same time as *A Boy's Will.* Scornful of social institutions, including motherhood, she dwelled on theories of genetic perfection through sound heredity. She may or may not have heard from the publisher Thomas Bird Mosher in America or from John Drinkwater in England about RF's potential as a poet, but she never let on. There is no evidence to support an introduction of any kind here or elsewhere in England. Determined to hold him to four books, refusing to provide him with either royalties or an accounting, and having rejected any settlement offered, Madame Nutt opened the way in New York for Henry Holt & Co. to pirate both volumes of verse. Madame Nutt eventually would return to France, bankrupt and impoverished.

The freshness and surprise shared by the whole Frost family just before Christmas 1912 are revealed in Mother's recollections of the historic moment: "But actually it was not until a morning in 1912 when a card came to a cottage . . . in Beaconsfield, that we knew *A Boy's Will* had been accepted for publication. That was splendid. We were pleased because our elders seemed pleased. We couldn't comprehend, because we had been given no foretaste of them, what resolve, what patience in waiting, had gone into that first book: what a climax, what a beginning, was signified by such a recognition coming at last."

My grandfather was almost forty years old at the time, and the euphoria in the Frost household did not translate into any income even after a second volume, *North of Boston,* was in print. In fact, just before Christmas 1913, with no down payment on the recently signed contract with David Nutt, and with no other income in sight for extra cash for presents, the Frost children descended upon the grocer's back room to barter with their three or four pennies each of spending money, for old wood to make one another presents. In "Good Relief," an uncollected poem, their father captures the poignancy of a child's longing at Christmas:

> But the two babes had stopped alone to look
> At Christmas toys behind a window pane,
> And play at having anything they chose.
> And when I lowered level with the two
> And asked them what they saw so much to like,
> One confidentially and raptly took
> His finger from his mouth and pointed, "Those!"
> A little locomotive with a train.
> And where he wet the window pane it froze.

Friends in England remarked on the resourcefulness of the Frost children in these straitened circumstances far from home. Attempts to place the children in the public schools were abandoned: the poverty, the class rigidity, and the submissiveness of so many of the other children led, once again, to a decision to keep the Frost children out of school. The at-home education by their parents continued, and they soon found writing projects that built on the early Derry journals. They would move freely between friends of their own age and the adults who came and went. Besides the writing, they joined in picnics and long walks in and around both Beaconsfield and Dymock. Despite the crowded housing and the depressing amount of rain and mud, the countryside with its lush trees and flowers created a hospitable environment for the whole family.

RF longed for critical acclaim but was nevertheless amazed by the outpouring that greeted his first published volumes: *A Boy's Will* and *North of Boston*. Although a number of his poems had appeared individually in various journals in America before the family moved to England, finding a publisher and receiving good reviews changed everything. RF quickly embraced public recognition (thus far without remuneration) when it presented itself in England and America in 1913–15, and, for the first time, he and his family were able to enjoy the promise of a steady income.

Having been encouraged by his mother's love of poetry and her Swedenborgian sensitivity, as well as by his own success as a writer in high school, RF had overcome moments of despair. Resisting the pressure from his grandfather and well-meaning friends to leave what had thus far proved a frustrated career, he had stuck to his desire to become a recognized poet, to excel at his chosen craft. Besides cultivating a sense of humor that allowed him to mock the nonsense out of himself, he took steps to avoid activities and groups that tried to divert his efforts: he reminded those who bid for his time that he was a "gyroscope," not a "spin top" and that he was playing "for mortal stakes." What he soon discovered was how difficult it was to achieve a balance between pursuing his ambition and providing for his growing family. The result was a fascinating balancing act, performed on very limited resources and with little encouragement outside the immediate family.

I am puzzled every time I hear academics interpret RF's life as a myth-making, as a deliberate attempt to go to England and "infiltrate" the English scene of poetry, publish his books, and return to America a famous poet—an interpretation that fits neatly into the *mis*interpretation of his famous poem "The Road Not Taken," failing to take into account the "not" in the poem's title or the poem's use of key words charged with emotion: "sorry" and "sigh." We tend to reshape our pasts, to mythologize them after the fact; choosing the right path looking forward is an entirely different matter.

In fact, before leaving the States, my grandfather was very close to submitting his poems for possible publication as collections rather than individual poems in scattered journals. We know that RF had been in touch with Thomas Bird Mosher, a well-known publisher in Portland, Maine. In November 1912, he wrote Mosher from England to alert him to the dramatic turn of events: "I have three other books of verse somewhere near completion . . . and I wanted to be alone with them for a while. If I ever published anything, I fully expected it would be through some American publisher. *But see how little I knew myself*" (emphasis added). He is writing from Beaconsfield at the time that he is negotiating the contract with David Nutt. We will never know when or whether Mosher or some other publisher in America would have published the first three volumes without the events in England. But I believe it was about to happen here, as well.

In the meantime, RF had met other poets for the first time at the opening of Harold Monro's Poetry Bookshop in London: F. S. Flint, in particular, who, in turn, led him to a meeting with his fellow American, the expatriate Ezra Pound, with whom he would enjoy a brief friendship. The circle of literary friends, whose families befriended the entire Frost family, quickly expanded to include W. B. Yeats and the Georgian poets Lascelles Abercrombie, Wilfrid W. Gibson, W. H. Davies, John Drinkwater, Jack Haines, Eleanor Farjeon, and Rupert Brooke.

RF also met at the Poetry Bookshop an aspiring poetess, Mary Gardner, wife of the noted classical archaeologist Ernest A. Gardner. It was through their friendship—at times the source of considerable tension between the archaeologist and the poet—that the entire Frost family was invited during the summer of 1913 to join the Gardners at Kingsbarns, a seaport town near Edinburgh. RF would remember his mother, Belle Moodie: "But Scotland was my mother's country," he wrote home, "and I felt as if we ought to get a glimpse of it. My mother used to sing a song that said she couldn't: 'Oh I cannot get a blink o'my ain countree.'" *My* mother, Lesley, and her sisters and brothers had been exposed to their grandmother's love of Scotland and its literature since early childhood, listening to tales and ballads from the old country during the late-evening family gatherings. My mother wrote of Belle Moodie's influence:

> My grandmother harked back to the shores of the Orkney Isles, to the moors of Bruce and Wallace, to the Border Wars and sailing ships. Her forebears listened to tales as legendary as those of Homer. The shepherds on her Highlands watched the stars as curiously and reverently as had the Wise Men. The captains of her great seaports sailed away, like Sir Patrick Spens, never to return except in balladry. In later years, yielding to an atavistic tide, I, too, was to sail the coasts of Scotland, through the Hebrides, the Orkneys, through Pentland Firth, and come to understand Odysseus and his Sirens. Islands on a "wine-dark" sea as the "many-fingered dawn" appeared, these were his seducers, and mine. I, too, was to plead with my captain to permit

me to go ashore, perhaps forever. For hadn't I heard, as a child in England, our friend Wilfrid Gibson read, or rather chant,

> You sing, and my soul is borne
> To the isles of the outer seas
> To the far, wind-scarred, wave-worn
> Outer Hebrides.

Like any true Highlander or Celt, my grandmother was a mystic. She "heard voices." She believed in "second sight." She dwelt in the "double lives" of Emmanuel Swedenborg, her mentor; the outer and the inner; the actual and the spiritual. The lines he and she faintly drew between fact and fantasy, nature and the nature of man, were all but invisible.

Much of RF's early derivative verse—"La Noche Triste," "Caesar's Lost Transport Ships," "A Dream of Julius Caesar," "A Heart in Charge"—is rooted in such historical sources as Homer, Virgil, Scott, and Prescott, referencing legendary heroes. "A Heart in Charge," never collected, appeared in *A Boy's Will* as "In Equal Sacrifice" and reflects Robert's reading in Scottish history and legend:

> Thus of old the Douglas did:
> He left his land as he was bid
> With the royal heart of Robert the Bruce
> In a golden case with a golden lid.

One of Belle's and Robert's favorite poets was Robert Burns: often considered an artless, natural genius, Burns was, in fact, a well-read intellect and craftsman who broke clear of the decayed British neoclassicism in favor of folklore and song and the strong Scottish literary tradition. No surprise, then, that Robert and Elinor chose the name for their eldest daughter from Burns's well-known lyric "Ye Bonnie Lesley":

> O saw ye bonnie Lesley
>   As she gaed o'er the border?
> She's gane, like Alexander,
>   To spread her conquests farther.

Back in London, RF's historic meeting with Edward Thomas—and his wife, Helen; their daughters, Bronwen and Myfanwy; and son, Merfyn— was the most telling event in 1914; this was *their* year. Their intense literary friendship surfaces as a compelling leitmotiv through the lives of the Frosts and their friends in poetry throughout 1914, in the years until Edward's death at Arras in 1917, and in the ache of memory.

Whenever I read—with my adult students or alone—the beautiful poem "Iris by Night," my voice cracks when we come to the lines, "And then we were vouchsafed the miracle/That never yet to other two befell/And I alone of us has lived to tell." My grandfather was right: "No tears in the writer, no tears in the reader." He was right, too, to move beyond the tribute to Thomas in "To E. T.," allowing the period of mourning to gather the rainbow witnessed by both men into a circle "in a relation of elected friends." The truly romantic friendship that grew and never died between the two poets is one of the more remarkable in literary history.

As Thomas faced the harsh decision to enlist and go to the front, family and friends debated over his choice. He had hoped to join RF in America, where they had planned to put together an anthology and open a summer literary camp not unlike the Bread Loaf Writers' Conference; in any event, Thomas was old enough to avoid the draft. His particular love of country, closely tied to the land, drove him to a deep sense of patriotism. Once Edward was killed at the front, RF wrote a remarkable letter of condolence to his widow, Helen, praising his bravery. He concludes: "I want to see him to tell him something. I want to tell him, what I think he liked to hear from me, that he was a poet. . . . It was beautiful how he did it. And I don't suppose there is anything for us to do to show our admiration but to love him forever. Robert."

RF knew he had lost "the only brother" he ever had. Yet, perhaps better than did her husband, Elinor plumbed the complexities of Edward's choice to enlist and serve at the front, where death was almost certain. She thought money worries had not been a factor. "I think he went in the end," she wrote her daughter Lesley at Wellesley, "because he thought as he was physically fit to go, he ought to go. He thought he could be of just as much use as a younger man. Then, too, his anxiety to try himself in danger." She discounts her husband's belief that Edward's strained relations with his wife and son had a good deal to do with it.

In her college composition, my mother echoed her mother's sentiments: "Then, when the war broke out, after a long and bitter struggle with himself, his strong sense of duty and love of country, for he loved England with that love that few men in this country ever learn, he enlisted in the Field Artillery Corps." After several incidents in No Man's Land—hearing a baby's cry from a house on the front line and watching "a great grey hawk that had been slowly circling above the clouds of smoke swoop down . . . and pick up a tiny field mouse"—suddenly death came. It was Easter Monday, and Edward was killed instantly by a bursting shell. "The relief found him there, dead, and word was sent home to his wife and three children."

While favorable reviews by Edward Thomas (perhaps the best RF ever received), Ezra Pound, and others in England helped promote his reputation, RF strongly resisted the implication that he had been mistreated by U.S. editors and that he should be accepted in England as an expatriate like Pound or Eliot. He felt he had done everything to be accepted back home.

Nostalgia for the sheer wonder and innocence left behind on the Derry Farm had followed them to England and back to New Hampshire. I associate the line from "The Tuft of Flowers" celebrating "sheer morning gladness at the brim" with the early years at Derry and in England. Times were very hard for the Frost family and the aspiring poet. But, at least in those early years, Robert and Elinor consciously sustained the illusion, as mentioned earlier, of "a life that goes rather poetically." Once back in America, however, the suspension of disbelief, the sense of life that allows for elves and fairies, was gone, replaced by the complexities that accompanied the emergence of Robert Frost as a publicly recognized figure.

Franconia, New Hampshire

Welcomed back to America in 1915 as a recognized poet, RF and his family enjoyed a period of rest with the John Lynches in Bethlehem, New Hampshire, where they had visited summers while on the Derry Farm, avoiding the hay fever season and exploring the White Mountains. Walking out along the back roads high above the valley, RF found a small farm overlooking the Franconia Range—the idyllic scenery described in his poem "'Out, Out—'": "five mountain ranges one behind the other / Under the sunset far into Vermont." It was primitive, with no indoor plumbing or electricity. A woodstove in the kitchen and a Franklin stove provided heat for the house, which was smaller than the house at Derry, and an uphill spring supplied water. There was an upper pasture and hayfield, and a barn for hens and one or two cows. Among several woodlots were stands of birch, maple (a sugar orchard), poplar, tamarack, and spruce. As it does today, the farmhouse porch overlooked the peaks of Liberty, Haystack, Garfield, Cannon, Lincoln, and (RF's favorite) Lafayette. A branch of the Gale River flows below the farm, and above it is former pasture now grown up with fir, alder, maple, and birch. Here the family lived off the land for five years, from 1915 to 1920.

Years later, at the same time Mother was busy with the restoration of the Derry Farm, she offered to provide her support for the Franconia project, making it clear that she could not participate in any fund-raising. She wrote a letter, "To the Franconia Place—from the Derry Place," in which she describes the acquisition of the Franconia property: "Well, I remember the day my father and I walked up a hill road out of Franconia and came on the Willis Herbert farm facing one of those spectacular mountain views that the White Mountains provide—this time the Lafayette Range, and my father said 'this is it.' He walked across the lawn to a man digging the spring earth and went straight to the point: 'You wouldn't want to sell me this place would you?'" The sale was soon negotiated; the family moved in, building a shed in the back, a porch at the front.

In summer, the home *was* idyllic. Besides tending the two cows, two calves, and the few hens, the children shared their father's love of botanizing and helped plant a good-sized vegetable garden: peas, corn, beets, squash, cucumber, turnips, and cauliflower. The children helped transplant wildflowers, trees, and shrubs from the woods and meadows to their backyard or to the side of the brook that flowed from their spring. And they were looking forward to entering school in the fall, at the grammar school in Franconia and, for the older children, at the Dow Academy.

In subsequent years, as Lesley, Carol, and Irma spent more and more time away from Franconia, Marjorie, the youngest—only ten on her return from England in 1915—developed a deep attachment to their new home. Upon her tragic death in 1934, her parents ordered the printing by the Spiral Press of a small book of her poems entitled *Franconia* (1936). Here is Marjorie's title poem:

> Long, long ago a little child,
> Bare headed in the snow,
> Lay back against the wind—and smiled,
> Then let her footsteps blow.

> Lighter than leaves they blew about,
> Until she sank to rest
> Down where no wind could blow her out,
> Deep in a mountain nest.

> And to this day she's smiling there
> With eyes alert and wild,
> For she has lived on mountain air
> And stayed a little child.

Above all, the setting provided RF with the time to renew the rhythm of his poetry, to listen to the live speech of local people, to work "as a poet, in the margins of farm life." He had not written seriously since leaving England; now he experienced a renewed burst of creativity that included "Brown's Descent," "The Gum Gatherer," and "The Vanishing Red."

But by late August, a northern chill blew down from the north, and by September the first freeze left nothing but beets and turnips to harvest. RF and Carol struggled to build a henhouse as winter descended—and with it, illness. In addition to frequent colds for the entire family, Elinor found herself pregnant and extremely unwell. RF wrote Lascelles Abercrombie in England: "You will be sorry to hear that Elinor is altogether out of health and we are in for our share of trouble." This, her seventh pregnancy, ended when, in late November, she had a miscarriage that further weakened her heart.

By Christmas week, Elinor was recovering her strength, and the children were enjoying winter sports during the school holidays. Years later, my mother recalled the importance of Christmas in her childhood:

> I doubt whether any children, in any clime, in any Christian land, could have anticipated the joy of Christmas Eve and Christmas dawn (early dawn!) with any more excitement than was felt by the four Frost children. . . . Christmas was for us a long-drawn-out anticipation. It began as early as October-November,
>
>> "When between whirls of snow not come to lie,
>> And whirls of foliage not yet laid," [lines from "Christmas Trees"]
>
> we went scouting for a well-shaped pine or balsam or spruce through our own wood lot. . . . The proud child was the one who had spotted the "perfect tree," the one symmetrically rounded, slimly tapered, and not too tall for the bay window of our front living room. It became, long before it was cut, a sort of symbol, the *raison d'etre* of our Christmas preparations.

From my mother's Derry journals, we have two entries for January 1907 by the eight-year-old Lesley that reinforce the importance of Christmas as a family event (unedited):

> This year all the children were anxshus to know what they were going to have for Cristmas, espechily Irma. Every time Mr. Pirkins [the mailman] drove into the yard Irma would ask mama what he had brought us for Cristmas, but mama wouldn't tell. When Cristmas night came we children hung up our stockings and went to bed. We were expecting santa claus to come in the front room that night and give us things. We went to sleep as quick as we could.
>
> The next morning we woke up early to see what we had for Cristmas, but mama wouldn't let us go down intill the sun came up. When we came down stairs we ran to the kitchen door to go out and dress. As soon as we got out there we found that santa claus had come out there instead of in the front

room. After we had looked at all the things, there was a rocking chair and doll and a dog with a little bell tied around his neck and pichures for Irma, and there was a train or cars and a pig and a pigs trogh and a pig pen and a little boat and a ball and some pichures for Carol and a ball and a doll and a rocking chair and a kitty and some pichures for Marjorie, and some dominoes and some dice and a ruler and a little tracing and drawing book and two dolls and a rabbit for me, and there was a blackboard and some candy for all of us together. After we had looked at them all a minute we dressed and ate breakfast and had a happy time all day long playing with our toys. That night papa played dominoes with me and Carol, then we had supper and went to bed very happy.

Papa Goes to See Santa Claus

One day before Christmas papa said to us I am going out in the alders to see santa claus and I must take the axe. I tried to make him tell me what he was going to do with the axe but he would not. After he had gone we went out on the hill and shouted about santa claus till papa could not stand it and he sent us home. Pretty soon papa came home. But he would not tell us what santa claus said. And we never knew till Christmas what papa went out there for. It was a Christmas tree. jan 17 1907

Besides the entries in her Derry journals and her article "Our Family Christmas" in *Redbook Magazine,* my mother edited an anthology, *Come Christmas* (1929); in a subsequent printing, her father gave her permission to include as a frontispiece the uncollected poem "Good Relief," quoted earlier as a reflection of the real hardship for the children at Christmastime.

Come Christmas 1915 in Franconia, we have a record of letters from both Lesley and her father shedding light on two contemporaneous poems: "Two Look at Two" and "Christmas Trees." The first, dated December 20, from Lesley to a young friend in England, Delphis Gardner, was miraculously discovered in Ireland this past year.

In her letter, Lesley touches upon a variety of relevant topics: reference to the *Rein,* a magazine produced by Delphis Gardner paralleling Lesley's *Bouquet* (both now in Special Collections at the University of Virginia); mention of the war and of Belgian children; a vivid description of the wintry weather and the children's activities, including sliding, skating, and school; how "a deer ran across the pasture behind the house a short time ago and when mama and papa went up in the woods a few minutes after *a buck and doe stood within a few feet of them and looked quietly at them and then softly trotted off among the firs*" (emphasis added); a description of "*Christmas trees* this year, for we have many acres of lovely firs of different sizes" (emphasis added); a nostalgic comparison of the New Hampshire "winter of snow and ice and white trees and mountains and sunny days" and the "daffodils and pale blue skies of the English springs and the green grass all year round"; and, at the end, reference to her mother's illness and slow recovery.

Here we have, then, in 1915, a clear description of an event that in all likelihood inspired her father's poem "Two Look at Two." It wasn't until 1920 that the poet distributed early drafts containing an additional fourteen lines that were deleted from the first published copy in 1923 (*Mountain Interval*). Lesley was still typing her father's poems (as she did in assembling *A Boy's Will* and *North of Boston* in Beaconsfield) on the old Blickensderfer that accompanied the family to and from England and had been reassembled by Carol in Franconia.

"Two Look at Two" is a lyric/narrative poem in which a couple, late in the day and about to turn back down the wooded mountainside, stands facing first a doe and then a buck as they emerge singly from behind a spruce and then as each "passed unscared along the wall." The poem goes beyond the direct observation of the quiet passing of the deer to create a balance between the impulses of the heart and the mind; despite the distance and tension between the human and the natural, the lovers project their tenderness on the doe and buck, in an exalted and unifying moment of wonder devoid of sentimentality. The poem ends in one of the poet's "as if" moments, confirming the couple's human love by advancing a powerful illusion of earthly response: "Still they stood, / A great wave from it going over them, / As if the earth in one unlooked for favor / Had made them certain earth returned their love."

No less felicitous from a literary viewpoint is Lesley's loving description of the Christmas trees: "We have enough of Christmas trees this year, for we have many acres of lovely firs of different sizes. I wish we could bring one in with the white snow heavy on its branches. It would be prettier than if it was decorated with paper and tinsel." What an enchanting prelude to her father's poem "Christmas Trees," apparently written during the holidays. As noted, on December 19, RF sent a handwritten copy of the poem to Lois Frances Tilley, who, together with her parents, Mabel L. and Morris Palmer, was a neighbor of the Frosts in Franconia. Her father was a professor of English at the University of Michigan, where RF later taught. And, on December 24, RF sent another copy to his friend Louis Untermeyer. Each copy of the poem carried a distinct watercolor illustration signed "Lesley" by my mother. In his cover letter to Miss Tilley, RF apologized for not repaying her and her mother's kindness "with something better than this Christmas thing the *children and I have been playing with* [emphasis added].

. . . We are in better spirits here than we have been, for we have Mrs. Frost up and around with us again." He ends the poem:

A thousand Christmas trees I didn't know I had!—
Worth more it seemed to give away than sell.
Too bad I cannot lay one in a letter.
I can't help wishing I could send you one
(I could spare one and never feel the difference)
In wishing you herewith
A Merry Christmas
   For
      Miss Tilley and her mother
       from
         Robert Frost
          and the children.

And Mrs. Frost wishes to be remembered though she had no part in this nonsense.

In 1929, "Christmas Trees" was chosen by Joseph Blumenthal at the fledgling Spiral Press to print as a Christmas card (with sewn silver-coated wrapper) from him and his wife, Ann. Of the 275 copies, Blumenthal kept 75 for himself; the rest he gave to RF's publisher, Henry Holt & Co. Apparently, Blumenthal failed to include RF in the printing; gently admonished by the poet, Blumenthal was able to recover several copies and send them to Frost. This idea of a Christmas greeting—subsequently using an as-yet unpublished poem and with RF's input—resulted in a tradition most years until 1962, shortly before the poet's death. (By 1962, the press run was for 17,055 copies with twenty-one variant names imprinted!)

What I find remarkable about these Christmas events in Franconia is how they reinforce my understanding of the sharing of impressions, ideas, images, even metaphors, in the give-and-take between Robert Frost—as poet, teacher, husband, and father—and his wife and children. Not only did RF consider Elinor a part of each poem, he found delightful ways to bring the children into the world of the imagination as part of their daily lives. The shared family experience that had begun in Derry with the at-home education, the "education by poetry" offered by Elinor and Robert, was built upon in England and continued in Franconia. Despite constant worries about money and illness, the shared love of place and the feeling of wonder survived.

The Stone House and the Gully

RF had purchased the eighteenth-century "Peleg Cole" house in July 1920 at the urging of Dorothy Canfield Fisher, a close friend in nearby Arlington. The family had found the Frost Place in Franconia, located in the White Mountains in northern New Hampshire, inhospitable to the plantings of apple trees and other farm products. Mother no longer lived at home, but Irma and Marjorie needed better and more accessible schools, and Carol wanted to farm. Furthermore, Dorothy Canfield Fisher convinced him that the charming, historic stone house in South Shaftsbury would make the perfect home for his son, Carol, and Carol's wife, Lillian. The property featured eighty acres of land for farming, and Vermont had a warmer climate for orchards and gardens; New York and the railroad were nearby. RF wrote friends that he planned to plant a "new Garden of Eden with a thousand apple trees of some unforbidden variety." That same year, 1920, *Harper's Magazine* published his poem "Good-by and Keep Cold," about "an orchard so young in the bark/Reminds me of all that can happen to harm/An orchard away at the end of the farm/All winter. . . ." Carol and Lillian's son was born there in 1927: their only child, Prescott. It would be Prescott alone in the Stone House—his mother seriously ill in hospital—when his father committed suicide, and it would be RF who praised the young teenager for his extraordinary courage.

At Christmas 1928 RF purchased the Gully farm, only a mile away, where he and Elinor could avoid crowding the children. It was a poor little cottage built in a high hollow that ran between two ridges—hence the gully—on a lot of 153 acres, 50 of them in woods. Although there was no brook, a live spring was later developed as a frog pond.

Recently returned the same year from a trip to England and France, taking Marjorie with them, the Frosts decided to invite several artists—artists in need of help during the Depression—to live at the Gully and help convert the farm into a more livable space: Wade Van Dore and J[ulius] J. Lankes accepted the invitation. Van Dore, a young poet from Ann Arbor and a former student of RF's at Amherst College, whose philosophical precepts of Thoreau made him more than happy to serve as caretaker and handyman of the property, later published *A Life of the Hired Man,* which describes his friendship with RF as fellow naturalists. At the Gully, he was soon joined by Lankes, a struggling artist known primarily for his woodcuts, who had completed the illustrations for two of RF's books, *New Hampshire* and *West-Running Brook.* Both men were buoyed by the strenuous outdoor and indoor renovations they undertook. Although their arrangement at the

Gully was short-lived, Frost and Lankes's close, symbiotic friendship would last for decades, until Lankes's death in 1960.

The Gully became another one of those houses we children loved to visit, walking back and forth from Carol and Lillian's home in South Shaftsbury, swimming in the pond (full of pollywogs and frogs), and roaming freely the delightful countryside.

Robert Frost and Women

At home, RF found himself surrounded by women. His mother, Isabelle Moodie, was born in Leith, Scotland; her father having been lost at sea and her mother having abandoned her family, Belle traveled with her grandmother to America sometime between the ages of eight and twelve. Left with an uncle, Thomas Moodie, who was married to a Scottish woman, Belle was raised in Columbus, Ohio, where she became a successful schoolteacher. Invited by RF's father, William Prescott Frost Jr., who, upon his graduation from Harvard, had been appointed principal of the very small Lewistown Academy in Pennsylvania, Belle joined him at the academy for the year 1872–73. Belle, several years older than William, had a hint of a burr in her musical and lively conversation as well as a strong social and cultural background, an aristocratic bearing, beautiful deep-set dark brown eyes, and a mass of auburn hair. She was soon courted by the principal, who overcame her religious convictions with his own charms: he was extremely gifted, capable, strong-minded, handsome, and athletic, with penetrating, cold blue eyes. They were soon married.

The Board found itself unable to pay its staff, forcing the resignation of the young couple. Belle would follow her husband to San Francisco, where he had long hoped to enjoy an adventurous life in journalism. Belle's mystical devotion to her Swedenborgian faith and her deep response to poetry and other literature drew the couple apart, and their children, Robert and his sister, Jeanie, would be raised in the shadow of her powerful personality. Her artistic idealism and spiritual sensibilities revealed themselves in her poem "An Artist's Motive" (published in her husband's paper, the *Daily Evening Post*, on March 29, 1882) and in her prose fairy tale *The Land of Crystal; or, Christmas Day with the Fairies* (a booklet printed on December 10, 1884). The early death of her husband from consumption left Belle and the children penniless, and they were forced to return to his family in Lawrence.

RF's sister, Jeanie, born in Lawrence, Massachusetts, during a brief separation of her parents, was a very bright child; she graduated from Lawrence High School and the University of Michigan, starting a career as a schoolteacher. Tragically, during World War I, Jeanie was arrested in Portland, Maine, for the exhibition of severe symptoms of paranoia. Under her brother's guardianship, she was committed in 1920 to the Augusta, Maine, state hospital, where RF continued to visit her until her death in 1924.

And, of course, his wife, Elinor, co-valedictorian with Robert of their Lawrence High School class, joined her sister Leona in developing skills as an artist, which she passed along to her children. Marjorie would write some fine poems before her untimely death; Irma and Carol, overcome by mental illness, both tried to write. Carol dreamed of becoming a poet himself; Irma tried to study sculpture before succumbing to her bipolar delusions. Robert and Elinor did everything they could to help their troubled children.

The fact remains: in the Frost family, my mother, Lesley, stood alone and strong for a life of adventure, stimulated by her parents as a child but ready to fly as soon as age and circumstance allowed. She alone lived to return over and over again to the motivating ambitions of the literary life. She alone, in sharp contrast to her father, and despite ongoing financial challenges, embraced a life of constant physical activity in which she told me she "never suffered from depression."

As a working poet, during the years prior to Elinor's death in 1938, RF found himself in the company of professional women dedicated to poetry, like-minded in their search for "ulteriorities" and active participants in the struggle for public recognition of their art.

The simple fact was that women were often the enthusiasts for poetry: my grandfather remarked that it was not unusual for a man to approach him at a public gathering, shake his hand, and sheepishly declare, "My wife loves your poetry." Women in general often embraced the arts or were found in low-paid editorial positions. While both men and women enjoyed the poet's often witty and philosophically driven conversation and friendship, very little attention has been given to RF's understanding and appreciation of women, stemming in part from his home life, but no less so from his study and teaching of William James's *Principles of Psychology*, as well as from the direct observation of the farmhands in his adopted region of New England.

Besides noting the close personal support of his family, it is not difficult to name others who informed both my grandfather's and my own journey: Susan Hayes Ward, Harriet Vaughn Moodie, Amy Lowell, Eleanor Farjeon, Kathleen Morrison, and, in my family, my aunt Lillian, my sister, Elinor Francis Wilber, and, first and foremost, as central to *my* story, my mother, Lesley Frost, the natural link between my grandfather and me. There are,

I am sure, others worthy of mention—Marjorie Kinnan Rawlings and Elizabeth Shepley Sergeant come to mind. But those I spend time with *here* extended their friendship beyond literary considerations to an empathetic participation in the lives of the Frost family as a whole.

Narrative Verse (*North of Boston* and *Mountain Interval*)

Once I started sharing my grandfather's poems with others (in lectures and my adult classes), my admiration for his awareness of the psychology of women grew, both in general and in particular—clearly and brilliantly portrayed in his narrative verse. He seemed keenly aware of the raw deal many women were dealt, often frozen into demeaning, monotonous functions as wives or caretakers and often with no one to blame.

Focusing on the *North of Boston* and *Mountain Interval* narratives, it is easy to illustrate the powerful, highly individualized portraits of women: in "The Death of the Hired Man," "Home Burial," "The Black Cottage," "A Servant to Servants," "The Housekeeper," "The Fear," and, from *Mountain Interval*, "In the Home Stretch" and "The Hill Wife."

"The Death of the Hired Man" deals with a farmhand who has come "home" to die. In human and humane terms, the dialogue contrasts, without villains and with both love and understanding, the two viewpoints: Warren's concern that he and Mary will have to put up with Silas's failing efforts to farm his land rather than seeking help from his better-off relatives; Mary's realization that Silas has come "home" to die: "home is the place where, when you have to go there,/They have to take you in," we are told. Before Warren goes to check on Silas himself, his wife's tenderness and concern for Silas seem to transfer to the man she loves. He returns: "'Warren?' she questioned./'Dead,' was all he answered."

Because "Home Burial" deals with events all too familiar to Robert and Elinor Frost, in the loss of their first son, it is a painful document to read; RF seldom referred to it or recited it in public. What we might look at here is the powerful and remarkably balanced portrait of parental anguish: there are no villains, no winners in the battle over how best to express one's grief. Both viewpoints are passionate, hurtful, yet loving at the same time: ". . . in the face of love," the husband reminds his wife, Amy. It would take a strong woman—Elinor Frost—to read or listen to this poem, yet she fully understood its dramatic power.

"The Black Cottage" shows how strong the image of the sons' mother (since died) prevailed in her innocence over the race issue raised by the Civil War. She had supposed that the war had decided that:

What are you going to do with such a person?
Strange how such innocence gets its own way.
I shouldn't be surprised if in this world
It were the force that would at last prevail.

The minister who accompanies the narrator goes on to explain that he would not change the Creed, with its unpopular, pagan reference to Hades. He is stopped by "the bare thought/Of her old tremulous bonnet in the pew." Of course, RF uses the opportunity to expound on his belief that truths go in and out of favor: "Why abandon a belief/Merely because it ceases to be true?" the minister adds.

Richard Poirier's assessment that "Frost's sense of the plight of women who have nothing to do but a home to keep . . . is responsible for a series of remarkable poems about the frustrations of the imagination and its consequent expression in the distorted forms of obsession, lies, or madness expression" clearly applies to "A Servant to Servants," in which a woman and her husband, Len, have moved to a lakeside property where she cares for the handymen. She unburdens herself to a stranger, realizing that she has nowhere to go, she will always be behind in her work, and may end up where her insane uncle did, in a cage in the attic. Her loneliness and the unending pointlessness of her life are overwhelming.

In "The Housekeeper," Estelle's mother is also trapped by circumstance. Her daughter has run off and married another man, leaving her common-law husband, John Hall, behind on the farm, no longer of any worth. There seems to be no escape for him, either. What interests the reader (as it does the unidentified narrator, a friend of John's, apparently) is what kind of a life the three of them have had together and will not have in the future. Estelle's mother ("the housekeeper") plans to join her daughter as soon as possible, leaving John, whether rightly or wrongly, all alone.

During RF's poultry days on the Derry Farm, John Hall was a friend of RF's who helped him in the raising of poultry and was a subject in his poultry essays and poems. As poet, RF leaves these troublesome relationships unresolved. In a rural setting where making a living is difficult at best, RF gives us a portrayal of his characters that is neither flattering nor villainous.

In "The Fear," the wife and Joel contemplate the possibility of a threatening visitor late at night whose face she says she has seen. It is left ambiguous just what she is afraid of, perhaps an extra- or premarital lover or simply an intruder. The circumstances with the lantern light, a real man and child out walking on a lonely road at night, and the mounting tension with her husband add to the drama.

"In the Home Stretch" also reflects the wife's sense of entrapment in a domestic setting. The first lines establish the metaphor of the kitchen window over the sink: "She stood against the kitchen sink / And looked out through a dusty window / At weeds the water from the sink made tall." Here is where she will come to stand "and go the round / Of many plates with many towels many times." She realizes that when she and her husband, Joe, decided to move to the farm, the daily routine would not change, but she is pleased that he is pleased. They try to reassure each other as the movers help them settle in. Joe talks of going the rounds—after a night's sleep—"of apple, cherry, peach / Pine, alder, pasture, mowing, well, and brook. / All of a farm it is." With the couple having retired exhausted from the move, and only the stove throwing off light, the poem ends on a comforting metaphor: "The fire got out through crannies in the stove / And danced in yellow wrigglers on the ceiling / As much at home as if they'd always danced there."

The headings for the five parts of "The Hill Wife" tell it all: "Loneliness"; "House Fear"; "The Smile"; "The Oft-Repeated Dream"; "The Impulse." Culminating in the impulse, a young bride, in loneliness and fear, strays away from home and never returns:

> Sudden and swift and light as that
>   The ties gave,
> And he learned of finalities
>   Besides the grave.

If we include "The Witch of Coös," published much later in *New Hampshire*, where the wife's former lover rattles around in the old farmhouse as a skeleton in the attic, we can imagine a whole chorus of female voices, soft and tender to obsessed and shrill; where one wife abandons her partner, another loves and endures. At times lonely and estranged himself, RF balances the impact of drama, fear, and abandonment with empathy and understanding.

Whether we search for RF's female characters in his dramatic narratives or return to such love poems as "Two Look at Two" and "West Running Brook," I would agree with Dana Gioia that there is nothing "antiquarian about Frost's dramatic narratives, which are more rooted in realist fiction and theater than in neo-classical pastoral verse." RF expresses an affinity for his diverse characters, representing, as they do, his northern Yankee region, and to whom he never condescends. Avoiding judgment, his dramatic poems mostly just end rather than conclude. Gioia brings Frost's dramatic verse into the Modernist tradition. While he describes a series of bases for this interpretation, of special interest for this discussion of the women in the poems, his reference to RF's "powerfully psychological characterizations" is of particular relevance here.

His Equals in Poetry: Susan Hayes Ward, Harriet Monroe, and Amy Lowell

A parallel aspect of my research on the broad topic of the role of women in RF's search for recognition are his expressions of warmth and appreciation for the genuine affection and moral support a number of literary women provided him in his struggles. I soon identified three women outside the immediate family—Susan Hayes Ward, Harriet Monroe, and Amy Lowell—who stand out for their personal courage as women and as taste setters in poetry, and who, at the same time, extended their concern and affection to the entire Frost family.

The long, empathetic correspondence between my grandfather and Susan Hayes Ward began in 1894 with the acceptance of "My Butterfly: An Elegy" for publication in the *New York Independent,* of which Miss Ward was literary editor. The aspiring poet had maintained a considerable distance from the debate over the direction his poetic efforts were taking. Determination to be his own editor and to develop a coherent aesthetic doctrine and disciplined craft was tempered by shifting moods and occasional irritability, by a wry and often self-deprecating humor, and by the complex process of maturing not only in his technique and idiom but as well in the more profound areas of philosophical and spiritual convictions. Given his youth, his inner toughness was remarkable.

RF's poetic ambitions led him to submit his poems for publication even before his graduation from Lawrence High School. Having received his share of rejections, he was buoyed by Miss Ward's acceptance of "My Butterfly," and even more so by its appearance on the front page of the November 8 issue of the *Independent.* The semi-religious weekly had been expanded to cover politics, social and economic trends, history, literature, and the arts under the guidance of Miss Ward's brother, the Reverend Dr. William Hayes Ward, who had joined the paper in 1868 as associate editor, advancing to superintending and then honorary editor before his death in 1916.

The Ward siblings were from an archetypal New England family. William Hayes Ward, a progressive missionary and a scholar in the classics and archaeology, also wrote religious poetry and literary criticism, including a lengthy memorial to Sidney Lanier, whom he and Susan greatly admired and promoted in literary circles. Neither Susan nor her sister, Hetta, married. Having graduated from the Berwick Academy in Maine and from

Wheaton College in Massachusetts, Susan and her sister studied art and foreign languages in a number of European capitals before joining their brother in the Old Stone House in Newark, New Jersey, where they wrote on a variety of subjects for the *Independent*. Miss Ward's contributions reflected her lectures on American and English poets and philanthropic subjects related to her service on charitable boards.

RF doubtless stood in awe of the illustrious Ward family, but he instinctively trusted Susan's spiritual strength and intelligence. Her encouragement was vital to the still tentative poet and made him feel he "could afford to be modest" and could convey, at least to her, his fluctuating moods of elation and self-doubt. Besides strong feelings of gratitude, the early letters to Miss Ward reveal a willingness to accept her suggestions for revising his poems, although Susan did not herself attempt to alter his verses.

Miss Ward had shown "My Butterfly" to her brother and had read the elegy to Bliss Carman and Charles Roberts in Washington, D.C., for their approval. The poem was also sent to Maurice Thompson in Indiana and to the Reverend William E. Wolcott in Lawrence. Through Miss Ward, RF received the praise for which he yearned; he also received stern remonstrations (similar to those heaped on him by his grandfather): to go back to Dartmouth and complete his classical training; to find gainful employment and avert a life of penury the absence of independent wealth assured him; and, from Dr. Ward, urgings to improve both his theoretical base and sense of moral purpose by studying Sidney Lanier's verses and his recently published treatise *The Science of English Verse*.

When he submitted "My Butterfly" to the *Independent*, RF was aware that its editor had a predilection for the high lyrical music of the elegy (in the vein of Richard Hovey). As he later learned, Dr. Ward had praised Lanier in his memorial as one of the "first princes of American song," whose passion for music and search for moral beauty and truth he considered sterling attributes. Dr. Ward believed, in fact, that "My Butterfly" had been directly influenced by Lanier. Embarrassed, RF quickly explained: "I have never read Lanier's poetry nor the volume of his you mention"; he described, by contrast, an interest in Kipling's verse and the importance of sound as an element of poetry. Little surprise, then, when his other poems, which he showed to the Wards and to Wolcott, were viewed as inferior for their "flatness of tone" and for "sounding too much like talk."

Miss Ward, more astute perhaps than her brother in her tolerance and understanding of RF's developing idiom, included his work in her review entitled "A Decade of Poetry, 1889–1899": "'My Butterfly' (November 5, 1894)," she wrote, "which read as if written by a practiced pen, was, I believe the first poem its author, Robert Lee Frost, ever offered for publication. He was hardly past boyhood at the time, and the poem was written, he says, when it first dawned upon him that poetry ought to sound well." The literary editor of the *Independent* years later would recall that preliminary assessment: "I congratulate you on the recognition you are receiving, but far more on the pluck and ability. I remember with what delight I carried your 'Butterfly' down to Washington and read it to Bliss Carman and Charles Roberts and asked if that wasn't the real thing. I was sure you had it in you then. Possibly you may not remember but you told me that you wrote that poem when you first began to realize that poetry ought to 'sound well.'"

In discussions with the Wards and with Wolcott, RF was just beginning to formulate his peculiar approach to the "sound of sense"; he only vaguely understood that the musicality his would-be benefactors were urging upon him was almost diametrically opposed to a sought-for diction, rooted in experience and reflecting the vernacular (whether in prose or verse, in Hardy or Shakespeare).

Although periodically disheartened by an inability to find renewed inspiration and fearing that he was "not a poet, or but a very incomprehensible one," RF acknowledged the "new courage" he gained from Miss Ward's kindness. She seemed to know when to withhold criticism and when to make constructive suggestions; she followed his swings of mood and was consistent in her belief in his future success. RF thanked his friend and benefactor: "You have encouraged my poor Muse with interest when you couldn't with praise."

A series of visits between the Frost family and the Wards reinforced the friendship begun in correspondence. How often the visits occurred is unclear. RF had met Miss Ward in Boston's North Station to receive the fifteen-dollar payment for "My Butterfly." Putting the timid poet at ease, Miss Ward opened the way for a friendship spanning almost four decades. Elinor Frost did not go with her husband on this occasion, although that had been her intention. However, in 1906, while living in Derry, Elinor traveled by herself to visit Miss Ward in Pocantico Hills, New York. Her visit coincided with Miss Ward's acceptance of RF's poem "The Trial by Existence," and RF's increasing confidence is evident in letters to his editor and friend during the Derry years. He was able to joke about typos in the manuscripts and about his colleagues' mysterious silence after the poem's appearance in the *Independent,* a silence provoked, it turned out, by his failure to cite Pinkerton Academy in the credits.

Detailed plans for Miss Ward to pay a return visit to Bethlehem, New Hampshire, where the Frosts had been staying with Mrs. John Lynch during the summer months, were completed in September 1907. Within a few weeks after Miss Ward had come and gone, RF wrote her of the visit's special significance in a way revealing of an intense poetic nature:

> How long ago and far away Bethlehem is already. Our summer was one of the pleasantest we have had for years. But it is almost hard for me to believe in the reality of it now. I have been that way from boyhood. The feeling of time and space is perennially strange to me. I used to lie awake at night imagining the places I had traversed in the day and doubting in simple wonderment that I who was here could possibly have been there and there. I can't look at my little slope of field here with leaves in the half dead grass, or at the bare trees the birds have left us with, and fully believe there were ever such things as the snug downhill churning room with the view over the ranges of mountains, our talks under the hanging lamp and over the fat blue book, the tea-inspired Mrs. Lynch, baseball, and the blue black Lafayette [Mountain]. There is a pang there that makes poetry. I rather like to gloat over it.

In a letter to Miss Ward written in 1922 from Ann Arbor, Elinor's recollection complemented yet made more immediate her husband's account of their brief time together:

> We likewise remember with pleasure your visit to us in Bethlehem when the children were little. . . . Always when someone takes me for a drive through Franconia Notch I think of the day you and I spent there. It was a cloudy day late in the season, you remember, and the place was deserted except for us, and everything combined to make the lake, and the effect of the cliffs, and the Old Man himself, more impressive. The place is spoiled now, by touring automobilists. Also, I remember gratefully how kind you were about the children all coming down with a bad cold while you were with us. You laughed at the row of them, busily blowing their noses, with friendly amusement, and not a bit of concern for yourself.

Elinor shared with Miss Ward intimacies of her family life—the chronic illnesses, lack of money, the hardships associated with growing children, a miscarriage from a late pregnancy. Miss Ward responded with genuine concern for the Frost "bairns," as she affectionately called them, asking for recent snapshots and details of their doings. She described life in retirement at the old Hayes House in South Berwick. Efforts to restore the garden as it was in the days of Judge Hayes were hampered, she said, by financial constraints (imposed by having to maintain two houses), her brother's physical decline since a bad fall from a carriage, Hetta's blindness, and her own increasing deafness, which, she assured RF, was "no laughing matter."

Correspondence between the families had become sufficiently casual that Frost twitted Miss Ward about her need to journey to Bethlehem to buy potatoes:

> I am moved to melancholy reflexion by the news that comes to us that you have been buying potatoes in Bethlehem. When you were an editor, do I think for a moment that you ever went that far out of your way for a poem? No. The poetry sought you, not you the poetry—else you got along famously on prose. And what are potatoes, pray? Starch. You may ask the man who writes the advertisements for Grape-nuts [sic(k)] I cannot help but think. One of my apple trees, standing stock still and rooted, earns more money in a year than I can earn with all my locomotion and artistic detachment. The moral seems to be that I must write more and better poetry if I hope to compete in the market with things to eat.

It would be some time after RF's return from England before he found lasting relief from the penury of his farming days.

The familiar dimension between RF and Miss Ward was deeply reassuring to the poet. In 1911, RF wrote the editor of a pressing need to see her in Newark: "For how are we going to continue to read each other's letters satisfactorily unless we renew in memory from time to time the image of the living voice that informs the sentences." With his request for an invitation, RF forwarded a packet of seventeen of his unpublished poems folded into sheets stitched together in a heavy blue binding. The as-yet-unrecognized poet referred to his offering as from a "minor poet" and candidly critiqued its significance. "It represents, needless to tell you, not the long deferred forward movement you are living in wait for, but only the grim stand it was necessary for me to make until I should gather myself together. The forward momentum is to begin next year," he announced prophetically.

RF took the train to Newark alone a few days after Christmas. The two-day visit sharpened existing differences and tensions between the striving nonconformist and the Reverend Ward, a severe theologian who was anxious to tutor the less scholarly and considerably junior aspirant. Household readings in the Bible took place daily in several languages (Hebrew, Greek, Latin, and Sanskrit), and one of the poems contained in the Christmas packet, entitled "My Giving," could be understood to ridicule the do-good, Christian ideals cherished by the missionary family. RF was surprised and hurt by the minister's attack on Henri Bergson, whose *Creative Evolution* he had been reading on the train and whose dualistic approach to science and religion appealed to him. With unyielding dogmatism, Dr. Ward denounced the book as an atheistic tract; RF left the next day without daring to confront the stern, bearded, and bespectacled scholar with textual passages he had marked during the night in defense of Bergson.

The next year, having decided to "abandon teaching for poetry," RF turned his back on a highly successful teaching debut at the Plymouth Normal School and, with his wife and four children, set sail for England. Settled in Beaconsfield, he wrote anxiously to Miss Ward: "Perhaps I ought to conceal from you, as one of the few mortals I feel in any sense answerable to, that I am in the mood called aberrant. . . . So slight is my consideration," he lamented. "I may be too old to write the song that once I dreamed about ('the tender touching thing'). . . . If there is any virtue in Location—but don't think I think there is. I know where the poetry must come from if it comes."

Since the appearance of "My Butterfly" in the *Independent*, only a smattering of RF's poems had been printed in U.S. magazines and periodicals. He was understandably elated when *A Boy's Will* was accepted for publication shortly after his arrival in England. He quickly mailed copies to two friends in America: Ernest Clarence Jewell, editor of the *Lawrence High School Bulletin*, which had carried his first poem, "La Noche Triste," and Susan Hayes Ward. He wanted to share his success and with this first small volume to vindicate himself in the eyes of those whose belief in his poetic talents had sustained him.

A family friend brought Miss Ward reports of RF's lecturing triumphs upon his return to America and a copy of his second book, *North of Boston*. Miss Suzy, as she was known to intimates, wrote RF of her plans to read aloud from the new volume to her blind sister. "I have a sort of motherly feeling about you and your wife," she confided; "and I often wish I could do something for those children." Miss Ward was by now living out her days in the old Hayes House in South Berwick, keeping busy with her readings of the poets, her missionary work, and providing hospitality for the many guests to the family homestead.

RF visited the Hayes House at least once after his return from England, and after William, Hetta, and Susan had retired there from the Old Stone House in Newark, perhaps soon after William's death in 1916. During one such visit, RF was importuned by Miss Ward to compose a poem based on some childhood memory of hers about a "little boyish girl" who couldn't let go of the birch tree while trying to reach the fox grapes growing there.

Although RF insisted that he did not write and should not be asked to write poems on demand or for special occasions, he had conceded in at least two instances: the "Class Hymn" for his graduation from Lawrence High School in 1892 and "Wild Grapes," first published in *Harper's Magazine*

(December 1920) and subsequently in *New Hampshire* (1923). "The Master Speed," intended by the poet to celebrate his daughter Irma's marriage to John Cone, while associated with a specific event, was not commissioned. The occasion of President John F. Kennedy's inauguration would prompt a third.

"Birches," Miss Ward explained, about a boy too far from town to play baseball but who has learned to tame the young birch, should be accompanied by a poem about a girl. She gave RF her story of when, as a young girl, she was caught up in a birch tree in search of the wild grapes growing there and had to be saved by her older brother. RF had watched Miss Ward's hands clench and unclench as she recounted the young girl's plight. The closing lines of "Wild Grapes," in the words of an older and wiser Susan Hayes Ward, convey the poet's own tenderness toward his subject:

> It wasn't my not weighing anything
> So much as my not knowing anything—
> My brother had been nearer right before.
> I had not taken the first step in knowledge;
> I had not learned to let go with the hands,
> As still I have not learned to with the heart,
> And have no wish to with the heart—nor need,
> That I can see. The mind—is not the heart.
> I may yet live, as I know others live,
> To wish in vain to let go with the mind—
> Of cares, at night, to sleep; but nothing tells me
> That I need learn to let go with the heart.

Writing to Miss Ward's nephew in December 1923, shortly after his aunt's passing, RF acknowledged the source of inspiration for "Wild Grapes." A warm tribute to a dear friend, the letter lamented Miss Susan's failing health and recalled their final visit:

> We had a grand talk about poetry together the last time I went to South Berwick. I didn't notice that her faculties were failing then. She gave me the only material I was ever able to make a poem to order out of—some childhood memory of her own. . . . I wish I had published the fact it was written by request of Susan Hayes Ward as a companion piece of another poem of mine called Birches. She said Birches was for boys and she wanted me to do another like it on nearly the same subject for girls. For all we so seldom saw each other we were great friends. My wife and I both cared for her more than I can tell you.

The friendship between RF and Susan Hayes Ward brought out in the struggling poet qualities of devotion, humor, artistic integrity, and, above all, courage. Miss Ward's motherly instincts and sound editorial judgment combined to enhance their relations. What had been from his late teens the centrality of poetry in RF's life benefited from the understanding and reassurance provided by this remarkable woman during a crucial period in his development.

The importance of Susan Hayes Ward to the emergence of Robert Frost as a recognized poet cannot be overstated. Another poetry editor of outstanding merit, Harriet Monroe, had immediate impact on RF's search for recognition that was less all-embracing but equally significant in the history of modern American poetry, including, of course, in the recognition of the New England poet in his home country.

Monroe's family background is important in defining her contribution to the arts, as it would prove to be, as well, in the case of Amy Lowell. Born into distinguished families, both women were shy and withdrawn as children, dominated by their more assertive relatives; left to their own devices, they found solace in their fathers' fine libraries. Harriet's older sister, Dora, married John Welborn Root, one of the leaders in the vanguard of brilliant architects who rebuilt Chicago after the great fire of 1871. His early death in 1891 inspired Harriet to write a memoir of his career. Her younger sister, Lucy, married William J. Calhoun, U.S. minister to China under William Howard Taft; Harriet visited them in Peking in 1910, recalling in a letter to RF her time in China as "a glorious memory."

Harriet's impatience with the scant attention given to poetry by editors of magazines and papers prompted the founding of *Poetry: A Magazine of Verse* in 1912 under adverse financial circumstances. She first secured five-year pledges of fifty dollars each from more than one hundred Chicagoans. Besides Frost, Carl Sandburg, and Vachel Lindsay, such poets as Joyce Kilmer, Rabindranath Tagore, and Rupert Brooke were introduced to the public through her magazine.

Even before Harriet founded *Poetry*, she could claim a place in Chicago, not only as member of a distinguished family but also as a poet. She made her literary debut in 1891, when she was invited to write the dedication poem for the Columbian Exhibition in Chicago celebrating the four-hundredth anniversary of the discovery of America. At the opening of the World's Fair the following year, she read—with parts sung—her "Columbian Ode." She subsequently published several volumes of verse, and, with Alice Corbin Henderson, edited *The New Poetry*, touted as the first anthology of twentieth-century poetry. The anthology appeared in 1917 and rivaled Amy Lowell's anthology, *Some Imagist Poets*. It was said that she "reigned in Chicago as 'autocrat of all the poetries.'"

In Monroe's posthumously published autobiography, *A Poet's Life*, she recalled including RF's long, blank verse poem "The Code-Heroics" in the February 1914 issue of *Poetry*, nine months after Ezra Pound had favorably reviewed *A Boy's Will* as a foreign correspondent for her magazine. She was pleased that her magazine had given RF "an introduction to his native land while, disgusted with American refusals, he was still spending a few years of better luck in England."

The catalytic role played by Ezra Pound in the discovery and promotion of the new poets and the New Poetry after 1912 is well documented. Besides Frost, Pound introduced H. D. Aldington, Yeats, and Ford Maddox Ford to the U.S. public. He turned away from the Imagist movement in mid-1914 but continued to supply poems to *Poetry* until 1919 (when his name was dropped from the roster of editors). Harriet Monroe had run across Pound's writings while in Europe in 1910 and had asked the expatriate to serve as foreign correspondent for her fledgling magazine. RF met Pound through Frank S. Flint at Monro's Poetry Bookshop in London.

Although he strenuously objected to Pound's efforts to edit his work and to portray him as a companion expatriate snubbed by American editors, RF acknowledged his well-meaning promotion of his poetry. When *Poetry* editors (other than Monroe, apparently) rejected two poems he submitted in 1913, Harriet told Pound that she was contrite over the incident. By the following year, after the publication of *North of Boston*, *Poetry* was enthusiastic about Frost. Where Monroe freely rewrote, revised, and corrected the verses submitted by other poets, this was not the case with RF's poems, which she left unaltered. Their letters, while initially somewhat detached and ambivalent, were uniformly cordial and respectful in tone. They came to share regret over the split between Pound and the others, Harriet recalling in a 1916 letter to RF Pound's "real loyalty to the arts and even to *Poetry*, in spite of all his slams and damns." It would be this loyalty that would influence the successful effort to free Pound from St. Elizabeths Hospital long after his incarceration at the end of the Second World War.

During the early years of publication in *Poetry*, both before and immediately after the Frosts' return from England, RF was continually preoccupied with the need for money. In 1914, he submitted two more poems to *Poetry*: "The Code" and "The Black Cottage." In a letter returning an unsigned check left lying around, he asks Monroe to consider publishing

"Black Cottage" in the May or June issue; while "The Code" appeared in the February 1914 issue, "Black Cottage" was withheld only because *North of Boston* was already on the stands.

In March 1916, having settled in Franconia, New Hampshire, RF submitted the long narrative "Snow" to *Poetry*, seeking two hundred dollars; Monroe offered him one hundred. He didn't want to be greedy or to haggle, RF assured her; he suggested they "talk the matter over, as the Germans would say to Wilson." Asking that "Snow" be held over until fall, he urged Monroe to have no anxiety about the money: "Where we are now we can live on our debts. I wouldn't play into your hands by admitting so much if I were writing to you merely as an editor. It is between poets I say it and I make no bones of it." He wrote her that he had "his heart set on having another poem in *Poetry* before I turned to play- and novel-writing."

RF soon received a telegram telling him that *Poetry* had awarded "Snow" a cash prize of one hundred dollars. His reply was telegraphed the same day:

> Dear Miss Monroe, My congratulations to you and your fellow editors of *Poetry* on what is bound to prove a very popular award in this family. I was feeling blue when like a bolt from the blue came so much wealth and glory. I am the more sensible of it all that it is my first real prize in a long life. Hitherto my utmost has been a few dollars for running at a Caledonia Club picnic, a part interest in a pair of ear-rings, and a part interest in a gold-headed cane for impersonations at a masquerade, a gold medal for sheer goodness in a high school, and a Detur for scholarship at Harvard. Always sincerely yours Robert Frost.

RF was especially gratified by the interest Harriet Monroe took in several poems written by his close English friend Edward Thomas that he had submitted to her anonymously in September 1916: "After you've got me off your mind," he wrote, "I wish you could find time to look at a few little poems an English friend of mine has been writing since he turned soldier. He is known for prose rather than verse. If you care at all for what I enclose I shall be tempted to tell you who he is. He has a quality."

Monroe replied that she liked "Tall Nettles"—also "When We Two Walked in Lent," except she thought the latter let down at the end when it ought to be strongest. "But who is the illustrious author?" Encouraged by her response, RF explained his fears that "I shall be suspected of admiring them for love of their author" and that Edward Eastaway (the pseudonym he insisted be used in placing his poems) might be killed in the war, in which case "there will be plenty found to like them and then where will my credit be for having liked them first: After all is it any worse for me to like them because I knew their author (but I don't like them for that reason) than for others to like them because they know he is dead. . . . 'Old Man' is the flower of the lot, isn't it?" A selection of Edward Thomas's poems, including "Old Man," appeared in the February 1917 issue of *Poetry*.

Harriet Monroe soon developed a respect for RF's critical acumen. Among others, she asked for his comment on Pound's "Three Cantos," which he confessed he found perplexing:

> I'm not so much ashamed of having kept this too long as of having kept it too long to no purpose. I don't really feel as if I had gone anywhere with it, even helped by wifely counsel. There's stir in the poem of the Poundian kind and I can't say that I don't like it. But it leaves me partly baffled. I suppose that is the Sordello of it: I grant him the Sordello form. I suppose the meaning is meant just to elude one going out as you come in. . . . You're not asking me whether you ought to publish it are you? All you want is my impression of the poem as a poem and not as a magazine availability.

By 1917, the rocky start between RF and Harriet seemed forgotten. As he liked to remind her: "I always think of you as the champion of the cause of poetry with a little no less than with a big P." He accepted her help in arranging poetry readings in the Chicago area. "I realize that this is making you my agent in a troublesome business," he wrote. "But back out without notice whenever you please. Your kindness has gotten you into this." In accepting an offer of $150 for his first Chicago reading, he thanked her: "The money would be much—we won't say it wouldn't—but the great thing would be to see you and Vachel Lindsay."

RF and Monroe shared, as well, admiration for such Midwest poets as Lew Garrett, Ridgley Torrence, and William Vaughn Moody, whose widow, Harriet Moody, opened her luxurious Chicago home (and her New York City apartment) to visiting poets. As late as 1935, when no longer in need of *Poetry* as an outlet for his verse, he acknowledged that "*Poetry* is one of the few places it would seriously bother me to be left out of for good and all."

In late 1921, RF offered Monroe "The Witch of Coös," another long poem in blank verse. "Coös is the next county above where you were in the White Mountains," he told her. Regional differences often were the topic of playful exchanges. RF quoted Van Wyck Brooks as arguing that "the future lies with the East in art. . . . But I thought I would look around Detroit and Chicago a little before I came to any conclusions for myself. Of course I am hopelessly Eastern in my accent: I have half a mind to call my next book 'The Upper Right Hand Corner.' . . . I'll let you know when I am ready to award the palm to any section." It was at this time that RF accepted a post at the University of Michigan, moving his family to Ann Arbor for the years 1921–23, returning for one last year in 1925–26.

The debate over which region of the country would dominate the poetry scene in America provided light touches to their letters, but the ongoing business of advancing the cause of poetry and of publishing in *Poetry* was a serious matter between them. "The Witch of Coös" appeared in the January 1922 issue of *Poetry* and received the two-hundred-dollar Magazine Prize the next fall. RF was pleased: "I don't care what people think of my poetry as long as they award it prizes. You couldn't have pleased me more if you had gone deliberately to work to please me. Some have friends, some have luck, and some have nothing but merit. We'll assume me to have whatever of these will reflect most credit on all concerned. Yours more than ever Robert Frost."

In 1922, as *Poetry* celebrated its tenth anniversary, RF generously acknowledged the decade as "the best ten years of literature any Magazine has had in America." He protested when Monroe sought permission to publish his praise: "Aren't you afraid," he chided, "that, if you publish it right now, people will think one of two things, either I got the prize [for the 'Witch of Coös'] for the good opinion of you or you got the good opinion for the prize? I hate to have them make such underground connections. But absolutely as you please in the matter."

Back in Amherst, RF received from Harriet Monroe an essay she had written about him and his poetry (later included in her volume *Poets and Their Art*). Concerned how he might receive some of her more personal observations, she sought his opinion. "Your letter need not have been so worried about your article," he responded:

> It is a good article and a real Christmas present, if I may take it as such done up as it comes in red. I had been hinting round to the family for something simple to wear in my hair when I am out with the Opera Club this winter toadying to various and sundry Continental pretenders; and here I get a whole crown. Nay but seriously I am pleased with your article especially where it warns people against taking me too seriously. My debt to you has piled up to some altitude above sea level since you first printed blank verse of mine in 1913 [*sic*]. We have grown to be old, if not quite first name, friends. May we never be less.

RF often responded in jest to Harriet Monroe's importunate requests. When Monroe invited him to participate in the Poets' Day ceremonies to be held August 11, 1924, in Philadelphia, suggesting he preside over the special event, RF declined:

I just haven't the courage to undertake it. I never have any luck of any kind in August, especially if I am in clothes. The only way I outwit the jinx is by staying strictly in overalls and one shirt—absolutely coatless. It is a sad admission to make, but the reason for this is not half as mysterious poetical and spiritual as I wish it were. It is flatly physical. In August I am given up to hay fever and my refuge is in the very opposite direction from Philadelphia. Why in the name of Liberty are we poets invited to Philadelphia in August anyway? Because we are sure not to come or because we are sure not to have any audience and then the editors can all say they told us so—poetry is no longer a factor in life—or because all the other months are preempted for science religion business and politics? Seriousness aside, I shall have to let this honor pass.

When Harriet Monroe sought RF's counsel in editing the anniversary anthology of *The New Poetry*, RF persuaded his publisher, Henry Holt & Co., to reduce the fees, reminding Monroe that the publishers "have been hardening their hearts a little against the anthologists. . . . But you're special. And it's not that I am just willing to be in your book; I'm eager to be in it." Sixteen of RF's poems were included in the 1923 edition, and four more were added to a later edition.

Over time, however, Monroe and her associates found it increasingly difficult to coax submissions to *Poetry*. She and her associate Morton Zabel continued to prod RF in anticipation of his next volume, *A Further Range*, with some success. With an assist from his daughter Lesley, RF submitted "Ten Mills." When Monroe was not satisfied, he wrote out and submitted the longer "At Woodward's Garden" in time for both poems to appear in the April 1926 issue of *Poetry*. Subsequently, Monroe scolded RF for not even stopping by if in Chicago, and she was still hoping for some poems for the twentieth birthday number in 1932. "So please get busy and send them—I suspect you of laziness," she wrote.

As editor of *Poetry*, Harriet Monroe was naturally reticent and eager to embrace, without apparent malice or envy, vastly differing styles and personalities. As poet, she entered with RF into the vigorous debate over poetic technique in America.

RF had grown (since "My Butterfly" was published in the *Independent*) ever more sharply away from Imagist poetry and related arts and away from Sidney Lanier's contention that language is a species of music. Conversely, in such essays as "Rhythms of English Verse" and "The Free Verse Movement," Monroe made clear her predilection for *vers libre* and the Imagists, especially Richard Aldington. Taking off from Lanier's *Science and the English Verse*, she argued that "the best way of clearing our minds of error is to think of verse in terms of music." She criticized the modern acceptance of the "pseudo-science of prosody, which we have inherited from the unscientific past and from languages of different structure." She believed free verse has a wider range of expressiveness than the exact metrics so long in vogue. She encouraged closer affiliation between poetry and the allied arts of music and drama—and perhaps the dance. In her essay "The Poet and the Composer," she urged closer collaboration between the two professions to allow for musical settings for the best poems.

Monroe therefore approached RF's poetry as if it were a form of music, rich in timbres, antiphonal tones, and half-interval scales, all part of a lyric chorus of songs. She praised "the musical essence of [RF's] neighbors' talk . . . those slow and simple, but oh, elusive and difficult, rhythms." She noted the absence in his poetry of free verse experiments but found subtle originality "in his weaving of cadences over the basic meter."

Although RF preferred to maintain a certain distance in the mock-serious debate over aesthetic technique, he shared with Monroe a common effort to gain the public's acceptance of the experimenter in art. Along with RF, these friends of the new movement in poetry could recall how desperately hard they had to struggle in the early years for recognition from a callous public, a factor that brought them together but one that critics and biographers often ignore. In two of her essays, "Frugality and Deprecation" and "The Poet's Bread and Butter," Harriet Monroe decried the paltry rates that rewarded poets in America. Out of the public's fear that "favor would undermine the precarious vitality of the poet" and in order to protect him from the "soiling hand of money-grubbing . . . the poet is lucky if he gets a mere pittance from editors, insufficient to support him on bread and water in a hermit's cave." A sum of two hundred dollars to Yeats for a poem was considered exorbitant (whereas John Singer Sargent received thousands for one painting). Harriet knew that poets become bitter and perverted if silenced by neglect.

RF kept as friends those with whom he could engage in the "play for mortal stakes," delighting in the late-night sessions, in Chicago as elsewhere. The circle of friends would argue the merits of cadence and confines of meter, over Lanier's, Monroe's, and RF's peculiar understandings of free verse. Elinor Frost and their daughter Lesley sometimes joined the circle. In this way, Monroe's relationship with RF had extended gradually to his family.

While at Ann Arbor, members of the Frost family traveled to Chicago, where they were entertained by Monroe and Harriet Moody. Harriet Vaughn Moody was the widow of the poet and playwright William Vaughn

Moody; they met in 1899 and married just one year before her husband died of a brain tumor, at age forty-one. An intimate friend of Harriet Monroe and a friend of poets, Harriet Moody often opened her three-story brick house on Groveland Avenue to poets, as well as her apartment at 107 Waverly Place in New York City and a farm she owned in West Cummington, Massachusetts, adjacent to the birthplace of William Cullen Bryant. Out of her home in Chicago she established the Home Delicacies Association, a catering service that supported a tearoom at the Chicago Little Theatre and that resulted in a very successful cookbook, *Mrs. William Vaughn Moody's Cook-Book*. William's letters to her have also been published. On October 12, 1915, the Chicago Little Theatre produced for the first time Rupert Brooke's play *Lithuania*; the young poet had recently visited Harriet Monroe and others in Chicago, and news of his death at sea on the way to Gallipoli had just reached the theater.

The various poets were often accompanied by members of their families and might stay weeks at a time in her luxuriant accommodations: "The guests and their hostess would sit up very late, sharing poetry and an interest in the poetic theatre. Candles would light them to a landing of the great staircase and a four-posted bed." Harriet Moody "was most completely herself with those who had the gifts of humor and gaiety," her friends reported. The live elements of companionship—often of whimsy and fantasy—had bonded her friendship with William, and she had found the qualities of "natural buoyancy" in Padraic Colum and Ridgely Torrence. The appeal soon extended to Robert Frost, "another poet after her own heart."

Anticipating one of his trips to Chicago, in 1921, RF writes Harriet Moody that he will be accompanied by his daughter Lesley rather than Elinor. He points out obvious differences between the two women, Lesley requiring entirely different treatment:

> She [Lesley] can be treated worse, though I shouldn't say there weren't bounds beyond which bad treatment ought not to go even in her case, young and tough as she is.... If it could be arranged I should like to leave her a little while with you in Chicago for the good you would do her. The poor kid is rather sick of the institutions and that through no fault of hers. She's had splendid marks and likes seventy-five percent of her teachers. But my line of talk isn't calculated to make her like any institution. You know how I'm always at it against colleges, in a vain attempt to reconcile myself to them.

His chief complaint in a life of strained relations with academia was that it sacrifices "initiative and independence." Harriet and Lesley became friends and maintained a spirited correspondence.

When Lesley submitted one of her own poems to *Poetry* in 1923, Monroe's handwritten rejection was both encouraging and compassionate. "I am interested in this poem," she wrote, "and in the fact that you are writing such good stuff, but do you want frank talk?" Following suggestions for reworking the poem and inviting her to resubmit it to her, she concluded: "Good luck to you and your muse she is starting off very well. And a happy summer to all the Frosts." Years later, in 1935, while teaching at Rockford College, my mother brought Monroe to the campus for readings at Maddox House, and there, under the auspices of President Gordon Keith Chalmers, Monroe was awarded the honorary degree of L.H.D. (Harriet Moody had died in 1932, at age seventy-eight.) Soon after the untimely death of another Frost child, their youngest daughter, Marjorie, Elinor sent Monroe a gift of Marjorie's privately printed verses: "We didn't want it to look like a memorial book, but I have had some small sized copies made of a photograph we like very much, and I will enclose one in your book, though you didn't know her. As a rule, I am putting it only in the copies I am sending to her intimate friends."

A short time after these exchanges, on September 26, 1936, Harriet Monroe died of a cerebral hemorrhage while attempting to climb Machu Picchu; she is buried in Arequipa, Peru. She had founded *Poetry* to give poets a place of their own where theories of craftsmanship could be discussed and where poems created in the new spirit and the new forms could be presented to an ever-expanding public. Her catholic tastes allowed her to accept a variety of forms: free verse rhapsodies, polyphonic prose, classical sonnets, and blank verse narratives. She looked back longingly to her time at *Poetry* as an era of clarification, of stripping art bare of rhetoric, eloquence, grandiloquence, bringing it closer to life, to modern subjects and speech, and to the new rhythms.

RF admired Monroe "as the most aesthetic intellectual of her sex" and was generous in acknowledging the importance of her contribution. He became impatient with her form of aesthetic idealism and her acceptance of Imagism and free verse. But because he and the other poets of his generation—as poets and not as editors or critics—championed a common cause, he could tell her in all sincerity, "Never mind."

It was also during this period of experimentation in poetry and in the debate over poetic technique that Robert Frost and Amy Lowell became acquainted. RF's and Amy's individual and often differing lifestyles and approaches to the writing of verse are revealed through an intense, lively relationship that spanned a brief but exciting decade in the emergence of the New Poetry in America.

As a child in the prominent Brookline Lowell family finding herself marginalized from a college education, Amy, like Harriet Monroe, took advantage of her father's large library to become an avid reader and collector of books. And it would be Ezra Pound who was instrumental in bringing together the poets Amy Lowell and Robert Frost, just as he had been in connecting Frost and Monroe. In 1914, Pound was in London, representing Harriet Monroe at *Poetry: A Magazine of Verse* and trying his damnedest to win RF over to free verse. Amy had been reading the expatriate's pronouncements on Imagism in the March 1913 issue of *Poetry,* and Pound's emphasis on the emotional impact of things seen strongly appealed to her.

Having traveled to England to meet Pound and the small band of Imagist poets he championed, Amy ran across a copy of RF's recently published *North of Boston* at the Poetry Bookshop, where, at its opening, RF had met, for the first time, F. S. Flint and a number of poets other than Pound, whom he would track down later. Amy would recall how that night she learned "a lesson I have never forgotten. For here was our vaunted *mot juste* embedded in a blank verse so fresh, living, and original that nothing on the score of vividness and straightforward presentation—our shibboleths—could be brought up against it. . . . I immediately took off my hat to the unknown poet, and I have been taking it off ever since in a positively wearying repetition." Back in America in 1915, Amy demanded the right to review *North of Boston* for the fledgling *New Republic.* Docking in New York harbor upon the Frost family's return from England, RF spotted Amy's review; its praise prompted him to call on her at Sevenels, her Brookline home, where, according to Amy, "at once began a friendship, which on my part, has been an ever-increasing admiration of his work, and a profound attachment to the man."

The friendship with Amy Lowell, begun at what RF jokingly called the "cutglass affairs" at Sevenels, soon expanded to include his wife, Elinor, and their children, on the one hand, and Ada Russell, Amy's lifelong companion, on the other. Elinor Frost's correspondence with Amy suggests the lengths to which the Frost household would go to accommodate the visitor from Brookline and her entourage; on at least one occasion the entire workings of the Frost house in Amherst were taken over to ensure Amy's comfort away from home. RF, sometimes accompanied by his wife, was a fairly frequent visitor at Sevenels. The two poets read and collected each other's books, and RF's personal library (housed at New York University) contains ten volumes autographed to the Frosts by either Amy or Ada.

From the first, Amy asserted her leadership in the new poetic movement. Alienated by Pound's odd manner and what seemed to her a greater interest in her money than her verse, she took under her wing a number of writers and other artists, some of whom had been working with Pound on his anthology *Des Imagistes*. She soon created her own anthology, *Some Imagist Poets*, with its famous Imagist credo (Amygist credo, Pound preferred to call it). Having shaped Pound's group to her own purposes back in America, she threw the full power of her personality and family prestige into the fight for a renewal of poetry in her homeland. She failed in her attempt to purchase from Margaret Anderson the poetry editorship at the *Little Review*, a competitor of Harriet Monroe's *Poetry*. But she was pleased to be elected the first president of the New England Poetry Society.

In "Memories of Amy Lowell" in *Poets and Their Art*, Harriet Monroe described her first encounter with the Bostonian Lowell. Amy's characteristically late entrance to an alumni banquet in honor of her brother Lawrence Lowell, president of Harvard—a banquet where the women were segregated from the men—had, according to Harriet, the desired effect. Miss Lowell's "ponderous and regal figure" descended the stairs and "took possession of the occasion." Scolded by Amy for not yet having published two of her poems that *Poetry* had accepted, Harriet nevertheless fell under the "spell of the half-magnificent, half-humorous personality." Although Harriet found Amy's at times overbearing personality to be her own worst enemy, her power to gain public acceptance for the New Poetry came close to Harriet's ideal of "organic, harmonious relations between bard and audience."

In England in 1914, Amy Lowell's lavishness in wooing away Pound's followers and developing her own coterie of artists was unheard of among poets. Amy handled poetry like any other big business—putting poetry "on the map," so to speak. "I made myself a poet," she was heard to say, "but the Lord made me a business man." Her family position made her an exception among the poets of her generation, but she understood the penury in which these poets—be they Symbolists, Imagists, or Georgians—searched for recognition. She heralded the "courageous little band who, when they could get themselves printed, which was seldom, . . . were either completely ignored or furiously lampooned." Amy knew from experience that the "stigma of oddness is the price a myopic world always exacts from genius. . . . How hard, how desperately hard is the way of the experimenter in art."

As propagandist and militant leader of the New Poetry, who often judged success in terms of monetary gain, Amy competed with RF for a best seller. "I do wish I could beat Frost on a book," she lamented when *Six French Poets* and *Men, Women, and Ghosts* did not outsell *North of Boston* and *Mountain Interval*. Late in life, she complained: "The more successful

I am, the more I am hated. . . . I meet with no jealousy from men who have arrived like Frost, Lindsay and Sandburg, but I meet with nothing else from those of lower rank."

Although Harriet Monroe marveled at how Amy put "the drive and urge of a rich and strong personality" and the sway of her ancestors at the service of poetry, her view of Amy's poems was more detached. Verses in such poems as "Spring Day" she thought fairly batter our eyes and ears in search of scientific rapture. "She delights," Harriet concluded, "in the rush and clatter of sounds, in the kaleidoscopic glitter of colors, even though the emotional or intellectual motive goes somewhat astray among them." Too much of Amy's poetry, Harriet seemed to be saying, springs from the will, not the heart, an appraisal strikingly similar to RF's memorial assessment:

> She helped to make it stirring times for a decade to those immediately concerned with art and to many not so immediately. The water in our eyes from her poetry is not warm with any suspicion of tears, it is water flung cold, bright and many-colored from flowers gathered in her formal garden in the morning. Her Imagism lay chiefly in images to the eyes. She flung flowers and everything else there. Her poetry was forever a clear resonant calling off of things seen. Amy was far more vocal in explaining her brand of Imagism and more prolific in terms of experimentation in verse than her competitors. As Pound moved to protect Harriet Monroe and *Poetry* from attack, Amy stepped up efforts to minimize both Pound's and Monroe's roles in revitalizing American poetry.

Amy Lowell had gone to France in search of the French poets—Baudelaire and Verlaine—who had inspired Pound's Imagism. She indulged a passion for modern French music, in particular the piano works of Eric Satie. Her verses would reflect the orchestral color and verbal music of this school. In "Can Grande's Castle," she used polyphonic prose in a contrapuntal form that reaches orchestral sonority; her poem "Sea Shell" was set to music and sung at Sevenels by a noted French tenor, much as the verses of Mallarmé and other Symbolist poets were used by Debussy in his ballet music. In the work that followed, *Six French Poets,* many of the verses translated did not in fact adhere to her credo, but she was skilled in bending these poets, as well, to her theories.

Amy Lowell hoped to retain natural rhythms or cadence in free verse and objected to the association with free love in the minds of her public. Her peculiar brand of Imagism was broad enough to embrace most modern American poets, including Frost. From the time of her review of *North of Boston* for the *New Republic,* she recognized the power of RF's blank verse in meeting the Imagist credo and conceded that he had transformed blank verse into a fluid instrument of his own idiomatic speech; but she never gave up trying to convince him "that cadence was much more effective than meter and that *his* variety of blank verse was merely a step away from cadence and free verse." She herself tended to walk through poetic movements, returning to set rhyme and meter in, for example, *A Critical Fable* and *Ballads for Sale*. RF, too, on occasion moved closer to Amy's unrhymed cadence, as he said he did with several poems (we have no record of which) he sent her: "Two of these are in very free verse for me. I call them experiments in vanishing meters."

Imagism and the New Poetry stressed sensuous and emotional immediacy, color and music, qualities of the fine arts rather than verse. Poets like Swinburne and Lanier practiced the rhythms of *vers libre* like musical virtuosos in search of tactile and visual effects. Even before his first poem, "My Butterfly: An Elegy," appeared in the *New York Independent* in 1894, RF had resisted the suggestion that verse is a series of musical sounds and of vowel- and tone-colors. "The music of poetry is not like the music of music," he would say. In "How Hard It Is to Keep from Being King," he describes the tension between the irregularity of the accent-stress and the regular beat of the meter as though they were equally matched contestants:

> I am not a free-verse singer. . . .
>
> . . . .
> I write real verse in numbers, as they say.
> I'm talking not free verse but blank verse now.
> Regular verse springs from the strain of rhythm
> Upon a meter, strict or loose iambic.
> From that strain comes the expression *strains of music*.
> The tune is not that meter, not that rhythm,
> But a resultant that rises from them.

He emphasized that "Numbers, numbers. Count. *Metronome*. Figures. Measure. That's verse." He conceded that just as there is probably more love outside marriage than in, more religion outside the church than in, there is probably more poetry outside verse than in. Nevertheless, for himself, he chose verse as "an institution of metrics."

RF's disagreements with Amy, which often took the form of light repartee, went beyond the debate over poetic technique. In August 1915, shortly after the appearance of *Some Imagist Poets*, RF mixed praise with a personal rebuke: "Yes I like your book," he wrote, "and all I lay up against you is that you will not allow me a sense of humor. Occurs to me a simple way to make you. I could make up my mind to stand outside your Poetry Society until you did."

Anxiety over Amy's appraisal of RF's first volumes intensified when her *Tendencies in Modern American Poetry* appeared in 1917. In her critique of RF's poetry, she lavishly praised what she called his "bucolic realism, his independence as an artist, and his 'unerring sense of fitness' in his choice of blank verse." While RF appreciated Amy's acclaim and her effective use of quotations from his and others' work and thanked her "for giving 'Old Man's Winter Night' its due," he quibbled over her characterization of *North of Boston* as a "very sad book" worked on an "exceedingly small canvas," and chided her again for her "groundless doubts" about his humor.

RF was no less annoyed by Amy's insistence that *North of Boston* was "an epitome of a decaying New England," populated by people who are "leftovers of the old stock, morbid, pursued by phantoms, slowly sinking to insanity." In "The Black Cottage," "A Servant to Servants," and "Home Burial," for instance, she detected a disease "which is eating into the vitals of our New England life, at least in its rural communities"; in "A Hundred Collars," she found a dullness and absence of the "pungency of thought or expression which is so ingrained in the New England temper."

Both poets shared an intense Yankeeism and conviction that their home-land was assuming a new lease on life; but, unlike Amy, RF maintained that his blank verse was derived from the living talk in villages and farms north of Boston. He sought to portray not rustic but real Yankees, and thus he deliberately avoided the picturesque raciness of a James Russell Low-ell. Amy, on the other hand, relying on her distant cousin as an authority, argued that the essence of New England was captured in its dialect, in its "picturesque words, quaintly turned to half conceal, half reveal a solemn truth." RF's retort to Amy's charge in *Tendencies* that he eschewed dialect in his poetry was pointed: "And for the fun of it you might record in the margin of your book that RF makes no merit of not having used dialect in *North of Boston*. He says he doesn't put dialect into the mouths of his people because not one of them, not one, spoke dialect." On another occasion, he chided her for her attempt to imitate New England speech in her poem "The Overgrown Pasture": "Trouble with you, Amy, is that you don't go out your back door often enough!" Years later, in describing the difference between their attitudes toward the natives of the New England country-side, Amy would concede that RF's was more sympathetic and tolerant of idiosyncratic behavior; in contrast, hers was one of pity. Having come late to New England rural life, she recognized that she was a "complete alien," her knowledge of the Yankee's language and psychology being "atavistic," and that the milieu depicted in "The Overgrown Pasture" seemed less native to her than the life of London or Paris.

Sparring over their differing uses of humor, dialect, and regional peculiarities in their verse, RF and Amy shared a "little weakness for dramatic tones." "I go so far," RF wrote Amy, "as to say that there is no poetry of any kind that is not made up of dramatic tones." Amy's response, although more literary in its derivation, took a similar tack: "It is strange," she wrote, "I come to feel that the dramatic is the great interest in poetry. Not plays, to me their limitations are hampering, but what Browning called 'Dramatic Lyric.'" Along with Harriet Monroe, RF preferred Amy's *Legends* to her more strenuous experiments in technique. Her friends agreed that, if not a poet, Amy was certainly "a great storyteller (*a la* Chaucer, Keats, Browning, and touched by Frost)." It was in the debate over the use of tragedy in the *North of Boston* narratives that RF's and Amy's mutual love of the dramatic erupted into a playful exchange recounted by RF at one of his readings: "I knew Amy Lowell very well, and she said one night to me in her great house in Brookline, she said: 'After all, what's the difference between your stories about New England and mine?' I said: 'Amy, you're more like Shakespeare. You can't have a tragedy without a villain and I do it without a villain.' She said: 'You don't like mine?' And I said: 'Yes, Amy, you are more like Shakespeare.'" RF took pride in putting people into tragic situations where no one was to blame, where—borrowing from George Meredith—"passions spin the plot." One critic, Van Wyck Brooks, saw the tragi-comic, comi-tragic view of life as part of Frost's "accomplishment in mediating New England in the mind of the rest of the nation."

While RF seemed most comfortable maintaining a certain distance, often through professional jest, in the mock-serious debate over aesthetic technique, his relations with Amy Lowell gradually became more familiar in tone and substance, reaching out to include members of his family.

Amy had treasured the praise she received from RF when *Six French Poets* appeared in 1915. "Do you know," RF had written her, Paul Fort is "the only one of your six who shows with any vividness the sounds I am after in poetry. I'll tell you what we did with the Henry III. My daughter [Lesley] and I read it together, I with my head tipped one way following your English aloud, she with her head tipped the other way following his French in silence, the book being open in two places at once you understand. And even under those unfavorable circumstances I brought tears of excitement to my daughter's eyes. And she is a young thing." Amy, elated, was quick to reply: "Of course you like Paul Fort best. 'Sound posturing,' well, well, call it what you like, it is dramatic, all the same."

William Prescott Frost Jr., RF's father,
San Francisco, 1876

Isabelle (Belle) Moodie Frost, RF's mother,
San Francisco, 1876

Elinor Miriam White, ca. 1892, upon her
graduation from Lawrence High School
as co-valedictorian with Robert Frost

The Frost children at the Derry Farm, 1907

The "Bouquet House," back of the Beaconsfield Bungalow, England, 1912–14; pencil drawing by Irma Frost, in the *Bouquet*, September 1914. (Courtesy of the Robert Frost Collection, Clifton Waller Barrett Library, Manuscripts Division, University of Virginia Library)

Pencil and color drawing by Lesley Frost of "the little grey house on the windy hill" from Matthew Arnold's "Forsaken Merman," in the *Bouquet*, June 1915. (Courtesy of the Robert Frost Collection, Clifton Waller Barrett Library, Manuscripts Division, University of Virginia Library)

Robert Frost, his wife, Elinor, and their children (Lesley, Irma, Marjorie, and Carol), Plymouth, New Hampshire, 1912. (Courtesy of the Plymouth State College Archives)

Robert Frost, first publicity photo, England, 1913–14

Rare photo of Susan Hayes Ward, poet and literary editor of the *New York Independent*. (Courtesy of the Wheaton College Library)

Hayes House, family home in South Berwick, Maine; currently the home of the headmaster at Berwick Academy. (Courtesy of the Old Berwick Historical Society)

Harriet Monroe, poet and founder in 1912 of *Poetry* magazine. (Courtesy of the Poetry Foundation)

Amy Lowell, poet. (Courtesy of the Poetry Foundation)

Robert Frost using his homemade writing board, Franconia, New Hampshire, 1915

Lesley Frost (*left*) during Greek Games, Barnard College, 1919

The "Knapsack of the Open Book," a bookmobile in which Lesley Frost, with her sister Marjorie, toured New England towns and camps during the summers of the late 1920s

Lesley Frost, New York City, ca. 1929

Marjorie Frost

Irma Frost

Carol Frost

Lillian LaBatt Frost (Mrs. Carol Frost)

Elinor and Lesley Lee Francis with their mother, Cambridge, Massachusetts,
ca. 1933

Elinor and Lesley Lee in
their Swedish dresses, ca.
1936

Poet And Granddaughters

—Morning Star Photo.

Robert Frost, one of America's foremost poets, and Mrs. Frost are visiting their daughter, Lesley Frost, and their two grandchildren, Elinor and Lee Francis, here. Elinor is at the left and Lee, perched on her grandfather's knee, is at the right.

Under the auspices of the William Arthur Maddox Memorial Lecture foundation, Mr. Frost will lecture in the Rockford college chapel Tuesday at 8:15 p. m. He spoke on the Beloit college campus Friday, and tomorrow at 2:30 p. m. he will be guest lecturer at the Janesville Woman's History club meeting.

Lesley Frost is on the Rockford college faculty and presides over Maddox house at the college.

Elinor and Lesley Lee with their grandfather, *Rockford Morning Star*, December 8, 1935. (Courtesy of the Rockford College Archives)

Elinor Frost at the Maddox House, Rockford College, 1935

Lesley Frost as director of the Maddox House, Rockford College, 1934–36

Lesley Lee and Elinor at the Hacienda de la Clementina (between Tampico and Victoria), Mexico, 1936

By December 1917, despite the tensions caused by the appearance of *Tendencies,* RF felt free to ask a personal favor of Amy: "A good way to show forgiveness if you are capable of having such an emotion would be to have my young daughter over from Wellesley [where Lesley was a freshman] some day to see where you sit enthroned. It would mean a lot to her for a long long time afterward not only to have seen you but to have heard you and yet to have been heard a little by you." RF betrayed a father's anxiety in a follow-up letter to Lesley, in which he instructed her to get a copy of Amy's recently published *Men, Women and Ghosts* in advance of her visit:

> You won't perhaps care for the longer poems and of course you won't go far in any poem that doesn't get hold of you. Find something to like though. I know you can. Be fairer to her than some people have been to you. She's not going to examine you and see how well you know and like her. You simply won't want to feel lost in the dark should she happen to illustrate what she means by cadence rhythm and such things from her own work. She won't talk about meter. She scorns the very word. Prosody, too, she hates the name of. She may try to tell you what determines the ending place of a line in free verse. She'll be interesting. You'll find there'll be a lot in what she says.

When admitted to Sevenels, Lesley found the ailing poet holding forth from her large, pillowed bed, chain-smoking her Manilas, and engrossed in her final work, the two-volume biography of John Keats.

For a time after the publication of *Tendencies,* RF was upset with Amy for the book's portrayal of his wife, Elinor. He wrote her a letter of cautious, sweeping praise: "Your generosity from the first has had so much to do with making me that if from now on you reversed yourself and tried to unmake me, I should never be brought to believe you were anything but my friend." He went on to correct a few factual errors in the biographical data and to make passing reference to her continuing reservations about his sense of humor. It was in a long letter to Louis Untermeyer (one of the many letters RF did everything he could, but failed, to keep his friend from publishing) that RF unburdened himself about Amy's description of his wife: "That's an unpardonable attempt to do her as the conventional helpmeet of genius." RF tried to make his longtime friend, at least, understand the complex nature of his marriage; he had been hurt by Amy's simplistic portrait, and so had Elinor, who tried unsuccessfully to have personal references omitted from later editions of the book.

In 1922, when RF extended an invitation to Amy to lead off a series of poetry readings at the University of Michigan, the verbal sparring between the two assumed notoriety. At the reading, 2,500 persons crowded the auditorium only to have a blown fuse cast them in total darkness, even before RF's introductory remarks. We are told that the impromptu jesting kept their invisible audience in howls of laughter, the hilarity having increased when RF tipped over the water pitcher.

Amy's reputation for subjecting contemporary poets, including Frost, to her satirical wit was enhanced when a long poem entitled *A Critical Fable*—composed in rhyme and meter in the style of James Russell Lowell—appeared anonymously and was later exposed as hers by the *New York Post* on a tip from RF.

Amy's critical judgment had by now placed RF high among his contemporaries, and her affection for him and his family never abated. In a letter to Untermeyer shortly before her death, Amy mentioned having seen RF "several times that year and having got to know both him and Elinor much better than before." "I must say," she concluded, "they wear well."

Like her friend Harriet Monroe, Amy Lowell passed away unexpectedly from an apparent cerebral hemorrhage on May 12, 1925, while working on her biography of Keats. She was fifty-one. In 1926 she was awarded posthumously the Pulitzer Prize for Poetry.

Elinor Frost's letters to Amy Lowell in the year before Amy's death reveal a constant concern for her overtaxed husband, who was finding it increasingly difficult to keep up with the demands on his time. She and RF were trying to help their daughters Lesley and Marjorie launch the bookshop—the Open Book—in Pittsfield, Massachusetts; and their son, Carol, and his wife, Lillian, needed assistance at their farm in South Shaftsbury, Vermont. Despite the openly affectionate tone of Elinor's letters, biographers have persisted in attributing mean-spirited motives to RF and Louis Untermeyer for failing to attend the "Complimentary Dinner in Honor of Amy Lowell" held only two days before her fatal stroke. In her tentative acceptance, Elinor alluded to RF's overcrowded schedule, "twelve or thirteen reading engagements ... (which means a lot of traveling, as you know) besides keeping up his college work [at the University of Michigan], and I just don't know how he is going to manage it. Then there is his own party on the 26th [of March], which will, of course, be a nervous strain, though a pleasure at the same time. I wonder if anyone will come to *his* party. Please change your mind and come yourself." Amy did not, in fact, attend RF's fiftieth birthday party, but her effusive "Tribute to Robert Frost" was read aloud. It is also true that Amy, in her most imperious manner, had tried to coach Untermeyer and Frost on what to say at her commemorative dinner, which may in part have prompted them to send their regrets. Nothing was particularly unusual, though, about such public figures missing one another's readings and honorary functions. On the day before her death, Amy received a sympathetic note from Lesley saying how sorry she was that Miss Lowell had been sick and had had to postpone her trip to England; she requested autographed copies of the Keats biography to place in the Open Book showcase. Surely, Amy must have realized that RF, unaware of the seriousness of her illness, had not intended to rupture their long-standing friendship.

In the memorial tribute that appeared in the *Christian Science Monitor,* RF spoke of how Amy Lowell "had helped make it stirring times to those immediately concerned with art and to many not so immediately." RF realized that their sparring was an important part of their active and passionate engagement in the debate over poetic technique in America. They had listened with excitement and at times with the anger of true friendship to each other's pronouncements, and they had benefited from opportunities to test their evolving idiom. RF knew that with the death of his friend Amy, a chapter in the debate was closed.

Although RF became impatient with Amy's pyrotechnics and her tendency to pervert his work to her theories, he respected her determination to place herself "at the head of a fighting movement in art," and he joined forces in a common rebellion against the trite Romantic attitudes and the outworn, false generalities of the previous generation. He shared a love of the dramatic, and they both tried with their students and the larger public to lodge poetry with them to stay. In a letter to Amy in 1915, RF summed up the feeling of that period: "The great thing is that you and some of the rest of us have landed with both feet on all the little chipping poetry of a while ago. We have busted 'em up as with cavalry. We have, we have, we have."

Elinor Miriam White Frost

Throughout these early years—both before and after her marriage—Elinor Miriam White Frost's personality and role in Robert's quest for recognition as a poet remained elusive. But that precisely was her wish. She had always detested the public exigencies of her husband's professional life and would have preferred to share the strength and beauty of his poetry in private, between the two of them, at least until after their deaths. She was passionate and unshaken in her belief in him as a poet; reluctantly she came to realize the need to reach out to his larger public, if for no other reason than the growing problems in the family that created financial pressures on Robert as breadwinner. Elinor held strong opinions she could defend, but she was quiet-spoken and shy in public and avoided celebrity.

Family members conceded that Elinor Frost was always a terrible cook who preferred to be anywhere other than in the kitchen. On the other hand, she was beloved by those close to her. Her daughter-in-law (Carol's wife, Lillian) loved Elinor, whom she remembered as a quiet gentlewoman whose silences disturbed her husband but seemed natural to her. Lillian spoke of Elinor's good sense of humor and her sweet little giggle; how she enjoyed reading and watching and listening to the evening card games and liked to play croquet; how she made all the children's clothes when they were young and never thought of her own needs as there was RF or her children or grandchildren to think about. Her love of painting was contagious, Lillian recalled, and she was certain Elinor had passed at least one landscape down to my mother. Her college friends at St. Lawrence University said she was in no way a mixer: she never thrust herself forward; she was always demure, quiet, contemplative, serious, and thoughtful. Her real life was her inner life. She tended to keep her actually rather strong opinions to herself. She seldom spoke of the past.

As a consequence, despite Elinor Frost's college degree, experience as a teacher, her artistic and literary talent, she is seldom discussed separately from her husband. We have a record of her at-home teaching of the children: the children's journals from the Derry Farm and England and, equally impressive, the children's delightful and precocious art, exemplified by its exhibition in the *Bouquet* and other writings from their time in England. The illustrations in the six surviving issues of the *Bouquet* attest not only to the children's love of art but also to the talent their mother awoke in them. Her direct involvement in the daily at-home education was by necessity far more intense and ongoing than that of her husband.

Remarkably for a woman in the late 1800s, and despite a childhood marred by rheumatic fever, Elinor announced that she would marry Robert only after she graduated from college. Her college transcript and graduation exercises documented at St. Lawrence University in Canton, New York, show that she completed her degree in liberal arts in three academic years, 1892–95. The curriculum she chose was very strong in Latin and English, history, and math and also included courses in German, French, economics, physics, psychology, parliamentary law, Cicero, Caesar, chemistry, sociology, debate, jurisprudence, and logic. There is no question that Elinor could hold her own intellectually.

Elinor was determined to complete her studies at St. Lawrence University before agreeing to marry the impatient suitor. Early in the fall of 1894, her final year at the university, she was understandably embarrassed when Robert showed up in Canton at her lodgings, bearing a gift of one of two copies of *Twilight,* a privately printed small book of several of his poems that included "Twilight" and "My Butterfly: An Elegy." Interpreting Elinor's discomfort as a rejection, RF destroyed his copy. (Elinor's copy was found by a collector many years later and today is part of the University of Virginia Library's Clifton Waller Barrett Collection.) Distraught, RF tried to lose himself in the Dismal Swamp of North Carolina. After several harrowing incidents, finding himself lost and without money, he called on his mother to help him find his way home. Although exhausted and frightened, he was elated to discover his "My Butterfly: An Elegy" had appeared on the front page of the *Independent* (November 8, 1894), where he would continue to publish. Despite RF's dramatic tactics to win Elinor's hand, or perhaps because of them, she agreed to marry him one year later, having completed her degree in three years, as planned.

Once married, Elinor focused her attention on the goal she and her husband had set for themselves, to enjoy a life of poetry together. Elinor had become her husband's number one partner, not as a helpmeet for genius but as a perceptive ear for the beautiful music of his poetry. He shared with her each poem as it was written; in a practical sense, as he stated, "she had a perfect ear for vowel sounds." It was to her the children went for comfort and understanding; she shared with Robert a constant preoccupation with family illness and financial worries. Her death in 1938 deprived the four children, especially the more troubled ones—Carol and Irma—the uninterrupted support they needed and craved.

Lesley Frost

SYMBOLISM

These hieroglyphs of snow
In wheelrut pond and ditch,
The tracks of quail and doe
Like quilting overstitch,
Can only just imply
The truth of what they say:
That bird and beast passed by
And winter came this way.
    (Lesley Frost)

In tracing my journey with my grandfather Robert Frost, everything I touched passed through my mother, Lesley Frost, who, like her father, left an extensive record. Her attachment to books and writing remained foremost throughout her life. Her papers reside at the University of New Hampshire, where they help us understand the influence of her father in her varied literary life, as well as in terms of the impact of her "education by poetry" in her search for adventure. The record of my journey will show that books, books, books, and all that they mean metaphorically, shaped my life, as well.

By the time I was growing up, my mother was enjoying a full life as teacher, author, and lecturer in her own right. Between adventures, she developed a successful network with several publishers in New York City, where her father had acquired over the years a number of literary friends. It was during the period 1927–34 that Mother edited an anthology, *Come Christmas,* for Coward McCann—bringing out a second edition in 1935 with a facsimile of the manuscript of RF's uncollected poem "Good Relief" in the frontispiece. In 1932, Coward McCann published her mystery novel, *Murder at Large,* a story she was convinced would be used by Agatha Christie in her *Ten Little Indians.*

Beginning in 1939, she would publish three volumes of children's stories around the mischief of her young daughters, dedicated to Elinor and Lesley Lee, "who helped make" the books. The first, *Not Really,* was published by Coward McCann; the second, *Really Not Really* (1962) by Channel Press; and the third, *Digging Down to China* (1968), by Devin-Adair, with charming illustrations by Marjorie Frost's daughter, Robin Fraser Hudnut. More later about the Airedale and the Giraffe as household pets. Devin-Adair also published *Going on Two* (1973, with drawings by my cousin Robin), a collection of humorous poems written as if by Mother's grandson Prescott Frost Wilber at that precocious and mischievous age. Other publications were articles on a variety of subjects such as education and travel, and several ghostwritten or cowritten volumes.

My mother emerges from RF's story as the early and natural link to my own involvement in the Frost biography. Through an interest in family history, and, just as important, through a sense of communication and mutual enrichment as a child, I understood that my mother, having assumed the mantle of her father's public image, had freed me in the next generation to pursue a more independent and scholarly approach to the family archives.

My mother's role as it regards her father, when treated by biographers, is seriously misunderstood. Although her politics and mine took different directions, I am enthusiastic about her talents: writing skills, encouraging family members to have successful lives; without money of her own, giving generously of her time and energy to projects that reinforce her love of both her parents. Because her mother, Elinor Frost, is obscured by her husband's ambitions, which she freely embraced from the time they met in high school, Mother went out of her way to open a tribute to her at St.

Lawrence University and to put her own papers at the University of New Hampshire, in her mother's name, where they would get treatment separate from those of her father.

Childhood and Schooling

From the beginning of her own life, on the farm at Derry, my mother was a part of her father's as yet ill-defined literary ambition. In her published Derry journals, we see a child who called her siblings "the children" and was concerned always with the need to care for her mother. By 1912, as mentioned earlier, she and her sisters and brother would be preparing in England the 120-page notebook "An Important Year by Four Children, Dedicated to Papa & Mamma." Once settled in the bungalow on Reynolds Road, in Beaconsfield, Lesley helped her father gather together a few of his poems, transcribing them on the Blickensderfer typewriter brought from America into two small manuscripts soon to be published by David Nutt as *A Boy's Will* and *North of Boston*.

The children's crowning achievement was the *Bouquet*—the previously mentioned in-house magazine to which the four Frost children and chosen friends (and several parents) contributed. A little house behind the Beaconsfield cottage was called "the *Bouquet* House," set aside for this purpose. As the mastermind and "managing editor," my mother would type and assemble the little magazine, a single copy of which was to be issued monthly, with stories, poems, essays, and illustrations by the invited contributors. At least two of Frost's poems, "Locked Out" and an early version of "Pea-Sticks" (later changed to "Pea Brush") appeared in the *Bouquet*, along with several early poems signed by Edward Thomas, whose children were also contributors.

Miraculously, Elinor Frost was able to preserve six of some fourteen issues of the *Bouquet:* the surviving issues were passed on to my mother, who tried without success to write about the English years in tandem with Myfanwy Thomas, the last surviving daughter of Edward and Helen Thomas. I found the papers in a small suitcase Mother carried around with her; shortly after, I donated them to the University of Virginia Library. The library assisted me in using the illustrations from the *Bouquet* in *As Told to a Child,* published by Cyder Press together with the stories by RF for his children.

The *Bouquet,* masterminded and edited by my mother, featured a body of compositions and artwork remarkable for its reflection of the children's powerful and imaginative response to their surroundings. Experimenting with various techniques, the children sought to convey a range of emotions (often on a moral plane), of anger, fear, revenge, joy, laziness, curiosity. The fluctuating moods and feelings, and the tricks they play on the brain, were used knowingly by these young writers for suspense and excitement, for surprise and wonder.

For visual effects, each issue of the *Bouquet* was enhanced by the generous use of illustrations, puzzles or riddles, and even advertisements. We know that the Frost children, encouraged by their mother, brought to England an interest in painting and drawing. The profusion of pencil drawings and watercolors, the use of cream wove paper and paperboard covers, when added to Lesley's typed manuscript, gave each issue of the *Bouquet* a finished look. Assembling the *Bouquet* was a logical continuation of and progression from the earlier journals and notebooks.

By the time Mother turned fifteen on April 28, 1914, she had caught the eye of a number of her father's new friends, with whom she found herself at ease. Having sent a copy of one of her stories—"The Valley of Mist"—to J. C. Smith, an educator and RF's Scottish friend, Smith wrote her father: "You are not only a poet yourself but (unless I am mistaken) the father of one. I read Lesley's last affusion (as Wordsworth would call it) with the greatest interest.... Yes, quite remarkable. Keep your eye on Lesley." And in another letter, he wrote: "Tell Lesley to keep on writing—we look forward to her letters. Lesley will be an ornament to American Literature one of these days." RF's botanist friend Jack Haines and his wife, Dorothy, received the Frosts in their Gloucester home. "Lesley at 15," Dorothy said, "was nearly grown up and well educated and very handsome. I fancy she read a great deal." Friend and poet Eleanor Farjeon, who joined the small circle of poets in Dymock just prior to the outbreak of war, observed in Lesley "a tall girl of noble promise, her mother's chief stand-by in the domestic chores." RF, who found the poet W. H. Davies, frequently a member of the group in Dymock, to be pretentious, wrote home that Davies "set about encouraging Lesley to write about nature. It would be good practice for a child.... Lesley is old enough to have to struggle to keep a straight face in such circumstances. There now, he said, see that little bird, that little green one, I wonder what kind he is. Says Lesley It's a sparrow and it isn't green, is it? And Davies stumped into the house." (Davies had lost a leg when hit by a train in his hobo days.)

Before returning to America, RF's close friend and soon-to-be fellow poet Edward Thomas gave my mother a 1912 edition of A. E. Housman's *A Shropshire Lad*, signed in his diminutive hand "Lesley Frost from Edward Thomas," a small volume I treasure in my home library. From my mother's little story in the *Bouquet*, "What a Swallow Is," Thomas had already asked

To her parents' dismay, Mother soon began dating men—in p[art]
Donald Schlesinger (spelled Slesinger at the time), and, more serious[ly,]
roll Hollister, an accomplished pianist—and hanging out with a left-le[aning]
group of students at museums, the theater, and many concerts.

In one adventure, she and Donald Schlesinger decided to "raid" t[he]
Columbia University publication *Columbia Literary Monthly* and tak[e]
charge of the editorship. The literary magazine, a student monthly, had
never admitted women to its editorial staff. Surprisingly, after considerable
comment by the administration, the Student Council gave Mother permission to serve as an associate editor. Writing home shortly after on the *Literary Monthly*'s letterhead, Mother explained the outcome: "The magazine
is over, at least till next year. At the last moment we had a terrible quarrel
with the college organizations (King's Crown and Student Government)
about a Jew being Editor in Chief, which held us up so long that when we
finally went to press the printer refused to print it in the time we gave
him. [Virgil] Markham is appointed Editor for next year." According to the
Columbia University Archives, the *Literary Monthly* was discontinued and
replaced by the *Varsity*, which would publish its first issue (volume 1, no. 1)
in December 1919. Lesley Frost is listed as a contributor: "During the war,"
the editors comment, "[Miss Lesley Frost] was employed in the manufacture of army aeroplanes, and after the armistice she returned to college,
where she is a leader in athletics. Miss Frost is the daughter of Robert Frost,
the noted New England poet." In this issue of *Varsity*, we find two poems
by Lesley, "Blue Heron" and "The Awakening," about the god Pan, which,
as mentioned, she had submitted earlier to a college competition. Virgil
Markham, who lived in the shadow of his father, Edwin Markham, the poet
laureate of Oregon known for his celebration of the downtrodden laborer
in his poem "The Man with the Hoe," did, indeed, become editor in chief;
there is no mention of Donald Schlesinger as a contributor or on the editorial staff.

Mother seemed to take unusual pride in her accomplishments as an
athlete. Representing the class of '21, she entered and won frequent tennis
matches; the Barnard College Athletic Association invited her to join the
Barnard Varsity Base Ball squad, where she played a number of positions,
including pitcher; she won the Torch Race and Hoop Race at the Greek
Games, a Barnard tradition; at two different Field Days (May 1919 and
October 1919), she excelled in individual events (second place in the 40-yard
dash and first in the javelin, a college record of 68 feet 10 1/2 inches; only ten
other American women had thrown farther), for which she received a gold
medallion now in my possession: next to a Greek goddess, perhaps Athena,

for and been granted permission to use the opening simile, "I think some-
body's bow and arrow must have flown away together," a simile Edward
later included in "Haymaking":

> While over them shrill shrieked in his fierce glee
> The swift with wings and tail as sharp and narrow
> As if the bow had flown off with the arrow.

RF was proud to echo his friends' assessment of his eldest daughter: "Lesley
will hardly be one of the children much longer. She is as tall as her mother
and reads a decent paragraph of Caesar off without looking up more than
a couple of words. Sometimes too she does a paragraph of English writing
I admire."

The road Mother chose—inspired by an early life of reading and writing, she would explain—gave full expression to her boundless energy, leaving room for an early assumption of her role as family caretaker, especially
where her mother and siblings were concerned. As the trajectory of her life
evolved, she came to understand the dominant role her father and other
poets would play in her public appearances and in her writings.

Having returned from England in 1915, she settled first in Franconia,
New Hampshire, and then with her parents in Amherst, Massachusetts,
where her father assumed a teaching position at Amherst College. In one
year, she had completed her high school studies and was admitted as a
freshman at Wellesley College for the fall semester of 1917.

Still very young, but mature for her years in the role she had assumed
within the Frost family and in her writing, she managed to be a source of
almost continual conflict at Wellesley. First, she found herself expelled
from the court in the middle of a tennis match she was winning, and soon
she was excluded from the tennis team altogether—without explanation.
Papa wants Lesley to demand an explanation. And then matters get worse
when her Latin teacher ridiculed her for having started Latin by reading
it as literature, and for having shared her translations with other students;
even worse, a French instructor marked her down for having composed a
poem in French without first having studied prosody.

Letters that passed furiously—like texting today—between my mother
and her parents in Amherst reveal how hard it was for RF and Elinor to stay
out of their daughter's crises. RF wrote first to her and then to Professor
Charles Lowell Young, a colleague in the Wellesley English Department
(December 7, 1917). In his effort to intervene, he took to task both the Latin
and French instructors, colorfully accusing them of stifling the spirit of a
naturally excited student; but the spirit, he wrote Young, "will not be put

off." He pointed out that just such a painful approach to learning he had experienced at Harvard—where his early poem "A Tuft of Flowers" received a "B" grade from his instructor; he shared with Young "four lines to the tune of Tararaboomdeay I once addressed to Sheffy [Alfred D. Sheffield] when I was a patient at Harvard:

> Perhaps you think I am going to wait
> Till I can write like a graduate
> Before I can write to my friends any more
> You prig stick, what do you take me for."

Years later Sheffield took the dig in good grace and asked to be forgiven his ignorance of young talent. While his message about the teaching of English, French, or Latin was a serious one, RF concluded his letter in a friendly appeal to an old friend: "But blast all this. What a father I am! I promise never to talk to you about my children again—any of them. That is if you will forgive my having talked this time and the last time and the time before that and so on back to the day on top of [Mt.] Lafayette. They are really not worth talking about. Lesley in particular is not. She is no good. You can tell her I said so." Let no one take the last quote literally—he was a poet, after all! Although it was true that, as the eldest and by far the most adventuresome of the Frost family's children, my mother never stopped worrying her parents, they soon realized that RF's well-intentioned meddling in the daily drama only made matters worse.

It would be my mother's rather fiercely independent lifestyle that defined the rest of her life and the extraordinary adventures it led to as my sister, Elinor, and I were growing up. And it was her imagination and particular sense of poetry as it guided the life that she shared with us and that I want to share with you.

Once again on her own, Mother sought ways to satisfy her passion for airplanes and flying and to express her hatred of Germany. With no money for flying lessons, she decided to find work in a Curtis airplane propeller factory in Marblehead, Massachusetts. Having picked up some last-minute tutoring in wood carving from a family friend who carved wooden toys, she was able to secure a drafting job at the factory, a job generally not open to women, and thereby raise her salary to fifteen dollars weekly, enough to cover her food and lodging nearby, working from seven in the morning to six at night, through to the signing of the Armistice. Her parents became increasingly worried upon learning that factory workers alongside her were succumbing to the lethal "Spanish flu" of 1918: Elinor Frost had become seriously ill, her husband less so.

The next two academic years, ones Mother would enjoy both academically and athletically, were spent at Barnard College in New York City. One puzzle for me—and for her later in life—is why she did not complete her studies at Barnard. She had transferred to Barnard from Wellesley for the spring semester of 1919, continuing her studies through the 1919–20 academic year as a junior in the class of '21 before joining her parents in Ann Arbor, where her father had accepted a teaching appointment. Yes, it was true that finances were a constant worry and also true that her father took a rather cavalier approach to any formal education, but Mother was a talented student and excelled at Barnard. The failure to complete the undergraduate degree would haunt her the rest of her life.

At Barnard she found herself challenged not only academically but also socially, culturally, and athletically. From the beginning, although she studied hard and suffered as any undergraduate over examinations and grades, her activities outside the classroom filled her letters home. And there were many letters, addressed sometimes to "Papa," sometimes to "Mama," or simply to "Everyone."

Residing her first year in Furnald Hall, she moved to Brooke Hall her second year. Through her father, she was able to spend valuable time with a number of literary friends and their families: Louis Untermeyer, Padraic Colum, James Chapin, Ridgely Torrence, Harriet Vaughn Moody (often visiting New York City from her home in Chicago). On one occasion, Harriet took her to the Ridgely Torrence Garrick Theater. After watching a performance of the Spanish play *Bonds of Interest* (*Los intereses creados*), she was taken backstage to meet what she called a "rottenly" behaved Edna St. Vincent Millay. She praised productions by the Shakespearean actors Walter Hampden in *Hamlet* and John Barrymore in *Richard III*, returning to several more performances for the thrill. She made passing reference in her letters home to the numerous luncheons and dinners spent with these and others associated with her father.

For a time, her sister Irma came to New York to study art at the Art Students League; while Mother accepted responsibility for her sister, they lived in two different worlds. Mother tried to keep her father out of her affairs at Barnard, but it seemed that everywhere she turned, RF and his relationship to her were noted. Louis Untermeyer embarrassed her, making her life at college more difficult, by praising as superior her poem "Pan," one of a number of student entries in a competition, in front of the actual winner and in front of her. Louis later apologized. When RF came to town, he often stayed in the apartment of the publisher Alfred Harcourt, but, here as well, the Frost family's perennial shortness of funds restricted his visits.

patroness of Barnard, holding a laurel branch and shield, we find in the school's color, blue, the capital letters *B* and *C* and the date 1920; on the reverse, it reads "First Place, 15 Points, Lesley Frost."

Not long before her departure from New York and Barnard, Mother summarized her success thus far: "Another thing I've discovered," she wrote her parents, "is that if you are liked by the girls and are very good in athletics or acting or anything else there the faculty like you better even if you spend time you ought to be studying." She also realized how precarious her financial situation was, and how much she was depending on her parents and her parents' friends to help her through, to the point of providing her with desperately needed clothes appropriate for the city. She had been transferred to Barnard from Wellesley on scholarship, but when she heard the tuition for the next year had been raised to $250, she started to talk about leaving and returning to full-time employment: "It's good I'm getting out," she wrote her parents.

Mother went on to complete more credits at the University of Michigan, where her father had accepted a teaching appointment. However, she never completed her degree; it was a time when, even with a college degree, women struggled to gain professional respect.

The Open Book and the Knapsack

Mother believed fervently in the individual and in work, hard work. She was raised by her parents to believe in the power of poetry, but she remained unaware of her father's desire to publish until he presented his manuscripts to David Nutt when she was thirteen and fourteen years old in England. As the four children wrote in their journals, there was simply a mutual sharing of experience in their artistic endeavors from a young age.

It was in this way that Mother only gradually came to look upon her life as an "adventure in poetry," or, as her father would say, "in metaphor": "After two long experiences with adventure by poetry, on the *New* England farm, and in old England itself, I was never going to really get far away from poetry again. But by the time I went back to the United States once more I was seventeen [*sic*], and it was time to begin a life of action and hard work of my very own."

Always looking for ways of putting books into a way of making a living, Mother entered the "business" side of books. Her parents had had a select library around which the family life revolved. It was by far the most important thing they possessed. RF and Elinor considered children ready for literature from their first reading days. RF tended to buy outright any book he wanted or wanted his children to read; he avoided the public library on the belief that if a book was good enough to read it was good enough to make one's own, and good enough to care for as a treasure. Books on the Derry Farm were treated as jewels, to be carefully and individually wrapped and placed in special boxes each time they moved—to Plymouth, to England, and back to Franconia.

Tragedy struck when a customs officer, replacing a board, drove a spike through board and books and all. One of the worst nightmares Mother would recall from her childhood was the dreamt terror of her house on fire in the pitch-black night. She knew instinctively that the first thing to be rescued were the books; but as she seized them frantically in great armfuls, they buckled in the middle and scattered in every direction. Her panic and heartbreak at this would awaken her in fright.

Separated from the family library, Mother soon found a way to combine books, schools, and publishing in one enterprise: a bookshop. The bookshop would kill two birds with one stone, so to speak: it would make her a living (maybe), and it would give her books all over the walls. Her first bookshop did this to perfection, appealing to the double play of her nature: the fundamental need for action, hard physical labor, and the other need for contemplative exercise—"a pendulum movement in all things," she would say. The alternative current from mental to physical and back again, she contended, gives poise and stability to one's life, avoiding the extremes and providing a sought-after balance between the outward exertion and the inward thought, reverie and exchange of ideas: "I saw a bookshop as a business in which there was enough hard work so that I could always feel physically stretched and enough of the ivory tower so that I could always feel the world well lost in a good book":

> But yield who will to their separation,
> My object in living is to unite
> My avocation and my vocation
> As my two eyes make one in sight.
> Only where love and need are one,
> And the work is play for mortal stakes,
> Is the deed ever really done
> For Heaven and the future's sake.
>   (from "Two Tramps in Mud Time," Robert Frost)

She and a friend, Mary Ellen Hager, leased a lovely old New England house at 124 South Street in Pittsfield, Massachusetts, furnishing it with antique colonial furniture Mary Ellen was trying to sell. They made a library bookshop out of several of the living rooms and settled in "happily and luxuriously" in the midst. Announcements were sent for the formal opening on June 2, 1924. They called the whole affair the Open Book, an invitation to come in. The flyer carried lines from Yeats: "Then nowise worship dusty deeds. . . . For words alone are certain good."

In the house they entertained with dinners, luncheons, teas. They set aside a children's room full of books for the young and toys, with storytelling one afternoon a week after school; in conjunction with the Pittsfield public library, they offered a circulating library. They had roundtable forums in the evening or gatherings for poetry readings around the huge fireplace. To this house came Robert Frost, who was delighted to share in his daughter's business venture. He and others—Carl Sandburg, Edna St. Vincent Millay, Edwin Arlington Robinson, Amy Lowell, Louis Untermeyer, and Walter de la Mare from England, who read and talked about reading and writing. In this atmosphere, there was opportunity to listen to the animated exchange of ideas, for dreaming and reverie, and for self-awareness.

> He ate and drank the previous words
>   His spirit grew robust;
> He knew no more that he was poor,
>   Nor that his frame was dust.
> He danced along the dingy days;
>   And this bequest of wings
> Was but a book. What liberty
>   A loosen'd spirit brings!
>   ("A Book," Emily Dickinson)

The many literary contacts Mother had made over the years, in part as her father's surrogate, in part through her editorial work in New York City, opened the way for these extraordinary visitors to the Open Book.

At the time of the opening, however, the sense of euphoria dissipated as "the play quickly became play for mortal stakes." Mother had had to borrow a large sum of money in advance—some of it from her father—since the publishers had consigned an enormous number of books and since she was starting a business in a completely strange city within weeks of setting foot in it for the first time. She quickly overcame her worries with the optimism of youth, when "nothing ventured nothing gained really meant something," and determined to let neither bills nor publishers nor the attitude of the public bother her.

Pride took over when she, Ellen, and sister Marjorie stood back and gazed upon the freshly painted shelves overflowing with more books than they had hoped for, with the furnishings and pictures a perfect setting for the books themselves. They stood and admired the handsome and original sign, designed and executed by one of America's foremost modern painters, James Chapin, swinging from a post in the front yard like an English tavern sign. But, of course, pride goeth before the fall. Mother describes the moment: "Among the first enthusiastic customers I noticed one who seemed, from her back at least, not so enthusiastic. She was going along the shelves with near-sighted conscientiousness, her eyes only an inch or so from the titles. And her expression boded no good. Finally she turned and introduced herself as an assistant librarian in the City's Public Library. The Librarian, she said, Mr. Ballard, had sent her to look us over. Then dropping her voice to a stage whisper she said 'I see you have a great many KNOPF books.'" It seems that in those days the publishing house of Alfred Knopf stood for everything a little in advance of the times, often startling in design and text—radical enough to worry the old and conservative. Mother's reaction to the librarian's hushed warning was immediate. That same evening she went to work weeding out all the Knopf titles from the shelves, storing them discreetly in a closet. Fortunately, as far as the Pittsfield public was concerned, her fears were unfounded.

According to Mother's account, it turned out that Mr. Ballard was "a blot on the town's escutcheon . . . a relic of the Middle Ages or earlier." Long since the author of a translation of the *Odyssey,* he sat in a musty back office and saw no one if he could help it. He would send his nearsighted minion to look into the modern book situation. Each month Mother sent over some ten books for inspection. Most were returned without comment. On one occasion, however, Warwick Deeping's *Sorrell and Son*—at that time the leading best seller—was returned with a note from Mr. Ballard insisting that "it be consigned to the furnace where it belongs."

But things at the library would change dramatically when Mr. Ballard died. "Mr. Ballard, the Librarian at Pittsfield, has just died (something I've been waiting for for years and never thought would happen)," Mother exulted. Fearing Ballard's replacement would be an unknown from out of town, she was in fact thrilled with the board's choice: a brilliant young librarian from California who "opened [the Library] up to the sun and air," disposing of "the rubbish of a hundred years." A younger, more vigorous and exciting staff helped the Open Book run a bookshop/lending library through the city's hospitals and office buildings on Main Street.

Mother soon had her finger in several bookshops. The Open Book had its own branch in Williamstown, only twenty miles away, where Williams College made the town three-fourths Williams and one-fourth town and where a lot of wealthy American boys did a lot of book buying. And she became part owner, with Leonora Harris and Anna Lloyd, of the Print and Book Shop at 521 Jefferson Street in Ann Arbor, Michigan, where her father was teaching at the university. Shifting stock around between shops often helped books that did not sell in one market to sell in another.

At the time Mother opened the bookstore in Pittsfield, her younger sister Marjorie joined her initially as a partner. Over time, however, she was forced to give up any hard physical work. Following a serious bout with pneumonia and surgery, Marjorie was unable to continue to help in the bookshop.

In 1926, at the time of Mary Ellen's mysterious death in the Bahamas, where she had gone to open a tea salon, two friends, Leonora O'Herron and Catherine Manion, assumed an ever-greater role in the bookshop, permitting Mother to commute back and forth from New York, where she worked primarily for Doubleday, Doran & Co., 244 Madison Avenue. Mother was able to lease the other half of the house they were in at 124 South Street, moving Leonora and her antiques in with her. The house was thoroughly renovated. "I can't tell you how lovely it is. But neither can I tell you how we've worked," my mother wrote Mary Ellen's father, Charles Hager, who would agree to continue to lend a sum of money to keep the business going. "I wish I could express to you," Mother wrote: "how my heart hurts me a million times a day when I think how Mary Ellen would have been so wonderfully happy to see things as they are now. She loved Leonora and Leonora her. . . . But some way I can't help the feeling that she is wandering about these rooms with us."

Leonora O'Herron had two antique businesses—one at 120 South Street next to Mother in Pittsfield, the other at 25 Lewis Street in Hartford, Connecticut. Although she never became part owner of the Open Book, she was Mother's close friend and confidant during this period. When Mother was away, she kept tabs on the Open Book and its finances. She was supportive when my sister, Elinor, was born May 11, 1929, at the Harbor Hospital Sanitarium, Sixty-First and Madison Avenue, urging Mother to get out of the city for the summer.

It wasn't long before the Open Book needed a means of transportation. "So with scarcely any greater purpose than package delivery and social calls and shop publicity," Mother explained, "I purchased the car, a half ton Ford truck, which set us back by installments at the rate of a hundred and fifty down and thirty dollars a month to five hundred."

The new owners fastened irregularly shaped, brilliantly colored lettering across the side curtains to read "The Knapsack of the Open Book," with the address (124 South Street) attached. Called a "she" by her owners, like a ship, the book caravan was launched. At the cost of yet another fifty dollars, Mother ordered two bookcases to be built "the length of the truck, facing outward, and built at an inward slope from bottom to top"; each shelf was divided into small sections with the books wedged in tight. Between the bookcases, in the center of the truck, was a long triangular-shaped space extending from back to front. This they equipped with mattresses and blankets and all things necessary for sleeping out in case they were caught far from an inn or a friend's house.

Mother had been bitten by wanderlust, and the Knapsack was the means to satisfy the urge of a modern gypsy:

> The railroad track is miles away,
>   And the day is loud with voices speaking
> Yet there isn't a train goes by all day
>   But I hear its whistle shrieking.
>
> All night there isn't a train goes by,
>   Though the night is still for sleep and dreaming,
> But I see its cinders red on the sky
>   And hear its engine steaming.
>
> My heart is warm with the friends I make,
>   And better friends I'll not be knowing;
> Yet there isn't a train I wouldn't take,
>   No matter where it's going.
>   ("Travel," Edna St. Vincent Millay)

With some three to four hundred books, Mother and Marjorie took to the roads of New England and New York State. Having quickly discovered that the front-door and hotel approach was met with the glare reserved for peddlers and that the town squares proved too "unliterary," they tried to make it to the home of a friend for the night. Here they could display the books on the porch or street curb, where people would drift over and sit on the lawn or the steps to look at books and be served tea and cake (if available).

However, their biggest summer trade was done in the children's summer camps: a week on the Cape, another in the White Mountains or in the Berkshires. Boys and girls between the ages of eight and fifteen or sixteen flocked to the camps for six weeks in the summer. At the boys' camps, Mother's Knapsack was often headed off at the door by the directors, who maintained that boys should be spared the unnecessary distraction of books and be kept out of mischief by being exercised until they fell into bed exhausted.

Mother soon learned that it was the girls' camps where she received a more enthusiastic welcome, and where the counselors had to restrain the girls from spending their entire summer allowance on books. The girls loved modern poetry in particular: Edna Millay, of course, because her poetry is written for the young, and Carl Sandburg for the way he calls a spade a spade, and Edwin Arlington Robinson for his satiric humor, and Robert Frost for his human warmth and love of nature, and Stephen Benet for his romantic fervor, and even T. S. Eliot. Often the books were autographed, adding to the thrill. The counselors seemed to love the arts generally—literature, painting, music, handicrafts—and they would read aloud to the younger children and allow them to submit their original poems and stories for inclusion in the camp's bulletin.

All this set a welcoming background for Mother's arrival, usually for a stay of two or three days. She loved to talk and recite poetry, especially before the campfire at night, on a pitch-dark hillside, or along the lake shore under high black pines, with the smells of resin and needles and smoke:

> With the flames licking upward and lighting the faces of the children in a circle, what a delight it was to see their seriousness, hear their laughter and make them shiver with pleasure or fear. They had their favorites, often the ones they had memorized at school, and would call for them by name. But most of all, perhaps, they loved to have their skins turned inside out by the way I would really let go, in the wilderness of the jungle, and say the poetry of Vachel Lindsay: "The Congo," "Simon Legree," "John Brown." I knew they liked being scared. (Lesley Frost—Notes)

Mother admitted that she preferred selling books to "the person who can speculate *about* books. . . . I don't care particularly to sell a book except as a token of understanding between me and the customer—like confidential winks." She found it difficult to talk of the commercial side, but of course she understood that "behind our book mood *is* our money mood": She came to realize that the caravan provided "a nice summer-extension trade to the book-shop, of perhaps eight hundred to a thousand dollar turnover a month." The base of operations remained the bookshop in Pittsfield, and resupplying the caravan with books from New York proved difficult. In the off-season for camps, which closed by the end of August, Mother found a book outlet in schools, libraries, clubs, and private exhibits—anywhere "the introduction of books meets the proper sympathy."

She learned early on that there is much to commend the life of a "wandering bard." There are always pleasant things to be done "in whatever port one comes to anchor." Besides the usual resort activities, one can read aloud from one's own or someone else's work; she soon found that lecturing is especially exciting where the audience changes from day to day: "Oh, there's adventure enough in caravaning with books—even if it's only of the kind that finds you on your knees in the road-dust blackening the only shirt to your back over an exhausted tire."

Unless they had engine trouble or found themselves delayed on a particularly lonely stretch, they could find lodging with a friend in town. But, at one time or another, before the summer was over, they would have managed to sleep in every conceivable type of place, from inside the truck itself, to the floor of a gas station, to the tent of a camper, to the barn of a farmhouse. Once in the dead heat of August, Mother had four blowouts along the fifty barren miles of sand dunes at the end of Cape Cod:

> It wasn't all changing tires or being caught in blizzards, or cloudbursts, though these played their part. Most of it, however, was all one could ask of the vagrant gypsy life, of the satisfying of my urge to travel. Our Ford truck was indeed a sort of Parnassus on wheels, as Christopher Morley so aptly phrased it. And although a Ford truck could hardly be said to have wings, we could often feel that we were galloping cross country on Parnassus himself with a bundle of books in the saddle bags.

Having been brought up on a farm, Mother had a particular craving for nature. On the road, she could watch the seasons come and go at close and intimate range.

> Nature's first green is gold,
> Her hardest hue to hold.
> Her early leaf's a flower;
> But only so an hour.
> Then leaf subsides to leaf.
> So Eden sank to grief,
> So dawn goes down to day.
> Nothing gold can stay.
>   ("Nothing Gold Can Stay," Robert Frost)

In the spring, driving down a narrow road in the Berkshire Hills, between birch and poplar trees, or among the cherry and peach orchards of the Pelham Hills, farther south, she could have her fill:

> Loveliest of trees, the cherry now
> Is hung with bloom along the bough,
> And stands about the woodland ride
> Wearing white for Eastertide.

Now, of my threescore years and ten,
Twenty will not come again,
And take from seventy springs a score,
It only leaves me fifty more.

And since to look at things in bloom
Fifty springs are little room,
About the woodlands I will go
To see the cherry hung with snow.
    ("Loveliest of Trees," A. E. Housman)

Then there would be the richness of summer, the smell of juniper and bal-
sam in the mountain pastures as Mother forced the heavy truck up over
stony, washed-out roads, making shortcuts from one New Hampshire valley
into another. And then all too soon would come the autumn, Keats's "season of mists and mellow fruitfulness":

Season of mists and mellow fruitfulness!
    Close bosom-friend of the maturing sun;
Conspiring with him how to load and bless
    With fruit the vines that round the thatch-eaves run;
To bend with apples the moss'd cottage-trees
    And fill all fruit with ripeness to the core;
        To swell the gourd, and plump the hazel shells
    With a sweet kernel; to set budding more,
And still more, later flowers for the bees,
Until they think warm days will never cease,
    For Summer has o'er-brimm'd their clammy cells.
        (from "Ode to Autumn," John Keats)

And Mother would respond to the feelings nature had inspired in her:

A thrush would sing, piercing and almost too sweet among the arches of the
mountain pines. Or a white heron would rise with a whiteness as piercing as
sound from the desolate marshes along the Massachusetts or Maine coast,
fraught with the terrible and haunting emotion of Benet's poem:

I flung my soul to the air like a falcon flying.
I said, "Wait on, wait on, while I ride below!
    I shall start a heron soon
    In the marsh beneath the moon—

A strange white heron rising with silver on its wings,
    Rising and crying
    Wordless, wondrous things;

> The secret of the stars, of the world's heart-strings
>   The answer to their woe
> Then stoop thou upon him, and grip and hold him so!"
>   (from "The Falconer of God," William Rose Benet)

And all the time, Mother recalled, she would say the poem out loud to the woods and hills, knowing that she had the very book in which it was printed right at her elbow, on her back, so to speak, in her knapsack. It was a "good and righteous" feeling, she said, that helped her along greatly toward her next marketplace.

The Lure of the Sea

It was through poetry that members of the Frost family first experienced the romantic lure of the open sea. Lesley, as the eldest and most exposed to her father's "lover's quarrel with the world," had developed as a child on a farm far removed from the ocean. But her at-home education by poetry had given free rein to her imagination, often engaged in the nature at hand on long walks with her father but no less so in the world beyond their grasp, a world she included in her daily journals and in her artwork. One of her later poems, "The Lonely of Heart," reflects both her and her father's sensitivity to isolated worlds, such as Easter Island, Tristan da Cunha, Pitcairn Island, and the Hebrides:

> I am encumbered with the loneliness
> Of those in alien places, strange and far,
> Whose season's rigors I can only guess—
> How vast the distances. Perhaps they are
> Not lost except as I conceive them so;
> But I can think them lonely past belief,
> Can think the storms more bitter from their seas,
>   And closing in with snow;
> Can feel the darkness widening reef from reef
> And hear the winds torment the foreign trees.
>
> The road above the rainy Hebrides
> That chalks the cliff from Wrath to Pentland Firth,
> Where one dark figure in a doorway sees
> How raveled fog blindfolds a phantom earth.
>
> . . . .
>
> So far from here the winds and waves go by,
> So far beyond these still New England fields,
> Where spruce woods point their steeples on the sky

And on the hills the savin lays its shields
And lights prick out like stars from farm to farm.
Yet being safe in what is understood
In blood and sinew and the deeper bone
   But brings a fierce alarm:
What of the realms beyond *all* earthly good,
Even of storm, uncharted and unknown.

It wasn't until 1935, after four distinct sea voyages, that Mother edited a personal anthology of verse entitled "Look Homeward, Heart," never published, in which she includes a section of poems evoking the mysteries of the sea, including two poems by her father: "Once by the Pacific" and "Sand Dunes." She introduces the section she calls "To the Scattered Waters" with a postcard painting (by Frank Vining Smith) of the pilot schooner *Wander Bird* and writes out each poem in careful longhand: "All Day I Hear" (James Joyce), "The Crying of Water" (Arthur Symons), "The Sea Waves" (Sara Teasdale), "Old Ships" (David Morton), "The Mariners" (Margaret L. Woods), "Windward Rock" (Kenneth Leslie), "The Shell" (James Stephens), from "Tristan da Cunha" (Roy Campbell), "A Wanderer's Song" (John Mansfield), "The Lake Isle of Innisfree" (W. B. Yeats), "Far Lake" (Wade van Dore), "Song for All Seas, All Ships" (Walt Whitman), "Atavism" (Elinor Wylie), "A Visit from the Sea" (R. L. Stevenson), "LII" (A. E. Housman), "Low Tide" (Sara Teasdale), "A Passer-By" (Robert Bridges).

Although the call of the sea reflected in her choice of poems was never extinguished, she would describe her first sea voyage in very down-to-earth terms. The SS *Parisian* left Boston harbor on August 24, 1912, destination Glasgow (Scotland), carrying, besides a full passenger list, a cargo that included 211 barrels of apples and 46,665 bushels of wheat. Robert and Elinor Frost were accompanied on board by their four children, Lesley (13), Carol (10), Irma (9), and Marjorie (7). Once in England, Elinor mentioned the crossing only in passing: "We sailed from Boston to Glasgow, and enjoyed the ocean trip on the whole, though Mr. Frost, Lesley and I were quite seasick for a few days. The younger children escaped with only a few hours discomfort." In the composition notebook the children put together soon afterward—"An Important Year by Four Children, Dedicated to Papa & Mamma"—Lesley's description of her discomfort is far more vivid: "Rose, sunk! Up, down! High, low! Back, forth. I woke with a horrible feeling in my stomach and a whirling head. Great green waves went over the port-hole, a wind roared outside and I shut my eyes at every sinking of the ship. How far down is she going? When will she start to rise? Then suddenly she would be caught at the bottom of [a] steep moving green gulf between two waves and would start her ascent. Up, up, up and the higher she went the more I dreaded the next drop. This was a storm and I knew it."

She employs similar language in describing the ever-present seagulls, especially the small pearly-white ones "dropping like stones" to the water in search of fish or food thrown overboard. "All the way over," she concludes, "I never saw any kind of gull catch a fish, although once I saw one at the top of the mast with one under his foot, if I didn't dream it." She includes an ode "To the Seagull" and a drawing in color of a gull floating on the water.

Not to be outdone by her father's often humorous treatment of such matters, Lesley goes on to describe three Scotsmen on board: a Scotch schoolteacher, guided by his resentment of British rule; the disagreeable captain of the ship, forever yelling at them, "You little kiddies, get below"; and a nagging, whining Scots boy who wouldn't stop following them everywhere.

Once back in America, and having finished high school in Amherst, Massachusetts, Lesley entered Wellesley College in the fall of 1917. Her talent for interpreting her early experiences through the prism of her poetic, somewhat romanticized imagination is evidenced in a series of compositions written for her freshman English class. In one, she recalls being seasick: "I came up on deck early in the morning to try to overcome the first attack of sea-sickness by breathing and swallowing the strong wind and rain that were sweeping across the ship." In another, she describes her somewhat exalted response to nature's stormy mood: "When on board ship out upon the sea, sandwiched between grey waves and grey clouds, I have exulted in nature's mood. I have stood on the windward deck and let the fine cold rain beat against my face as it was beating upon the glassy waves and beating up along the deck so furiously that it whitened as it struck. Just as the wild dismal fog-horn blowing out into the grey answered to the wildness of the day, so I responded. A white gull wet its wing tips in a near wave. By the curve and dash of its flight I imagined that it, too, felt and gloried in the storm."

Writing home from Beaconsfield, Elinor had recalled how, on the last day of the crossing to Glasgow, the SS *Parisian* "skirted along the north coast of Ireland, and [I] thought the dark, wild looking headlands and blue mountains very beautiful." In a college composition on W. B. Yeats's play *Land of Heart's Desire,* Lesley invokes the mystery of the same rugged Irish coastline:

> I remember the day when we sailed up the northern coast of Ireland on our way to England. The blue bare hills with no trees on them, not to mention a house, nothing but heather and flying gulls, rose out of a bare sea against a bare sky. Cutting into the hills was a bay where lay some warships as lonely and deserted if not more so than they would have been out of sight of land.

The increased swell off the land that rocked the boat sideways added to the wildness of it all. It certainly was a place for fairies

> . . . to ride upon the winds
> Run on the top of the dishevelled tides
> And dance upon the mountains like a flame.

With the outbreak of war the previous August, the Frost family headed for home, sailing from Liverpool on the SS *St. Paul* on February 13, 1915, and taking with them Edward Thomas's teenage son, Merfyn. They were shaken by the proximity of the blockade and the uncertainty of war. In pitch darkness and rain, with the SS *Lusitania* nearby, the *St. Paul* was escorted by two battleships out into the Atlantic. Lesley's college composition captures the harrowing scene:

> Standing in a fine cold grey rain that blew down the Mercy river from the sea, we watched our boat, the St. Paul, come slowly in to the wharf, rubbing against the great buffers. They lowered a gangplank. A hard-faced official took our passports, glanced at them swiftly with hard eagle eyes, and pushed us on board. For the next two hours we stood about on deck watching the Lusitania anchored near, and waiting for us, as two battleships were going to take her and the St. Paul around the coast of Ireland in the night. Night came and we sailed. It was so dark we could see nothing through the sifting rain but a few twinkling shore lights and the long restless rays of two searchlights that felt of us again and again, as with fingers. The next morning we were far out in the Atlantic.

By way of contrast, once settled in New Hampshire, Robert sent Lascelles Abercrombie a more witty description of the "inspector at the gangway in Liverpool who was for keeping us in England till our greatness ripened a little more. Very well says I, maybe you know more about what's good for me than I do myself. I like England and I'm willing to stay if some one else will take the responsibility. But I give you fair warning: if I don't go now I won't go at all. I shall become a British subject and 'run for' the Laureateship. That seemed to make him think. He let us go on board—muttering." Just prior to departure from England, the Frost family moved from Little Iddens to the home of Lascelles Abercrombie and his family at the nearby Gallows. In February 1915, the family hastily packed their possessions into a huge crate. The attached label read "For SS St. Paul. Sailing Feb 13, American Line, Liverpool. Please forward with dispatch." Ninety-nine years later, the crate's lid and label were discovered shoved into a back closet under the stairs at their new home in Franconia.

Around the World with a Bookstore on the SS *Franconia*

Because everything Mother undertook she viewed as an "adventure," we should not be surprised to learn that the tours of the Knapsack led directly to further excitement—an adventure at sea, of course. It would happen at one of her periodic visits to the Institute of Politics at Williamstown; having stopped the truck at the front door of the Institute's grand dining room while waiting to join friends for lunch, she opened her shop.

As a group of interested browsers gathered around the truck, she began arguing loudly with a professor from Columbia University about the education of the young. He said memorizing was not good; Mother replied that a certain amount of it *was* good, particularly if one memorized *good* poetry. Neither of them could explain what good it had done them, but Mother was glad she had, even long poems like Coleridge's "Ancient Mariner" and Lord Macaulay's "Horatius at the Bridge" (from *The Lays of Ancient Rome,* 1842).

A little old man had been standing at the edge of the crowd; with snow-white hair, a white goatee, white spats and a cane, he looked like a character out of Dickens's *Pickwick Papers.* "I learned 'Horatius at the Bridge' too when I was a boy," he said, challenging Mother, "and I'll wager I can say more of it now than you can." Soon the two of them were competing to see who would break down first:

I

Lars Porsena of Clusium
  By the Nine Gods he swore
That the great house of Tarquin
  Should suffer wrong no more.

By the Nine Gods he swore it,
  And named a trysting day,
And bade his messengers ride forth,
East and west and south and north,
  To summon his array.

II

East and west and south and north
  The messengers ride fast,
And tower and town and cottage
  Have heard the trumpet's blast.
Shame on the false Etruscan
  Who lingers in his home,

When Porsena of Clusium
  Is on the march for Rome.

The long poem narrates the courage of Horatius in saving the Bridge Gate in battle against the Etruscans over the Tiber River, when "the Romans were like brothers, in the brave days of old." Both Mother and her father were great storytellers, and they loved story poems like this one.

With the two challengers reciting lickety-split, it wasn't long before both they and the crowd broke down laughing. It was then that another gentleman came forward and told Mother she was just the person he was looking for to take her books on an around-the-world tour. "Shake hands on it quickly," Mother said, "because it sounds so wonderful and I'm afraid you might change your mind." At the moment of his asking and Mother's instantaneous acceptance, neither knew the other's name. He was, in fact, director of the Cook's Southern Hemisphere 1927 Cruise, and he had been looking for someone to join the cruise as a lecturer; when he saw Mother's bookshop, he saw the advantage of having books on board as a resource for passengers to research the different ports of call.

"And it was given to me," Mother said, "because I was having fun with poetry." Later she would tell her audiences that there are all kinds of ways to get joy and adventure out of life, many paths to the same end: the path of the scientist (Eve Curie), of the thinker and scholar (Ralph Waldo Emerson), of the nurse (Florence Nightingale), of the missionary (Junípero Serra), of the explorer (Christopher Columbus), of teaching (Aristotle). Returning to the path of poetry, the path of her father, she often quoted Wordsworth: "Effort and expectation and desire / And something evermore about to be." Living that way, Mother would conclude, was the highest expression of the individual as he or she tries to live likewise.

Having quickly accepted the unexpected offer to take her books on board the SS *Franconia* on what would be a five-month around-the-world cruise in the Southern Hemisphere, she at once threw herself into the preparations for the voyage leaving New York January 12 and returning June 2, 1927.

It was already mid-August, and the hardest work had to be done before they left port. Placed in charge of the bookstore, Mother had to choose books with complete finality—no changes, no renewals. She would be committed to the stock she had. After consulting with the lecturers hired to provide orientation for the many ports of call, she soon had sifted and organized book lists totaling some three thousand volumes.

Her travel library would, they decided, include "required" reading for the lectures: a marvel of geography and information. Knowing that she had agreed to give an occasional lecture herself, she also included a large collection in the field of literature—novels and poetry. Next she had to persuade each publisher in turn to consign the books to her for the duration, allowing her to pay for the books she sold only after her return, and to return any unsold books to the publishers. Through her many contacts in the New York publishing business and her enthusiastic salesmanship, she managed to sell the idea. In fact, she said, not a single publisher disappointed her.

The previous year Mother had met my father, J. Dwight Francis, who lived with his family in Pittsfield and who frequented the Open Book. She and Dwight would marry upon her return to New York. The love affair was in full bloom when Mother boarded the cruise liner; her long, passionate letters to Dwight contain many details about the voyage and were returned to her years later; she passed them on to me.

The SS *Franconia* had designated certain cabins by number in which the books could be stored and unpacked, and the publishers had been directed to address the boxes to these cabins. The cruise ship was programmed to leave port at midnight on January 12. Imagine Mother's horror upon coming aboard earlier in the evening and finding no trace of the books in the space allotted to them. A big farewell party was in progress on board that included relatives and friends; instead of joining the festivities, Mother found herself snooping about belowdecks and up and down the bitterly cold windy Cunard docks with a couple of deckhands and longshoremen with a lantern hunting her lost stock-in-trade. They found nothing. Overwhelmed with exhaustion, she fell into her bunk bed, not caring whether or not they decided to evict her in Kingston, Jamaica, the first port of call.

Mother's recollection of the voyage on the SS *Franconia* comes to us through the many lengthy letters sent home, to her parents and to Dwight. Her perspective here, as at other times in her life, is one of finding in each circumstance the poetry, the romance, the seeds of adventure. Besides the correspondence, she left us the official logbook, two albums of photos of the voyage, invitations from other passengers, and memorabilia of the many ports of call.

The SS *Franconia* sailed at midnight out into a stormy North Atlantic, making her way through wind, snow, and ice as Mother slept. Once the ship dropped southward into the Gulf Stream and the sun came out, Mother emerged on deck. After a systematic search for the crated books, they were finally located far from the assigned cabins. Unpacked and checked, the books were found to be all there. For the books' display, the *Franconia* had outdone herself. Two large adjoining salons—the card room and writing room well forward on B deck—had been lined with built-in book-cases, transforming two rather cold-looking ship's lounges into attractive, homelike, colorful libraries. She was permitted to set up exhibits whenever and wherever on board she pleased. In port, the fun was to arrange for the residents to browse among the books at leisure. In ports such as Fiji, Port Moresby, and Zanzibar, few residents were interested in books, but those who were, were passionately so, having been isolated for so long from the book world; in such ports as Honolulu, Melbourne, Singapore, Cape Town, and Buenos Aires, there was a veritable run on the bank.

Mother shared a large six-passenger cabin, from which four of the six bunks had been removed, with one other woman, the assistant hostess Mildred Delnoce. Mildred turned out to be an excellent companion with a compatible sense of humor; both enjoyed the many incredible, outrageous, melodramatic things that happened in those almost five months at sea. Together they looked over the other passengers. There were only roughly five hundred passengers on a ship whose usual quota for an Atlantic crossing was more than two thousand. The extraordinary accumulation of wealth during the "Roaring Twenties" meant that, on such a cruise as this, the space was sold not by the bunk but by the cabin or suite, allowing for the luxury of space. Situations developed, nevertheless—often interesting, sometimes disastrous, never exactly peaceful.

Mother provides a running commentary on the odd assortment on board. Here were elderly people retired from business or professional lives. Here were spinster women who made a habit of travel, who set up rocking chairs in their cabins and deck chairs on deck and wore a path between the two, knitting, gossiping, reading, "like cats curled up on a stoop." Here were a few businessmen with rice or sugar or oil interests on the other side of the world and who combined business with pleasure—"9/10 pleasure and 1/10 business"—in order to confer with their managers in Java, India, South Africa. Here were a few parents who had briefly escaped their job responsibilities in order to give a son or daughter a journey that would be an education in itself. And here were the sons and daughters, losing their heads over so much leisure, romance, and opportunity for mischief. There were even a few shady characters—women who hoped to land a millionaire, men who were professional gamblers and card sharks or who might be smugglers of drugs or jewels, seldom seen, except ashore in certain ports or in odd corners of the ship at odd hours. One young man of twenty or so had just been adopted by one of the millionaires on board after being the man's chauffeur for several years. The millionaire was offering the boy a cruise by way of background and education. And here was the hard woman, stiff with diamonds and emeralds, who had once been a secretary who married the boss. He had died, cause unknown, and she was spending the fortune left her. There was the representative of old England, a fine colonial of the old school, returning for a last visit at seventy to the Malayan rubber country and to visit friends in Singapore. Mother admired him for his energy and humor, which, she said, was way out in front of most of the men: he played a hard and brilliant game of deck tennis every day in the blazing tropic sun. He fell in love with a young American widow, and they were married on the return to England. Then there was the couple "of mystery" from whom the mystery never lifted. At first they were thought to be brother and sister, but when it was found they were not, nothing changed: "They were loved and respected for what they were," Mother said: "There was a sense about them of past and future tragedy. They were sad in their happiness together, and also strangely happy in their sadness. He was obviously a cripple of the last war, and she might have been his nurse at some time along the way. Now they were sharing a brief illusion of life together. He committed suicide the day the journey ended." And then there was the seventeen-year-old who had been whisked away from a romance opposed by her family. She lived the whole trip only for his cables and letters at every port, and they were married the day they were reunited. Absence had made the heart grow fonder.

One of the more dramatic events, Mother recalled, was when a famous retired surgeon from Cincinnati, Ohio, was called upon to perform an emergency appendectomy at 2:00 a.m. in the middle of the Indian Ocean on the hottest night of the year. It seems that the ship's surgeon was too out of practice to be of any help. Of course, the retired surgeon, Dr. W. D. Haines, and his wife made the most of his accomplishment.

One of the lecturers was Branson de Cou, the staff photographer, who frequently displayed his colored stills in the movie salon at night. Mr. De Cou actually weighed about three hundred pounds. Once, in a narrow-gauge African train, he became wedged in, and it was a serious matter to extricate him. A lot of glass was broken, and he fainted several times before it was managed. But he was saved to return to the States with another rare and beautiful collection of moon rainbows over Victoria Falls, sunsets over the Taj Mahal, and sunrises over Malaya.

Dancing all night and buying Spanish shawls by day in Old Panama and Balboa made Mother feel they "were walking around in a Somerset Maugham short story," a feeling later intensified in the South Seas and India, she said. They were already in the tropics, where the heat and super-charged atmosphere meant anything could happen, "from Cinderella to riches, from murder to romance." Turning out of Panama into the broad Pacific, those passengers experiencing it for the first time felt the thrill that John Keats had in his "On First Looking into Chapman's Homer":

> Much have I travell'd in the realms of gold,
>   And many goodly states and kingdoms seen;
>   Round many western islands have I been
> Which bards in fealty to Apollo hold.
> Oft of one wide expanse had I been told
>   That deep-brow'd Homer ruled as his demesne:
>   Yet did I never breathe its pure serene
> Till I heard Chapman speak out loud and bold.
>
> —Then felt I like some watcher of the skies
>   When a new planet swims into his ken;
> Or like stout Cortez, when with eagle eyes
>   He stared at the Pacific—and all his men
> Look'd at each other with a wild surmise—
>   Silent, upon a peak in Darien.

Despite Keats's obvious error in identifying Cortés as the Spanish explorer, the sentiment prevails.

After disappointing stops in Los Angeles, including a bird's-eye rush through Hollywood, and on a trash-strewn Waikiki Beach in Hawaii, the SS *Franconia* left Honolulu and headed for Apia (Samoan Islands). On the way, she crossed the equator. As part of the traditional festivities, Mother and the other passengers each received "A Proclamation" from Neptunus Rex (Captain Melsom), which reads in part:

> Greeting: Know ye that on this the 8th day of February I have deigned
> to hold my court upon the decks of the good ship FRANCONIA, in
> latitude o and Longitude 166, on her voyage around the world.
> BE IT KNOWN that on this day Miss Lesley Frost, a landlubber and minion
>   of Terrestrial Rulers, hath found favor in my eyes. . . .
> Given under my Fin and Seal this Eighth day of February 1927.

"Of all the islands we saw," Mother recalled, "Samoa, Robert Louis Stevenson's island, seemed to me the loveliest, and all that a South Sea island should be." She experienced the enchantment found in Stevenson's *Island Night's Entertainments* or *South Sea Island Tales*. Circumstances added to the excitement, for coming off Samoa, Captain Melsom received radio warnings of a hurricane.

With no docking facilities available for big liners, the plan had been to anchor offshore and send the passengers ashore by long boat. As the waves increased in size and the wind in violence, the skipper said no boats could be lowered. Several passengers, including Mother, created such a scene that the skipper finally relented, allowing one boat to attempt it. Mother, of course, was on board, leaving Captain Melsom to fume and fret. Although he tried to signal the handful of passengers who made it onto the island to return to the ship, Mother noted that they "weren't very good at reading signals" and thus had the island to themselves for the twelve hours as programmed. Once onshore, the small party made its way up the hill at Vailimia to Stevenson's tomb. At the highest point on the island, the tomb is a huge oblong granite stone on which is carved Stevenson's "Requiem," as epitaph:

> Under the wide and starry sky
> Dig the grave and let me lie.
> Glad did I live and gladly die,
> And I laid me down with a will.
>
> This be the verse you grave for me:
> *Here he lies where he longed to be;*
> *Home is the sailor, home from the sea,*
> *And the hunter home from the hill.*

Mother described the intensity of the moment as her group made its way down the mountain: "We came down the mountain to swim in the deep jungle pool near his home where he had swum many and many a time. We walked around the island on footpaths under palms and breadfruit and papaya trees, and the Samoans, a beautiful and quiet people, with all the gentle characteristics that Stevenson so loved them for, gazed at us with quiet brown eyes as they sat cross-legged on the pebble floors of their open round thatch roofed houses, or under the trees beating their tapa into cloth. They were Gauguin's pictures in the flesh."

Moving South from Samoa, the SS *Franconia* entered tropical water, with porpoises and sharks riding along the phosphorescence of the waves. As the sea changed, so did the sky. Mother was accustomed to the stars and constellations of the north—the Dipper, Pleiades, Orion, Aldebaran, and the North Star—but the sky above her now held Canopus, Antares, Peacock, and Polaris. She remembered Byron's "Stars":

> Ye stars! which are the poetry of heaven,
> If in your bright leaves we could read the fate
> Of men and empires,—'tis to be forgiven

That in our aspirations to be great
Our destinies o'erleap their mortal state,
And claim a kindred with you; for ye are
A beauty and a mystery, and create
In us such love and reverence from afar,
That fortune, fame, power, life, have named themselves a star.

By way of Fiji, Australia, New Zealand, and New Guinea, the SS *Franconia* made her way to Singapore. In Fiji, when visitors from the island came on board, the staff was overwhelmed trying to keep them out of the engine room and galleys or kitchens. Cooking paraphernalia and steam engines and roaring furnaces attracted them, and there was danger of their getting permanently trapped with piston rings and pressure cookers. In New Guinea, on the other hand, the natives were drawn to the fascinating array of mirrors. The elevators, in particular, were coated with mirrors; the visitors couldn't resist seeing themselves repeated on all sides with their bracelet-size earrings and their shark-bone nose rings.

After having raised anchor, the crew found a huddle of the islanders packed into an elevator. A lot of hand gestures were necessary to convince them to leave: they soon jumped overboard and swam ashore.

Reaching Batavia in Java, Mother was driven into the Java hinterland, up among the rice terraces and green mountains of tropical forest, where she encountered "worlds of beauty and imagination that surpass description." In Singapore, her group danced in a flowered patio until three in the morning, then drove back to the ship for their bathing suits. At the harbor entrance, they swam out to a float in mid-channel. Here they watched the sunrise, and "the little boats of every kind and shape, and the sampans with their colored sails of saffron, sea blue, pale rose—the ships of all ages and all places, come sailing past us against the ripening sky." Mother recalled another poem, "Cargoes," by John Masefield:

Quinquireme of Nineveh from distant Ophir,
Rowing home to haven in sunny Palestine,
With a cargo of ivory,
And apes and peacocks,
Sandalwood, cedarwood, and sweet white wine.

Stately Spanish galleon coming from the Isthmus,
Dipping through the Tropics by the palm-green shores,
With a cargo of diamonds,
Emeralds, amethysts,
Topazes, and cinnamon, and gold moidores.

Dirty British coaster with a salt-caked smokestack,
Butting through the Channel in the mad March days,
With a cargo of Tyne coal,
Road-rail, pig-lead,
Firewood, iron-ware, and cheap tin trays.

Mother saw a short story in each of these events. She could not resist adding one such final episode from her voyage on board the SS *Franconia*. She recounted how, while ashore in Sydney, Australia, two of the more ardent women welfare workers—"probably pillars of women's clubs in Springfield, Ohio, or Rutland, Vermont"—discovered and purchased a little red paper-bound volume that proved to be the spark that would set off a wild chain of events. The book had been written, it seems, by the last brave missionary to leave the South Pacific island of Tristan da Cunha. He had left the island, given its residents up as impossible to reform or even alleviate, and his book was his apologia. It made a terrible and sad story of misery, disease, crime, insanity, starvation, and cold.

To appreciate the impact of the little volume, one needs to know a little of the background of Tristan da Cunha. It is an extinct volcano that once rose hissing from the ocean bed. It is solid volcanic rock rising sheer out of the sea to a height of 7,500 feet, with scarcely room for a human being to cling to its side. Around 1816, a half dozen shipwrecked English sailors dragged themselves up out of a raging sea onto the rock. A ship off course found them several years later and offered to remove them. But they had grown attached to the place and had no homes to return to. They asked only that some women be brought out to share their hardships. The women brought were African, the roots of a colony of desperate souls: beachcombers, criminals, lepers. Yet children are born there, and life goes on, with their self-imposed sentence of isolation.

The women of the SS *Franconia,* who were kindly disposed, saw in this island "the perfect answer to a longing to do good works." The result was explosive. One fine morning just off Australia, Mr. Skinner, the Cook's cruise director, and Mr. Hawkes, the Cunard cruise director, while making the ship's rounds arm in arm, came upon Mother's two library rooms, where bedlam had let loose. Bolts and bolts of material were draped over every chair; patterns were being cut from heaps of old newspapers and magazines; sewing machines had appeared out of nowhere. "What goes on here?" the men asked in dismay. "Oh, nothing. We're just making some clothes for the island of Tristan da Cunha." "The *what* island?" shouted Mr. Skinner. "The island of Tristan da Cunha," someone explained patiently. "Don't you know about it? You should. This will explain," and he was quickly handed the little red book. Mr. Skinner scorned to touch it. "But my dear ladies," he said, trying to restrain his voice. "How do you expect the residents of this island to receive these things?" "Why, we are going to stop there," he was told. "It's somewhere between Africa and South America." "Impossible," shouted Mr. Hawkes, now also thoroughly roused. "This ship has a certain run, a certain schedule, and it can't be tampered with. Tristan da Cunha is a thousand miles off our course. It's in the Antarctic. It's—it's impossible." "Oh, I don't believe so, Mr. Hawkes," said Mrs. Springfield Illinois, very gently. "I'm sure Captain Melsom will be only too glad to stop and do a kindness for these poor people." "Then *you* ask Captain Melsom," shouted Skinner and Hawkes in unison. They asked Captain Melsom, by special envoy. Captain Melsom said no, certainly not.

Captain Melsom was a dour old Scotch sea captain who had long since lost his faith in human nature and who never descended from the bridge even for meals. The bridge was his home. He lived there, did his own washing, hanging his shirts and underwear out on a line, and knitting for relaxation. However, he didn't succeed in dampening the enthusiasm for the Tristan da Cunha project. The cutting and sewing continued unabated, and every week another delegation was sent to Captain Melsom. After a half dozen such visits, they wore him down. He yielded but with bitterness. "You'll be sorry," he said, using some good Scotch oaths. "Wait till you hit an Antarctic storm!"

So the sewing committees went to work with renewed energy. Victory was theirs. Committees were formed within committees. The committee from Illinois was working against time and competing with other state committees; New England had its own group, quite exclusive, making little nightgowns of sheer white batiste. Then someone had another brilliant idea. It was decided to announce in every port, from Batavia to Cape Town, that the SS *Franconia* was open to contributions. Everything would be and *was* welcome. The campaign, organized by fresh committees, was successful beyond measure. Contributions poured aboard: barrels of sugar, bags of potatoes, bales of old clothes, live pigs and hens, furniture and toys. The women organizers of the project became heroines.

Life on board revolved around their efforts. Even Mr. Skinner and Mr. Hawkes, finding that it kept so many problem women out of trouble, gave it their official blessing. When the question arose as to how precisely all this booty could be sent ashore on Tristan since both sanitary and safety regulations restricted access to the island of Tristan to within three miles, it was Hawkes who suggested they build rafts, lashing the supplies to them, and trusting the island's fishermen to retrieve them from the sea. The rafts were built by the crew on the open deck, where they attracted a large audience. Because the missionary had written of semi-worthless radios on the island, radio stations in Durban and Cape Town were asked to broadcast the SS *Franconia*'s approach.

The sad outcome of this reckless adventure was foreordained. Stormy weather made the approach impossible, and Mother said she could only hope that the islanders on Tristan da Cunha never received the radio announcements. The perishable parts of the collection went into the ship's own larder. The clothes and other furnishings were stowed away in the hold with the idea that some other ship, in some other year, might take them to Tristan. No other ship ever did. Mother said she could not help but think of these lines from the poem "Tristan da Cunha," by Roy Campbell:

> Snore in the foam; the night is vast and blind;
> The blanket of the mist about your shoulders,
> Sleep your old sleep of rock, snore in the wind,
> Snore in the spray! the storm your slumber lulls,
> His wings are folded on your nest of boulders,
> As on their eggs the gray wings of your gulls.
>
> No more as when, ten thousand years ago,
> You hissed a giant cinder from the ocean,
> Around your rocks you furl the shawling snow
> Half sunk in your own darkness, vast and grim,
> And round you on the deep with surly motion
> Pivot your league-long shadow as you swim.
>
> Why should you haunt me thus but that I know
> My surly heart is in your own displayed,
> Round whom such wastes in endless circuit flow,
> Whose hours in such a gloomy compass run—
> A dial with its league-long arm of shade
> Slowly revolving to the moon and sun.
>
> My pride has sunk like your grey-fissured crags,
> By its own strength o'ertoppled and betrayed:
> I, too, have burned the wind with fiery flags
> Who now am but a roost for empty words,
> An island of the sea whose only trade
> Is in the voyages of its wandering birds.

And so the SS *Franconia* headed for home by way of Montevideo and Buenos Aires, on schedule in spite of the detour and the delay. The passengers, Mother included, began to think only of the day they would see their friends and families once more:

> Much as we had loved the world as a whole, yet the sky scrapers of New York and the spring-green hills of the Hudson Valley would be the *most* exciting, the most beautiful sights to see. And as we sailed that last lap from the Island of Martinique our thoughts were only of the United States of America. I wanted my Vermont mountain of Camel's Hump—not Table Mountain or Mont Pelée—my roommate wanted the little stone walls of Virginia—not the walls of Morro Castle or the Great Wall of China. And so it was with every passenger aboard.

The Death of Marjorie Frost Fraser

Lesley's younger sister Marjorie never enjoyed good health. Upon the family's return from England in 1915, my mother soon went on to college and an active life; Marjorie, only ten at the time, stayed behind to continue her schooling in Franconia and Bennington. In subsequent years, she joined my mother in launching the Open Book in Pittsfield but was unable to endure the physical demands. In the summer of 1928, Marjorie accompanied her parents on a return trip to England. While her parents undertook visits with old acquaintances in Great Britain, Marjorie indulged her love of French by remaining with a family in France. Back home, her health continued to deteriorate, and she was admitted for extensive treatment at the Johns Hopkins University Hospital in Baltimore. The following year, her parents enrolled her in a nursing program at Johns Hopkins, but she was soon hospitalized in Baltimore with signs of tuberculosis. A decision was reached to send her to a sanatorium near Boulder, Colorado.

It was in Boulder that Marjorie met Willard Fraser, and they were soon married. Their daughter, Marjorie Robin Fraser, was born on March 16, 1934, in Billings, Montana. Tragically, Marjorie soon became seriously ill with puerperal fever. She was flown to the Mayo Clinic in Rochester; despite massive injections and transfusions, she succumbed to the infection on May 2, both parents at her side. In the meantime, Carol's wife, Lillian, had become ill with tuberculosis and was undergoing treatment in a sanatorium in Monrovia, California.

The Frost family was devastated by these events, traveling back and forth across the country; Elinor, suffering from extreme exhaustion, experienced what would be one of many attacks of angina. Adding to her parents' dismay, Mother's marriage ended shortly after my birth, and her divorce became final in the year of her sister's death. Besides the poems of Marjorie's published in a book called *Franconia*, mentioned earlier, Charles Sullivan, an anthologist and poet, included another of her poems in his book *Imaginary Gardens: Poetry and Art for Young People* (1989), in which he pairs Marjorie's poem "Spring" with Andrew Wyeth's painting *Christina's World:*

> To tangled grass I cling
> When in the fields I lie,
> For fear of taking wing.
>
> When mountain torrents bring
> The last of winter by,
> In tangled grass I cling.
>
> When maple tassles swing
> Pure gold against the sky,
> To tangled grass I cling.
>
> Alighted robins sing
> A song I dare not try
> For fear of taking wing.

For me, Marjorie's abbreviated life was a sad and moving mix of joy and loneliness; for the Frost family, a treasure lost.

Crossing the Atlantic on the Schooner *Wander Bird*

And so it came to pass, in the summer of 1934, shortly after her divorce from Dwight became final and mourning with her parents the tragic death of her sister Marjorie, Mother fulfilled another dream—at the very moment she needed a break from personal anguish. Invited by the skipper and his wife, she set sail on the 85-foot pilot schooner *Wander Bird,* crossing the Atlantic from Gloucester to the Baltic Sea (Göteborg, Sweden) without benefit of wireless or motor, one of a crew of six men and two women. Warwick Tompkins owned the schooner, serving as her captain; he was accompanied by his wife, Gwen, and their two children, Ann and Warwick Jr., then ages two and four. Mother left me and my sister, just toddlers, with friends in Cambridge, Massachusetts, where she was living at the time.

John Masefield, Henry Thoreau, and Jack London were among the artists who had inspired Tompkins and other young men to leave everything behind and go to sea. Sterling Hayden, for example, dedicated his autobiography, *Wanderer,* to his wife, but also to Warwick Tompkins and Rockwell

Kent, "sailormen, artists, radicals." He quotes Masefield's "Sea Fever" and Thoreau's essay "Life without Principle":

I must go down to the seas again, to the lonely sea and the sky;
And all I ask is a tall ship and a star to steer her by,
And the wheel's kick and the wind's song and the white sail's shaking,
And a gray mist on the sea's face and a gray dawn breaking.

I must go down to the seas again, for the call of the running tide
Is a wild call and a clear call that may not be denied;
And all I ask is a windy day with the white clouds flying,
And the flung spray and the blown spume, and the sea-gulls crying.

I must go down to the seas again to the vagrant gypsy life
To the gull's way and the whale's way where the wind's like a whetted
knife,
And quiet sleep and a sweet dream when the long trick's over.
     ("Sea Fever," John Masefield)

Wherever a man separates from the multitude and goes his own way in this mood, there indeed is a fork in the road, though ordinary travelers may see only a gap in the paling. His solitary path across-lots will turn out the higher way of the two.
     (from "Life without Principle," Henry David Thoreau)

For Hayden, books and the sea "had more than a little in common: both were distilled of silence and solitude." The lure of the sea both inspires and explains his peculiar view of life.

For Mother, the voyage on *Wander Bird* was the culmination of years of longing to experience the adventure and danger of the sea. One poet, in particular, Henry Wadsworth Longfellow, brought her back to the sea from her inland home in New Hampshire, to the sea where her ancestors had landed and been seamen for several generations in the seventeenth century. Longfellow also led her to Spain. She found that the sea and Spain were inextricably interwoven in her earliest dreams, congealing into a longing to know both worlds, expressed in Longfellow's translation of a Spanish ballad, "The Secret of the Sea" or "The Galley of Count Arnaldos":

Ah! what pleasant visions haunt me
As I gaze upon the sea!
All the old romantic legends,
All my dreams, come back to me.

> Sails of silk and ropes of sandal,
> Such as gleam in ancient lore;
> That the sailing sea-bird slowly
> Poised upon the mast to hear.
>
> Till his soul was full of longing,
> And he cried, with impulse strong,—
> "Helmsman! for the love of heaven
> Teach me, too, that wondrous song!"
>
> "Wouldst thou!—so the helmsman answered,—
> "Learn the secret of the sea?
> Only those who brave its dangers
> Comprehend its mystery!"

And it was Longfellow's "My Lost Youth" that had provided her father with the title of his first book, *A Boy's Will*.

"There is a tide in the affairs of men," as Shakespeare says. Mother's tide, she told us, drew her out to sea several times in the ebb and flow, or pendulum movement that—she would remind us—dominated her own life. She spoke of her need to seek rest and renewal and strength by way of the hard facts of physical exertion, the war and peace that comes when nature herself is the noble opponent.

Warwick was a super navigator, a master mariner. He pushed *Wander Bird* to give all she could give, and he cared for her with a certain exultant pride and joy. To see him, as Mother did, when he had a strong wind abeam and *Wander Bird* was cutting the seas at ten knots (fast for a boat of her build), or when he was maneuvering her in and out of a narrow harbor mouth (when sailing becomes a fine art) or in a storm that required the most precise action and stretched every mental and physical fiber in him, was to see a man in every sense of the word. You knew how he felt about ships, although he might not be able to say it so well as Robert Bridges in "Ships":

> I cannot tell their wonder nor make known
> Magic that once thrilled through me to the bone
> But all men praise some beauty, tell some tale,
>   Vent a high mood which makes the rest seem pale,
> Pour their heart's blood to flourish one green leaf,
> Follow some Helen for her gift of grief,
> And fail in what they mean, whate'er they do:
> You should have seen, man cannot tell you
> The beauty of the ships of that my city.

After graduating from the University of California, Warwick managed to make his way to Manila; once there he started a newspaper that proved very successful. Tiring of it after several years, he shipped aboard a Chinese junk for Singapore. He took his first command, at age twenty-three, of the sixty-five-foot yacht *Sir Arthur,* a vessel used to recruit cheap labor, making good money until the boat went down under him. He worked his way back to Paris. He knew by now that "neither the mechanized navy nor the stupidly dull merchant marine" held any attraction for him. He gave up the sea temporarily and went in for art and journalism; it wasn't long before he had several engraved woodcuts hung in the Grand Palais.

It was there, in Paris, that he met Gwendolyn Bohning Carter, a beautiful girl from Fort Worth, Texas, recently graduated from Smith College. Gwen urged Warwick to find a way to obtain his own ship. Soon married and living in a Paris garret, Warwick hoped he could amass enough money to purchase his dream boat, a pilot schooner.

The couple made their way to Hamburg, the birthplace of so many of the fine pilot schooners. There in the docks were abandoned ships in varying degrees of decay. It seemed as if Fate had foreordained the couple's first discovery of the name *Wandervogel—Wander Bird—*under the accumulated grime. The ship was sad, disheveled, but sound; it would take little more than soap and water, paint, varnish, and new gear to put her back in action. Warwick proudly pointed to the schooner's distinguishing design: "Alone of all the world's working craft," he wrote, "they are designed to sail on a fixed waterline. They are shaped, framed, planked and fastened to meet any test of the sea. They are virtually super-yachts, born of centuries of trial and error, fruit of immeasurable sea experience, unquestionably the ablest craft afloat."

Launched on August 9, 1883, at the H. C. Stulcken yard in Hamburg, Germany, *Elbe 5* joined the imperial German government's fleet of pilot vessels at the mouth of the Elbe River. Weather conditions were often severe, with gales intensified by a funnel of currents across the North Sea. The competition was tough and *Elbe 5* had to race to be the first to meet incoming ships. For forty years, *Elbe 5* had sailed with pilots tending clipper ships, whalers, colliers and coasters, ocean liners and the big windjammers; in 1924, *Elbe 5* was abandoned and left to rot in the backwaters of Hamburg. Lacking funds but well supplied with determination and enthusiasm, Warwick and Gwen purchased *Wander Bird* for $1,500. Borrowing money from friends, they were able to refit the schooner and sail for America.

Running a parallel life at sea, another avid sailor, Irving Johnson, whom

Mother had befriended as a teenager in Amherst, Massachusetts, had been
no less infected by the fever of wanderlust:

> I am fevered with the sunset,
> I am fretful with the bay,
> For the wander-thirst is on me
> And my soul is in Cathay.
>
> There's a schooner in the offing,
> With her topsails shot with fire,
> And my heart has gone aboard her
> For the Islands of Desire.
>
> I must forth again to-morrow!
> With the sunset I must be
> Hull down on the trail of rapture
> In the wonder of the Sea.
> ("The Sea Gypsy," Richard Hovey)

Having signed on as mate to Captain Tompkins on *Wander Bird*, Johnson would soon meet Electa (Exy) Search, a college friend of Gwen Tompkins. While visiting her friend on board *Wander Bird* in Boston harbor, Exy
had been fascinated by "the incomprehensible sailing talk" and the strong
appeal of the ship herself. She managed to board *Wander Bird* in France,
met and fell in love with Irving, and they were soon married. She and
Irving made plans to purchase a schooner and sail her, like *Wander Bird*,
with a number of young people who could share the expenses and labor of
a long cruise. They settled on a pilot schooner they renamed *Yankee*; once
she was refitted, they returned to America. Just outside of Gloucester a last
bit of fog lifted, "and then the most beautiful day of the cruise and a clear
starry night with a yellow half moon as the *Yankee* came into her new home
port" and rested at anchor:

> And I have loved thee, Ocean! and my joy
> Of youthful sports was on thy breast to be
> Borne, like thy bubbles, onward.
> From a young man I wanton'd with thy breakers,
> And trusted to thy billows far and near,
> And laid my hand upon thy name—as I do here.
> (from Canto IV, *Childe Harold's Pilgrimage*, Lord Byron)

Shortly after the *Yankee*'s arrival in Gloucester, in the summer of 1933,
Mother ran into Electa and Irving, who were frantically preparing for their
first round-the-world cruise. They tried to persuade Mother to accompany

them, but she realized that she could not be away from me and my sister, two and four years old at the time, for what would be some eighteen months at sea. "But I have to admit," Mother recalls, "I wept salt tears into the salt sea as we trailed the *Yankee* down Gloucester harbor the day she set sail."

Before leaving, Electa and Irving had left Mother an introduction to Warwick and Gwen Tompkins, scheduled to arrive on *Wander Bird* sometime in the fall. When she went aboard and met the Tompkins family, Mother knew she must cross the Atlantic with them or she "would never trust my lucky star again!" They had anchored *Wander Bird* in the Cambridge River, not far from Mother's home in Cambridge. She would slip aboard many a night across the river ice where the ship lay frozen in for the winter, snow and ice and darkness shrouding her decks. Stooping down a little doorway under a coping, Mother would bend double and drop down a companionway into the captain's quarters: "There, in a cabin as snug and cozy as a bug in a rug, bright with copper and tiles and woven goods from many a distant port, we would sit around the open-front stove (a tile fireplace made in Amsterdam in 1631), and we would talk of the battles lost and won and the beauty and mystery of the ships while we heard the whispering of the snow across the decks above, and the sleeping children turning in their bunks at our elbow."

Writing to her parents, Mother refers to "this sea fever business" and the Tompkinses of the *Wander Bird,* whom "I like so much and am seeing so much of." She describes Warwick's book, *Fifty South to Fifty South,* in which he tries to explain his love of a sail, a rope, a mast, a wheel, and stars and moons and suns: "Ships and the sea I have loved passionately longer than I can recall. Why this should be is hard to say, for my ancestors, sturdy landsmen who made excellent teachers, engineers and farmers, knew and cared nothing for the sea. Welsh-English they were, and happily they left me a measure of their proverbial tenacity." A companion book, *Two Sailors,* provides a charming account of the life of the children aboard the schooner.

Mother was drawn to these two women, Gwen and Electa, in large measure because of their courage and adventurousness in following their husbands into what for them had been an absolute unknown. Yes, they had been attracted to the cozy, intimate way of life belowdecks on *Wander Bird,* but they knew nothing about sails and rigging, sheets or seasickness, and even less about the driving ambition of the serious skipper, requiring often harsh discipline at sea.

Clearly, Gwen does not share her husband's rising ebullience with each gale and squall. She prefers to stay belowdecks with her chores: teaching the children, preparing for Christmas or the Fourth of July, storing the sup-

plies, tending to her knitting, sorting the laundry, and helping the chef in the galley and at mealtime. While there are times when she mans the watch to relieve the others for more strenuous work in the rigging, she feels no joy as does the skipper when *Wander Bird* is striving for top speed in a roaring gale or taking shortcuts through rocky straights. Warwick and Gwen's daughter, Ann, only a child at the time, later recalled: "As I look back on our life at sea, I think my mother was really incredible—among pioneers, brave, even if she preferred even-keel sailing to pushing hard with the lee rail underwater. She let her children climb the rigging and go out on the bowsprit, after all!"

Mother, not unlike Gwen and Electa, would join for one brief voyage those "adventurous young women." But first she had to persuade this seemingly driven man to let her work under him. It wasn't going to be easy, she knew. Warwick didn't think much of women on the whole, still less of them as sailors on the North Atlantic run. Gwen and Mother wore him down over time, and he reluctantly agreed. In a letter to Mother sent just before the sailing date of June 26 out of Gloucester, Gwen describes final preparations as under way—washing and painting and reaching "a deliciously weary state." Warwick had found it difficult to sign up enough young men who could pay their way, so Mother will be welcome, Gwen adds, as long as she is willing to go at $250, and she warns that they "may be eating S. S. Pierce groceries." Warwick, it seems, was not in a very cheerful mood: "I'll enjoy having you no end," she concludes, "and Warwick will just have to bear up under us and will probably like it in the end."

On April 9, 1934, the *Washington Post* carried an announcement of *Wander Bird*'s planned voyage: "A crew of young American yachtsmen, including William Phillips, Jr., son of the Undersecretary of State, will sail 10,000 miles this summer in a schooner to pay the respects of American seamen to an old Finnish sailor [Capt. Gustaf Erikson, a sea cook who has become a sea king and who from the little port of Mariehamm, Finland, sends to sea the last fleet of windjammers left in the world.] . . . . They will sail north of Scotland, cross the North Sea, and after navigating the narrow Skagerrak between Denmark and Sweden will turn northward into the Baltic." They sailed out of Gloucester at noon on June 26, 1934, destination Göteborg, Sweden: "So *Wander Bird* spread her great white wings to the winds and went racing away to the eastward," Tompkins wrote in *Two Sailors*. "The steeples, masts, and towers of Gloucester quickly faded to mere pinpoints against the sky and then vanished altogether. The green fields and gay rocks of the shore merged into a thin, faint blue line more like a low sunset cloud than anything else."

The skipper and his wife kept with them at all times their two young children, both hardened sailors. Ann had already been nicknamed "Queen Ann" and Warwick Jr., "Commodore." Warwick Jr. later recounted how a visitor, after being given a tour of the boat, pulled out the top drawer of a chest of drawers, only to find the infant Warwick asleep inside: "I've already met the captain," said the visitor, "so this must be the commodore." The nickname took.

Ann and Commodore were sea babies with such unbabylike playthings as ropes and marlinspikes. But Ann also had a love of fluffy dolls and Teddy bears and woolly dogs in a nursery full of saltwater-stained toys accumulated in a score of different ports of call. They slept in the built-in bunks once used by the Hamburg pilots, and their parents slept in the after cabin. Their father marveled at how easily they adapted to their environment, navigating ladders and rigging without a life jacket and more sure of foot when under way than when motionless in port. Unlike the less experienced crew, they were seldom seasick.

Their at-home schooling using the Calvert method started very young. Gwen was provided a box of supplies, including pens, pencils, paper, etc. Warwick built a special desk for them, a traditional model except for the raised edge to keep supplies from flying off in stormy weather. Recess permitted them to go on deck to study whatever sea mammals came by, such as whales or porpoises. They studied the passing ships by outline: tankers carrying explosive loads of oil and gasoline, battleships like sharks with hunched-up shoulders, rusty-sided freighters with cranes and cargo booms, or high-sided liners with rows of portholes. The skipper placed items left strewn around deck into a lucky bag for prizes. The only way to retrieve a lost item was to do a job or pay money. The money collected was used to buy something everyone could enjoy such as ice cream or records for the phonograph. Skipper liked to play hide-and-seek with his children. Commodore would hide in a lifeboat, Ann in a tight corner, while Warwick would move from side to side among the sails and rigging to avoid detection. He also taught the children to play chess. Part of their schooling was to learn with the rest of the crew to identify sheets (ropes) and sails (e.g., halyards) by name and when blindfolded. They learned to tell time by the bells at four, eight, and twelve o'clock, how to measure the nautical mile, and how to use knots to measure distance in the water.

Once at sea, it fell to the Skipper to put his green crew to work, teaching them to hand, reef, and steer. Sails, running rigging, and belaying pins had to be memorized—both their locations and how they worked. Mother and the other hands had to learn to walk, then run blindfolded, to the various blocks and ring bolts from any spot on deck, this in case it had to be done in a pitch-black stormy night off the reef of Norman's Woe, or Cape Wrath, or the Butt of Lewis. Bruised from ankle to elbow, from shin to shoulder, Mother winced but felt her wounds were worth it, agreeing with Carlyle that "in all true labor, were it but hand labor, there is something of divineness."

The watches were immediately set up—three hours on, nine off, the clock round, two on watch at a stretch with one at the wheel and the other in the bow lookout. There was no wheelhouse or bridge, compass and wheel being open to the sky, wind and wave, rain or shine. As the rhythm of the sea took over my mother's life, its color and the silence, she felt she had been away for years, had never known that other life of newspapers, cars, crowds, and politics. Whole passages of verse flooded her mind, from Masefield, Keats, Stevenson, and others:

> Out of the air a time of quiet came.
> There the two spires of leaning canvas rose,
> Mainsail and topsail, lifting, gently lifting,
> White like the brightness that a great fish blows
> When billows are at peace and ships are drifting, and
> There the great skyline made her perfect round
> Notched now and then by the sea's deeper blue.
> (from *Dauber,* John Masefield)

> Oh ye! who have your eye-balls vexed and tired,
> Feast them upon the wideness of the Sea;
> Oh ye! whose ears are dinned with uproar rude,
> Or fed too much with cloying melody,
> (from "Sonnet of the Sea," John Keats)

> And truly there is nothing else. I had literally forgotten what happiness was, and the full mind—full of external and physical things, not full of cares and nonsense about a fellow's behaviour. My heart literally sang: I truly care for nothing so much as that.
> (from *At Sea*, Robert Louis Stevenson)

Mother believed that the eight people on board were not only congenial but shared her romantic attachment to *Wander Bird:* "We had become a unit in a matter of hours, understanding each other in silence as in talk, loving *Wander Bird* with a passionate and jealous love."

Meanwhile *Wander Bird,* under the vigilant eye of its skipper, headed northwest on the great circle course—NW by W 2 points south. Then, on the fifth night out, came a strange encounter with that other world they had left so far behind. Mother was at the wheel on the midnight watch—twelve to three—. She recalled that a full moon, riding high, made the sea a blue-black brilliance from horizon to horizon. The wind was a fine strong one in exactly the right quarter for speed. Every sail was set, and the log was reading a brisk 101/2 knots. The waves ran very high but slid under like great soft pillows on which they seemed to have risen instead of to rise.

It was at this point that they marked the first transatlantic liner they had seen since leaving the States. She was headed for New York, a long beetle of lighted superstructure moving slowly at the horizon's rim. Warwick, on deck whether it was his watch or not, decided to practice his hand-operated signal light on them, a flashlight with which he could do Morse code. He signaled the liner: "Yacht *Wander Bird*, five days out of Gloucester. Report us to the *Boston Herald*" (where they were expecting an occasional report of *Wander Bird*'s whereabouts). After repeating the signal several times, they received some answering flashes from the liner that made no sense. Warwick gave up in disgust, cursing all modern radio operators who can't understand Morse code except on some modern gadget like a wireless set. Then they all stood aghast. The liner was making a turn—a great arc—and returning to them. Apparently they had misunderstood the skipper's signals and feared that *Wander Bird* was in some distress and needed help.

To turn a liner around at sea seemed reckless at best; it seemed unlikely that Lloyd's would cover the cost and might bill poor *Wander Bird* for misleading a liner. Mother stood at the wheel while all hands were called on deck. They stood around anxiously in a huddle waiting for the blowup and the blast of indignation from the rescuers when the truth was revealed. The porthole lights came on one by one all over the liner, and the decks filled with people. She even listed to port as the passengers gathered along one rail to have a look at the schooner. Dwarfed and embarrassed, the *Wander Bird* and its crew felt guilty in the face of the approaching skyscraper.

The liner came in close above them, and someone came forward on their bridge with a megaphone: "Hello," shouted a voice. "A beautiful ship you have there. Who are you, and where are you bound for?" So it turned out that they had just come over to have a look, to give a lot of transatlantic tourists a thrill. They carried on a conversation with what turned out to be the Dutch liner *New Amsterdam*, bound for New York and well ahead of schedule. Their captain, seeing a sailing ship under full sail in the bright moonlight, had been impressed, his imagination stirred: on board the *Wander Bird*, relief and pride restored.

Mother and the others each said a word of greeting through the ship's megaphone. Then, in farewell, this Leviathan of the deep blew her foghorn at them. The blast almost lifted them out of the sea. The crew of *Wander Bird* pumped its little hand-held foghorn in reply. With cheers on both sides, one drowning out the other, the liner crossed their bow and headed for America. Ships that pass in the night:

> Whither, O splendid ship, thy white sails crowding,
>   Leaning across the bosom of the urgent West,
> That fearest nor sea rising, nor sky clouding,
>   Whither away, fair rover, and what thy quest?
>   (from "A Passer-By," Robert Bridges)

Before long, *Wander Bird* was off Newfoundland, heading into the Great Banks. Warned before leaving the States that icebergs were running farther south than usual, the crew was put on special alert. Unfortunately, dense fog—never lifting, never changing, wrapping them solidly in with a wet wool blanket—separated port from starboard, fore from aft, and night was not much darker than day. The man at the wheel was as separated from the man at the prow as if they were from different worlds. In such foul weather, whoever manned the prow had to work hour after hour, pumping the little foghorn. After several cranks of the handle, a mournful cry went out into the mist; whoever was on watch strained his ears for an answer. But from whom? From another ship? From an iceberg? Because an iceberg reflects an echo from some distance, that is what they listened for most anxiously.

> Listening lest ice should make the note resound.
> She bayed there like a solitary hound
> Lost in covert. All the watch she bayed.
> The fog came closelier down, no answer made.
> Denser it grew until the ship was lost.
> The elemental hid her.
>   (from *Dauber,* John Masefield)

Mother wrote home that she was "literally scared cold. Between ships and icebergs," she couldn't see how they could miss.

After fourteen days at sea without sight of land, Warwick said, "If any-one of you wants to climb to the masthead he will be able to see the peak of St. Kilda directly over the bowsprit." Some of them, not quite believing, went up into the rigging, and there it was, the different blue of a mountain just showing at the edge of ocean blue. A cheer went up, and once again they saluted the navigational skills of their skipper, his ability to tell where land was to be seen by only a mast-height's difference of viewpoint.

St. Kilda is the outermost island of the Hebrides, a solitary mountain island where storm and cold are the norm nine months of the year. Not unlike Pitcairn and Tristan da Cunha, a handful of people cling to it, half-starved, half-frozen. England, to whom they belong, once removed them for their own sakes, but they came right back. Mother saw them as another proof that you can't reform people who don't want to be reformed. "It only makes them *more* stubborn," she said. She wanted terribly to stop and enjoy "the many lovely tranquil bays, green green valleys running off into purple hills, white white cottages in protected valleys, and whiter beaches with their still whiter breakers."

But Warwick was bound for the Baltic, and he had no intention of stopping by the wayside. Also his logbook was telling him that he was making an Atlantic crossing in record sailing time. So he was anxious to put on speed and more speed to cut the times even further. He looked for short-cuts as they steered in close to the coast of Scotland. The wind let up, and the clouds vanished. Mother wrote home about how the Scottish coast, range on range of the loveliest, most barren-looking Benwarlocks, took her breath away: "Right along the cliffs between the mountains and a rough sea, a narrow lonely road runs from the lighthouse at Cape Wrath to Pentland Firth, some fifty miles or more. And along that road, five, ten, fifteen miles apart, a house or two, sometimes half a dozen houses in a group, and two little villages of perhaps thirty or forty houses and a kirk. Not a tree for God knows how many miles. And grass only on the sheltered side of rocks or a steep slope, with one or two cows or a half dozen sheep grazing. Never a soul in sight. How I longed to go ashore and see the people who lived like that." When they came off Cape Wrath, one of the most famous danger spots, Warwick knew he was taking a calculated chance, the odds good only as long as the weather stayed calm. He sought a record-breaking passage by taking a shortcut along a lee shore when a vicious squall caught them flying too much sail.

Thrown bodily from her berth, for the first time she heard the cry of "All hands on deck"; she knew it was serious. She went on deck, fast. Rain and wind pinned her to the deck, as it was pinning the ship to the sea—even under the sea. As *Wander Bird* went down and down, Mother wondered if she would ever come up. Then a sheet of the main topsail gave way; the sail came loose with a terrible shudder and noise, throwing them into unspeakable blackness and confusion. If she had been giving the orders, Mother said, she would have ordered the sail cut away entirely as an offering to Father Neptune. But not Warwick Tompkins. He would never dream of losing a sail. He ordered all hands, all the men that is, up the mast. Mother and

Gwen were left alone at the helm in the wet and roaring blackness to keep the ship's nose into the wind. The sail was saved, and the squall passed over them before they ran aground on a reef. Even Warwick acknowledged that it had been a close call, and for a while he wasn't quite so free with his sail.

Little of Warwick's precious time had been lost, however, for *Wander Bird* came off Pentland Firth, at the northern tip of Scotland, eighteen days out of Gloucester—an incredible sailing feat. (The following year, 1935, *Wander Bird* would sail in sixteen days, twenty-one hours from Gloucester to Pentland Firth, believed to be the fastest passage ever made by a vessel of one hundred feet or less in length.)

Reaching Pentland Firth, *Wander Bird* was facing one of the most treacherous riptides in the world. Instead of going around, Warwick pointed his little ship into the narrow, rocky straits, where the tide was going seven knots through a knothole. With a wind at their backs, carrying them neatly along at nine knots, he figured he could lick the seven-knot tide and even perhaps advance at two knots. So in they drove. The roar was so loud that all communication other than sign language ceased. It took every effort, every muscle, every nerve to hold the ship front-end front through the channel. Any swing of the ship's broadside meant a possible shipwreck on the rocks. Mother realized that they probably could have swum ashore, and, anyway, there was a good stalwart bunch of Scottish fisher folk on the treeless green landscape watching them from the dooryards of their immaculate white houses, ready to take care of them. She felt, however, that the fisher folk were looking at them with dour disapproval, and, seeing the American flag flying from our masthead, were probably saying, "Those crazy Americans. They *would* do a thing like this."

Fortunately, right in front of their watchful eyes, *Wander Bird* went through. Several times the ship had stood absolutely still in her tracks and may even have done a little backing up. But the tide gradually slackened, and when the tide did a right about-face, the *Bird* actually shot through into the North Sea as if fired from a cannon. It was a great victory for Warwick, and he stalked the deck like an Admiral Nelson after a good day. Gwen, on the other hand, was less than pleased. Mother found her in her bunk with pillows over her head and told her the worst was over. "What's the matter?" Mother asked. "You took Cape Wrath calmly enough." "That's because," Gwen said, "at Cape Wrath I knew that if the worst came to the worst all I had to do was take one child under each arm and we would all go to the bottom together. But here we'd lose the ship and the ship is our *home*. Don't you realize that?" Mother guessed she did if it upset her that much.

Realizing that *Wander Bird* was not far from its destination, Mother found a last ounce of energy to write home to her parents. It was July 20, and they had been at sea more than three weeks. "Dear Mama and Papa— Here we are becalmed in the North Sea for the best part of four days." She speaks of the record run from Gloucester to Pentland Firth and notes that Warwick hopes to make up the lost time in the last fifty miles to Göteborg.

The North Sea is typically treacherous and unpredictable. At first, *Wander Bird* found herself in a dead calm; she sat under slatting sails, in a hot sun and breathless air, whistling for a breeze. Warwick, being a good seaman, was quite superstitious: one of his superstitions was that playing the game of "Ghosts" would bring on a wind. So for two days and nights Mother joined the others in playing "Ghosts" to the point of exasperation. On the third day the wind came; Mother had a strong suspicion that "it was coming anyway."

If playing "Ghosts" had brought the wind, Mother sincerely wished they hadn't played the game so conscientiously. Because the wind that came was a gale: little rain—in squalls only—but a terrible blow. The waves stood up and hung over the ship, and then lay across her decks in water ten feet deep. Once battened down, they stayed below when possible, hanging on with their teeth and fingernails when forced to go on deck. It wasn't much better below. You couldn't stand or sit. You braced yourself in a narrow passage and used all your strength to stay put as a wave had the ship on her side.

To make matters worse, as they approached Stockholm's narrow Skagerrak, the wind veered, and waves and wind were at cross purposes. For Mother, this was the worst sailing experience of her life. They would mount to the top of a wave, where the wind would take them by the throat, holding them there trembling and shaking. As the ship went into a bucking motion, Mother went into a tailspin of seasickness: getting into her bunk, she stayed for hours on her hands and knees, so desperately and constantly ill she thought she would die. She had been seasick on other occasions and thought she wouldn't care if she died. But that was because in her heart of hearts she knew she wouldn't die. Now, when she thought she might, she didn't want to die in the least.

Meanwhile, Warwick was having the time of his life. Instead of taking in sail and riding it out, he had added canvas wholesale, and *Wander Bird* was breaking all her own records for speed—11.4 knots was what they were doing. Every hour Warwick would open the bulkhead door; he and a lot of water would come below so that he could write up the log. He was gloating, Mother noticed, as she was perishing. Even Gwen was ill for the first time in her sea life.

Wander Bird flew into the strait between Denmark and Norway. While she was still seasick below, Mother recalls, sometime in the wee small hours, Warwick stuck his head into her and Gwen's cabin: "You girls have got to come on deck. Something too beautiful, too tremendous to miss. A square rigger, all sails set, is coming up the Skagerrak behind us, with the moonlight on her. It's something out of a world of dreams. Come along!"

But Mother couldn't make it. It was a strange sensation: wanting to do something as much as she wanted to go on deck and finding her body wouldn't answer. She lay there in a fierce frustration. Every time Warwick came below, she called out: "Where is she now? Perhaps I can make it before she actually passes us." Warwick said she was gaining on them slowly, and he would let them know when she was almost alongside. By that time, *Wander Bird* had come a little into the lea of an island, and the ship's motion had slackened a bit. She dragged herself out of the bunk, crawled to the galley and drank some hot soup left in a thermos for such occasions. Then, weak as a rag, she made her way up the ladder and pushed up the door to the deck. When she had emerged halfway, a wave came over the ship and washed her against the rail like a drowned puppy. There she clung until the water receded. She opened her eyes, and there, in full moonlight, looming against the sky, was that ship of another day, of another century—a square-rigger with every inch of canvas displayed. And at that moment a voice came from the deck of the pitch-black hull. She and the others saw no one but heard the cry: "Ahoy! The *Leif Erickson*, 104 days out of Australia, bound for Marieham, Finland. What ship are you?" Mother was thrilled. "All the poetry of the sea poured over me with the next wave," she said, and she repeated:

> "Wouldst thou!"—so the helmsman answered,—
> "Learn the secret of the sea?
> Only those who brave its dangers
> Comprehend its mystery!"

For that brief moment, she felt as though she had understood.

Rockford College and Maddox House

Mother's sister Marjorie had died just before *Wander Bird* set sail. Writing home on her return trip by liner, Mother wrote of her loneliness at sea, and the family's mourning of their loss: "If only one's zest in living, or *belief* in living, would return. Do you think we can rise above what has happened? I am terrified most of the time that I can't. Being alone with the loneliness of the elements this way may not be the best way. Perhaps *plunging* into things at Rockford [College] may be my salvation."

Before leaving Gloucester, Mother had accepted a teaching position at Rockford College, Illinois, where RF was a friend of the president and his wife, Gordon and Roberta Chalmers. Gordon Keith Chalmers, a graduate of Brown, Oxford (Rhodes Scholar), and Harvard, a scholar in seventeenth-century thought and letters, entered a second marriage with the poet Roberta Teale Swartz. Having taught for several years at Mount Holyoke College, in 1934 Chalmers was appointed president of Rockford College. As a friend of my grandfather, he facilitated my mother's appointment to the English faculty.

Along with her teaching and other faculty duties, Mother was responsible for the Maddox House cultural center; in that capacity, she would invite to the campus a series of speakers that included her father, Harriet Monroe of *Poetry* magazine, Ridgley Torrence, Carl Sandburg, and others. Her many duties provided a great deal of press in Rockford. Besides a photo of Mother taken together with Harriet Monroe, there appeared locally a photo of me and my sister, Elinor, sitting on RF's knee, a photo I pull out in my classes to demonstrate my traditional role as granddaughter.

It would be here, in Rockford, that Mother recognized, as a working single parent, the need to enter us in the local school system; I entered pre-kindergarten, my sister, first grade. A pattern was established: to put us in the best schools possible wherever we found ourselves: briefly in Mexico; Rockford; Gainesville; Washington, D.C.; on to Putney School in Vermont; Radcliffe College in Cambridge; and, for me, on to the University of Miami and Duke University. Mother continued the practice of reading to us, helping us with our writing, and, in general, passing along the love of books, literature, and art. None of our elders sang, but somehow we became familiar with Scottish ballads and legends (including Harry Lauder) and recordings of folk music. And her children's stories grew directly out of our early childhood interaction with our mother.

While my sister and I, now three and five, were content in our new school environment, Mother was restless. She returned home at night emotionally and physically drained. She believed that her status in academia would never improve until she completed an undergraduate or master's degree. The Ted Davisons and others at the University of Colorado had offered to assist her in continuing her formal education. But Mother's drive lay elsewhere.

During her years in the New York publishing business, Mother had edited an anthology of poems, *Come Christmas*; had published several stories under the pseudonym Leslie Field; and saw a mystery novel, *Murder at Large*, into print. And two short essays (one on the Open Book caravan, the other on Maddox House) had appeared in *Publishers Weekly*.

At Christmas 1935, Mother was offered a round-trip ticket on a U.S. Airways flight from Chicago to New York in exchange for writing an article on the thrill of flying. The article deals at length with what she calls the "lure of flying," not unlike the lure of the sea. Picking up on her deep admiration of Charles and Anne Lindbergh and Amelia Earhart, she describes the lure as one of danger and of beauty. Because by this time commercial flight has become relatively safe, the adventure of flying is less concerned with danger. "It has to do," she writes, "with the particular sensations that derive from coming to grips with wind and fog, earth and stars, rain and snow and distance, the known and the unknown. It is romance—if one is allowed to mean by the word what was meant when St. George met the dragon." Summing up, she refers the readers to the pioneers, to Columbus, and others. She describes the flight itself: "So, on the Boeing monoplane, with her 550 H.P. Wasp engines, making one of the eleven daily runs from Chicago to New York . . . I was constantly aware of those who have lived, and are living, on the horizon's edge, the growing edge, of discovery. . . . And everything I beheld, from the moment I rose off the earth at the Chicago airport until I touched it again at the Newark field, had a film of the adventurous past of aviation superimposed on it, as a double exposure."

She describes the clean line of the plane, its two three-pronged propellers. She compares these propellers to those from the single-piece mahogany ones "whose tips I cut by hand for their slight metal reinforcements" at the Curtis factory in Marblehead in 1918. Entering the plane, she admires the comfort enjoyed by both crew and passengers, the distribution of newspapers and a meal. She realizes this flight cannot compare to the "poignant beauty" that Earhart experienced flying across the Atlantic or over the Himalayas by moonlight. And, of course, she marvels at the speed: "three miles a minute," altering the horizon's outline as if racing the turn of the earth—three and a half hours flying time from Chicago to Newark!

Leaving the romance of flying behind, she soon discovered that her academic duties, combined with trying to raise two children without adequate resources, presented a serious distraction from her writing. She had assistance at home only sporadically; child care was a constant struggle. In the meantime, her parents, especially her mother, Elinor, since the death of Marjorie, were being advised by their physician in Amherst to seek rest and quiet in a southern clime during the winter months—what RF termed "the pneumonia season." They first took up residence in Florida's Key West for the winter months of 1934–35. The visit proved enjoyable, but there were problems: they found little privacy on the beach; and, while Carol, Lillian, and their son Prescott (born in 1927), and Robin (Marjorie's daughter, born at the time of her mother's death in 1934) had joined them, they found it impossible to keep Carol occupied. The following winter, 1935–36, her parents returned to Florida; RF lectured in March and again the following January at the University of Miami.

Mother's final semester at Rockford, spring of 1936, was full of indecision. President Chalmers, with his wife, Roberta, a strong supporter of my mother's employment, accepted a position as president of Kenyon College and suggested she might follow them. Friends at Rockford, however, urged Mother to retreat to Mexico, staying for a time with their dear friends Nadine and Robert Miller on their ranch, La Hacienda de la Clementina, between Victoria and Tampico. Just the sound of the name excited Mother. From an early age, she had been attracted to her father's readings in precolonial history in Mexico, Peru, and elsewhere, an attraction I would also find irresistible. Despite the turmoil of those final months at Rockford College, the Chalmers and Frosts remained close friends; Gordon went on to an illustrious career at Kenyon College, dying unexpectedly at the age of fifty-two.

Escape to Mexico

While in Rockford, Mother had acquired a Model A Ford. She loved to drive. By December 1936, she was ready to put the two of us in the back of the car and head first for San Antonio, where her parents were seeking a warmer climate. It would be her parents who not only encouraged their daughter to get away for a while to write but also helped finance the venture. Before making it to the Mexican border, however, we encountered serious flooding from a storm as we approached the Mississippi River; I have been told, as an adult, that the three of us were forced to spend a night protected from the storm by "the ladies of the night" in a brothel. And we were grateful! As we continued south, Mother's plan was simple: live cheaply, write, and learn the language.

In frequent letters home, Mother describes the beginning of what would be a yearlong adventure south of the border. "Well, here we are in Mexico— and I mean Mexico!" she wrote. Having made our way south on the Laredo/ Mexico City road (the only paved road in Mexico at that time), we turned onto a road that, to Mother, just wasn't a road. We made our way some ten miles over "a hard freshly-plowed field, only worse in a way because of the terrifying bridges made of small worn logs. Not one of them looked able to hold a car up." Yet the local population considered the bridges an advance. Making our way through a dense orange and grapefruit orchard, we arrived after dark on Friday (New Year's Eve, 1936) at two broken-down gates tied up with ropes that our Mexican boy guide (whom Mother had commandeered for the last six miles of the way) alighted to untie. With a half dozen dogs barking furiously, a man emerged with a flashlight to meet us. We had been unable to call ahead; there were no telephones off the main highway, and we had been told the road running to Tampico was impassable. But we *made* it! Robert Miller, Mother wrote her parents, "is one of the best known—perhaps the best known—English rancher in Mexico. He has been at it for more than thirty years—oil, corn, fruit." At sixty-four, he was tall, perfectly built, with snow-white hair and a young face. He rode horseback miles a day, putting in long hours of hard physical labor building a dam, or shoveling out irrigation canals. His seventy-six-year-old maiden sister had joined her brother and was a hard worker—all day long. In the years since the Revolution, Miller had resisted the government's acquisition of his land, gradually losing the ability to sustain a profitable fruit business. His wife, Nadine, aged about fifty, "with the strength and activity of half of that," had been a successful businesswoman when she married Miller some eight years earlier, having lived most of her life in the San Antonio/Browns-ville areas of Texas. Mother was delighted to be with these people "who know everyone, from the President down, and are deep in the agriculture, politics, and literature of the country."

Settling in at the Millers' ranch, Mother was to pay only 150 pesos a month—about forty-five dollars—for everything. Possessing the only car in the area, she quickly agreed to drive her hosts to Victoria or Tampico as needed. News was hard to come by because the Millers had no money for extras. Once a week they saw the local news in a Tampico paper. Nadine was the ranch doctor, and Mother was able to transport several of her patients to a doctor in Victoria, get the groceries for two or three weeks, and even help her attend to matters in their land case.

The ranch covered three thousand acres, with some three hundred peons (men, women, and children) living on it, the men working it. There was help for cleaning up after meals, but the whole family swept and dusted and scrubbed: "yet nothing seems clean, at least until you're used to it, and then you accept it as 'clean dirt.'" Actually, that first night when we went to our bedroom, there was, placed between my sister's and my bed, "a spider such as one could only imagine seeing in a nightmare drinking from the water jug. Its body was over an inch in width and from stem to stern of its legs was over three inches. It was dark brown and heavy looking. In fact an *animal,* not a spider. It was harmless—needless to say!"

The room assigned to us opened up onto a pleasant veranda, affording privacy and easy accessibility. It gave one a grand peace to be apart from what was going on in the house. Mother could "sit in the room just inside the window and door screens, or in the shade on the porch, or in the sun on the porch, or out further still in the garden." Despite the fleas, ticks, cockroaches, and, of course, spiders, the natural beauty was intoxicating: "A flock of parrots just flew over making a noise like a loose board being jumped on. The pet macaw on the round perch in the yard yelled back at them. The bougainvillea is in full bloom, and a tree of it is at every corner of the porch. The smell of avocado pear blossoms comes in gusts. And the oranges, the last of this crop, lie neglected on the green grass."

"The food is wonderful," Mother added. "Mrs. Miller does the cooking—on the biggest range you ever beheld." Venison and duck roasts, Mexican preparations of rice, orange juice by the pitcher, papaya in several different ways (including pie), cake with so many pecans as to be almost one pecan, pancakes with homemade cane syrup. "I hadn't known venison could be the best meat ever tasted, but let Mr. Miller spend three hours baking and basting a venison ham and there never was anything better to eat."

And, not to be forgotten, the children. My sister, Elinor, and I were totally engrossed with two Chinese/Mexican children—Josefina, thirteen, and Querentino, nine—whom the Millers had practically adopted. After their Mexican mother eloped with another man down the road, their Chinese father died of heartbreak. Together with the children, we were having a grand time: "climbing the trees for oranges and grapefruit, feeding the chickens (some just hatched), collecting gourds for dolls dishes, and riding on the horses in front of the workmen on the place." We only rode "jog-trotting mares," but it was a thrill nevertheless; we went six miles horseback one day and were sore the next.

Leaving the children well attended on the ranch, Mother and Nadine would drive in Mother's car to Mexico City to pick up her mail and get money at the Wells Fargo Co. Letters sent to the hacienda were getting routinely lost or returned to the United States. The nearest Mexican post office in Forlon was little more than a shack and not reliable. No packages got through in either direction.

From Tamalipas Province by car, the climb to Mexico City defied description. Mother doubted there could be anything like it in America or even Europe. Although she wished her parents, so near in San Antonio, yet so far from the strain and rigors of a foreign land, could join her and experience these wonders, she admitted that she was comforted by having a Mexican resident, fluent in Spanish, by her side:

But five hours along edges on hairpin turns was enough. I couldn't have stood another minute it seemed to me. For so much of it the Montezuma

River, flowing down from Mexico City, wound along a thousand feet below (sheer drop) and looking up at the peak ahead one would say it just *couldn't* be climbed—and then it was. Yet the grading was such that the car never had to be put in second, barring a truck or something ahead. But the traffic is scarce—not more than thirty cars in two hundred miles. . . . And with any imagination—I seem to be pestered with it—that tiny thread of road that runs hundreds of miles from one civilization to another looks breakable in a hundred places. The villages strung along it at great distances don't even seem attached to it. And what villages!

Mother and Nadine had discussed at length what were termed the "agrarian difficulties," the land reform that had been so violently set in motion by the Mexican Revolution of 1910. The term "agrarian difficulties," with which the Millers were still very much involved, was a kind of "password, an expression uttered with a drop of the voice as there might be eavesdroppers, or as Bostonians might speak of the 'condition' of a woman expecting a baby. Something awful but exclusive." By Mother's understanding, the situation was driven by inconsistencies and political rigmarole and intrigue. She described Josephus Daniels, the U.S. ambassador to Mexico (1933–41), as "no good to anybody" because he wouldn't even listen to their troubles, and efforts by those like the Millers to take their concerns to Vice President John Nance Garner had proved futile.

Since the Texan had become vice president, under President Franklin Roosevelt, he and Ambassador Daniels had made an about-face. Robert Miller was said to be the only foreigner who ever got any money as compensation for his initial claim, but the Mexican government had continued to chip away at the remaining acres, allowing only six hundred acres per holding. Of course, Miller had since carried his appeal to the United States in his wife's name. In his interview with Garner, the vice president, referring to "that dirty ignorant country of Mexico," simply echoed the president's attitude: "If you *will* gamble, my boy. It's a great game isn't it—speculation? I got burned myself. Bought several thousand acres on the wrong side of the Rio Grande and they aren't worth a cent now—except to the Mexican government!" And Daniels reinforced the "hands-off" policy by doing whatever he could to help restore to Mexico its own land. While still seizing land without restitution and giving it to the peons, the government made no effort to sow communistic principles in the federally run schools, one of which was operated on the Millers' ranch. The Millers believed Cárdenas had let Trotsky into Mexico to show the people what was wrong with Soviet Russia.

Three centuries of colonialism had left a land divided by race and religion: Spaniards, creoles, *mestizos,* and the Indian masses (regarded as a valuable natural resource in mining and in agriculture and working as landless peasants). Since the disastrous intervention of the United States in an underdeveloped Mexico—during the Mexican War of 1847 under Scott and Lee and again in the 1916 Punitive Expedition in search of Pancho Villa under General Pershing—foreign holdings in Mexico counted for as many as 100 million acres, not to mention the powerful foreign-owned industries. Using brute force, intrigue, and deep patriotism, a number of powerful factions strove against each other with a common goal: land reform, political and economic stability, and social justice.

There was increasing strife between radicals and the Church, and between Obregón and his chief rival, Plutarco Elías Calles. Civil war seemed inevitable. With the election of Lázaro Cárdenas in 1934, the new president's popularity put an end to Calles's domination of Mexican politics.

Cárdenas had been a skilled battlefield commander and revolutionary general, puritanical, sober, soft-spoken. He showed no interest in wealth or privilege. In 1928, having been elected governor of the province of Michoacán, he initiated an ambitious reform program: schools, roads, irrigation projects, land distribution. Three-quarters of the population depended on agriculture, but only 3 percent owned the land they worked. The need for party- rather than personality-driven politics had led to the formation of the PNR (Partido Nacional Revolucionario, which, in 1938, became the PRM, or Partido de la Revolución Mexicana), helping to stabilize the electoral process.

In 1933, Cárdenas won the PNR nomination for the presidency and was swept into office the following year with 98.19 percent of the popular vote. His pro-labor stance and concern for the treatment of Mexican workers led to the expropriation of the oil companies and national debt. Despite the economic depression of the 1930s and the continual threat of strikes, Cárdenas reorganized the twenty-one oil workers' organizations into one large syndicate. Land redistribution accelerated, addressing the welfare of the peasants and workers and making them part of the political process.

Mother tended to side with Cárdenas in the ongoing dispute over the treatment of foreign landowners in Mexico. She thought he had proved to be an excellent leader of the slowly emerging state, in terms of education, irrigation, and the overall modernization and industrialization of the nation, bringing the agricultural revolution to an end. But she feared his attitude toward foreigners was softening. She hated to see him "browbeaten by American money—or English. The silly old argument that 'enlightened' people bring up, that an ignorant race is too ignorant to take care of itself."

It was at this time, in March 1937, that Mother was faced with the first of a series of nagging medical exigencies in the family. My sister and I had picked up a nasty blood infection—probably from the irrigation water or unsterilized drinking water—and we found ourselves driven to Victoria not once but twice to be examined by a Hungarian doctor from Budapest. "It meant continuous attention," Mother complained to her parents, "potassium permanganate baths every day, a plaster of white mercuric oxide salve several times a day, and being waited on hand and foot because the sores were so painful." None of the homeopathic remedies worked, and, in the absence of antibiotics, I would continue to have outbreaks of boils for several more years.

It was time to move up to Mexico City to stay for a few months. On April 2, 1937, we made our way to another lifestyle in a big, exciting city. For seven pesos a day (ca. $1.85), we joined several other renters, mostly foreigners, in the home of Señora Mariano Solgado at Calle Hamburgo, 39. "Here we are in a place," Mother wrote her parents, "so utterly different from the ranch that it takes a few breaths to adjust—to the altitude and the kind of life." The Solgado family is "up to its ears" in old Spanish customs.

The Solgados used to be very wealthy by Mexican standards. Mr. Solgado was head of the Customs Department; he had died just one month earlier at the age of ninety-six. His small pension was soon reduced by half. Both middle-aged daughters were forced to leave their sheltered existence and go out to work, one as a nurse with the Rockefeller Foundation, the other as a secretary in the government offices. The Solgados' married son worked for an oil company in Tampico; his seven-year-old son was staying with the grandmother to escape the tropical diseases of Tampico. The grandson and a two-and-a-half-year-old Indian baby, along with four other boarders—two women and two men—would take part in the great event of the day: the night meal, served at about eight thirty and lasting until ten.

The three of us were given a *huge* room on the ground floor, with sun flooding into it all day through windows that opened from floor to ceiling. At night, the windows were closed and locked and shut off with immense wooden shutters that folded out of the walls and were double-locked; the bedroom doors were all left open, and air circulated by way of a big central skylight over the patio. The front door was triple-locked.

The Señora, in her eighties, would go "up and down and around the house all day long with a bunch of heavy keys, about 30, on a key ring the size and weight of a horseshoe, doling out a bit of spice from this chest, a towel from that cupboard, a bottle of iodine from that cabinet." And, of course, there were Indian servants: a washwoman, a cook, a cleaning woman, and a serving woman, working long hours from six in the morning until eleven at night, or later. We ate well, Mexican food in the Vera Cruz tradition, we were told. On the ranch, we ate American-style food, with an occasional Mexican touch. In general, we avoided the Mexican cooking, but the Salgados' cuisine was excellent. In fact, my sister and I soon put on weight. Mother was pleased: "I've never seen Lee with such a huge and sustained appetite. And supper here being just another five or six course dinner, she gets plenty of chance to eat."

Within a few days, my sister and I began attending the Maddox School, considered the best English school in the city. The school hours were only from nine to one, which we liked, during which they had two periods of Spanish and three of English. Located a block from our house, it was run by two English women—"oh *so* English," Mother said—but Spanish prevailed as the spoken language. It stayed open all summer, with the long vacation in November, December, and January. My sister was put in third grade (and was expected to know her tables up to 14), and I was put in the lower half of first grade. Although it was a private school, the tuition was only twenty pesos a month, about six dollars. In fact, Mother found she could get by on a hundred dollars a month—barring the unforeseen.

Once settled in Mexico City, Mother complained of tonsillitis, which she treated with gargles and paintings. This was soon followed by a badly infected finger, not only painful but making her penmanship an ordeal. Thorough treatments for the infection followed; the abscess came to a head and was mercifully lanced. But that was not all. In our room at Avenida Hamburgo, I had been working on fashioning some material into doll's clothing, using a pair of scissors to make holes in the fabric. Pushing through from underneath, the point of the scissors penetrated my left eye. Horrified, Mother wrote her mother in Amherst, explaining her feelings: "I have been pulling myself together the last day or so, and can begin to eat again. No matter how I prepare myself for just such accidents with thinking of the things that *could* happen and don't, of how much worse almost any could be than it actually is, and of how fortunate Elinor and Lee have been to have had so few, yet when this struck it bowled me over. Blindness, even of one eye, makes me fairly faint to think of."

Learning of my accident, Mother had rushed me to an internationally known ophthalmologist, Dr. Caryl Bauer. People came to him from all over the world for cures. He would welcome his patients, often lined up outside, into his tiny, shabby workroom located in a poor part of town. He was wonderful to them and with them; he took a little money if they had any to give. Four months of every year he would lock up and go to Paris, Berlin, or New

York to study. A sixty-five-year-old bachelor, he spoke fluently at least five languages. During the consultation, Dr. Bauer could see a cataract forming over my left eye. Taking precautions to prevent infection that might spread from one eye to the other, he was hopeful that with a five-year-old patient so extremely strong and healthy, the cataract might be absorbed naturally, thus precluding surgery. But it did not absorb. There in that tiny work-room, I was strapped down on the table, given a local anesthetic, and the cataract was successfully removed, leaving permanently blurred vision in that eye. Mother assessed my handling of the situation:

> Lee goes on accepting in her quiet way. Emergencies, like this or the ton-sils [removed the previous year in the States], she meets with such superb gallantry, while she goes into a tantrum if she can't tie her shoe lace! The days we go to the doctor she only says "Let's go as soon as I get dressed so I won't have to think about it before hand." She has of course cried a couple of times when he was hurting her badly. The first time he said "If you won't cry I have something in the drawer for you." She didn't stop, but when he was through he went to the drawer and gave her a chocolate. She looked at him in a puzzled way, and said to me afterward "I went on crying so I wonder why he gave me the chocolate." The second time she cried he said nothing but gave her the chocolate again when she left. After that, she said "I guess he gives people the candy because they get hurt and not because they are good about it."

"Other than the eye (which really doesn't *seem* to be in Lee's way at all)," Mother wrote her parents, "the children are extremely well. Lee has gained five pounds, and Elinor two, since we came to the Solgados."

Since moving to Mexico City, Mother had been struggling with the rap-id-fire Spanish she was exposed to. She felt panicky when trying to con-verse with educated Mexicans but did well, she said, "with shop keepers and garage men!" By staying through the summer months, she hoped to take advantage of classes offered to the many foreigners who would arrive to study Spanish and Spanish art and history at the university.

Mother did, in fact, register for a course on Mexican art that ran from mid-July to mid-August. Her copious notes covered the precolonial (Aztec and Mayan uses of copper, gold, and silver), colonial, Renaissance, and Moorish (*mudejar*) influences, and on into the Churrigueresque and mod-ern revolutionary periods. The course covered major works in architecture (especially the cathedrals in Mexico City and Oaxaca), painting, sculpture, and ceramics. She was sent to the Antigua Librería Robredo (at the inter-section of Argentina and Guatemala in the city) to purchase recommended texts for further study. Although much of the three hundred years of colonial art is lost, the large output of the eighteenth century was inferior in quality and focused on commissioned religious canvases. The intervention of foreign powers—Spain, United States, and France—helped shape Mexican art until we reach the great mural painters (propagandists) of the Revolution: David Alfaro Siquieros, José Clemente Orozco, Diego Rivera, and Dr. Atl.

Brought back to reality by a gasoline workers' strike in the city, Mother was down to a couple of liters. Less gasoline, fewer cars, but more reckless driving, Mother soon found. Having adopted the Mexican love of intrigue and secret assignations, Mother managed to wrangle one liter at a time from hoarders out for a quick profit. "I spent three-quarters of an hour 'persuading' two bandits and a pleasant policeman who was aiding and abetting them into giving me two liters. . . . We all had all the time in the world. . . . They would have been deeply hurt if I had given up the game."

Mother knew from experience that keeping one's temper was important; she confessed that she had flown off the handle at times: "the Post Office and the police and the civil service are all too much for human flesh and blood to stand *all* the time." Strikes and even revolutions didn't seem to bother the Mexicans, who seemed to enjoy something that clears the heat temporarily: "People of all classes say, 'It's time to have another Revolution—we need it,' in just the tone we'd use to say 'A good rain right now would help the garden.'"

Our next move was to Cuernavaca, a place that had attracted Mother since the first visit there with Nadine Miller, a place she described as "a Mexican Eden." Less than a month after our arrival at the Rancho Amanalco, she wrote a brief essay on her surroundings that soon appeared in the Pittsfield, Massachusetts, newspaper, the *Berkshire Evening Eagle* on October 8, 1937, and in the *Rockford Morning Star* on October 12:

> Here we are in a spot we can't believe in yet. . . . I sit in a sun almost too bright for writing, with a palm that took only ten years to grow its 40 feet at one elbow, and at the other a banana tree with flower and fruit at one and the same time. Near by are three varieties of cactus roses in bloom, bougainvillea falling over a low roof, and the bright blue-green of the swimming pool against the dark jungle-green of orange and *aguacate* trees.

Across a steep ravine was the village of Cuernavaca with the Palace of Cortés in the foreground—palace and nearby church dating back more than four hundred years. And, of course, the mountains:

Beyond the village we are hemmed in by mountains—those rising immediately at our backs being a link in the ring that circles the high plateau of
Mexico City, those southward, where Taxco hangs on a cliff, being part and
parcel of the long Sierra Madre range that stretches from Southern California to the Isthmus; while to the east the cone of Popocatépetl and the massive reclining shoulders of Ixtaccíhuatl hold up white snow between green
valley and blue sky.

We would sometimes accompany the Indian servants across the ravine to
the open market, where we bargained for a kilo of peas at twenty-five centa-
vos, offer twenty, and end up giving twenty-five as a compromise, suffering
at the thought of the farmer's lack of profit. The glorious heaps of tropic
fruit—mangos, plums, bananas, melons—and the abundance of tomatoes,
eggs, spring chickens, and other fresh produce were covered in layers of
mud and rotted material. We were overwhelmed with the smell of entrails
that hung in heavy festoons and disturbed by the "troubling gaze of shawl-
wrapped, pock-marked women who squat on their heels" and seek you out
from a place of "poverty, illness, and a gentle, even cheerful, endurance":

> It has been said so often that Mexico is a country of contrasts that it mustn't
> be said again, but it has to be. In order to withstand the shock of divergent
> impressions, I go about like one of these ancient lizards with eyes half closed
> against an over-brilliant landscape on one side and the human misery on the
> other, the childlike simplicity and sweetness of the Mexican temperament
> as opposed to its terrible childlike cruelty, the blazing calm of the midday
> sun against the shattering violence of the nightly rain.

The ranch was owned by Albert Harmsen, the "saber-scarred, war-
scarred, Mexican Revolution–scarred, wiry little" German expatriate.
Harmsen never stopped talking about the coming revolution, occasionally
displaying one of his many pistols, machine guns, rifles, swords, and knives,
an arsenal he sometimes drew on to shoot a scavenging ring-tailed raccoon.
The gardener, the sad-eyed Alberto, could often be seen sweeping up the
leaves with a broom made of tiny twigs tied to a stick; two Indian women
nearby would scrub clothes on a granite slab, dipping the water from an
irrigation canal running loudly through the grounds and under one of the
houses, one of several dwelling places surrounding the garden.

It was like what the Britishers within the gates called "a private compound," in which they would hoarsely demand that the children be quiet
at all times. Actually, under all this luxuriant beauty lurked a number of
deadly insects: black widows, kept as pets by an occasional boarder; the

stalking "*vinegrío*," built like a nightmare wasp without wings, but with an evil tail like a unicorn's horn behind and lobster-claw jaws up ahead; an innocent-looking fuzzy caterpillar that emits poison from his hairs that causes the heart to race for several days (but is not fatal!). As for the adorably ferocious-looking lizards forever sliding up and down the walls and trunks of trees, they were considered harmless additions to the picturesque landscape.

More disturbing was a battle to the death between two large-breed dogs, one a Dalmatian, the other, I believe, a Great Dane. They opened each other's throats, and I understand they died of their wounds. Picture also my sister and me swimming in the well-kept pool but dragging a little sack of chlorine attached to our bathing suits for protection.

Mother soon realized that we must rely on our American sense of humor: when the paper boy says there is no paper today, Saturday ("¿Por qué? ¡Quién sabe!") but has for sale the first half of the Sunday's paper, the rest of which can be purchased the next day, but only when bought as part of the whole paper, "one goes away simply convulsed with delight at having such advance news of the world"; or when your license plates are taken away ("as a favor to you") by some bureaucratic officer and then lost, and you are accused of entering the country illegally without plates, and then the *jefe* locates them in his desk drawer—"indeed you do laugh because it fairly surpasses the tragic, and anything that does that is funny."

By now, Mother had succumbed to the Mexican rhythm of life; she couldn't "remember ever feeling before such a state of mental and physical relaxation," a state where the sense of time is lost, and each day flows into the next. She noticed, as well, that my sister and I had adjusted to the new life to such a point of callousness that she felt positively hurt: "When I point out a hummingbird that is standing off an hibiscus three yards away, or shriek to look at a white butterfly twice the size of the humming bird, Lee answers in light derision, 'Oh, there are simply scads of those things around here.' And if the *criada* (servant) pours a rapid flow of indistinguishable Spanish that leaves me gasping, Elinor 'translates' with a note of scarcely veiled contempt—something to do with how to cut up the zanahorias (carrots)." Mother thought it better that we learn "kitchen" Spanish than no foreign language: "And at least they now know a lot more about the inequalities of the human race, about differences in vegetation and animal life and points of view and, within the 'compound,' about international relations, since we are English, American, German, Canadian, and Mexican."

Despite all the physical beauty of Cuernavaca and the Rancho Amanalco, the perfect setting for writing and relaxing, Mother felt a mounting concern for family back home in the States—especially for her mother. Each letter from her parents only heightened her anxiety.

At first, the letters home debated where her parents might best spend the winter months of 1937–38. They had plans to leave Amherst on or around December 1. They had loved San Antonio, but there had been far too little sun. Maybe Arizona or New Mexico or Florida. Any one of these was fine with Mother. The Southwest would permit Robin to visit from Montana, and they might find a ranch with horses, something my sister and I would have loved. However, the repeated suggestion by her parents that we consider a family gathering in Gainesville, where her father had friends at the University of Florida, wasn't too pleasing to the three of us, who frankly longed to be on the water and not in "an inland Florida city."

There was further debate over whether or not it would be feasible for the family to meet in Mexico, possibly in Cuernavaca. But Mother quickly discouraged the idea, citing a long list of obstacles. Transportation to and from central Mexico was difficult, as was getting around within Mexico. A long journey over ten-thousand-foot mountains, with a drop of five thousand feet to Cuernavaca, would add to the exhaustion after the long plane ride, and it would be even worse if sailing down the coast to the malaria-ridden ports of Acapulco or Mazatlán, especially in light of her parents' dread of seasickness. She went on to stress the torture of mosquitoes and other insects, as well as rumors of an epidemic of bubonic plague along the coast. Keeping the water and food safe was always an issue—boiled water, canned milk, vegetables disinfected with iodine—even in the Amanalco compound. Amoebic dysentery was rampant. These conditions, she added, were aggravated by the prevalence of trashy Mexican teenagers who attract British and American men, who then denounce their families and sink to the lowest level. No place for Carol, she concluded: "It would be too great a risk for the *whole* family to come in right now. And you'd hate the fleas!"

Mother felt compelled to mention the ever-present threat throughout Mexico of political and criminal violence. There was every indication that most English and American oil companies might soon pull out of the country, tying the country up in knots. The natives were very sweet and kind to the *"yanquis,"* she wrote, but the immigration authorities were another matter altogether: generally hard-boiled and suspicious in the extreme. If Mexico were ever to be swept clean, it would be overrun by Americans, and there would be no peaceful, untroubled spots like Cuernavaca!

II · AFTER 1938

THE FAMILY DEBATE came to an end abruptly as 1937 drew to a close. Mother received word from her father: her mother had undergone surgery for breast cancer at the Springfield (Massachusetts) Hospital. Her doctors were fearful that her damaged heart would not withstand the anesthesia, but despite her general weakness, she was given ether, "and she lived through it." RF cautioned his daughter: "Be careful to give her all the courage you can for the future and at the same time all the credit she deserves for having come through a worse ordeal than we expected." The surgery was deemed successful, however, and Elinor began to make a slow recovery during November. Their home in Amherst was reorganized to reduce the need to climb stairs.

"The way you've staged a recovery is too thrilling, mama," Mother wrote. But she was worried sick, and her parents soon gave up any romantic notion of exploring the west coast of Mexico, Robert admitting in a letter to his daughter that "we are no longer young and rugged. We mustn't be ambitious to live too dangerously." Mother agreed that the family simply must not try to travel to Mexico and that she must get back to the States before her visa expired, to be with her mother during her convalescence and in time to conduct a serious job search in the fall. "So I think Florida is really best," she wrote. "It strikes a spot about halfway between us, isn't such a difficult journey for you, and has more *chance* at something to occupy Carol." She planned to leave around mid-November and arrive in Gainesville in time to rent two lodgings, one for the three of us and her parents, another for Lillian, Carol, Prescott, and Robin.

Gainesville and the Death of Elinor Frost

Arriving from Mexico, my sister and I shared with our mother the downstairs of a rented house at 743 Bay Street; our aunt and cousins—Lillian, Carol, Prescott, and Robin—leased a home nearby. Our grandparents were enjoying the mild Florida weather: "Our weather has been sunnily lovely except for a rain or two to start spring in the grass," RF wrote, and they were anticipating their fiftieth wedding anniversary. But it was here—on March 20, 1938—that Elinor Frost would succumb to a series of heart attacks.

When Elinor collapsed, Mother accused her father of bringing on her mother's heart failure by having insisted upon living upstairs where he would not hear the children running above him. In an emotional state, she tried and succeeded in keeping her father from Elinor's bedside until it was too late. My sister and I (ages eight and six at the time) were escorted into our grandmother's room for a final good-bye. Elinor was too weak to respond; she lay quietly on the pillow and apparently did not call for her husband, who waited impatiently outside. After a brief visit, we children were sent to a neighbor's house to play until the crisis passed.

As young children, we felt the sorrow at the unfolding events but were incapable of processing them in a meaningful way. It was clear my mother, in her sad-angry confrontation with her father, feared and resented his overpowering needs and, like her father, did not want to give up her independence or that of her daughters. These hurtful encounters would affect Mother's relations with her father over the years; she expressed to me frequently her regret over her mother's unfulfilled life as a woman married to a struggling poet, dedicated to both him and her children, and all of them demanding of her limited strength.

Grieving and distraught, the widowed poet was unable either to participate in the cremation or to make the memorial arrangements back at Amherst. He soon resigned his position on the faculty and sold the home he and Elinor had owned on Sunset Avenue. RF kept the urn in a closet, where he would bring an occasional orchid, a flower they both loved.

When it came time to scatter Elinor's ashes at the Derry Farm, in accordance with her wishes, RF went to the house to seek permission from the current owners. Having received a chilly reception, and noting the poorly maintained property near Hyla Brook, he decided to abandon the mission and, instead, to purchase a plot outside the Congregational Church in Old Bennington, Vermont, a family plot still maintained by his heirs. Etched on the plaque we find Robert Frost's name and dates, followed by the line from "A Lesson for Today": "I had a lover's quarrel with the world." Underneath we find his wife's name and dates, followed by the line from "The Master Speed": "Together wing to wing and oar to oar." Simple memorial tributes for Carol and Lillian, Irma Cone, Lesley Frost, and Malcolm Wilber have brought the family together.

To understand RF's breakdown upon his wife's death, we trace his love of Elinor back to his high school days in Lawrence. As a teenager, Robert's love of poetry and his determination to be a poet had grown as strong and lasting as his love for Elinor Miriam White, co-valedictorian of his high school graduating class. When chosen for the honor—to celebrate his roles as athlete, class poet, and editor of the high school *Bulletin*—he refused to accept the honor unless his sweetheart shared it with him; this was the only time the school named two valedictorians. Both seniors had to give speeches, both suffering from terrifying shyness. Elinor never got over her timidity in public, and it would be many years in the limelight before RF would be comfortable in front of an audience.

As noted earlier, Elinor had agreed to marry Robert only after completing a college degree from St. Lawrence University. She was an important partner in RF's long and difficult journey toward public recognition as a poet: raising a family; farming and writing on the Derry Homestead; teaching at the Pinkerton Academy and Plymouth State College; becoming part of a poetic renaissance in London that led to the publication and favorable reviews of his first two volumes of verse, *A Boy's Will* (1913) and *North of Boston* (1914); and, upon the family's return to America the following year, his establishment as a celebrated writer and teacher. Because of her belief in him, Elinor endured the hardships and applauded his successes. The loss of such a partner was devastating.

In the aftermath of his wife's death, just short of their fiftieth wedding anniversary, Robert lamented to family and friends: "She is the unspoken half of everything I ever wrote, and both halves of many a thing"; "pretty near every one of my poems will be found to be about her if rightly read." He wrote his daughter Lesley that Elinor "dominated my art with the power of her character and nature" and that her sorrow in a sad life "overcasts my poetry." He agonized to his friend Louis Untermeyer: "I am so quickened by what has happened that I can't touch my mind with a memory of any kind. I can't touch my skin anywhere with my finger but it hurts like a sad inspiration." To another close friend, Hervey Allen, he wrote out the lines from Tennyson: "And I, the last, go forth companionless,/And the days darken round me, and the years."

The voice of the grieving lover reached a new intensity in *A Witness Tree* (1942): "Happiness Makes Up in Height for What It Lacks in Length"; "Carpe Diem"; "The Silken Tent"; "Never Again Would Birds' Songs Be the Same." Because it has been disputed for whom "The Silken Tent" was written, Mother insisted that it was composed for Elinor and that she herself had typed it for her father before her mother's death.

Kathleen Morrison and the Homer Noble Farm

Following Elinor's death, we watched in amazement the reemergence of my grandfather as a teacher and public persona, who, by the time of his own death in January 1963, was revered nationally and internationally, four-time winner of the Pulitzer Prize and of many other honors. But, in 1938, it was clear to all of us that RF was in need of immediate help to restore balance to his life. Besides family members, Merrill Moore; Louis Untermeyer; Hervey

Allen, author of *Anthony Adverse* and a frequent Bread Loaf lecturer; the Iowa poet Paul Engle; and other close friends worried that RF was suffering a permanent breakdown. Kathleen Morrison came forward to provide anchor to the stricken poet.

Within the Frost family there were other strong women who would support and encourage my grandfather through his final years, helping to fill the vacuum left by the loss of his wife: besides Kay Morrison, my aunt Lillian LaBatt Frost, Carol's wife; and my sister, Elinor Francis Wilber. In her own fashion, my mother provided further anchor, as did the memory of Elinor Frost and her quiet strength in the poet's life and imagination after her passing.

Students and friends over the years ask me what I think of Kay (and her husband, Theodore, and two children). My usual reply: "If she had not existed, we would have to invent her." It is true, as he himself said, that my grandfather soon fell in love with Kay and asked her to leave her husband and marry him; it is also true that this stage of their relationship was short-lived and that she agreed to serve as his secretary (with the blessing of her husband and daughter, their son having died tragically) for the remainder of his life. He expanded upon his dilemma and on the much-needed help of his longtime friend Louis Untermeyer: "[Louis] and I have reached a point of frankness where we can tell each other exactly what we want of each other. . . . He recognizes that all my thinking must start from the obligations I am under to Kathleen and she under to me for what she has done to bring me back to life. He thinks as I think all can be managed right and seemly."

It was during the first visits to Florida, where the Frosts spent time at Key West in a rented house on the beach and later at the Casa Marina, that the Engles took RF with them to Cuba for a week's complete change of scenery: "We went down to Camaguey saw several cities besides Havana and plenty of sugar cane and royal palms. The land is rich; the people are miserably poor. Everywhere beggars and beggar-vendors. We saw one great beach to beat the world . . . by the most transparent ocean water I have ever looked into. . . . To me the best of the excursion was the flight both ways in the big Pan American plane and especially the swoop and mighty splash into the bays on arrival."

Letters from my mother to Kay Morrison, especially in the years immediately following Elinor's death, are written with affection and a full understanding of the enormous effort required to stabilize her father in his despair. She repeatedly thanked and congratulated Kay on the work she did to find RF a home, first in Boston at 88 Mt. Vernon Street and then in Cambridge at 35 Brewster Street.

In his letters to Lesley, RF asks his daughter to be grateful to Kathleen, who "has made my apartment pleasant and taken an interest in my mail and my lecture engagements," and who has "helped me through a bad time." Mother realized that she could and would continue to make suggestions on how to manage RF and his troubled children, in particular Carol and Irma, while also working with Kay to help her cousins, Hilda and Vera Harvey, all of whom needed both financial and emotional support.

The relationship was beneficial to both Kay and Ted, who was on the English faculty at Harvard, and no less beneficial to RF. Kay and her family resided in the farmhouse at the Homer Noble Farm in Ripton, Vermont, first rented the summer of 1938. RF soon purchased the farm, leaving the large farmhouse to the Morrisons. For himself, RF chose to live in a rustic, three-room log cabin a few hundred yards up the hill, overlooking the north pasture, often coming down to eat with the Morrison family. There he did his writing, as he did elsewhere, on a lapboard while seated in a Morris chair. The arrangement lasted for twenty-three summers. He would enjoy the companionship, the land, the horses and dogs of the farm, and the privacy the cabin afforded him for his work. Equally important, the Bread Loaf Writers' conference—which RF had helped launch, joining the Morrisons in its development—was a short walk or drive downhill from the farm.

RF owned another home near his cabin they called the Eubar, where friends and relatives could stay for lengthy visits: I remember Alfred Edwards, James Chapin, each with families, as well as RF's grandson Prescott's in-laws, the Gordons, who ultimately purchased the home. Getting to the Eubar was a delightful walk over from the Homer Noble Farm and cabin along a wooded path.

One summer, while I was still at the Putney School, Mother arranged for me to stay at the Eubar with the artist James Chapin, his wife, Mary, and their two-year-old son, to serve as a model for a planned oil painting and as an in-house baby sitter. The artist made sketches of me for his painting, but I, the emotional teenager, was rankled by his highly temperamental demands. I was soon dismissed and returned to the Homer Noble Farm to stay with the Morrisons and my grandfather. The oil painting was never completed, but Chapin gave me a study he did for the painting. Chapin painted RF and Elinor, as well, but the condition of both paintings has deteriorated badly.

Our family visits to the Homer Noble Farm were delightful. We slept in the main farmhouse down from the cabin and up from the main road. Kay and Ted always had one or two wonderful riding horses—one was called

Black Beauty, another, Sugarbush—in the barn nearby. We children rode horseback, hunted for snakes under strategically placed boards in the field, and participated in games of baseball and tennis. RF would come down for meals, enjoyed by all at a large table; sometimes we were invited up to the cabin to talk or walk or play games with our grandfather.

Mounting Family Tragedies

Even before Carol Frost's suicide in 1940, personal tragedies had overwhelmed Robert and Elinor Frost. Elinor had found it increasingly difficult to overcome her own depression and physical limitations brought on by frequent illnesses and pregnancies, weakening further a heart already damaged by childhood rheumatic fever. She never fully recovered from the loss of their first son, Elliott, in 1900 just before their move to Derry. She and Robert exchanged harsh words at the time, but they were never estranged. Elinor soon renounced any Supreme Being, distancing herself from her mother and eldest sister, Ada, devout Christian Scientists who had urged the Frosts not to call the doctor when Elliott became ill; eventually summoned, the doctor said it was too late to save the child. She had come to echo the sentiment of the wife in "Home Burial": "the world is evil."

Although RF's powerfully dramatic poem "Home Burial" was based factually on a neighbor's tragic loss of a first child—and the Frosts would never use their property as a burial ground, a practice common in rural New England—the raw, self-accusatory emotions expressed in the poem's dialogue clearly were drawn from personal experience; RF never read the poem in public for that reason. Elinor's avowed atheism and RF's deep exploration of man's spirituality outside of institutional religions were a source of conflict. Over time they came to respect each other's differing views, RF claiming to prefer to debate the views of an atheist as more of an affirmation than those of a wavering agnostic.

Elinor's endurance had been further weakened by the tragic loss of Marjorie following the birth of her daughter, Robin. Her extended family adopted Robin from the beginning; besides her father and grandmother, Willard Fraser and his mother, Elinor Frost and Lillian participated in Robin's early development. Later in life, Robin, as an accomplished artist, would illustrate some of her aunt's stories for children. My sister, Elinor, and I were frequent visitors at South Shaftsbury. Lillian had been hospitalized for major surgery at the time of her husband's death in 1940, and she and Prescott moved in with close friends for a lengthy period of recovery.

Lillian was a remarkable woman. She had lost a lung overcoming tuberculosis as a young wife (the only patient in her California TB ward to survive); she was almost totally deaf with white hair in her early twenties. The first years I knew her she had a horn she held to one ear into which we would have to yell to be understood. Over her lifetime, however, she graduated to a hand-held box she carried around and finally to a smaller and smaller device she could hide in her clothing. Despite her handicaps, she outlived not only her husband but her son and daughter-in-law. More important, she was extraordinarily generous with her dedication to family and her tireless energy. Having suffered through her husband's tragic death, she opened her home—in South Shaftsbury and Bennington—to me and my sister.

Having lost his mother, and with his wife hospitalized, Carol succumbed to his long-held suicidal thoughts. Although RF continued to encourage his son in his craving for success as a poet, he must have realized that it was not to be, aware of the cruel fact that it was Carol's sister Marjorie who had been born with a lyrical voice, snuffed out too early. As his despairing father, RF had come to visit repeatedly in long night vigils alone with his son, trying desperately to reassure him and help him out of his depression. But Carol returned to his irrational insistence that his inability to have more than the one child, as well as his dependence upon the family for support, made him useless. Little was known then about an illness that appeared to be manic depression and for which there was no known cure. Rather than being institutionalized, Carol had enjoyed many years of freedom to farm and be a loving caretaker of his family. As his father sadly acknowledged, he was at home with animals and children.

Once Lillian was back on her feet, she and her son, Prescott, moved into an apartment in Bennington. Elinor and I spent a year during the war (1941–42) with them, attending public school and enjoying a happy outdoor life with new English bikes Mother had brought us. I skipped a grade into sixth grade and made lots of friends shooting marbles and entering into the rhythm of a smaller town and more informal schooling. We even had "boyfriends." Mine was John Crawford; we would meet outside the movie theater Saturday mornings in time to watch cartoons, war news, and a feature film, usually a Western. (A few years later, I learned that John had fallen off the back of a truck and been killed.)

After the one year in Bennington, my sister and I returned to Washington; Prescott would go on to MIT and, after a brief military service during which he was permanently disabled by a bout with pneumonia, became a naval engineer and inventor, settling with his wife and children first in Panama City and then in Oregon, a state he had come to love and where he tried to market some of his inventions, in particular an above-ground irrigation system.

In 1952, just before the release of the Salk vaccine, my sister, Elinor, contracted polio (both spinal and bulbar). During the Korean Conflict, she had moved to Pensacola, Florida, with her three young children to be with her husband, Malcolm, who was serving in the Naval Reserve. (As an orphan whose only sibling had perished in Italy, he could not be sent into combat.) In all likelihood the virus was transmitted by the children, who did not get sick. It would be Lillian who moved in with the family back in Fairfield, Connecticut, caring for the children while their mother spent ten months in the New York State Rehabilitation Hospital, learning to cope with her serious paralysis. My sister recovered sufficient mobility to permit her to enter local politics in Fairfield and ultimately win election to the state legislature from the 133rd General Assembly District, where she served for twenty years before her retirement in 1992 to care for her husband, who was suffering from Alzheimer's. A press clipping shows her office at the time, located, for convenience's sake, at her home on Lalley Boulevard: a collage of clipped newspaper articles, correspondence, General Assembly brochures, and memos are spread across a massive carved oak table. The table had once belonged to her grandfather at his residence in Cambridge, Massachusetts, and now fills the dining room of my youngest daughter's home in Virginia. At her retirement, Elinor was hailed as "no less than poetry in politics and the peerless pride of Fairfield." But Elinor was not a romantic stargazer; she was a patient legislative leader. Her concerns for better health care and improved transportation dominated her legislative agenda. Although RF's poems are not central to her chosen profession, she often referred the interviewer to "The Gift Outright" or "Take Something Like a Star" to encourage her constituents to reach beyond themselves. Elinor was lauded as a mentor and for her honesty, fairness, and a willingness to stick up for what she believed in; she was praised no less for her dedication to the citizens in her district and in Connecticut, serving as a model for all who would attempt to get into public service. It was noted that her peers annually recognized her as a leader, and, according to the *Connecticut Magazine* polls, she ranked among the top ten legislators.

As a member of the Public Health and Safety Commission, Elinor was and remains sensitive to the problems faced by the handicapped. While serving in Hartford, Elinor relied on crutches; later in life she was restricted to a wheelchair, neither of which has slowed her down: sixty-three when she retired, she is now eighty-six. Driving a hand-controlled pickup truck into which a pulley carries her collapsed wheelchair into a crawl space behind the front seat, she takes herself around the Fairfield/Bridgeport area entirely on her own. She flies out of Hartford airport for trips to visit family in Seattle, Los Angeles, Nebraska, Washington, D.C., and Atlanta. She urges more women to run for office, hoping that further services for the handicapped will help increase participation. In the *Fairfield Citizen-News* of March 30, 1977, she commented on the challenges faced by the handicapped: "Physically handicapped people are prevented from obtaining jobs because of stairs, narrow doorways, high curbs, escalators, and poor parking. . . . It's the most extraordinary thing to me that we have to legislate what I would call thoughtfulness." When asked how she managed to keep up the hectic pace of travel, she lightheartedly replied: "I just start a little earlier."

Once Elinor could again manage her family's needs, her aunt Lillian returned to her children and grandchildren in Oregon. These four family members—Elinor Frost; Lillian; my mother, Lesley; and my sister, Elinor—each in her own way, continued to show remarkable fortitude in keeping a troubled family together.

Robert Frost's Religious Views

Given the constant emotional turmoil in the poet's private life, reflected in his poetry and in his relations with his wife, Elinor, RF's religious views became the subject of debate, inspiring a great deal of print. I had long since concluded that a fervent, metaphorically driven dualism had, to the end of his life, given my grandfather the power, sentiment, and core beliefs of his worldview, which expanded metaphorically to a universal scientific/ religious view of man's purpose. The purpose or design of our journey lies not in the unity itself, he tells us, but in the search for truth. In such poems as "Neither Out Far Nor In Deep," "For Once, Then, Something," "Once by the Pacific," and "Our Hold on the Planet," despite the enormous limitations he sees on man's ability to reason, his search for the ulteriorities never falters. Further summarized in his meditative monologue "Education by Poetry," the core beliefs, that is "the self-belief, the love-belief, and the art-belief," are all inextricably related to the God-belief, "that the belief in God is a relationship you enter into with Him to bring about the future."

RF's poems provide the poet's own delight and surprise "of remembering something I didn't know I knew"; the dualism, the two-endedness, his love of the couplet and contrariness, the conflict, coexistence, and interdependence between good and evil, between justice and mercy, between spirit and matter, seem so intuitively natural to me from my appreciation of the poems and essays: elements that come to the poet out of the history of Western civilization and the great thinkers going back to Greek and Roman times—to include Plato, Darwin (and the Huxleys), Bergson, William James, Santayana, Thoreau, and Emerson, in particular.

The late Peter Stanlis, an Edmund Burke scholar and professor of English at Rockford, spent considerable time with the poet at his cabin in Ripton, Vermont. His book, *Robert Frost: The Poet as Philosopher*, provides additional comments on this vexing topic. He correctly observes RF's lifelong fascination with the sciences—evolutionary theories, geology, astronomy, physics (Einstein)—as he seeks to harmonize aesthetically a belief in evolution with idealistic philosophy. And he correctly points to troublesome errors in Thompson's "official" biography: an inability to understand metaphorical thinking, a total lack of wit or humor, and a heavy-handed reliance on psychoanalytical theories to organize his materials into a breathtakingly negative portrait. Even when RF wrote to his biographer, "I am a Dualist," it seems not to have registered in Thompson's assessment.

Stanlis also places emphasis on the cliché-free originality and depth of RF's intellectual grappling with the great mysteries of life, resulting in a brilliant gathering metaphor of dualism and the exciting tensions reflected in his verse. Scholars acquire their knowledge systematically, RF tells us; poets acquire theirs haphazardly, letting "what will stick to them like burrs in the field." RF the poet concludes: "I have wanted in late years to go further and further in making the metaphor the whole of thinking," in risking the spiritual in the material.

It is significant, I think, that RF always preferred those moments of excitement, of drama and adventure, such as Darwin's actual discovery of "natural selection," logged into his journal *The Voyage of the Beagle*, as compared to the more scholarly *The Origin of Species*. RF was a man of "passionate preference" in all matters of the heart.

My grandfather never embraced any institutionalized religion, noting, as he did occasionally, that there is "more religion out of church than in." He knew the Bible extremely well and often referred to himself as an Old Testament Christian. He approved of the teachings of Christ but did not speak of Christ as the son of God. God, for RF, not only existed but was the foundation for his humble acceptance of the trials of life, reflected in his interpretation of the Book of Job.

We are given a more sentimental approach in Dorothy Judd Hall's *Robert Frost: Contours of Belief*, finding, as she does, a consistent pattern of belief in a cosmic structure, of spirituality in an incongruous world in which good and evil are interdependent. The book is dedicated to her longtime friend Lesley Frost. In her introduction, my mother notes the influence of Robert's mother, Belle Moodie Frost, a Scottish Presbyterian turned Swedenborgian, on the impressionable child, especially after the death of his father:

"Dorothy has so ably stated the case in the affirmative, in God's favor, and I find it so easy to agree with her, that I am wondering how we all became involved with the question in the beginning."

RF, I think, would want us to come back down to earth even at the end, in the spirit of "After Apple-Picking" and "Birches," where a reaching *toward* Heaven matters, but where "earth's the right place for love." Although RF argued in favor of the power of artistic creativity, will, and reason in man, and although he acknowledged that something must be left to God, in whose sight he yearned to be accepted, he had a "lover's quarrel with the world" as he found it; his perception of reality, I believe, remained secular and devoid of any religiosity:

> Grant me intention, purpose, and design—
> That's near enough for me to the Divine
> And yet for all this help of head and brain
> How happily instinctive we remain,
> Our best guide upward further to the light,
> Passionate preference such as love at sight.
>   ("Accidentally on Purpose")

In my correspondence with Seamus Heaney, whose essay "Above the Brim" is one of three independently composed tributes included in the volume *Homage to Robert Frost* (along with those of two other Nobel laureates, Joseph Brodsky and Derek Walcott), we discussed the line "But from sheer morning gladness at the brim" in "The Tuft of Flowers" (and included in the original title of my earlier book), together with the well-known lines in "Birches":

> ... He always kept his poise
> To the top branches, climbing carefully
> With the same pains you use to fill a cup
> Up to the brim, and even above the brim.

Commenting on the seesawing between heaven and earth (here as in "After Apple Picking"), Heaney draws our attention to the "upward waft of Frost's poems, and the different ways in which he releases the feeling ... of airy vernal daring, an overbrimming of invention." In a great dramatic poem like "Home Burial," Heaney shows how the cruel downward pressure of tragedy leads to its own buoyancy, with all the "rigor and dispatch of Greek tragedy."

I had written Heaney prior to the publication of *Homage to Robert Frost,* pointing out the coincidence between my use of "brim" and his, as well as the coincidence of location: Derry, New Hampshire, and his roots in Derry County, Northern Ireland. His response was friendly: "I am as proud as punch to think that those salutes to the genius of Robert Frost should have touched you and found assent. And, of course, the 'brimming' element in it all—I mean the coincidence of our titles—makes it all the more heartsome." Referring to the imminent release of *Homage,* he calls it "a kind of retroactive tribute, a coded message to say that he [Frost] too should have heard from Stockholm that we are his pupils."

With his letter, Heaney enclosed a signed copy of "Crediting Poetry," his Nobel lecture, in which he recalled those poets in his childhood who most stood for "that truth to life." "I loved Robert Frost," he said, "for his farmer's accuracy and his wily down-to-earthiness." I was most fortunate to meet informally with the Irish poet, both here (where he taught at Harvard) and in Dublin (where a mutual friend arranged a reception at his home for Heaney and his wife, Marie, in my honor).

In such late poems as those in the "Cluster of Faith" and "Kitty Hawk," the poet further explores God's descent "Into flesh was meant / As a demonstration / That the supreme merit / Lay in risking spirit / In substantiation." Substantiation of the spirit in the flesh "in birth after birth," substantiation of the "the soul's ethereal / Into the material." In the two masques, *A Masque of Reason* and *A Masque of Mercy,* the Old Testament Christian explores the still-unresolved dilemma: "How can we be just in a world that needs mercy and merciful in a world that needs justice" (Frost to G. R. and Alma Elliot).

Yet, while RF was exposed to the Swedenborgian mysticism of his mother, he was no less exposed to the tragic sense of life shared with his wife, Elinor, who was heard to deny the existence of a caring or loving God. She and her husband, Robert, were very private people, and we may never be able to establish a rational basis for religious conviction. We do know RF showed remarkable courage in the face of seemingly unendurable personal tragedies; surely, a belief in God, however shrouded in figurative language, could have provided the strength such loss requires. *Nota bene:* He has not yet returned, dissatisfied from what he learned "from having died" ("Away").

The War Years in Washington, D.C.

The year 1938 became a watershed year in our lives. Upon my grandmother's untimely death in March, our small family of three moved to Washington, D.C. As both RF and Mother were struggling to get back to work—and to life in general—RF wrote his daughter: "It is a lot to me that you are having things so much your way these days. . . . Won't it be great if you can get a book of children stories going. You are late in overcoming your self consciousness in writing. It's about time you came out in writing with the naturalness you have in talk. You aren't as happy in talk when I am present I guess. It is as if I was always present when you wrote. You have me to get over." RF takes the opportunity to add: "Me—I am miserable living around with people all the time. I have always had hours and days to myself alone. . . . The future of Europe is easier for me to see than my own future." He reminds his daughter of the hardships of getting ahead in the academic world without advanced degrees. He tells her: "I wish you could get away from schools entirely. We seem to hang round them unwanted. I mean our family." RF goes on to explain that his mother, Belle Moodie, never earned more than $400 a year teaching while raising two children; lacking a degree, he, RF, was paid $300 a year part-time, and $800 and $1,100 full-time at Pinkerton Academy. In his mid-thirties, finding himself "on the ragged edge of the profession," he looked into the possibility of finishing his degree at Harvard; he was advised to read Shakespeare: "Even my kindest patrons in education were suspicious of me for my irregularity."

It follows, RF would explain, that he hated to see his daughter being subjected to the same institutional rejection. "Your appointed way should be more and more clear to you. It will be by knowledge or achievement you will make your mark, you mark my words. Spanish is the plain and simple way perhaps," RF concludes. While for my mother, the burden unintentionally imposed by a famous father was considerable, she felt strong enough to deal with and eventually overcome the obstacles posed by her inheritance. The burden, however, may have contributed to her seeming reluctance to sustain attention to or focus on any one of her many gifts. She never fully "got over" her father, as he had advised. For me, the burden that seemed to set me apart in ways hard to understand while young was certainly felt but could be handled far more easily one generation later. With maturity, the blessings of a caring grandfather and a great poet could be embraced and celebrated. It seems to me that we all have to come to terms with our parents as adults. We never fully understand them or, for that matter, ourselves. The issue of "understanding" is, at best, complex. Thus *I* would have "to get over" my mother, just as she had to get over her father. In a poem, I wrote:

TANGLED

More than anything else it was
The memory of her mother.

Try, try as she would to recover
The time her heart was free of guilt,
She soon discovered that no feeling—
Not even the absence of feeling—
Could, in isolation, be rebuilt.

The weeds that tangled with the phlox
Tangled with the rose
Along the climbing stem of thorns,
And from the mix,
Distinguishable, but long since grafted there,
New motives for each twist and turn were born.

Try, try as she did to extract
The stubborn roots
That held both soil and plants,
She had found anew

(Only this time she revered her mother)
That the flower she grew or picked
Proved different from any other.

While immersed in the study of my grandfather's life and work, not unexpectedly I kept running up against my mother's strong personality, as well as an overwhelming desire to both understand and please her. Opening and reading the myriad of documents (some published, others not, of course), my curiosity led the way. Even with the publication of a score of articles on Frost the poet, I resisted coming to terms with my mother's rich and varied life, except as it interrelated with her father's ambitions in the name of poetry.

And then it was too late. Taken by complications from Parkinson's disease, in 1983, her eighty-fourth year, she took with her many parts of the puzzle as she had perceived them. In another sense, however, her departure permitted me the freedom to explore with greater ease the written record and to dare to create my own take on her passionate and adventurous life and to take notice of the many obstacles she had had to overcome.

The King-Smith Studio School, the Frost School, the TWA Night Shift

Once settled in Washington, D.C., my sister, Elinor, and I often accompanied Mother to visit with her many friends in New England. It was mid-afternoon when we found ourselves driving from South Hadley—the home of Mother's close friends Traute and Robert Barrett—to Hartford, to visit

Vachel Lindsay's widow, Elizabeth Connor; that same afternoon, the Great Hurricane of 1938 came ashore in New England with extraordinary violence. It was September 21, and landfall occurred, we learned later, on Long Island as a category 5 hurricane, killing more than six hundred people.

Barely able to stay on the road, Mother turned down her window to ask a traffic cop, fully hidden in his orange slickers, what was going on: "Just a little blow," he yelled, waylaying cars headed dangerously toward the Connecticut River. Forced to abandon the car off Route 5, we crawled on hands and knees across a field to a farmhouse. There, we sought refuge with some forty others. Having lost power, the owner called upon us to help milk his distraught cows, the three of us joining the others in doing what had to be done. We soon felt part of a B movie script as one of the stranded women chose the moment to give birth to her baby.

Back in Washington, for the almost three years leading up to our country's involvement in the war, Mother taught and helped direct the King-Smith Studio School at 1751 New Hampshire Avenue. It was a good outlet for my mother: beginning in the 1940–41 academic year, she gave a popular creative writing class and poetry seminars to the many young women relocating to Washington to do war work. In effect, as a school of the arts, the work primarily took place in the studios. The curriculum was strong in music, dramatic and theater arts, fine and applied arts, photography, history of art, literature and creative writing, and foreign languages. (A photo taken by Masha Arms, an excellent photographer and family friend, shows me and my sister with our grandfather walking along New Hampshire Avenue, near the Studio School.)

But, of course, Mother wanted to open her *own* school. Having rented an attached house on Kalorama Road (just off Connecticut Avenue), she opened her new home as the Frost School for young women who, finding themselves in the capital to do war work, longed for the chance to continue their studies in the company of other similarly motivated women. Besides conducting her own round table based on the St. John's "Great Books" series, Mother offered other discussion groups: Joseph Auslander led a "Poetry Round Table," Warren Mullin, a "Current Affairs Round Table," and there was always one notable personality or another—such as my grandfather, Vice President Henry Wallace, the painter Enit Kaufman, or the author Padraic Colum—who would come by informally and might be invited to stay several days. The evening meal was part of the attraction. The young women who had suitors entertained them at our home: there was a lot of romance. Mother was delighted that we had a good cook and plenty of help.

Mother was soon involved in politics. She befriended Eleanor Roosevelt and Henry Wallace, with whom she played tennis at his home several times a week and who gave her jars of his hybrid corn seeds. It followed that she wanted to help in the war effort, replicating if possible her time late in World War I drafting wooden propellers at a factory in Marblehead, Massachusetts; now, in World War II, after a brief stint in an airplane factory in Maryland where she resigned over the company policy that she join the union, she found work as a mechanic on the Trans World Airways (TWA) airplanes at what is today Reagan National Airport. Just as in 1918, her entrance into the labor force as part of a wartime shift—often as the lone woman—made her the object of media attention.

Once again, she was driven by a pioneer spirit. Writing home in July 1943, she explains that because she has been at her TWA job for only two months, she cannot get leave to go on vacation in Vermont:

> My work with TWA is just exactly what I wanted and more so. I just couldn't have imagined that I would actually be working on the overhaul of the planes themselves on one of the busiest and most exciting airports. A plane comes in from Natal, Brazil, from Preswick, Scotland, from Alaska, from Russia (with Joseph Davies) or from China (having taken la Chiang Kai-Shek home), and we go to work on it the moment of arrival. I am on ignition—that is the electrical maintenance—and it is frightfully *hard* work.
>
> After advertising for women mechanical trainees all spring long they accepted five and now only two of those remain—another woman (from Pittsfield, Mass.!) and myself. Two of the others were fired, and the third broke down physically. I have just had two weeks on a night shift—11:30 p.m.–8 a.m. but have gone back onto day (7:30 a.m.–4 p.m.) again and hope to stay there. I was the only woman out there at night except for some poor soul in the stockroom whom I never saw. And also I was only averaging four hours a day of sleep! . . .
>
> Of course they *have* to be A+ for efficiency and ability and speed. Then their attitude toward women is really as man to man. They want women to succeed, and they take pains to instruct them and encourage them—and we all work like *dogs* and anyone who doesn't, man or woman, just doesn't last. Salaries are good, the spirit is good, and I am conscious for the first time in the war, in or out of government, of being on or near enough a firing line so that everyone works *with* everyone else to get a job done.

Mother's enthusiasm for the job survived, but she *did* complain to us children that there were no restroom facilities for women—*and* that she had called in the AFL/CIO to address the situation in spite of a long-held anti-union sentiment. She also mentioned the added pressure of local report-ers who noticed her representation of women undertaking war work and also because of her now famous father. She mentions "an article done by a publicity man at TWA for their monthly 'organ,'" and that the *Daily News* in Washington will have a feature article with excellent pictures, "one of which will appear in a *Collier*'s article about women at the National Air-port." The nationally distributed press release is entitled "Robert Frost's Daughter Mends Planes and Runs School for Open Minds":

> The boys on the graveyard shift at the TWA maintenance hangar are unan-imous in their approval: "Lesley Frost? She's tops!" They are referring to the lithe, blue-eyed lady in coveralls, precariously a-straddle the nose of a huge four-engine Army transport. Maybe she's checking wires that must be per-fectly attuned, maybe she's changing some of the 28 giant spark plugs in a 2000-H P. Engine. Whatever she's doing, she's doing it well. At the han-gar, she's No. J-10291 on the maintenance crew, only woman on the grave-yard shift; a skillful team member getting a man's salary, doing a man's job. She knows the work. In World War I she carved mahogany propellers for wooden planes. In this war, she worked up from trainee ranks. . . . Now she's an electrical "man."
>
> Out of her working clothes, you meet a different Lesley Frost. You meet the daughter of one of America's foremost poets, Robert Frost. You see imag-ination, vitality. . . . Out of her coveralls . . . Lesley runs a "pension" that is unique in the busy annals of Washington life. With 10 girls from all parts of the world, Robert Frost's daughter conducts a "school for the open mind" where college graduates continue their education by informed round-table discussions. . . . All the girls work during the day at war jobs, return at night for seminars. Sometimes Robert Frost drops in for a few days, sometimes his crony, Padraic Colum, holds forth on Irish mysticism. . . . Enit Kaufman from Vienna—a Wellesley professor who fought in the Spanish war—a Mexican political hero—all mingle in discussions at Lesley's school.

Mother's daytime and nighttime activities meant that Elinor and I were left to our own devices. We had already become accustomed to what in today's parlance is debated in the press as "free-ranging" activities for young children encouraged by their parents. Washington in wartime seemed sur-prisingly provincial and safe; we would walk down Columbia Road on our own to the Potomac School, an outstanding private elementary school that later moved out into Virginia. By eighth grade I was attending the Holton Arms School, also located walking distance from home and that later moved out into Maryland.

It was during my single year at Holton Arms that I became aware of what it might mean to be closely related to Robert Frost. Jacqueline Bouvier (President Kennedy's future wife) attended the school one year ahead of me; one year behind was her sister, Lee Bouvier. All three of us were published in the *Scroll,* the school's literary journal. Four of my juvenilia were included in the May 1943 issue. But before they were accepted, my mother and I were questioned as to whether or not I had received help in writing the poems. I had not. With obvious parental pride, Mother reported to her father that "Lee finished school [at Holton Arms] in a blaze of glory with nothing less than a B average for the year, a lot of her work on display at the final reception, and with four poems in the school year book—more entries than anyone including the work of the High School group."

After I moved on to the Putney School late the following year, my English teacher, Gabriel Jackson, commented disdainfully about my response to an assignment to write a psalm: "This is the first time I notice your inheritance in your writing." And again, at Radcliffe College, I learned that a paper I had submitted to both my English and British history classes on Daniel Defoe was being considered for a freshman writing prize; this time, I was called in by the faculty and asked whether or not I had had help. Mortified, my murmured denial did little to convince them of my innocence; in any event, there was no prize.

When several of my poems were published many years later, I was careful to hide any connection to a famous poet; otherwise, I surmised, I would be held to too high a standard. My mother decided as a young woman not to submit her poems for editorial review; instead, first with a pseudonym but eventually with the professional name Lesley Frost, she revealed her identity in future publications, mostly in prose. Besides the poems in *Going on Two,* she left behind a small file of unpublished poems, several quoted here.

Family Pets

Moving to Washington, D.C., we took with us a gift from Hervey Allen of a purebred Airedale terrier puppy we named Ricky. Once cured of a stubborn and painful case of mange, he became an important part of our lives and even a lead character in our mother's stories: *Not Really* (1939), with an introduction by Louis Untermeyer; *Really Not Really* (1962), illustrated by Barbara Remington; and *Digging Down to China* (1968), illustrated by Marjorie Frost's daughter, Robin Fraser Hudnut. Of course, in these stories, the animals can talk for themselves, really!

Robert Frost with Lesley Lee (*left*) and Elinor on New Hampshire Avenue NW, Washington, D.C., walking in front of the King-Smith Studio School, ca. 1941–42

Lesley Frost, conducting a poetry reading class at the King-Smith Studio School, ca. 1941–42

Lesley Frost, working the night shift as an aircraft mechanic for Trans World Airways at National Airport, during World War II

Watercolor portrait of Lesley
Frost, a gift from the Czech
artist Enit Kaufman, during the
war years in Washington, D.C.

Enit Kaufman and
Lesley Frost at Lesley's
home and school at 2003
Kalorama Road NW,
Washington, D.C.

Lesley Lee (*left*) and Elinor with
a giraffe at the National Zoo, a
character in their mother's books
for children

Robert Frost playing Pick-Up Sticks with his daughter Lesley and granddaughters
Lesley Lee (*left*) and Elinor at the poet's cabin, Ripton, Vermont, 1942; the family
Airedale Ricky is resting on the cabin floor

Robert Frost (*second from left*) with Theodore Morrison (*far right*) and Kay Morrison (*front left*) at the Bread Loaf Writers' Conference, Middlebury College, 1940s. (Courtesy of the Middlebury College Archives)

Robert Frost's cabin on the Homer Noble Farm, Ripton, Vermont, summers after 1941

Robert Frost with his border collie Gillie, ca. 1950. (Courtesy of the Middlebury College Archives)

Elinor and Lesley Lee with their mother (*center*) and their cocker spaniel Pito, Madrid, Spain, 1945

Lesley Lee's graduation photo, Radcliffe College, June 1952

Lesley Lee joins her grandfather in England, where the poet received honorary degrees at Oxford, Cambridge, Durham, and Dublin universities; photo at Oxford, June 1957. (Courtesy of the Dartmouth College Library)

Robert Frost at the walls of the Old City of Jerusalem while visiting as the first Samuel Paley Lecturer at Hebrew University, 1961. (Photo by H. E. Howland)

Robert Frost as a guest of the Kennedys at the White House, 1962. (Courtesy of the John F. Kennedy Library)

Elinor Francis Wilber in a campaign
photo for the Connecticut state
legislature, 1975

Robert Frost admiring a
carved threshing fork from
rural Spain, ca. 1962

Students from the Escuela de la Tahona visiting El Escorial, the monastery and palace of King Philip II

Lesley Frost, as director of the Escuela, seated on the school patio, during the summer program, La Granja (Segovia), Spain

Lesley Lee seated on the Escuela patio, during the summer program,
La Granja (Segovia), Spain

Really Not Really: In "Ricky Arrives—Really!" a young Airedale terrier shows up in a crate at 6:00 a.m., and the two children, Elinor and Lee, introduce him to their pet Giraffe, who is horrified at being challenged as the primary pet and hides under the bed. A name has to be found; coaxed out, the Giraffe suggests Ricky. "Ricky!" Lee said. "Why that's a wonderful name, like hay-rick because of his hair, and like Ricki-Ticki, because he will protect us, and like rickety because he can hardly stand up yet." The charming and amusing drawings highlight the hilarious adventures and misadventures of Lesley Frost, her two daughters—Elinor and Lee—and, of course, the Giraffe and Ricky.

My most vivid memory of the real-life Ricky was the day a young friend—Elizabeth Jackson's son—and I took him down behind our home at 2003 Kalorama Road, into Rock Creek Park. Standing in the middle of one of the creek's crossways, we threw a stick upstream, waiting for Ricky to fetch it and to climb back up to where we stood. After several successful throws, we watched in horror as Ricky was sucked under; I stood paralyzed as my friend leapt into the creek in a futile attempt to rescue the dog, and both dog and boy were blasted through a large culvert that fortuitously was free of debris. Dragging themselves out of the rushing water, they both survived the near-drowning adventure. We were later reassured by the city's health department that the pollution need not concern us.

We took Ricky with us to Ripton, where he was photographed lying on Grandfather's cabin floor while he, Mother, my sister, Elinor, and I played pick-up-sticks: a family portrait frequently reproduced, often with half of the dog cut out. Once Elinor and I went away to Putney School in Vermont, Mother found it more and more difficult to care for a big, active dog. In late 1943, she wrote from Washington: "Ricky is getting along—but he has so much pent up energy because he doesn't have enough exercise that he behaves as wildly as a puppy in the house, and jumps all over us like a tornado." Seared in my memory was the anguish of looking out the back window of the car while driving down a dirt road that led away from a farm where Mother had left Ricky behind, a feeling that recurred many times in my life but that, at that young age, I was not yet fortified to process. We were sorry to learn later that Ricky had been struck by a truck and killed.

Animals, pets of all kinds, had become an important part of our family life. Living during the war years in our mother's school on Kalorama Road in Washington, D.C., my sister and I made the most of our freedom to come and go. We would catch the trolley car to the horse stables (the name forgotten and the stables long gone) out Connecticut Avenue in Bethesda.

We remember clearly the happy use we made of the thoroughbred racing horses, retired from the racetrack. As light, young riders, we were allowed to help with the training of the young fillies and geldings, usually riding bareback in circles on a lead rope.

Elinor was injured twice during the months of frequent visits. The first fall was from a young, spirited filly she was riding around the indoor rink when the horse got tangled in some carelessly discarded wire. Elinor suffered a severe concussion requiring weeks of rest and possibly a broken collarbone never diagnosed or treated. The second time was during a more adventuresome ride out into Rock Creek Park.

On a brisk fall day, some ten of us left the stables in a trainer-led group. The horses had been trained to stop if the rider slid off around the horse's neck, a precaution that was soon put to the test. As we made our way at a trot into an open field, the leader yelled something, words lost in the wind; the horses, sensing a call to race, took off at a full gallop for the distant barn. As a group, we inexperienced riders, fearing disaster among the tree branches fast approaching, rolled off the horses' necks; naturally, the horses jumped over our bodies and left us in the dust. Elinor suffered a deep gash on a leg; I was fine. By the time we had made our long, embarrassing walk back, the horses were already in their stalls, enjoying their feed.

Elinor, two years older, left for the Putney School in 1942; I joined her there the following year. I was in a hurry to join my sister because RF had paid for a lovely Morgan horse that Elinor had picked out once at the school. He was a bay gelding named Rhubarb, Rhuby for short. I can't recall whether I fell in love first with my grandfather's poem "The Runaway" or fell first for Rhuby:

> Once when the snow of the year was beginning to fall,
> We stopped by a mountain pasture to say "Whose colt?"
> A little Morgan had one forefoot on the wall,
> The other curled at his breast. He dipped his head
> And snorted at us. . . .

I loved to ride Rhuby bareback, enjoying the rhythmic movement and quiet surroundings. And I was one of the children in eighth grade assigned to the predawn mucking of the stalls, part of the school's practice of asking the students to participate in all the farm activities as part of our so-called "progressive education." But in the spring, happily released out to pasture, Rhuby stepped in a hole and broke his leg. Despite attempts to save his life, ultimately the farm director ordered him out into the woods to be shot. My sister and I were devastated; only twelve years old at the time,

I found my grief especially hard to endure. Only recently, I named a new puppy—described by the Rescue League as a hound mix—Rhubarb, Rhuby for short, in memory of that beloved horse.

We can trace family pets back to the Derry years. Not surprisingly, on the Derry Farm the animals assumed an unusual importance, not so much as farm animals but as the recipients of careful care and affection. In my mother's journals, she refers to bulls, a calf, cats, a cow, deer, dogs, a fox, horses, a raccoon, a rat, a skunk, squirrels, wolves, a woodchuck. We can see the animals reflected in RF's verse from the Derry period, and in the little stories RF wrote for his children (ca. 1906), using a technique that later proved irresistible to my mother in her stories for children. Never intended for publication, RF's stories were written casually to entertain the children, who often appear in them as characters, as they do in his collected poems "Maple" and "The Last Word of a Bluebird." Here is one of several in which the family dog Schneider (a gift from Mr. Schneider, but referred to as Snider by the children) appears:

> One day Lesley met a squirrel in the woods and she said: "Do you live here? Why don't you come and live in the nest in the woodbine on our piazza 'long a' folks?"
>
> And the squirrel said: "Ain't you Schneider's Lesley?" And she said she was. And the squirrel said: "Well, I'd like to come but I guess I couldn't."
>
> And Lesley said: "I won't let him bark at you."
>
> "Well, if he don't bark at me perhaps I can stand the rest. I'll come down and see about it"
>
> So the squirrel came, but when he saw the nest in the woodbine he said: "My, my, whose was it? And Lesley said: "A sparrid's."
>
> "Well, I'd have to do a lot to it before I could live in it. But if you'll do what you said about Schneider, perhaps I'll try."
>
> So he went to work bringing grasses in his mouth like reins in Billy's. And when he got through the nest was as big as a pumpkin and he lived in the middle of it somewhere but you couldn't tell whether he was in or out until you called him.
>
> And when Lesley wanted to know anything about anything, all she had to do was open the window and ask him.

And here is one more of RF's tales about Schneider I love to share:

> One day Schneider chased a woodchuck down his hole and began digging after him like everything.
>
> But the woodchuck had two holes and he came up out of the other one and sat up and said: "I see your tail, Schneider, I see your tail."

Schneider ran over and chased him down that hole and began digging there.

Then the woodchuck came up out of the first hole and sat up and called again: "I see your tail, Schneider, I see your tail."

Schneider was so mad he gave up and went home.

The woodchuck laughed and said: "Goodbye, Schneider. Come again."

Schneider said: "Oh, stop talking—woodchucks can't talk." And the woodchuck said: "Neither can dogs."

That's so; they can't.

Schneider was a beloved family pet at the Derry Farm; several of the Frost children learned to walk by holding onto his silky fur, and my mother mentions long walks with the collie on and near the farm. Important details, compiled by the local historian Rick Holmes, clarify what had become something of a mystery surrounding Schneider's death. In 1907, during a serious rabies outbreak in the Derry area, while no one died of the disease, at that time usually fatal, a number of dogs had to be euthanized. When Schneider was attacked and badly injured by a stray dog, RF confined him to a pen in the barn. There Robert tenderly cared for all the dog's needs. Within a couple of days the collie died. Local authorities took the dog's head to the bacteriologist at the state laboratory of hygiene. Test results showed that the brains of Schneider and another dog *were infected with hydrophobia*. The grieving family held a funeral, described by Lawrance Thompson: "Schneider's headless body was given tender burial in a flower-garden near the front steps and inside the quince-hedge in the front yard of the Frost farmhouse. His grave was marked by a little spruce tree, transplanted to that spot from the nearby woods. It seemed significant to the mourning Lesley that even the spruce tree died." Here, and in connection with the later death of Winnie during the removal of porcupine quills, Thompson twists the facts to reflect badly on the poet, a pattern of interpretation prevalent throughout the "official biography."

The horses, cow, and chickens also assumed a strong presence on the farm. At first, RF tried to make a living from a flock of Wyandotte fowls. He and his friend Carl Burell built hen coops and launched a business in poultry farming. The hens on the farm ran free, having been bred and raised for eggs and fancy (that is, for show). Thanks to the publication of *Robert Frost: Farm-Poultryman*, we can learn about and enjoy some of the poet's finest prose writing: between 1903 and 1905, a total of eleven articles were published in two well-established journals, the *Eastern Poultryman* and *Farm Poultry*. The essays display RF as an engaging spinner of lively tales and humorous homilies. In them, we become acquainted with some of RF's new friends, in particular Charlemagne Bricault, a French Canadian poultryman and veterinarian who sold RF the first flock, and John Amos Hall, a poultry exhibitor, featured in "The Housekeeper," "A Blue Ribbon at Amesbury," and "New Hampshire."

The Frost family owned three horses, all of whom are mentioned in Mother's journals: the first horse they had was Billy (nicknamed Tuckup), whom she called an "old red horse" but a plug; the second horse was Eunice, a gray sprinter who liked to run away; the last horse she describes as another red horse named Roy, a name Mama liked, but that Papa preferred to call Billy the Second. I always thought RF's poem "The Runaway" might be about Eunice.

Once settled in the Gully farm in 1929, RF wrote to his friend J. J. Lankes about a Newfoundland puppy he had acquired:

Elinor [Frost] and I are alone here with nothing but a black Newfoundland pup—in breathless quiet after our stormy life. Having failed to educate my own children and other people's children I propose to end up as a teacher training a pup. . . . The aim is to subdue to polite usages without breaking the pride or spirit. I know the idea all right. I want one last chance to see if I can't carry it out. Given a pup that comes all over you with affection and knocks you in the face with her teeth. In two months we'll see if I don't have her so she walks toward me with her pleasure all in her eye and tail, takes her place beside me as an equal uncowed by any sound of my voice or motion of my hand. If I fail with her I will resign my professorship at Amherst College. (qtd. in Thompson, *Robert Frost: The Years of Triumph, 1915–1938*, 373)

Ignoring her pedigree name, they called her simply Winnie. She had been taught manners before misfortune struck, that is, until she tangled with a porcupine. RF administered chloroform in an effort to remove the quills from her face and mouth; her heart gave out. Heartbroken, RF wrote: "No dog could ever take her place in our affections. No dog will have a chance to." Of course, like most of us who lose a beloved pet, RF would, years later, learn to love another dog.

After World War II, RF acquired Gillie, a large black, tan, and white border collie, born at Martha's Vineyard around 1940–41, dying of cancer in Cambridge in 1952–53. The name originated in Scotland, where the gillie—often a male attendant to a Scottish chieftain—scouts the preserve in preparation for the hunt. RF kept Gillie with him most of the time, in his primary home in Cambridge, and also in Ripton and Pencil Pines in Florida. Heading south in winter, he would take Gillie with him on the train, making stops at some of his favorite haunts, especially Chapel Hill (University of North Carolina) and Atlanta (Agnes Scott College), where for more than twenty years the campuses came to anticipate his annual visits, during which he entertained faculty, friends, and students. I spent time with Gillie at my grandfather's home in Cambridge and occasionally helped with his care. His usual diet was Western beef, hard to find, mixed with shredded wheat biscuits.

Professor Reginald Cook (Middlebury College), a close friend of the poet's, recounts their many walks together, accompanied by a loyal and well-behaved Gillie. On one occasion, walking Indian file over a windy, rocky path through the woods between the Homer Noble Farm and the Ivy Dow place (that RF called Eubar), Gillie stayed close. Annoyed, RF told him, "Go on ahead!" Gillie disappeared, but at a turnoff into the heavy woods, he could be seen up ahead. RF said the wild woods inspired his poem "Closed for Good." Cook mentions elsewhere that he and RF agreed that a winter photo by Eric Schall, in a *Time* article (October 9, 1950) showing RF and Gillie starting up the path to the cabin "was one of the best we'd ever seen." Another friend, Hyde Cox, quoting RF, said that "'All Revelation,' stanza 1, lines 1 and 2, are suggestive of Gillie's head looking inquiringly around the door into the room.

Surely, RF's deep attachment to Gillie—and, I imagine, in recollection of Schneider at Derry and Winnie at the Gully—would inspire his poem "One More Brevity," about a Dalmatian dog named Augustus (Gustie for short). He would experience sleepwalking in search of Gillie at his home in Cambridge for years after the dog was gone. Kay Morrison owned two toy Schnauzers that she would bring with her to RF's home on Brewster Street. Understanding, as she did, RF's sense of loss, she gradually lengthened the time she would leave her dogs with him—and, as she hoped, RF soon formed an attachment in spite of himself. In my family, the poem "One More Brevity" would inspire the names of two later dogs: a Dalmatian named Gusti, and a collie mix named Gillie II.

On Assignment in Spain

As the war came to an end, Mother found work with what was called the Office of War Information (OWI), later merged with the United States Information Service (USIS); soon she was prepared for a major assignment out of the country, in Madrid, Spain. As the Germans left, the Americans arrived, so to speak.

Assigned as director of the library and other activities of the American embassy's Casa Americana, my mother made full use of her years in Madrid—1946–49—to put a strong cultural imprint on a Spain struggling with the devastation of the Civil War (1936–39) and the demoralizing effect of the Nazi influence on the ruling junta of Generalísimo Francisco Franco. She went in search of American books and soon discovered a large cache of used paperbacks abandoned at war's end. The Spaniards who frequented the U.S. embassy and the Casa Americana in those years were hungry for American books and literary interaction. The library and its corollary events associated with American literature and the arts attracted a sizeable public from literary and educational circles and *tertulias,* many of whom were drawn to all things American, having found similar offerings of the British embassy less exciting and politically less enticing. One of the most admired literary journals, *Insula,* edited by Enrique Canito, carried articles written by my mother on American poetry and other genres; her lectures at the Casa were well attended.

Isabel de Lafuente, Mother's administrative assistant in the Casa, and Margaret Cole, from the British embassy, would join the school Mother operated years later in La Granja (Segovia). Mother befriended noted contemporary artists such as Eduardo Vicente and Joaquín Vaquero Palacios and his equally successful son Joaquín Vaquero Turcios, as well as a group of prominent women associated with the American embassy: Helen Liencres, Eva Fromkes, and Jane Cabanyes, among others.

It was decided in the fall of 1945 that I would join Mother in Madrid for what would have been my third, or sophomore, year at Putney School—a decision taken over the strenuous objections of Carmelita Hinton, for whom Spain was no more than a Fascist dictatorship. I flew alone to Madrid; my sister, Elinor, would join us for the summer. In those days, the propeller-driven airplanes customarily made two stops for refueling: in Gander, Newfoundland, and Shannon, Ireland.

Once landed in Madrid, I settled in Mother's top-floor apartment on Calle Serrano, sublet from a university professor. Beautifully furnished and with a spectacular terrace, it provided us comfort and easy access; shielded from the hardships suffered by the survivors of the Civil War, we even had an *"asistenta"* who cooked our meals. Here, too, we had a beloved dog, a blond cocker spaniel named Pito (whistle, in Spanish), who would fly back with us to the States in the main cabin.

I attended classes at the Colegio de las Irlandesas, an excellent program run by Irish nuns where I was warmly received; I had a tutor at home to improve my Spanish. I would jump on and off the easily accessible trolleys to and from class. Because I am not a Catholic, I was excused from religious activities. One of the nuns *did* call me aside and asked nicely that I not mention to the other girls that my parents were divorced. Most of the girls were Spanish and Catholic; I recall my friend Juana María and others being required to enter the chapel on their knees as some form of penitence. In class, we memorized long passages from Shakespeare's *Henry V.* More important, I made a number of Spanish friends with whom I enjoyed hanging out for hours in the city's streets and parks: the Retiro, Prado Museum, Plaza Mayor. When my youngest daughter, Melanie Zimic, married Isidoro Reverte Alarcón in Madrid, it turned out her mother-in-law, Pilar Alarcón, had graduated from the Colegio and was there when I was there, although we had not met.

We also traveled outside the capital: Tangier, Morocco; the beautiful beach at a British resort at Torremolinos, near Malaga. Our most exciting trip was on a Spanish freighter that carried cork and cattle along the eastern coast of Spain from Malaga. Normally, the crew did not carry passengers, but our dollars were irresistible, and I think we were the source of great entertainment. Everything went smoothly until we unloaded at the port of Barcelona. There an immigration officer seemed to be overly anxious to check documents; he never said a word except whispered commands to his assistant we could not understand. Mother tried everything to soften the gentleman's demeanor. Finally, after a number of futile efforts, the officer shamefacedly confessed to having a painful sore throat. Relieved and amused, we went on our way.

I traveled to Mallorca with Mother's friend and colleague Helen de Liencres, who had married a Spaniard she met while she was on tour in the United States, performing as a high-board diver; she later excelled in sharing a deep knowledge of Spanish history and painting and continued to work as a tour guide long after retiring from the Casa and the death of her husband. Another Casa employee, Isabel de Lafuente, was the sister-in-law of the famous art historian Enrique de Lafuente; in 1901, her father in the Philippines helped track down the notorious rebel Emilio Aguinaldo on behalf of the U.S. government during its takeover from the Spaniards following the Spanish-American War. In later years, when we were running a school in the mountains north of Madrid, both women would visit us and take part in our activities.

Lesley Lee: Education and Employment

My last two years at the Putney School, upon my return from a year in Madrid, were filled with drama. My grandfather's home in Cambridge was a personal refuge; Mother was still in Spain. Putney was a strange mix of Puritanism and a John Dewey progressive philosophy of education. We enjoyed the work: we assisted in the making of maple syrup, lived among birches and elm trees, skied every day in winter, and received an exposure to interesting if controversial teachers and a fine music program. However, neither we nor our parents saw our grades, receiving instead individual notes from our instructors that tended to engage in amateur psychoanalysis. As my attitude toward the so-called "Putney spirit" was less than enthusiastic during my attendance from ages twelve to sixteen, I got little encouragement from either teachers or farmhands. I mention this in connection with the decision to have me join my mother in Madrid for my sophomore year, returning for my final two years, 1946–48.

In my absence, my sister, Elinor, graduated in the spring of 1946 from Putney, and Grandfather gave the commencement talk—all about reading, Elinor tells me. As early as 1943, my first year at Putney, RF had visited us at the school: Mother wrote me soon after, pleased to read my description of "being lost in the woods [with RF] in the dark, and of going down to the barns with Grandfather, and hearing Grandfather talk at Hinton House." She adds that "[G]randfather loved seeing you and Elinor but he didn't see *enough* of you." RF would return to Putney other times during our time there, staying involved with not only his children but his grandchildren—in terms of both personal affection and financial support.

Early in the fall of 1946, I settled in once again with new roommates. Smoking was prohibited for all the students at Putney, unless, in your senior year, you had the permission of your parents and a physician; if granted permission, the girls were assigned to a small storage room, the boys to a basement. I was a junior, and I neither knew how to smoke nor had permission. Several of the girls in my dormitory (actually, just an old house on campus) snuck out at night, went down behind some construction, and we each lit a cigarette. You see, I had bet that I could exhale through my nose without inhaling; I won my bet. However, when one of the boys was caught smoking in a lavatory, word was sent down from Carmelita Hinton's office that anyone who had smoked should come to her as director and confess. My friends made sure I was one of those who went up to the main building and told my story. Carmelita, who knew my mother, currently in Spain, expressed her disappointment in me. And, of course, no one believed me when I mentioned the bet and that it was the only time because I did not yet know how to smoke. One at a time, we were called—almost half the student body—before a committee of faculty and staff to repeat our confessions. And then I was sentenced to one week's suspension preceding the Christmas break, during which I was to complete a project of my choosing.

During the suspension, I sought refuge in my grandfather's Cambridge home. In fact, there was nowhere else for me to go over the holidays. RF was away, so I stayed there by myself, painting watercolor Christmas cards of dubious quality, one of which showed up recently in my sister's papers. Except for a brief visit from my aunt Irma and one of her two sons, and the company of RF's magnificent dog Gillie, for a few days in my care, I was alone; grateful, of course, to have a place to go. Grandfather wrote Mother that she should come back from Spain and take care of her children. We managed. Elinor was enrolled at Radcliffe College and was dating her future husband; I returned to Putney for the spring semester. We were told the suspension might appear on our records for college. I suspect there were too many of us, some very well connected, to recommend a collective condemnation. One consequence, I learned to smoke by my senior year and did not give it up until I was married.

In the fall of 1947, Mother drove me back to Putney for the opening of my senior year and attended the ceremonial student assembly. Later she would write a long memo, recounting her time in Madrid (1945–47) followed by a lecture tour of Central and South America for the State Department (1948). Besides lamenting the many problems she confronted in her attempts to show the people of these countries the rich literary life of our country, she also expressed concerns she attributed to the Cold War and the advance of Russia and Communist/Marxist ideologies.

Although my mother was a personal friend of Carmelita Hinton, the school's director, she was aware that Carmelita's three children had abandoned the United States for China as part of the agrarian reform movement there. Mother's strongly held anti-Communist views, not uncommon during the Cold War, are reflected in this contemporary account:

When I returned from Europe in the fall of 1947, Mrs. Hinton had just returned from the Prague Festival of the summer of 1947, together with the Lattimore boy and several other students. The first evening at the school, Mrs. Hinton lectured on the wonders and the enthusiasm of the young Czech, Russian and Balkan Countries for the new idea, having lined the room of the auditorium [school assembly] with posters which might have come out of Nuremberg they were so identical to the old Hitler Nuremberg Festival. After the lecture we went to Mrs. Hinton's home and Owen Lattimore talked on the marvels of Red China. Toward the end of the evening, I said to Mr. Lattimore, "I have not been in China and that part of the Far East, but I have been in many other countries of the world watching the Communist menace coming on and I do not know how you could say Red China is not tied to Moscow." He swung on me in total rage and said, "Any damn fool would know that there was no connection between Communist China and Moscow whatsoever."

This was in September 1947. I can recall vividly the excitement of the assembly in question, as well as the posters and Carmelita's support of the Russian takeover of Czechoslovakia. She could do little, however, when the two Czech students, probably those who returned with her from Prague, bravely addressed the assembly to condemn the entry of Russian tanks into Prague. One of these students, David Zdenek, served from 2002 until his retirement as a senior scholar and librarian at the Wilson Center in Washington, D.C.

In our family, we remained aware of the headline-making activities of Owen Lattimore, less so of the Hinton children who had left for China. It was rumored—although I have thus far been unable to verify these accounts—that "Billy" Hinton had left a wife and son in China and made his way to North Korea, where he was reported to have been involved in the "brainwashing" of American troops, before making his way back to the United States through Canada. It appears that, upon his return, his notes were confiscated and that his efforts failed to have them returned. His mother and others continued to defend his actions.

Because the political tensions with the school never lessened, my family offered me the opportunity not to return for my senior year. I decided on my own to return: Putney had an excellent record getting most of their students into good colleges; I wanted to follow my sister to Radcliffe College; and changing schools in a final year might create new problems.

Having graduated from Putney in the spring of 1948, I joined my mother in an ongoing search for opportunities to return to Spain and/or any other Spanish-speaking country. My first opportunity came when I was able to fly to South America, where Mother was carrying out a six-month tour of our USIS cultural centers in certain Central and South American capitals. I followed her to Bogotá, Colombia, Caracas, Venezuela, and Mexico City. The State Department grant included visits to Latin American Institutes in Santiago and Valparaiso, Chile; Lima, Peru; and Guatemala City in Central America. In each center, Mother gave a series of lectures on American literature.

Returning from her assignment, Mother reported on the generally inadequate efforts to develop the cultural centers, especially when compared to, let's say, the British and German institutes. For me, the visits offered a chance to improve my Spanish and learn some excellent typing skills in both languages at a popular typing school in Bogotá, where we repeated endless drills on what I call "high-rise" typewriters scattered around a large room. Otherwise, my strongest memory of the trip was a debilitating altitude sickness.

The summer following my freshman year at Radcliffe College (1949) another opportunity arose: in typical fashion, coming as a surprise the way it did, Mother informed me that I had been accepted as a teacher at the English-American School in Guatemala City. Traveling by myself, I flew to Yucatán by way of New Orleans. Before leaving the city, I made a point of boarding a ferry that would take me round-trip across the Mississippi River, a river I had seen only once before, driving to Mexico through San Antonio and Jackson, Mississippi. But it would be my first direct contact with racial segregation. Once on board, an African American gentleman approached me on deck to tell me gently that I was in the wrong section of the ferry. Greatly embarrassed, I took his suggestion to move over into the "whites only" section.

In Yucatán, I boarded a local bus in Cancún to take me to the Mayan ruins at Chichén Itzá. The bus carried rural farmers, many with chickens and other livestock; the wild, smelly scene constituted my idea of fun at the time. There were virtually no tourists at the ruins, and one of the guides offered me a ride back into the city. I was only eighteen, and it wasn't until I was told of the dangers of getting into a car with a stranger that I was the least concerned. I would return to Chichén Itzá many years later, during a visit to attend an Elizabeth Bishop Society meeting in Cancún. RF admired Elizabeth and visited her briefly when attending the World Congress of Writers in São Paulo.

Once in Guatemala City, I rented a room in a pension and started my job. All went smoothly until there was what you might call a noisy, unsuccessful coup d'état attempt. As far as I could tell, it was one military group against another, using tanks against the palace to make their point. It didn't last long, but we teachers and other citizens caught in the middle went up on our balconies and rooftops to watch the fireworks. Many buildings were pockmarked with bullet holes, but there was little loss of life; I believe one of the generals was assassinated.

The following summer, I had the possibility of a part-time job in Spain. I bought a ticket on the one-class American Export passenger/cargo liner the SS *Excalibur*, leaving New York harbor on June 27, 1950. After my mother dropped me off at the dock, I, as a seasoned traveler, took my suitcase belowdecks to my cabin and unpacked. It was a beautiful, clear, early-summer day; as we nosed out of the harbor—the time 12:30 p.m.—there was a terrible sound of metal scraping on metal as I was thrown across the cabin. I grabbed my purse and went on deck.

Informing us that our liner had collided with the incoming Danish freighter *Columbia*, the crew ordered us to secure a life jacket from our cabins; since the collision had caused the flooding of the cabin I occupied, I was given a life jacket on deck. As water poured through a 38-foot hole between the *Excalibur*'s no. 2 and no. 3 holds, Captain Samuel Groves rang up full speed, beaching her on the mud bottom off Bay Ridge, Brooklyn. The ship was sinking, but within an hour all 114 passengers had been taken off on tugboats.

Back on land, I called Mother, who thought I was calling from a phone at sea—for emergencies only and very costly, she reminded me—and I made my way later to her apartment on East Tenth Street. I found myself in Manhattan for the summer, having little else to wear and less money until we were reimbursed for the loss of ticket and the "limited liability"—of two hundred dollars, as I recall—due to the fact that in court the Danish freighter was found blameless. I stayed home and indulged my love of painting at the Art Students League. Late in the summer, the American Export Line invited us to dockside to search through the oil- and saltwater-drenched items rescued when the *Excalibur* resurfaced: there was nothing worth saving except, in my case, a small box containing a few pieces of cheap costume jewelry and some memorabilia worthless to anyone else.

I took only one course in Spanish literature while at Radcliffe. Furthermore, the dean of liberal arts, another of Mother's many friends in academia, called me to her office. Knowing of my grandfather's success as a poet, she gave me the well-intentioned advice to concentrate in English and be assured of a good academic record. I did not respond.

Thinking it over, however, I turned stubborn, remembering RF's objections to the laid-on approach to literature *he* had experienced at Harvard: I did not take a single English course once I completed the freshman requirement. I had hoped to study studio art (especially watercolor and sculpture/pottery), but, once at the college, I learned to my chagrin—I had failed to examine the catalogue before applying for admission!—that Harvard/Radcliffe did not offer *any* studio art; instead, I signed up for the only non–history of art course: "The Theory of Drawing and Painting and the Principles of Design," an uninspiring classroom study of principles we would have no opportunity to apply. I decided then and there to concentrate in modern European history.

After graduating in 1952, I needed to seek gainful employment to alleviate the ongoing shortfall in our family finances. Moving to Washington, D.C., I first resided with a group of working women in a house near the cathedral in Northwest D.C. and later in my own apartment down Connecticut Avenue, I quickly found a job; in fact, I secured several jobs in quick succession: as a typist with the Pan American Union; as an assistant with the American Political Science Association, and as a secretarial assistant with a former classmate of JFK and a specialist on the Hill.

My single purpose was to find employment in Madrid. The search did not go well because I had little to offer besides the AB degree and good typing skills. I quickly added speed writing, a barely adequate substitute for dictation, which I had never studied. The name of my grandfather was never mentioned. But I was persistent. I had heard that Senator Kennedy's classmate, Langdon Parker Marvin Jr., USNR, Air Transportation Economics Specialist, had been given a small but highly prized office space in the Library of Congress. More significant, he was reputed always to be looking for secretarial assistance, initially paying well but decreasing the amount as disenchantment kicked in, and to offer very irregular hours. Perfect for me. And being a Harvard/Radcliffe graduate gave me a certain entrée.

During the interview, Mr. Marvin dictated a letter almost incomprehensible to me; he then excused himself, saying he would return shortly. While I struggled to transcribe the letter, making up whole sentences as needed, several other women showed up to interview for the same position. By this time, Mr. Marvin had called, instructing me to send the others home and noting that as he would not be returning, would I please turn off the lights and lock the door upon leaving? I left the transcribed letter on his desk.

Early the next Sunday morning, Mr. Marvin called and ordered me to come to his office right away. I jumped on the trolley that ran down to the Capitol from my apartment; I was hired. I continued to use my not-very-fast speed writing to cope with an overloaded Harvard vocabulary. I also served as a messenger to Senator Kennedy's office; he would not have remembered meeting me.

Over the next few months, my relationship with Mr. Marvin gradually deteriorated. But, as I had expected, the break I hoped for materialized. My stepfather, Joseph W. Ballantine, by now married to my mother and settled in a small, historic home in Silver Spring, Maryland, was friends with Senator Francis H. Case (who served as a representative and senator from South Dakota from 1937 until his death in 1962). As a favor to his friend, Joe welcomed Senator Case's horse to graze on their property. One thing led to another, including a word from Senator Case, and I was offered a secretarial position in the American embassy in Madrid with what was then the Foreign Operations Administration, later International Cooperation Administration, and, more recently, Administration for International Development; I left home in February 1954.

After a difficult flight from the States by way of the Azores and Lisbon, I arrived exhausted in Madrid. No one in the embassy seemed prepared for my arrival. Hurriedly, I was assigned to the agricultural attaché for the first three days. But over the first weekend, on a Sunday evening, I became ill. Because of my long record of excellent health, I assumed I was suffering from "Madrid tummy" and that it would pass. It did not; the couple where I was living—a British Olga Lagarde and her Spanish husband, who took in pensioners—called their personal physician, Dr. Francisco Sastre Clemente. He was sure it was appendicitis. Because he had concert tickets, he ordered his assistant to take the blood test, and he returned at a little after 1:00 a.m., confirmed the diagnosis, and took me in his car to the sanatorium.

I was still in my red cotton, Chinese-style pajamas with an embroidered dragon when wheeled into the operating theater, accompanied by a medical team drummed up at the last minute on a Sunday night. The table proved too short; an extension was put in place. Through gauze placed over my nose, the ether finally took effect, and one hour later I awoke with nuns and others trying to keep me from kicking myself free of the tightly wrapped bedcovers. No sedatives were used before or after, and I spent sleepless nights.

Besides the flow of flowers, next to my bed was a bottle that contained my appendix. Like the part taken from a car being repaired, the organ was returned as proof of removal. No one seemed bothered. Visitors were allowed twenty-four hours a day from the first morning, and there were plenty of them: friends of my mother's, friends from my year in Madrid, strangers from the embassy, the surgeon, Dr. Tamames, an impassioned bullfight surgeon. And, of course, frantic phone calls and cables flying back and forth to the United States, including garbled calls from my then current boyfriend, Marvin Payne, suggesting I return home.

My mother was concerned because I had gone without extra cash, expecting to be paid. After the surgery, I discovered that the embassy was prepared to reimburse me only after I had paid up front the medical costs; furthermore, I had no money to pay for my food and lodging as I was expecting an allowance. Reminding me that I had no medical or personal leave accumulated, the personnel director advanced me leave to cover my ten days of absence. Consequently months went by before I could take a single day of vacation.

Mercifully, the initial turmoil and confusion subsided. I returned to a different boss, and I received some assistance in finding an apartment. I went to work for Charles P. Fossum, chief of the Food and Agriculture Division of the USOM. An extremely capable and compassionate man, Mr. Fossum, together with his family, helped me to survive the three and a half years and to benefit from and at times even enjoy my service.

I found I already had many contacts in the city through my mother's lengthy period of employment in the embassy and Casa Americana after World War II. In particular, I renewed contacts in the intellectual and artistic community, such as Eduardo Vicente, Joaquín Vaquero Palacios and his son Joaquín Vaquero Turcios, Enrique Canito at *Insula,* as well as colleagues and friends who spent time with me reminiscing. And, as I got older, I was better able to understand why, in Spain as elsewhere, the name of my grandfather opened eyes of surprise and appreciation, even doors to friendship. And it was from here, in early June 1957, I was able to fly to London to join my grandfather at Oxford and Cambridge Universities, as well as on a wild expedition to Dymock in Gloucestershire with the *Life* reporters. It would be a highlight of my tour in Spain.

Most of my life in Madrid, outside the office, was taking ballet classes, enjoying my first car, a VW Beetle (whose female driver, in high heels, struck amazement in the passing, mostly male, public); attending many concerts (often chamber music) and plays; eating at out-of-the-way restaurants; and taking frequent excursions to Segovia, Toledo, El Escorial, Granada, Sevilla, and many other beautiful and historic locations; visiting, as well, sites outside of Spain such as the Richard Wagner operas performed in Bayreuth, Mozart's Salzburg, the lakes of northern Italy, and touring along the Italian and French coastlines. Included among my Spanish friends was an aging bullfighter, Pepe Bienvenida, part of a large bull-raising and -fighting family; abandoned by his wife and unable to obtain a divorce, Pepe was dating a Spanish woman from a known Madrid family, a friend of mine through the American embassy. I learned a lot about bullfighting and saw some of the best execution of the balletic approach to the bull. There was respect for the bull: Pepe told me everything accomplished in the ring was "con permiso del toro" (with the bull's permission). It doesn't bother me now that the spectacle is being curtailed; during my time in Madrid, however, I could respond to the courage, artistry, and deep-rooted tradition, dating back to the Romans and Greeks, pursued relentlessly in the ring by these brave, often desperate young men.

I came away with a greater appreciation of the Spanish culture, especially her literature, history, and art, and an enhanced understanding of the life in post–Civil War Spain. I had also come to sense the need to make an effort to pull myself up and out of the work I was doing, work that had become effortless and repetitive, offering little or no challenge. I was determined to live on my own, without financial or other help from family. While I would learn to accept family contributions (from both the Frost and Francis families) for education, I was now prepared to attend graduate school at my own expense. By the time I flew home during my second two-year assignment, in 1957, I had accepted an offer for a graduate assistantship at the University of Miami.

I had chosen the University of Miami in order to be closer to my immediate family: to my mother, who had built—with her husband, Joseph Ballantine—a house on the same property as my grandfather's Pencil Pines, in South Miami. The three semesters I spent in residence, living in an apartment in Coral Gables, created the intellectual and emotional path to my future.

My grandfather was traveling frequently for his work and still had his permanent home in Cambridge, his summers in Ripton; only the severe winter months were spent in Miami. Yet his presence was always felt by family and neighbors. He occupied one of two prefabricated homes—that looked more like trailers than houses—keeping the second of the two for others, such as Kay Morrison, who would continue to serve as manager and secretary to the poet the rest of his life, or for friends and family who occupied the property in his absence. Mother and Joe did not last long in the hot climate, deciding after I left to move back to Manhattan as their permanent home.

Attending graduate courses in Spanish literature at the university, I soon met my future husband, fellow student Stanislav Zimic, both of us attending the classes of our mutually revered Professor José Balseiro. Stan and his parents had served as Partisans in Yugoslavia during the war, and Stan subsequently attended graduate school in Ljubljana. After the war, he had decided not to join the Communist Party, despite interrogatory pressure, thus precluding the diplomatic service he had envisioned. He left Yugoslavia for the States on a student's visa arranged by an uncle who lived in Miami. When the student's visa expired, the Yugoslav government, having decided not to count his Partisan service, cancelled his passport and demanded his return to fulfill his military service. In those years, graduate students committed to foreign-language teaching could be recommended by their professors for citizenship. This was how Stan was able to stay permanently in the United States.

It would be Professor José Balseiro, whose graduate program in Spanish we had entered at the University of Miami, who influenced me and Stan in our career choices. To understand how this happened requires a few words about Professor Balseiro: he joined the university faculty following a life and career in his native Puerto Rico. Besides entering politics, composing music, and writing novels and literary criticism, he had acquired a reputation as a scholar of Spanish literature. I like to think of him as a Renaissance man. His remarkable background permitted him to identify Stan as a potential graduate student.

Stan had earned a master's degree in Italian language and literature from the University of Ljubljana, but the office of admissions, unable to verify his record, had enrolled him as an undergraduate. Dr. Balseiro, during a casual conversation on campus, invited Stan to enter his graduate program and helped him find work in the cafeteria pending employment as a teaching assistant. Although fluent in Italian and Slovenian, both native languages, he also had a good knowledge of French, German, and Russian (the latter two the languages of unwelcome occupiers of his homeland). Recognizing a great opportunity, Stan agreed to switch to a master's program in both French and Spanish. His future research in the field of medieval and Golden Age literature would be written and published in Spanish, primarily in Spain.

While Stan went ahead to Duke University to complete his Ph.D. studies in Romance languages, I initially applied in Romance languages at the University of North Carolina at Chapel Hill. RF's longtime friend and chair of the English Department, Clifford Lyons, welcomed my application and took me over to meet his colleague in Romance languages. During the interview I was praised for my academic record and employment in Spain, and it was clear that there would be no obstacle to my joining the graduate program.

When I asked about the possibility of a graduate assistantship to defray my expenses, however, I was told that a woman could not be considered: the reason given was that the female undergraduates were taught the first two years at their campus in Greensboro, returning to Chapel Hill for their junior and senior years; consequently, I could not teach the freshmen and sophomores in what were all-male classes. After informing Cliff Lyons about my sense of the interview, I quickly decided to join Stan at nearby Duke University in Durham. There I was awarded a James B. Duke Fellowship, allowing me to study without employment and to complete the course requirements and comprehensive exams in record time, leaving to complete and defend the dissertation once settled in Austin, Texas, after my marriage.

I can recall only one other occasion when I faced overt gender discrimination. After completing my first year as an assistant professor of Spanish at Sweet Briar College, Stan and I were married. It was a simple affair, performed by Protestant clergy at my sister Elinor's home in Fairfield, Connecticut. Besides my mother and sister, RF and Louis Untermeyer and his wife attended the ceremony. Stan and I left the next day for Europe,

spending the summer honeymoon in Duino, Italy, not far from his family in
Deskle, Yugoslavia. Family members could visit us, but we could not safely
enter his homeland. In the meantime, Stan had landed a teaching position
in French and Spanish for the coming year at Washington and Lee University, across the mountain from Sweet Briar College.

Back from Europe in the fall, we settled in a delightful cottage on a farm
near Stan's appointment in Lexington, Virginia. Learning upon my return
to classes at Sweet Briar that I was expecting our first child the following
April, President Anne Gary Pannell decided to appoint a faculty committee (called the Sick Leave Committee), a typical administration response
to crisis, to determine my fate. Both the president and academic dean were
women: both informed me that I could not appear before the all-female
classes once my condition became visible and that it was in my best interest
to be free of teaching responsibilities upon the arrival of my first child. By
offering me most of my salary (while withholding a portion for my replacement) in the form of an "educational grant," I was released at the end of the
first semester.

Because of my position on the faculty, my grandfather had agreed to do
a reading at Sweet Briar in the spring. President Pannell absented herself
from campus, and I was unemployed at the time of my grandfather's scheduled visit. He, of course, enjoyed an enthusiastic audience and was housed
in the president's house.

Yes, the overt discrimination, while apparently legal at the time, was
both hurtful and embarrassing. The baby—Deborah Lee Zimic—arrived in
a Lynchburg hospital on April 13, 1962. As soon as Stan completed his academic year at Washington and Lee, we left for Austin, where my husband
would continue a successful career on the University of Texas faculty until
his death in August 2013. We were divorced in 1974; I left for Arlington,
Virginia, with our three young daughters to assume a position on the professional staff of the American Association of University Professors (AAUP)
in Washington, D.C.

Frost Studies and Lawrance Thompson

The shift toward a more scholarly approach to my grandfather's life and
work took place over a period of years, more so after my retirement in 1998
from the staff of the AAUP. I had written a master's thesis at the University
of Miami entitled "The Don Juan Theme in Contemporary Spanish
Drama," later completing my doctoral dissertation, "The Collective Protagonist in the Historical Novels of Unamuno, Baroja, and Valle Inclán" at
Duke University. RF had given me a portable typewriter on which I typed

my master's thesis near Pencil Pines, his winter residence in South Miami. When he read the result, he could not keep from observing that this academic writing was not what he preferred; mercifully, he was gone before I completed the painfully annotated five-hundred-page tome of my doctoral dissertation. His response to a packet of early poems I had sent him for Christmas in 1953 was entirely different:

> Your present was the best mail I got for Christmas. You'd think I might be weary of poetry and the ambitions of poetry after all I have seen and known of both in the last sixty five years since eighteen eighty nine when I wrote my very first poem and named it La Noche Triste in the language of your adoption. But I still prick up my attention to a fresh note of thought and feeling. These are true little poems, firm and shapely. You make your point every time as so few rhymesters seem to feel obliged to do nowadays. An Evening's Mood is one, with that splash of rain on the dirty window. At Home is another. You do it with delicate touches and gentle insights.
>
> > A different pattern in each heart
> > And mold to every thought
> > Have given life its secret part
> > Which man must not defy.
>
> You wouldn't have written that at any time but now and in any place but Washington among the One-worlders. They will learn the lesson. I shall keep the book, not among my books, but among the papers I pack with me wherever I go. I mean the things of my own I haven't yet published or haven't yet put the last touch on.

In order to make progress on the research, I had to confront the Lawrance Thompson three-volume biography and explore a number of formidable critics: Richard Poirier, William Pritchard, Reginald Cook, and Louis Mertins, among others. I had come to my grandfather's poetry as any young person might: not in school, where I read Shakespeare, Milton, and the Romantic poets for the most part, but at home, where I learned about Robert Frost and even memorized "Stopping by Woods on a Snowy Evening," "The Runaway," and "After Apple-Picking," among my favorites.

My encounters with my grandfather left an impression on me at an impressionable age, but I would be the mother of three before I could articulate a coherent response.

I recalled how we talked about "the sound of sense" and "the strain of rhythm upon meter"; together praised Henley's line "I am the master of my fate; I am the captain of my soul" as a high and demanding calling and praised Milton for the way he liked to face the harshness of our trial; and commented upon the apparent accessibility of the early ballads, of Mother Goose or Longfellow, and of other "popular" poets scorned by academic scholars. RF spoke of the difficulty in knowing when one has had an idea as one passes enthusiasm through the "prism of the intellect" and dams back and harnesses emotions by discipline "to the wit mill"; how you can never tell what you have said or done until you have seen it reflected in other people's minds; the danger of "losing one's sensitive fear of landing on the lovely too hard." We always came back to the need to just do it, in the face of fearful doubts and anxieties, by the braving of alien entanglements, in the best Jamesian tradition.

It would be years later before I applied these random philosophical thoughts to the problems of the Frost biography. What struck me through my own formal education and college teaching was how easy it was to abandon all touch with life as an adventure; life seemed to have purpose only when it achieved a tightly disciplined structure where I could feel safe, and perhaps a little smug and self-important. But wasn't I letting down my students by the lack of spontaneity and enthusiasm needed to be a good teacher? When I returned to the Frost biography, I was looking for answers to the questions, not only about the Frost family, but also about the meaning in my own life and the lives of my children and grandchildren.

It became apparent early on that the poet I knew was shockingly different from the one portrayed by RF's "official biographer," Lawrance Thompson. I knew Larry as a sociable fellow who came to detest his subject for a variety of reasons: the "old man" lived too long; he had pushed Larry aside once he realized the biographer's warped line of thinking, permitting the publication of Elizabeth Shepley Sergeant's brief—sympathetic but flawed—biography; and he had excluded Larry from RF's final journey to Russia shortly before his subject's death. Larry never understood that, indeed, as RF said, "It takes a lot of in and outdoor schooling to understand my kind of fooling." Overwhelmed by the vastness of his materials, collected over decades of following his subject and still rightly so an important source for Frost scholars, Larry turned to pseudopsychoanalysis for order, probably from his reading of Karen Horney, who suggested an outline of self-fulfilling neuroses. Reflecting its author's poor writing skills, complete humorlessness, and reluctance to let the poet speak for himself in the text, the three-volume biography, completed and published after the death of both the poet and his biographer, offered a grim portrait; the index alone, in a pattern already evident in the *Selected Letters,* created its own "monster" myth.

Despite the efforts of many friends and academicians—Sergeant, Pritchard, Poirier, Walsh, Richardson, and others to date—it seems the breathtakingly brutal Thompson analysis persists in the collective imagination. Eliot and Pound had planted the seeds of disapproval; the casual appraisal of the poet as superficial and too accessible—sort of like Longfellow and other good poets—reinforced the negative view.

I wanted to come to terms with the discrepancies between the official biographer's relentless and humorless portrayal and my own as yet unschooled awareness of a man always accessible for good talk, who presented an awesome yet human and often humorous presence, and who gave unselfishly to friends and family over the years. Would the record support my rejection of Thompson's thesis: that RF systematically and ruthlessly disregarded his family in a selfish and self-centered drive to achieve his own ends?

Clearly, genius and psychosis have common identifying features; the line between them is often blurred. All too often the artistic temperament lives on the perilous edge. There were, after all, signs of mental instability in the Frost family's history. To embark on a life as a poet, the artist and members of his family will be expected, especially where there is no financial security, to sacrifice collectively to reach a goal of public recognition. But the issue of motive is a tricky one. I realized how risky it is to seek definitive psychological explanations for events or for the dynamics of personality, a weakness, I believe, in many current biographies of public figures. The complexities and intangibles—mood, intent, patterns of behavior and inclination—are themselves the warp and woof of the subject's life, as of his art. Thompson himself, in notes for a lecture to the Literary Fellowship in October 1968, helps identify his own problem as biographer: "The ultimate problem of a Frost biographer is to see if the biographer can be enough of psychologist to get far enough back into the formative years of RF to try to understand and explain what forces were operative, back there, to create the curious forms of neurosis which RF had to struggle with throughout most of his life. Of course, such an approach, on the part of the biographer, is dangerous, very dangerous."

Thompson's crudely psychoanalytical interpretation had silenced the brilliant and self-deprecating humor of the living voice—a voice the biographer seldom quotes uninterrupted in his biography—and seriously misrepresented his relations with family and friends. Instead of characterizing my grandfather's unwavering (but doubt-ridden) ambition for poetry as a dark regression in the service of the ego, a selfish act of self-indulgence, I came to look upon RF's quest for recognition as a positive force—"a lover's quarrel with the world," if you wish—inseparable from his and Elinor's efforts to awaken the world of the imagination in their children (and grandchildren).

I knew from my own experience that my grandfather enjoyed domestic intimacy and the continuity of reassurance essential to his art that it provided him. He actively participated in shaping the young lives of his children and of his many students. He drew special strength from Elinor in joining together vocation and avocation, life and metaphor. Together they formed a pact to protect the integrity of his poetic talents, the subtlety and originality of his work, in spite of constant pressures from his grandfather and other family members, as well as well-meaning literary critics, to abandon the path of poetry.

Later RF pointed out to his public that he had sometimes wished he was a ready writer in prose, but never in verse. He had, he proclaimed, "never rhymed for parlor games or for exercises or from a sense of duty to keep the wolf from the door." Elinor knew he "hated to know he *must* write," and she was prepared to sacrifice to whatever extent proved necessary to shelter him from outside pressures and to vindicate her belief in him as a genuine poet. In July 1913, with the appearance in London of *A Boy's Will*, she wrote home: "How can they help seeing how exquisitely beautiful some of the poems are, and what original music there is in most of them?"

Unlike Elinor, RF saw no contradiction in the urge to go to market and to test one's skills against the other poets. Although Elinor resisted the public exposure, she supported her husband. As RF explained to Louis Untermeyer, "She's especially wary of honors that derogate from the poetic life she fancies us living."

Entering the debate, I soon focused on my grandfather's early, often frustrating quest for approval. Thanks to Susan Hayes Ward and others, he had had a smattering of his poems published in journals, but he had not been encouraged to submit a manuscript for a volume of poems. I was impressed by the peculiar dynamic of a literary family and the impetus to creativity in the symbiotic relationship between parents and children. I came to believe, with writers like Rollo May (in *The Courage to Create*) and Arthur Koestler (in his *Act of Creation*), that the artist—in this case, the poet—often beset by despair and self-doubt and inexplicable feelings of guilt, displays the creative and moral courage of the nonconformist to move ahead. He delves into "the smithy" of his soul, into the chaos from which he extricates form, to provide what he characterized as "a momentary stay against confusion."

Robert Frost and Harvard

It was during this time—while completing my doctoral studies at Duke University and initiating my teaching career at Sweet Briar College in Virginia; St. Edward's University in Austin, Texas; and summers at the Escuela de la Tahona in La Granja (Segovia), Spain—that I first undertook serious research on my grandfather, taking me back to the critical years immediately following the death of Elinor Frost in 1938 and RF's resignation from Amherst College.

Although my sister, mother, and I had moved on to a hectic life in wartime Washington, D.C., it had required the intervention of friends and family to restore RF to a productive life. The first of these restorative activities would be the appointment of the grieving poet to the faculty at Harvard College. In 1952, I would receive an AB from Radcliffe College, with a concentration in modern European history. Our classes—since the merging of the two faculties during World War II—were held on the Harvard campus in Cambridge. However, women were not permitted to enter the Lamont Library; there was very little in the way of athletics for women; and, of course, men and women did not share dormitory space.

One of the advantages of residing for four academic years in Cambridge was the opportunity to visit my grandfather's permanent home on Brewster Street. The attached house still stands, with a small plaque acknowledging RF's residence there.

During my college years, I could walk over from the Quad either to visit, when RF was in town, or simply to carry my books and enjoy, sometimes with a classmate, the quiet and comfort of the downstairs living and dining rooms, where we could spread out and fix snacks in the kitchen. Many pieces of the furnishings of the Brewster Street house are now in my home: a Boston College chair, two fine Persian rugs, a dresser, several antique tables and chairs. The dining room table and chairs are now in my youngest daughter's home; my sister has the bed; the late Bob Frost, Prescott Frost's son, acquired RF's desk.

Years later, when the editor of *Harvard Magazine* invited me to write a piece about RF's associations with Harvard College, I was delighted. Having gained access to many of the relevant files, as well as the archives at Houghton Library, I entitled the article "'Imperfectly Academic': Robert Frost and Harvard," which appeared in the March–April 1984 issue. By this time, there had been many changes at the college. My eldest daughter, Deborah Lee Zimic, was by then a senior at Harvard, where she concentrated in classics and was co-captain of the women's swim team. Women could be assigned to the Houses on campus, and all the facilities were coeducational, including Lamont Library.

This assignment took me back even further, to Robert Frost's father, William Prescott Frost. As a child in New Hampshire, RF's father became enamored of the idea of Robert E. Lee of Virginia, at that time courted by both sides in the conflict. (As we know, his father named his son, Robert Lee Frost, after the general. The poet dropped the middle name as a teenager; in fact, he and Elinor never gave middle names to their children, an issue addressed in the poem "Maple.") William Frost, a teenager, ran away from home to join the general but was caught in Philadelphia and returned to his parents. He would be turned down for entry at West Point, "for which I had tried very hard, and in which I was thwarted by political influence," he wrote in his Class Book. Instead, he entered Harvard College in July 1868 at the age of seventeen. Despite his initial reluctance and a somewhat flamboyant lifestyle, he held the Bowditch Scholarship, won the Bowditch Prize for his dissertation on the Hohenstaufens and a Detur for his outstanding academic achievement; he was elected to Phi Beta Kappa, delivering the commencement oration.

From the beginning, RF's feelings about his father's alma mater were ambivalent. He had passed the entrance exams before his brief stay at Dartmouth College, but at the age of twenty-three, he retook the entrance exams and sought admission a second time: "Let me say that if I enter college it must be this year or never," he wrote Dean LeBaron Russell Briggs. After making a series of self-deprecatory confessions concerning weaknesses in his former studies and expressing embarrassment over his unauthorized departure from Dartmouth College, he concluded: "All I ask is to be admitted. I don't care how many conditions you encumber me with."

From England, RF wrote Sidney Cox about obtaining a "quiet job in a small college where I should be allowed to teach something a little new on the technique of writing [and] where I should have some honor for what I suppose myself to have done in poetry. Well, but I mustn't dream." The dream persisted, however, and upon his return in 1915, acclaimed as a poet, he was called back to Harvard to deliver the Phi Beta Kappa poem (and receive honorary membership).

Still terrified of public speaking, yet eager for the recognition, RF delivered "The Bonfire" (which he called a "war poem") at the public exercises and "The Ax-Helve" (the "education poem") at the subsequent dinner. The line "war is for everyone, for children too" led to "The Bonfire" being greeted as an antiwar poem when it appeared in *Seven Arts*. "What disheartened me," RF wrote Louis Untermeyer, "was that it made everybody think that it was saying something on one side or the other of a 'question of the day.' Dammit." "The Ax-Helve," which he rarely read aloud because of its French-Canadian dialect, revealed much of the poet's maverick thinking about indoor and outdoor schooling, contrasting "laid-on education" with the ax-helve, in which "the lines . . . were native to the grain before the knife/Expressed them, and its curves were no false curves/Put on it from without." The event assured RF a triumphant return and critical acclaim. By 1917, he was ready to accept a faculty position at Amherst College.

In 1936, with the support of Robert Hillyer, David McCord, Bernard DeVoto, and others on the Harvard faculty, RF was selected to be the Charles Eliot Norton Professor in the spring of 1936, awarded to a man of high distinction and international reputation who would deliver (and later publish) six public lectures on poetry. The assignment filled the poet with a mixture of dread and excitement: "Of course I dread it," he wrote, "but I could hardly refuse the trial. There is still the name of having been the first American asked. Anyway it excites me a little. The University is one most people have heard of. It was mine after a fashion and my father's more than mine."

Arranged loosely under the heading of "The Renewal of Words," the titles of the six lectures, delivered without notes, convey the sweep of RF's poetic thinking: "The Old Way to Be New"; "Vocal Imagination—the Merger of Form and Content"; "Does Wisdom Signify?"; "Poetry as Prowess (Feat of Words)"; "Before the Beginning of a Poem"; and "After the End of a Poem." The attendance those April evenings was so overwhelming that, even after moving the event to the 1,200-seat Sanders Theater, the largest auditorium the university had to offer, the overflow climbed the fire escapes to listen through the windows.

Favorable press accounts were capped by the embarrassingly effusive praise in Robert Hillyer's Phi Beta Kappa poem, "A Letter to Robert Frost," delivered that spring at Columbia. But for RF himself, although he made and kept friends there as elsewhere, the sense of belonging at Harvard was still elusive:

> There was a moment in March when I thought perhaps they were giving me back my father's Harvard. But probably I was fooling myself. I'm imperfectly academic and no amount of association with the academic will make me perfect. It's too bad, for I like the academic in my way, and up to a certain point the academic likes me. Its patronage proves as much. I may be wrong in my suspicion that I haven't pleased Harvard as much as I have the encompassing barbarians. My whole impression may have come from the Pound-Eliot-Richards gang in Eliot House here. I had a really dreadful letter of abuse from Pound.

A severe attack of shingles prevented the poet from honoring a commitment to deliver another Phi Beta Kappa poem and an ode at the tercentenary celebration. In declining a follow-up invitation, RF drew a distinction between teaching and lecturing, on the one hand, and poetry: "I have kept poetry free thus far, and I have been punished for the mere thought of making it a duty or a business. . . . The way to use me is to let me come to their occasions with any approximation I happen to have on the shelf." In spite of his antipathy toward the "starchy stiffs," he was pleased to accept Harvard's honorary degree of Litt.D. at the 1937 commencement. President James Bryant Conant cited him as "The poet of New England: his friend-ship quickens the talent of tomorrow, his art perpetuates the inner spirit of our countryside." RF and Conant were initially friendly. But the scientist and the poet approached their tasks from opposing vantage points, and the distancing of their views would prove pivotal in shaping the long-term relations of poet and university.

With the shattering loss of Elinor in the spring of 1938, friends at Har-vard—in particular Theodore Morrison, David McCord, and Robert Hillyer—rallied around and proposed to President Conant that RF be offered a faculty position in the English Department. As he had already been elected to the Board of Overseers, Conant's response was chilly: "I am rather at a loss as to what to reply," he wrote. He questioned the reason for RF's resignation from Amherst College and wondered if he really is "inter-ested in doing much with students?" Acknowledging that the real diffi-culty was financial, President Conant suggested an appointment as curator of the Poetry Room or lecturer. He argued that the $5,000 salary suggested was a large sum to raise. He spoke of a "patched-up position at a low salary" between English and classics; he restricted the appointment to three years with salary not to exceed $2,500, necessary because RF would be sixty-six at the expiration of that time, and he would not want to run afoul of the retirement rules. There would be no pension, and RF would have to resign from the board, "to some extent robbing Peter to pay Paul."

As this in-house crisis dragged on, it was decided to send letters of appeal from the Friends of Robert Frost to prospective donors (including members of the Rockefeller, Roosevelt, Saltonstall, and Coolidge fami-lies) asking for donations of $250 or $500 to defray the $7,500 needed for a three-year appointment. At least one prospect protested: "It seems to me so obviously the sort of thing [Harvard] ought to do without being pushed or helped that I cannot quite understand why individuals have to do it."

Discussions were also under way with members of the Classics Depart-ment. On impulse, RF encouraged the move: "See what my impulse to flight has got me into—or almost into. . . . I feel as if I might find rest there if anywhere this side of urn burial," he wrote Hillyer. He described his dream of a course, more worldly than scholarly, that would treat the small Latin poems as if they were still "accessible to off-hand pleasure." Mischievously, he designated the course "Translations of Latin Poems into English verses not to be preserved," open to students with enough Latin to make their own translations, preferably into verse "or at least into free verse." Receiving a letter from the Latin professor Arthur Stanley Pease—a former president of Amherst—awakened him to the absurdity of his wish. Professor Pease, in welcoming him, suggests to the poet "that I [RF] might like John Finley as a watcher in my classes. Don't I know those bozos from old? They are too humanistic to be human." RF pulled back, recognizing his recklessness: "I must not bedevil my declining years with a wantonly falsified position anywhere."

When an offer was finally made for the 1938–39 academic year, it placed RF in the English Department. He was pleased to accept: "That would be a proud connection. And I think it would be much more sensible for Harvard to have me in the English Department than in the Latin Department.... It was a mere whim on my part to do something clear out of my province. Just so I have let myself dream lately of going to the Senate and learning to play tennis. I am in great need of being tied down by my friends to something regular." President Conant reappointed the poet as Ralph Waldo Emerson Fellow in Poetry for two years; for his final year on the Harvard faculty (1941–42) he was appointed Fellow in American Civilization.

Announcing Frost's return to Harvard as lecturer, one newspaper reported: "He will give marks, of a sort, but they will be secondary. Frost says he'll do most of the talking, but if mere talking won't stir up some enterprise among his hearers, 'I'll just keep silent, or even lie down on the desk, until it is realized that what I want is self-starters, not followers of a set routine.'" The catalogue carried a conference-group listing entitled simply "Poetry." As an associate of Adams House, RF convened the group of roughly forty students one evening a week in the fall semester. Students in his class attested retrospectively to the poet's extraordinary presence in the crowded Upper Common Room. RF would enter the room where students were sprawled haphazardly; he would slide down into an old chair directly before a large, wood-filled fireplace. During the four hours that followed—two-and-one-half hours of class, an hour and a half with some of his students afterward—he hunched lower, never appearing to change position. Students were transfixed as the poet ranged across contemporary poets and politics, Latin translations, and individual poems by lesser-known poets of England and America.

Equally successful were other contacts with students—at the seven Houses, with veterans from the war, and with the Nieman Fellows. Reaching out to the larger public on whom RF could always count, each year he participated in a Christmas program on WGBH-FM, Boston. In June 1941, RF broke precedent at Harvard by delivering a second Phi Beta Kappa poem, "The Lesson for Today," and an anti–New Deal poem, "Provide, Provide," inspired by a strike of Harvard charwomen. By the spring of 1942, things were sufficiently unpleasant that RF did not want to stay on unless Conant was "100 percent" for him. Their political views differed sharply, and Conant "did not find ways to make science and poetry congenial." RF objected to having a scientist as the head of a university:

> I told Conant once that it was mighty little he knew about humanities, or about poetry, or about philosophy—with his nose stuck in a test tube. . . . With all his science . . . with all his learning, which nobody begrudges or denies him, Conant was always a very "proper" individual, a Puritan and a prude if not a prig. He tried to regulate the lives of all his faculty. . . . He tried to interfere with their mores (and manners). . . . For myself I won't be shoved around. What's more to the point, I refuse to be directed by any outside force. My propulsion has got to come from inside myself. I'm a gyroscope, not a string top.

Just as RF had failed to publish the Charles Eliot Norton lectures in 1936— and a script was never found—there were similar assignments during his time at Harvard he did not fulfill.

The concept of a poet-in-residence had not yet taken hold as it has today. RF was, in effect, a pioneer in shaping his appointments (at extremely low salaries) along those lines. Limiting his official obligations at institutions such as Harvard, Dartmouth, and Amherst provided time for his writing, working with students, and taking part in a more national appreciation of poetry.

Despite the obvious tensions at Harvard, RF would recall with pride and considerable awe his many associations with his father's alma mater. When President Kennedy presented him with the Congressional Gold Medal on his eighty-eighth birthday at the White House, RF transferred the medal to Harvard's Houghton Library with the understanding that "it should be regarded as in memory of my father William Prescott Frost's days as a student at Harvard and my own days later as a student and a teacher there." Besides praising the instructors who "dumped knowledge" on him as a student—knowledge that became the raw material for many of his poems—he remembered the friends who supported him and invited him again and again to the campus; and he was pleased that family ties to the university, since his father's early achievements there, would be renewed in successive generations.

While still associated with Harvard, RF made his way to Dartmouth College in Hanover, New Hampshire, assuming some teaching and lecturing responsibilities. Finally, he made his way back to Amherst College, where, over the years before her death, he and Elinor had many homes: on Dana Street, Amity Street, Lincoln Avenue, and, finally, Sunset Avenue. Elinor's death in 1938 led to RF's resignation from the faculty and the sale of their last home together.

Writing his daughter in 1941, RF lamented his relations with Amherst. He said his faculty friend Otto Manthey-Zorn told him that "I had never had technical standing as a full professor. I could have been dropped at any time and I never had the least claim to a pension." RF imagined that he was being kept on from year to year with the largesse of some rich man's pockets, in all likelihood Stanley King himself. He would return to Amherst for the last time in 1949 with a full-time appointment as lecturer. As on previous occasions, RF acknowledged his ambivalent relationship with academia, continuing to teach students while, often at the same time, not discouraging them from leaving the academy. As early as 1920, he had admitted to the inconsistency of his views on education: "I believe in teaching," he wrote Sidney Cox that year, but I don't believe in going to school. Everyday I feel bound to save my consistency by advising my pupils to leave school. Then if they insist on coming to school it is not my fault. I can teach them with a clear conscience."

Robert Frost's Interest in Archaeology, Indians, and Pre-Columbian Artifacts

To the end, RF hated being a tourist and was never comfortable with air travel of any kind. With his family in England, in 1913, he had agreed to a vacation in Scotland only to please his wife and children. In an interview in the April 6, 1961, *Christian Science Monitor*, he remarked, "If I'd known seventy-one years ago that when I wrote those few verses they would have led me to this amount of travel I wouldn't have written them." Here, as mentioned earlier, RF throws us back on our Mother Goose and the cat that went to London to visit the queen: chasing a mouse instead, as RF points out, shows that "You could stay right at home and see it all."

It would be my mother, who, since her mother's death, having reached an unspoken understanding with her father, awakened in me a desire to "know more about it," to undertake a serious study of certain aspects of my grandfather's life and work. Upon her return from Brazil with her father, she had handed me—more correctly, laid forcefully on my desk in Austin—a pile of clippings from the São Paulo press, along with relevant State Department and consular/correspondence and photos, asking me to "do something with them." As most of them were in Portuguese (another Romance language I had studied a little), I said, "Sure."

The result was my first published article on my grandfather: "The Majesty of Stones upon Stones," which appeared in the 1981/82 issue of the *Journal of Modern Literature*. Because of my studies and teaching background in Spanish language, history, and literature, I was struck immediately by the recurring theme of stones laid upon stones and by the theme's apparent relationship to the poet's lifelong fascination with pre-Columbian artifacts and the search for man's origins in the cradle of civilization.

Not only is RF's poetry permeated by sources foreign to his English heritage, but, late in life, a number of official honors were bestowed on him outside the country. By formal invitation, he traveled to Brazil and Peru in August 1954; England and Ireland in 1957; Israel, Greece, and England in March 1961; and Russia in August 1962, shortly before his death.

Besides providing a sense of satisfaction in having carried out a goodwill mission for his country, the trips reinforced his interest in archaeology and in the ancient Indian civilizations of the Americas. The tangible traces of the distant past that he encountered on these expeditions interacted with the poet's intuitive response to history, prehistory, and geography, a complex interaction that had a profound impact on the richly metaphorical poetry that was the focus of his life.

RF was anything but a narrow regionalist, even though his metaphorical expression is drawn from New England speech. He often spoke of himself as one who prefers the part of speech in poetry that the Greeks call synecdoche: the philosophy of the part for the whole; skirting the hem of the goddess. As critics have noticed, he sought to intuit the very intention of the universe, to view the concrete in life as in a microcosm. In his poems, he creates a symbolic microcosm in which "fact is the sweetest dream that labor knows," in which the particular represents the general.

He also viewed himself as an artist rather than a scholar, as one who acquires knowledge unconsciously: "Scholars and artists differ most importantly in the way their knowledge is come by. Scholars get theirs with conscientious thoroughness along projected lines of logic; poets theirs cavalierly and as it happens in and out of books. They stick to nothing deliberately, but let what will stick to them like burrs where they walk in the fields."

He thrilled in the direct knowledge of flowers, trees, constellations, stars, Indian arrowheads, and stones—whether dating back to biblical times in and around Jerusalem, prehistoric cliff dwellings, uncut semiprecious stones mined in Brazil, or Inca, Maya, and Aztec ruins. He examined these artifacts not for their contributions to the pure sciences but for the homely and familiar details they provided of man's journey through time. He attributed to stones—often of his adopted New England—a special reality:

> Some may know what they seek in school and church,
> And why they seek it there; for what I search
> I must go measuring stone walls, perch on perch
>> ("A Star in a Stoneboat")

It followed that RF was drawn to the sciences—the laws of physics and relativity; Freudian psychology; Darwinian evolution; and the more general fields of geology, botany, astronomy, and archaeology—in and through their concrete manifestations in artifacts.

A significant number of RF's poems reflect the poet's peculiar, intuitive/archaeological measurement of time's passing. For example, in "A Missive Missile," he searches for motive in a little ochre pebble wheel dotted with red, sent to him "Across the barrier of ice . . . A million years," reaching him as metaphor. Other poems, such as "I Could Give All to Time" and "All Revelation," rely on different forms of measurement. "To an Ancient" takes us back to a nameless specimen of prehistoric man whose claim to immortality is the eolith and bone. For the poet, "Coming on such an ancient human trace / Seems as expressive of the human race / As meeting someone living, face to face." "Why Wait for Science" mockingly observes that the best way to leave the planet "should be the same / As fifty million years ago we came"; a similar preoccupation is revealed in "Accidentally on Purpose," where Man in the Universe "is just purpose coming to a head."

There are two books on Easter Island in RF's personal library. In his poem "The Bad Island—Easter," the poet treats his subject as he did the red pebble, the impervious geode, or a piece of meteorite. The rude, vast stone heads, with their scornfully curled lips, are examined not as primitive art, but as a "clinical chart," "easily read / For the woes of the past." My grandfather's interest—shared by my mother—later inspired my own take on Easter Island:

EASTER ISLAND

Huge stone faces were left behind
So that we might remember
Even if we cannot understand
Why they stand:
Mute seers on an island

Where the salt Pacific wind
Wears smooth, and all but effaces
Their pitted dreams.

One day they too will crumble:
First to rubble, then pebbles, sand,
And finally dust,
Their slow decay outlasting all our kind
To leave us just a hint,
Not of how they built them there or why,
But of a stubborn, pagan trust
In the spirit of mankind.

RF publicly cited both "To an Ancient" and "Closed for Good" as archaeological poems, the latter acknowledging a debt to the "passers of the past"
and the layer upon layer of footprints through time, a debt simply "For having once been there." His high school essay on Petra takes poetic form in "A
Cliff Dwelling," in which he imagines a spot of black on a limestone wall
as "a cavern hole / Where someone used to climb and crawl / . . . / Oh, years
ago—ten thousand years."

Like the dead seashell in "Does No One at All Ever Feel This Way in the
Least," each trace or artifact is "held forward for a symbol." By projecting
life forward into space and backward into antiquity, RF sought our place
among the infinities. Many of the poems mentioned contain a silent clue,
a sign, or, perhaps, a tangible representation of the human story. In them,
archaeology, cultural anthropology, and geography merge in a philosophic
penetration of earth and skies.

We can trace RF's interest in pre-Columbian American Indians and in
legendary heroes further back, to his early childhood and to his sensitive
reception of his mother's, Belle Moodie Frost's, imaginative storytelling
and reading aloud of tales that featured individual bravery in the face of
great odds. His mother read to him from Sir Walter Scott's *Tale of a Grandfather,* and the first book he read all the way through was probably Jane Por-
ter's *The Scottish Chiefs,* further enriching his understanding of his mother's
native Scotland and its history.

Through both his parents, the young Rob was also immersed in the
heroic myths of ancient Greece and Rome, and while attending the grammar school in Salem, New Hampshire, where his mother taught, one of
the first poems to attract him was Fitz Greene Halleck's "Marco Bozzaris,"
a poem on the Greek struggle for freedom that he found assigned in the
high school's reader and that he quickly memorized. The assigned readings

renewed his acquaintance with the Greek and Roman heroes: legendary stories about Greece in which RF sided with the Athenians in the Peloponnesian War, agonizing over the outcome. Several years later, he composed an occasional poem entitled "Greece" that appeared in the *Boston Evening Transcript* of April 23, 1897. It was inspired by Turkey's declaration of war against his beloved Greece and exhorted the country "not to let her glory fade" and to "Rise triumphant . . . once again."

In the summer of 1889, trying to catch up on his reading in American and English literature and to satisfy his interest in the fate of the American Indians, he read those volumes of James Fenimore Cooper's Leatherstocking Tales available to him: *The Deerslayer* and *The Last of the Mohicans*. The search for Indian stories led him to Mary Hartwell Catherwood's recently released and immensely popular *Romance of Dollard,* with an introduction by the noted historian Francis Parkman. He later expressed admiration for the authoritative chronicle *The Oregon Trail,* drawn from Parkman's life among the North American Indians.

The young Frost's regard for Henry Wadsworth Longfellow began in high school. He was heard to recite lines from "The Courtship of Miles Standish" and "Evangeline," and he may well have enjoyed its successor, "The Song of Hiawatha," an epic-lyric poem based in the curious legends of Henry Rowe Schoolcraft's *History, Condition, and Prospects of the Indian Tribes of the United States* (1857).

At Christmas 1953, RF elaborated on his passing interest in Spain: "I always like to hear about Spain for some reason. I wish I had the enterprise to go there. My interest is probably more due to [William Hickling] Prescott than to [Washington] Irving—the story of Cortez in Tenochtitlan rather than the Abenerrage [Abencerraje] in the Alhambra. I should be up and going to Peru and Yucatan among other places on earth I fail of. I take it out in reading. [Thor Heyerdahl's] *Kon Tiki* didn't attract me. But its successor *American Indians in the Pacific* is just my kind of travels."

The pleasure RF experienced in reading of deeds of prowess in a romantic vein was enhanced by his love of specific historical detail. After reading the three-volume *History of the Conquest of Mexico,* written by a distant cousin, William Hickling Prescott, and further inspired by his high school history teacher's rendering of William Collins's "How Sleep the Brave," RF wrote the twenty-five-quatrain ballad "La Noche Triste."

Speaking of its genesis, RF recalled that it was about that "bad night the Indians gave the Spaniards to my gratification when they drove them temporarily back from Tenochtitlan, that terrible night of June 30, 1520, when Hernán Cortés and his small band were pushed back across the causeways that led into what is today Mexico City and spent the long night of defeat under—or inside of, as the legend goes—an *ahuehuete* tree." The giant *ahuehuete* tree RF mentions is reported to have sheltered Hernán Cortés and some of his men in its cavity. Weakened over the years, it crashed to the ground in 1947.

"My sympathies were with the Indians," he recalled. "I had been grieving about the way Cortes treated Montezuma and his people. . . . My thoughts kept going back to the Indians trying to escape from the Spaniards. . . . People say 'You were interested in Indians the way children are interested in cops and robbers.' But it wasn't that way at all. I was interested in Indians because of the wrongs done to them. I was wishing the Indians would win all the battles."

The young poet certainly acknowledged the passages in Prescott depicting the moderation, justice, and valor of Cortés; those describing the romantic and chivalrous spirit of the Spanish enterprise; and those condemning the cruel excesses of the pagan sacrifices. He nevertheless sided with the Indians, suffering for their trusting helplessness at the hands of a ruthless soldiery, whose avarice and religious zeal marked the extinction of a free people. He was probably more deeply moved by Prescott's powerful eloquence in comparing the fate of the Aztec to that of the American Indian:

> The American Indian has something peculiarly sensitive in his nature. He shrinks instinctively from the rude touch of a foreign hand. Even when this foreign influence comes in the form of civilization, he seems to sink and pine away beneath it. It has been so with the Mexicans. Under the Spanish domination, their numbers silently melted away. Their energies are broken. They no longer tread their mountain plains with the conscious independence of their ancestors. In their faltering step, and meek and melancholy aspect, we read the sad characters of the conquered race. The cause of humanity, indeed, has gained. They live under a better system of laws, a more assured tranquility, a purer faith. But all does not avail. Their civilization was of the hardy character which belongs to the wilderness. The fierce virtues of the Aztec were all his own. They refused to submit to the European culture, —to be engrafted on a foreign stock. His outward form, his complexion, his lineaments, are substantially the same; but the moral characteristics of the nation, all that constituted its individuality as a race, are effaced forever.

The sense of fatalism that runs through Prescott's work, in which Cortés is portrayed as the selected "instrument of Providence to scatter terror among the barbarian monarchs of the Western World, and lay their empires in the dust," produced grief in the sensitive youth. In his uncollected ballad

"La Noche Triste," RF sets the stage in Tenochtitlán after the death of Montezuma. The tide has turned against the conqueror, who, "Now pressed by hunger by/The all-relentless foe,/Looks for some channel of escape." Cortes then gives the signal that "Will start the long retreat." The bravery of the Christians—Cortés and his lieutenants, Leon and Alvarado—is heralded in his flight across the causeway by night, trapped on both sides by the vengeful Aztec. Dead men lie "Trampled midst gold and gore," and the Aztec returns victorious to his temple. The ballad makes only passing reference to the conqueror's ultimate return and defeat of the Aztecs, concluding with praise for the Aztec's brief moment of glory before the end:

> The flame shines brightest e'er goes out,
> Thus with the Aztec throne.
> On that dark night before the end
> So o'er the fight it shone.

> The Montezumas are no more,
> Gone is their regal throne,
> And freemen live, and rule, and die,
> Where they have ruled alone.

"La Noche Triste" appeared in the April 1890 issue of the *Lawrence High School Bulletin*. The next fall, RF and his classmate Carl Burrell took opposing positions in the Debating Union's session on "a bill for removing the Indians from Indian Territory to more fertile districts and ceding said districts to the tribes forever; and for giving them some compensation for the losses already suffered." Speaking for the affirmative, RF drew extensive factual information from Helen Hunt Jackson's indictment *A Century of Dishonor: A Sketch of the United States Government's Dealings with Some of the Indian Tribes.* The *Bulletin*'s account of the debate states that "Mr. Frost . . . said some change should be made in the Indian's condition as it was very bad and growing worse. That the U.S. treaties were continually broken."

RF's friendship with Susan Hayes Ward led the poet to a special interest in the rich history of border wars in the region of South Berwick, Maine, the home of both Ms. Hayes and Sarah Orne Jewett. These writers and others had researched and admired their Protestant ancestors in the Berwick-Kittery township, and RF mock-seriously claimed the district for his own. Pinkerton Academy boys, he pointed out, played football against Berwick Academy students, and RF by chance had become knowledgeable about the notorious exploits of Major Charles Frost (1631–33–1697), eulogized as

> The last of that grand triumvirate
> Unflinching martyrs of a common fate,

Waldron and Pleisted and Frost these three
The flower of New England chivalry.

According to historical records, Charles Frost was a teenage conscript in the protection of the frontier from Indian raids in Kittery (now Eliot), Maine, at the property identified today as the Frost Homestead, still occupied by descendants. Advancing to lieutenant and grand juror in the province, Captain Frost was active in all military matters, culminating in King Philip's War, which ended with the king's death in 1676. In September of that year, Sergeant Major Waldron and Captain Frost invited a large number of Indians for a peaceful conference and military displays at Dover. During the seemingly peaceful exercises, the Indians were surrounded and taken prisoners. Most of them were sold into slavery and shipped to Barbados in the Windward Islands. This act the Indians never forgave, and for it Waldron and Frost paid with their lives.

Captain Frost was appointed councillor for a six-year term and made judge of the Common Pleas Court for life. Waldron was finally captured, tortured, and killed. Frost, having been promoted from captain to major, remained unharmed until the fateful Sunday, July 4, 1697, when, returning from church in Berwick, he and his wife and two sons were ambushed by Indians. Major Frost was killed. His family buried him on his farm, but he was disinterred, his head hung from a stake on a nearby hill, today known as Frost Hill, where the Indians dancing around the stake were ultimately repulsed by troops from the garrison. The funeral sermon for Major Frost pronounced by the Reverend Jeremiah Wise of Berwick was later published. It is believed that Frost's was the last bloodshed in New England in King William's War, the Treaty of Ryswick being signed only two months after these events, on September 11.

Major Frost's direct descendant, Robert Lee Frost, wrote what he described as a "Whitmanesque" piece in blank verse entitled "Genealogical." The lengthy, uncollected poem recounts the treacheries and ambush of Major Frost, and condemns the Hero of Great Hill as one "Who held that the end and means justify each other." The poem concludes with the major's secure reburial under a large boulder: "And there he lies in glory the ancestor of a good many of us / And I think he explains my lifelong liking for Indians."

RF's empathy with the Aztecs of Tenochtitlán and his deep compassion for the conquered Indians of North America were tempered in later years by patriotism and concern for America's destiny and purpose as a nation. Nevertheless, the poet drew inspiration throughout his life from the ancient Indian civilizations—north and south—and from their liberty-loving ways, displayed in their history and artifacts.

The reading in Prescott influenced the young Frost in another respect, noted by his biographer: "Prescott's early chapters on the Aztec Indian civilization exposed Rob for the first time to early phases of American archeology and thus established a foundation for his lifelong delight in Maya, Toltec, and Aztec cultures." And, in a December 1929 letter to Lincoln MacVeagh, RF observed, somewhat mischievously, I imagine, that "the first poem I ever wrote was on the Maya-Toltec-Aztec civilization and there is where my heart still is while outwardly I profess an interest more or less perfunctory in New England."

He also wrote a carefully researched historical/archaeological essay, for the December 1891 *Lawrence High School Bulletin*, entitled "Petra and Its Surroundings." The essay presents a vivid, pictorial view of the dead "City of Tombs," couched down among the peaks south of Mount Hor in Jordan. The Petra of the Edomites, Jews, Greeks, and Romans is painted as a wild and romantic location of varied hues of stone "alternately red and purple," columns of pink, and white mountains in the distance; of red cliffs and the Sik riverbed in summer, covered with tamarisk and oleander thickets, pale fern, ivy, and fig-tree roots; a place "for romance where everything is as vague as a rainbow half-faded in mid-air"; and where "To-day, all is ruin but the tombs that honey-comb the cliffs, and the city is a city of the dead."

Despite a romantic emphasis on the "grand sublimity" and "great, strange wildness" of Petra, the high school student demonstrated a parallel concern for precision of physical detail and historical accuracy. He revealed his considerable knowledge of geography and botany, together with a deep poetic response to ruins, cliffs, and "cave dwellers whose homes are now mere black squares upon the red crags." Suggestive of the mature poet's search for origins, it established RF's philosophical/anthropological approach to the land of the Bible, source for him of the west-northwest movement of civilization and the "on-penetration into earth and skies."

Established as a poet, RF began to collect books and drawings that sustained his interest in the precolonial civilizations. He picked up, at Goodspeed's in Boston, a large portfolio of Isher Catherwood's "Views in Central America, Chiapas, and Yucatan" and a book about Catherwood's architectural drawings of ancient Mayapan, and soon added John Lloyd Stephen's *Incidents of Travel in Yucatan*. He let it be known that he was looking for George Catlin's *Indians (A Series of Letters and Notes on the Manners, Customs, and Condition of the North American Indians)* and other relevant publications.

RF's personal library, housed at New York University, contains no fewer than twenty books on Mexico [Yucatán] and Central America, and another half dozen items on the ancient civilizations and Indian tribes of the Amazon and Andes in South America. Included in the collection are studies of Maya lands, cities, and hieroglyphics; excavations at Chichén Itzá and Uxmal; pre-Columbian art; and the true-life adventures of the Spanish conquistadors Pedro de Gamboa and Bernal Díaz del Castillo. Besides a number of fictional works that depict the North American Indian, and with which RF was acquainted since childhood, other volumes document the history and lore of Indian tribes in the continental United States.

Many of RF's friends and associates—Stewart Udall, Clifford Lyons, and Reginald Cook—with whom I had a chance to talk on occasion, shared with my grandfather their own fascination with Indian civilizations in precolonial times.

Elizabeth Shepley Sergeant was another fine woman who befriended the poet and whom I met at Bread Loaf. In her biography of RF, *Trial by Existence,* she tells the story of RF's visit to Santa Fe during the summer of 1935, where she was doing Pueblo Indian research under John Collier, the New Deal commissioner of Indian affairs. Invited to read his poems to the Writers' Edition, a regional group of poets, RF announced that Collier had promised him in Washington that Miss Sergeant would help him locate some live Indians.

Eager to indulge his "passion for archeology," Miss Sergeant and her Indian secretary offered to guide the poet the next day to the Puye cliff dwellings, the prehistoric home of the Santa Claras. They drove through the brilliant desert morning toward the Jemez Mountains, "along the sandy dry arroyos and waterless rivers, with their attendant rows of thin, trembling cottonwoods." The second verse of a song sung by the Indian secretary to the beat of his drum described the Puye cliffs, where "the bucks and the does, with their shepherd, had paused first on their descent from their Sacred Mountain to dance ritualistically in the Pueblo village."

Once in the mesa country below the peaks, Miss Sergeant and her companions climbed "sheer up the face of a cliff that rivals Delphi in beauty," where they could see the Puye caves "in the majestic curve of a canyon wall, spotted black with pinyons, grown with brilliant yellow and dull gray sage and rabbit brush." From the dizzying height of the narrow stone path, RF looked down into the Rio Grande Valley at the living Pueblo Indian villages. In that moment, Miss Sergeant saw the poet as "inscrutable as an Indian sun-priest" and wondered if a new poem would flow from his experience.

We find, then, in "A Cliff Dwelling," RF's treatment of the Pueblos as a prehistoric people threatened with extinction. He describes with serene detachment the Puye caves (and perhaps those of Petra) in a place where "sandy seems the golden sky / And golden seems the sandy plain" where the ancient race, ten thousand years ago, inhabited the limestone wall.

In the light of his love of archaeology, RF often counted archaeologists among his friends. William Hayes Ward, editor of the *New York Independent,* which carried several of his earliest poems, was noted in the field; in England, in 1912, Mary Wilson, wife of the classical archaeologist Ernest Arthur Gardner, introduced the poet to the Beveridge Circle; Campbell Bonner, a professor of Greek at the University of Michigan, was, as Elizabeth Sergeant pointed out, "interested in another of Frost's passions—archeology"; the archaeological studies of the ancient ruins of Yucatán by Alma Reed were known to RF through her friendship with my mother; and two renowned archaeologists—Albert Anthony Giesecke, residing in Peru, and Eleazar Lipa Sukenik (together with his archaeologist son, Igael Yadin) in Israel—were to figure prominently in RF's world travels late in life.

In the immediate family, RF's son-in-law Willard Fraser took a degree in archaeology at the University of Colorado and worked in the Southwest and Mexico under a grant from the Carnegie Institute. In 1932, upon Fraser's marriage to his daughter Marjorie, RF welcomed him into the family, proclaiming, "Archeology is one of the four things I wanted most to go into in life." The other three were astronomy, farming, and teaching.

More recently, an unpublished poem written into a first printing of *West-Running Brook* (1928) was donated to Amherst College by its owner, Dwight Whitney Morrow Jr., class of 1933 and a friend of the poet:

THE INSCRIPTION IN THE DESERT

These I suppose were words so deeply meant
They cut themselves in stone for permanent
Like wisdom in the brow above the eyes.
They were not wisdom: they were human lies.
"Forever" only meant a little while
And "mighty nation" not above a mile

The explanation for these lines indicates that the first three lines are a variant of the start of RF's "The Ingenuities of Debt" (*Steeple Bush,* 1947), which describes the decay of a city he names Cresiphon:

Which may a little while by war and trade
Have kept from being caught with the decayed,
Infirm, worn out, and broken on its hands.

Its losses having been met, overcome with sand, "And only rests, a serpent on its chin/Content with contemplating, taking in,/Till it can muster breath inside a hall/To rear against the inscription on the wall."

Mr. Morrow wrote the college that he received the inscription after a discussion with RF about Morrow's summer work on an archaeological dig in the American Southwest: "Robert Frost said he had always had two deep and important interests,—Astronomy and Archeology," and he reminded Morrow that his first poem, "La Noche Triste," was about archaeology.

In the dedication to his wife, Elinor, that prefaces *A Further Range*, RF speaks metaphorically of mountain ranges, including the Andes; the sub-title of a poem under "The Outlands" is "The Andes," which survives in later editions as "The Vindictives." Francisco Pizarro's exploration of Peru after 1531 and his founding of Lima in 1535 are associated with the obsessive pursuit by greedy Spaniards of El Dorado, of gold buried by Incas seeking to avenge the dishonorable execution by garroting of Atahualpa, their ransomed king.

> The king had scarce ceased to writhe
> When hate gave a terrible laugh,
> Like a manhole opened to Hell.

If gold was what pleased the conqueror, then "gold should be the one thing/The conqueror should lack." After the self-sack and self-overthrow, and after the conqueror had "Hunted and tortured and raged," the Incas "grew meek and still"; they died with their secrets, "Maliciously satisfied." One Inca speaks for all the oppressed Indians, telling how to hate effectively by wiping from the earth what the hated need most and letting them "die of unsatisfied greed." Besides an expression of sympathy for the Indians in their struggle against the oppressor, the poem is a comment on the reality of hate as an emotion that can modify the course of mankind.

In the Clearing (1963), RF's final book, reveals a greater unease about America's sense of national purpose. His poem "America Is Hard to See" is based on the exploits of Christopher Columbus, in his failed search for India. RF gives Columbus's confusion a modern-day interpretation:

> Had but Columbus known enough
> He might have boldly made the bluff
> That better than da Gama's gold
> He had been given to behold
> The race's future trial place,
> A fresh start for the human race.

Believing initially that Columbus's discovery was indeed a "fresh start for the human race," and that Columbus should be sung "As a God who had given us / A more than Moses Exodus," the poet is disillusioned. He concludes that by "Spreading out the room," Columbus only postponed the day when we would be in each other's way and "would have to put our mind / On how to crowd yet still be kind."

"La Noche Triste," "The Vindictives," and "America Is Hard to See" rely on sources where the lines between history and legend are not clearly drawn and where the poet's purpose of meaning and metaphor could be served.

In August 1951, my grandfather wrote me a letter that illuminates the relationships in the poem about Columbus:

> A funny thing happened to it with Douglas Freeman the Lee-historian when I was at his house in Richmond last spring. Two funny things in fact. To take up the first one first: "I venture to say," he said after hearing it read, "I would venture to say you were possibly months writing a historical piece like that." You can imagine my embarrassment. I should lose his respect if I confessed to a research man like him that I wrote the whole eighty-four lines of it without consulting a single book in one night. He would think I was talking literary mysticism if I told him what was true in a sense that I had been all my life writing it. So I stumbled round with "Yes in a way" and "Poetry is of course not managed just like history is it?" Then after a long pause the second thing happened. With true scholarly gravity he asked if I knew that Ferdinand and Isabella weren't making Madrid their capital in 1492. He got up and led me to the encyclopedia for correction. . . . But not a word from the old man for the idea of socialism in the "How to crowd yet still be kind." All he noticed was Madrid. I didn't defend it as I might by saying Madrid would serve well enough as a part for the whole of Spain. (Figure known as Synecdoche) But I'll tell you what I did do to show my slight knowledge of the country you seem to have adopted as your second best. I offered to make the line read "He might have fooled Valladolid." I couldn't give up "I was deceived by what he did"—the most emotional line of all.

Brazil and Peru

"In a sense . . . I had been all my life writing it," RF said. And so it is that, in a way, he had been preparing all his life for the trips to South America, Israel, and Greece: a fitting climax to a lifelong passion for precolonial history and archaeology that reinforced and made more vivid the knowledge that had stuck to him over the years like burrs in the field.

RF received an invitation from the State Department, sent to him by Assistant Secretary of State Henry F. Holland on July 24, 1954, to attend as a delegate, together with William Faulkner, the World Congress of Writers to be held in São Paulo on the occasion of the fourth centenary of the founding of that city:

> Your eminence as a poet, the admiration and affection with which your work is regarded abroad as well as at home, will make your participation in this meeting a memorable contribution toward intensifying the good will and friendship which have long united Brazil and the United States, and which is one of the bulwarks of hemisphere solidarity.
>
> In voicing American faith and American aspirations, your poetry has not only regional but hemispheric significance. It is a service to your country for you to undertake this mission as a cultural ambassador.

His daughter Lesley, who had lectured at the bicultural centers in Chile, Colombia, Mexico, and Venezuela, was invited to accompany her father and helped instill a sense of purpose for the difficult journey.

Arriving in Rio after a long and arduous nonstop flight aboard the Pan American Airways Clipper Super-6, the eighty-year-old poet was greeted by Ambassador James Scott Kemper and the cultural attaché Gordon Brown. They had arranged a series of receptions and conferences, to include an appearance before the Brazilian Academy of Letters and a meeting with the American poet Elizabeth Bishop, who resided in Rio and whom RF admired greatly.

One of the more exhilarating experiences, from the poet's perspective, was the chance to examine a collection of precious and semiprecious stones mined in Brazil. Rudolf Acton, a former student of philosophy at Harvard whom RF had advised to get away from it all—to some place, say Brazil— was now working in the University Programs section of the Ministry of Education and was an authority on gems. Acton showed RF some uncut stones, helping him with several purchases. Upon my grandfather's return to the United States, he presented me (and other family members) with several uncut semiprecious stones we later had made into jewelry.

The sessions of the World Congress of Writers were held in the auditorium of the municipal library in São Paulo. Of those delegates in attendance, RF later recalled being most impressed by Alvaro Julio da Costa Pimpao, a Portuguese count with whom he felt an affinity of ideas, and by Paul Rivet, a learned French anthropologist and the honorary director of the Musée de l'Homme in Paris, whom he found charming and knowledgeable in their mutual interests.

While RF, who spoke no Portuguese, delighted in meeting the press and through an interpreter managed to convey his infectious, if somewhat sardonic, sense of humor, the same was not true of his co-delegate, William Faulkner. According to press accounts brought home by my mother, Faulkner was seldom seen and ran shy of reporters. On one occasion, interviewed in his hotel room, he walked over—martini glass in hand—to the window overlooking downtown São Paulo, and exclaimed: "*My* how Chicago has changed!" He left the Congress shortly after in order to attend his daughter's wedding back in the States.

A second, dramatic flight of from eight to nine hours took the poet and my mother up the Amazon River and across the formidable Cordillera chain of the Andes: "I saw the wild parts of Brazil that I'd never dreamed of seeing," he commented; he saw unbroken wilderness and from there flew "right up among glaciers and peaks," where he looked down into the mouth of a live volcano to see "the Creator smoking," he later quipped. He flew over Lake Titicaca and near Vicuna, a "very famous little marble city," home of the Nobel Prize winner Gabriela Mistral.

Once he reached Peru, RF asserted at a news conference his "sincere admiration for the rugged, wild geography of South America." He noted the physical beauty of Lima, overhung by a low bank of clouds. A visit to the Anthropological Museum the next day was followed by a reading before the National Association of Writers and Artists.

Even more exciting was "half an afternoon in an ancient city"—in all likelihood the excavations and adobe ruins at Cajamarquilla in the Rimac Valley (where, at Cajamarca, Atahualpa was imprisoned and executed in 1533), and near Pachacamac, whose shrine was sought by Francisco Pizarro and his brother in the period of Spanish conquest.

As the poet and his daughter explored the burial grounds of the ancient Peruvians, RF must have recalled his poem "The Vindictives," published in 1936. My mother remembers seeing a rope-like object sticking out of the ground, then pulling it loose, and, as it disintegrated in her hand, discovering a skull underneath. Her father later described the object as "the edge of a skirt" and said that he saw "the cloth flutter in the wind."

They were guided on this archaeological excursion by the American expatriate Albert A. Giesecke, an authority on the Inca civilization, who, after many years as rector of the National University of Cuzco and as the city's mayor, established close ties with the American embassy in Lima. As the embassy's civil attaché, he accompanied dignitaries to the diggings at Lima, Cuzco, and Machu Picchu, sites of astounding Inca constructions of perfectly fitted rocks—of sacred stones built upon stones in fulfillment of an ancient legend.

RF returned to the United States from Corpac Airport aboard the plane *El Conquistador,* with a cob of Inca corn, several thousand years old, in his pocket. At a reading at Bread Loaf, he recalled his encounter with Dr. Giesecke, from whom he had requested an artifact of gold:

> I had an unlawful adventure, I think. I said to an archeologist who was a very, very fine man: "What I would like out of this country is a little piece of gold, you know, Inca gold," I said. "I suppose that never gets out." And he said, "Sometimes it does." Nothing else was said. And I got in the mail, without anything to mark it in any way from whom it came or anything, a little thin piece of gold ornament . . . must have come from him.

Israel and Greece

The inspiration for RF's March 1961 trip to Israel (followed by brief stop-overs in Greece and England) derived from an incident at the Morgan Library in New York in the spring of 1949. The Israeli archaeologist Dr. Eleazar Sukenik had brought four of the Dead Sea Scrolls to the library and to its librarian Frederick B. Adams to have infrared photographs made. The next morning, RF dropped by unexpectedly. Mr. Adams recalls the poet's excitement at seeing the Scrolls, so charged with history and for the most part so extraordinarily well preserved. RF and Professor Sukenik hit it off admirably; over lunch, RF said, "I've written a poem about archeol-ogy"—"Closed for Good" (the original six-stanza version); he promised to copy it out for Dr. Sukenik; Dr. Sukenik said RF must come to Israel, and so he did a dozen years later.

Having been invited to Jerusalem as the first Samuel Paley Lecturer at Hebrew University, he arrived at Lydda Airport on March 10, 1961. During the innumerable public receptions and news conferences, RF spoke of Pro-fessor Sukenik and the Dead Sea Scrolls; he noted that "the 'endless chain' dramatically connecting the ancient past with the present was best seen here," and that "Perhaps nothing in his long life had more vividly linked his entire career with the beginning of history than this visit."

A headline in the March 17 *Jerusalem Post* ran "Robert Frost Muses on Israel's Stones," especially at Ashkelon in Galilee, where the poet was reported to have exclaimed, "I thought there were many stones in Vermont, but this country is simply made of them." He visited the Sanhedria Tombs in the catacombs, the Mea Shearim in the old quarter of Jerusalem, and the Mandelbaum Gate, escorted by Harold E. Howland, the U.S. cultural attaché in Tel Aviv. At one session, Mr. Howland recalled, RF reflected on all these walls being used over and over again: "You have rocks piled on rocks. One civilization built another," he said.

RF still had stones and their metaphorical significance on his mind when he met with the Jerusalem Poetry Reading Group that evening at the home of Avivah and Naomi Zuckman, whose house, more than 150 years old, displayed giant flagstones and groined ceilings: "Frost at first was preoccupied with the house and its history, and we talked of Turkish architecture, of the permanency of stones linking Jerusalem and Vermont, of McIntosh apples and of what Lawrence Durrell calls the 'spirit of place.' His hand caressing the massive stones of the arched doorways, he said 'Someday even this will crumble.'"

The author and drama critic Mandel Kohansky commented on RF's entrancement with the Israeli landscape and the biblical associations it evoked. When RF walked along the beach of Ashkelon, he spoke of Samson and the Philistines, and, Kohansky observed, "he was profoundly impressed by the stony majesty of Jerusalem."

Indeed, the "Old Testament Christian" felt at home in the land of the exiled David, in the storied city of Ashkelon, and on the Hill of Healing, overlooking Judaea. He was reminded of his Swedenborgian upbringing, the Church of the New Jerusalem, to which his mother had belonged, and he remembered his *Lawrence High School Bulletin* essay on Petra when he crossed over into the Jordanian sector of Jerusalem and stayed at the Petra Hotel. Above all, he was deeply moved by the innumerable traces—stones like in Vermont, the vaulted Ain Feshka scrolls, a broken Corinthian column, the Sanhedria Tombs, and walls upon walls—of an ancient, biblical past.

In Athens a few days later, in his speech before the Greek Archeological Society, he recalled his readings in the Bible, Greek, and Latin, in that order. As on other occasions, he objected to translations that blur the idiom and are unsatisfactory in conveying the spirit of a culture. He talked of having enjoyed his studies in Greek and Latin in high school and at Dartmouth and Harvard Colleges, of his familiarity with Greek history and mythology as a young man, and of how "in the nineties [he] wrote a poem that was published in American papers . . . about the Greek war at that time."

Professor G. Armour Craig at Amherst College, coincidentally in Athens with his wife on a post-sabbatical vacation, remembers RF's visit to the Olympic Palace Hotel, where they were staying. As he walked out onto the two small balconies in Professor Craig's room, the strain from an unending succession of public appearances quickly vanished; he stood transfixed, moving from one corner to the other, identifying the monuments of classical antiquity spread out before him. He remarked that he had had to memorize the classical geography of Athens for his preliminary entrance exams into Harvard. He was truly happy and relaxed, Professor Craig observed, exulting in the sign of such archaeological treasures as the Erechtheum, the Parthenon, the Propylaea on the Acropolis, the Temple of Athena Nike, and the Olympieum, with which he already had intimate familiarity. The next day, RF and the Craigs climbed together the Acropolis, symbol for the poet of the ancient greatness of Athens. For the "Good Greek Out of New England," these were moments of great excitement and fulfillment.

Press accounts confirm that during the trips to South America and to Israel and Greece, RF was the object of considerable public attention, gave frequent conferences for the press, read his poems at formal and informal gatherings, and attended sessions of societies of writers and other intellectuals. Although pleased by the obvious popularity of his appearances, he often felt isolated by his advanced years, the tight, restrictive scheduling, and the barrier of language. His mind kept wandering back to his garden in Vermont and to his concern for its safety from encroaching deer. Once home, he was glad to be there.

Yet a rich residue of thought and feeling remained from his journeys. When recollecting the events of his world travels, it was around his passion for the artifacts and diggings, the ancient stone monuments and burial mounds, and all the other tangible signs of man's early passing that he spun his customary tales and anecdotes.

Robert and Lesley Frost: The Lure of Art

My grandfather enjoyed a lifelong interest in archaeology from biblical times through the precolonial evidences of passing civilizations such as the Aztecs and Mayas, as well as the Native Americans—what RF called "the majesty of stones upon stones." I have noted RF's private collection of precolonial prints by Isher Catherwood and the works of George Catlin and John Lloyd Stephens, providing illustrated views of the American Indians. Additional works covering these topics are scattered through my grandfather's personal library, housed at New York University.

The emotion and implicit meaning the Frosts found in the arts and that Elinor and the children developed with their drawing and painting pushed the family in yet another artistic direction, just one step away from the love of artifacts. Although they never attained the wealth necessary to purchase expensive furnishings of any kind, both father and daughter found different ways to be surrounded by high-quality original works of art: engravings, woodcuts, watercolors, oil paintings, and sculpture. It would be through friendship that they were permitted not only to help often-struggling artists but to relate in feeling with their aspirations and their artistic expression.

I was deeply moved when, shortly before his death in 1963, my grandfather gave me as a gift a packet of the Christmas poems, on which he wrote, "Christmas Cards by Robert Frost and Joseph Blumenthal," signing one of each year to me and securing them haphazardly with a blue ribbon. I believe it represents all of the Spiral Press collection that he still possessed at the time. Missing are the poems for 1934 ("Two Tramps in Mud Time") and 1938 ("Carpe Diem"). Whenever possible, RF sought the friendship of artists with whom he felt a spiritual and expressive kinship: notably, J. J. Lankes, whose woodcuts illustrate many of the poet's works, including three of his Spiral Press Christmas poems: "Neither Out Far Nor In Deep," "To a Young Wretch," and "I Could Give All to Time"; and Thomas W. Nason, (whose engravings appear in "Closed for Good," "From a Milkweed Pod," "A Wishing-Well," and "The Wood-Pile." The lives and reputations of both Lankes and Nason are forever intertwined with those of the poet: in their regionalism and rural realism, touched with a note of despair. A scattering of other artists are represented in other poems: Howard Cook, Leo Manso, Antonio Frasconi, Leonard Baskin, and Stefan Nartin. Closely paralleling these artistic associations was an early friendship with James Ormsbee Chapin, which resulted in Chapin's illustrating the Holt edition of *North of Boston,* and in a series of sketches and portraits of Robert and Elinor Frost—and even a sketch of me, preliminary to a never-completed oil painting. The first of two oil portraits of RF, dating from 1928, was purchased by Amherst College. In addition, Chapin helped my mother promote the Open Book in Pittsfield, using her business to increase the sale of his work.

Another important painter befriended by the poet in the 1920s was Leon Makielski, whom he met while teaching at the University of Michigan. The university purchased Makielski's oil portrait of Frost that hangs in the UM library, and RF purchased from Makielski his fall-foliage painting *The Red Tree,* a brilliant canvas now hanging in my sister Elinor's home, where it is greatly admired and sometimes lent for exhibits. In a July 8, 1922, letter to Makielski from the Stone House, RF shares a poetic moment:

> Well, I've just waked up from the deathly sleep that overcame me the minute I struck South Shaftsbury. I spent the morning between the shafts of a

wheelbarrow. That's the vehicle for me. When it comes to a full stop I can always get into it and sit looking back over the way we have come. In some ways it reminds me of a carriage, in some ways of a horse and in some ways of an automobile. Shall we say it combines the good qualities of all three? Last night I drove mine out at midnight to the height of land on our farm and then sat back into it to view the country o'er in the moonlight. In some ways it reminds me of an easy chair that accompanies me like a faithful dog. I guess I'll have to drop into verse to do justice to it. You know it was invented by Leonardo da Vinci, your artist.

Several other collaborative projects with favored artists were considered but abandoned. One, in particular, was an effort to work with Holt to produce an expanded version of *North of Boston*, accompanied by reproductions of Andrew Wyeth paintings. In his *Robert Frost and J. J. Lankes: Riders from Pegasus*, Welford Dunaway Taylor speaks of the wish to engage Wyeth: "It was a project that excited Frost's imagination, for in his eyes Wyeth occupied in painting a position comparable to that of Lankes in woodcutting. Moreover, he doubtlessly recognized in Wyeth's work that same strongly suggestive quality—a visual synecdoche, as it were—that distinguished that of Lankes." In her book *Abandoned New England: Landscape in the Works of Homer, Frost, Hopper, Wyeth, and Bishop*, Priscilla Paton explores important parallels between poet and artist. She points to the tendency to dismiss deeper or higher meaning in portrayals of rural settings. She quotes Wyeth: "I have a very strong feeling . . . that the more objects you use, the less there is in the picture. Robert Frost is deeper than his New England subjects." She references Frost's earlier work—*North of Boston*, primarily, where the regional, rural, and farm settings nourished his poems.

The association with Wyeth did not end here. While teaching at Amherst College, RF and Elinor frequented the home of Charles Hill Morgan, the founding director of the Mead Art Museum at Amherst. Morgan had purchased the painting by Wyeth entitled *Wind from the Sea*, a watercolor he displayed over the fireplace. Invited for lunch or dinner, RF would ask to be seated opposite the painting he so much admired, and Morgan offered to lend it to him whenever he and his wife were out of town. After Morgan's death, his heirs donated *Wind from the Sea* to the Smithsonian in Washington, D.C., where recently it was featured in an Andrew Wyeth exhibit entitled *Looking Out, Looking In*, a title inspired by such Frost poems as "Tree at My Window." In the meantime, Hyde Cox and several other friends, recognizing the intuitive, emotional, and psychological parallels between poet and artist, purchased from Wyeth a watercolor entitled *Winter Light*

(Winter Sunset) and presented it to my grandfather in 1954, on his eightieth birthday. RF left the painting to Kay Morrison; upon her death, it passed to her daughter, Anne Morrison Gentry. In 1987, Edward C. Lathem and his wife purchased the painting, donating it to the Hood Museum of Fine Arts at Dartmouth College. My mother, who had seen and admired *Winter Light* at her father's home in Cambridge, was naturally (as was I) disappointed to see the work pass out of the family. When I last visited the Hood Museum, by advance appointment, a few of us were given a private viewing of the Wyeth watercolor.

With the passing of my grandfather in 1963, works of art from his home in Cambridge made their way to me and my sister. We are fortunate to have a number of J. J. Lankes's engravings and woodcuts, as well as the watercolors *Sugar Bush* and *After Rain* by A. K. D. Healy, RF's friend at Middlebury College. *Sugar Bush,* one of my favorites, reminds me of my grandfather's love of bare trees (as seen in his early poem "My November Guest" and elsewhere). Nason's *Trees in Snow,* illustrating RF's Christmas poem, "The Wood-pile," has the same vertical lines in a winter scene.

In my home I have one of the sculptured busts of the poet by Leo Cherne. Another fine bust sculpted by Margaret C. Cassidy, wife of the sculptor Jim Paul Manship, is owned by Amherst College, while a bronze bust by Walter Hancock is displayed at Dartmouth College. A monumental stone of RF was sculpted by Jose Buscaglia during his undergraduate years at Harvard University, where it was later installed in Adams House. Of perhaps less artistic value are replicas of the statue sculpted by George Lundeen of RF sitting and writing on a tablet, located at a number of colleges—Dartmouth College, Agnes Scott College, and the University of Colorado—though it is certainly of no less worth than the one of my grandfather sitting on a park bench in the town of Amherst, engaged in conversation with Emily Dickinson!

Mother had begun acquiring original works of art as a young adult. Her uncle-in-law, Bob Francis, was a successful textile designer who turned to oil painting; Mother was allowed to choose several of his canvases from the museum in Pittsfield and to pass them along to us. While in Spain, Mother, through her work in the Casa Americana, met many artists and was given a lovely watercolor by Eduardo Vicente that features a small village with farmer and donkey.

During the 1940s, my mother sat for two large oil portraits, painted by two women friends, both accomplished artists. Enit Kaufman, born in Czechoslovakia, had escaped war-torn Europe with her husband in 1939 (leaving most of her work behind in Vienna) and started over in the United

States. She created her view of her new home through a series of watercolor portraits of many notable Americans, including Franklin D. Roosevelt, Dwight Eisenhower, Henry Wallace, Marian Anderson, Joe Lewis, and many others; she was widely exhibited at the Smithsonian and the New York Historical Society. Mother and Enit became close friends, and Enit gave Mother the extraordinary watercolor portrait, whose blues capture the blue of Mother's eyes along with her personality. The other portrait was by an Italian artist, Emma Barzini. Emma and Mother were friends in Madrid in the postwar period. The daughter of Luigi Barzini Sr. and brother to Luigi Barzini Jr.—both famous Italian journalists—Emma has received little critical notice. Enit's watercolor portrait is with me; the bold, dramatic oil painting by Barzini is with my sister, Elinor.

Artistic talent resurfaced in our family with Robin Fraser Hudnut, the only child of Marjorie Frost Fraser, who died shortly after her daughter's birth. Raised by her father and grandmother, Robin graduated from Smith College before marrying a corporate attorney and raising four children of her own. She became an accomplished artist and pianist, exhibiting her work in San Francisco, near her home in Tiburon, where she serves as a docent in several San Francisco museums. Robin was close to my mother and illustrated two of Mother's books, *Digging Down to China* and *Going on Two*. Each year she shares her artwork in a Christmas card, reminding us of Grandfather's annual Christmas poems. She also tracked down and photographed for me the painting of *Wander Bird* by Frank Vining Smith.

Over the final years of her life—she died in Fairfield, Connecticut, in 1983—Mother had settled in a charming Stanford White apartment in Lower Manhattan; she had loved New York ever since her time at Barnard College. Having ample wall space, she offered a number of artists a gallery in which to exhibit their artwork. Robert Maione, for example, during his exhibit, sold one of his oil landscapes, of a New England fall scene, to my sister, Elinor, to give to me as a wedding present. Frequently, Mother was given a print or painting by those exhibiting in her gallery. She acquired several oil paintings by the noted Spanish artist Joaquín Vaquero Turcios; he and his architect father, Joaquín Turcios Palacios, had been our friends in Segovia and assisted in teaching the young students in the Escuela de la Tahona, my mother's school in Spain. He went on to place multidiscipline works worldwide and is known in Madrid for his sculptured frescoes of the discovery of America adorning the central Plaza de Colón in Madrid. Besides paintings, Mother and I brought back many treasured items from Spain: pottery, illustrated missals, embroidered linen, antique jewelry, and furnishings from the eighteenth century. These multiple artistic associations, touched upon here, helped bring together the generations surrounding the poet from New England.

Robert Frost: The Spanish Connection

Except for his brief holiday in Cuba in 1939 and his visit to Lima, Peru, upon his return from Brazil in 1954, RF did not visit any Spanish-speaking countries. Because of his foundation in the classical languages—Latin and Greek—and a passing knowledge of French (studied at the time with his daughter Lesley), he could scan a Spanish text and understand a great deal. Actually, it was by choice that he did not study other modern languages for fear of losing his ear trained for the rhythms of speech essential to his craft, what he came to call "the sound of sense."

Yet RF's reputation in foreign countries was enhanced by his missions abroad, during which he met other poets and was covered extensively in the local media. In Russia, for example, he was made into a grandfather figure. By the 1930s, popular poems like "Birches," "Mending Wall," and "Stopping by Woods on a Snowy Evening" had been translated into Russian, and many educated Russians had studied English. Franklin D. Reeve, who accompanied RF to Russia in 1962, found that "because of the great difficulties in language his poems were frequently translated into homiletic rhymes where the wit and the conceits of the original become moralistic or aphoristic phrases of advice on living."

In Spain, where my family still maintains a home-away-from-home, I was gratified to learn that the poetry-reading public was aware of my grandfather's work. Doing research on this issue in Madrid, I met Professor Felix Martín Gutiérrez, at that time chairman of the English Department at the University of Madrid (Universidad Complutense) and president of the Spanish Association for American Studies. He spoke warmly of the American poet and said that Frost's poetry was fairly well known in literary circles. Felix was writing a dissertation that explores comparatively the work of Frost and Juan Ramón Jiménez. RF's poems remain difficult to translate, however, and anecdotal information suggests that other English-language poets—Walt Whitman, Emily Dickinson, W. B. Yeats, Ezra Pound, and T. S. Eliot, for example—are more accessible in translation in the foreign-language bookstores and library collections.

It wasn't until 1996 that *North of Boston* appeared in its entirety in Spanish. The timing of its appearance can be attributed partially to the lifting of copyright restrictions. In his introductory notes, Sebastiano Masó explains some of the difficulties he experienced in translating the sixteen poems, most of them dramatic dialogues:

In order that the poem preserve its original flavor, its own flight, that it not resemble, as so often occurs, the product of one of those inane translating machines, the poet who undertakes it (it has to be a poet, don't forget) must submerge himself in the original text as in a river and let himself penetrate to the bones for its meaning and its sound, and above all, as Frost postulates, through the "sound of sense," that complex counterpoint of rhythm and meanings, advance . . . from surprise to surprise, until the climax/revelation. (translated from the Spanish)

Masó points out in conclusion some of the technical problems presented by Frost's idiomatic speech and meter.

Biographical and artistic parallels are noted between RF and Antonio Machado (a contemporaneous Spanish poet of the so-called Generación del '98), but neither appears to have been aware of the other's work. The Argentinian writer Jorge Luis Borges, who often traveled to the United States, held the American poet, whom he never met, in high esteem. With a native command of English, Borges could quote certain poems he admired: "Stopping by Woods on a Snowy Evening," "Acquainted with the Night," "Birches," "The Bear," among others. He spoke of RF as "that great poet whose work is a mirror of man's essential loneliness"; he said he preferred him to Whitman and T. S. Eliot.

Although RF never visited these poets' homeland, he did have contact in the United States with two Hispanic poets, both Nobel laureates: Juan Ramón Jiménez, who left his native Andalucía in 1936, and Octavio Paz, from Mexico.

Jiménez became aware of Frost's poems in 1916, shortly after the first two volumes were published in England. While he and his bride, Zenobia Campudrí, were honeymooning in New York, the couple picked up a copy of the American edition of *North of Boston* and remained lifelong admirers of Frost's verse. No other poet represented in Jiménez's library received equal praise with the one he labeled "el cisne gris de Nueva Inglaterra" (the gray swan of New England). Juan Ramón found in Frost a profound sensibility to nature and a sincerity that he sought to emulate; he noted that Frost's blank verse was similar to the stark verse of Miguel de Unamuno, a compatriot influential in his own poetic development. It is not surprising, then, that my grandfather, upon reading, in a single night, a translation I gave him of Unamuno's *Del sentimiento trágico de la vida,* marveled at its deep philosophical play with words, its paradoxes and ironies, reminiscent of his own "play for mortal stakes."

Zenobia and Juan Ramón created between them an important sentimental and literary bond by sharing in the art of translation. Zenobia would prepare a literal translation that her husband later refined in poetic language, hoping to preserve the peculiar accent of the original, even the rhyme, as in the case of "The Pasture."

EL PASTO

Voy al pasto a limpiar la fuente; sólo
las hojas secas;—quizás esperara
un momento, hasta ver el agua clara—
sólo estaré un poquito, ¿Vienes tú?

Voy un instante, a ver si el ternerillo
que con la madre juega allí se viene;
—¡tan tierno! Ella lo lame y no se tiene—
sólo estaré un poquito. ¿Vienes tú?

My article "Robert Frost in Spanish Translation" included seven different translations of "The Pasture." Not only, in my opinion, did the Jiménez translation better express the original poem's intent; others were hard to identify as the same poem.

When the Jiménez translation of "The Hill Wife" ("La esposa de la colina") appeared in the University of Puerto Rico's *El liberal,* Zenobia, a name unknown to the American poet, sent Frost a copy and soon received a cordial reply dated January 20, 1919:

My dear Mrs. Jiminez [*sic*]

I should have answered your letter from Spain long ago but for something else from Spain [influenza], far less pleasant that, coming just after the letter, almost took my life and has left me rather badly off, I'm afraid, for the rest of the summer.

What I have carried in mind all this time to say to you is that so far as I am concerned you have all the permission in the world for the pleasant thing you propose, and I can't think my publishers will make the least difficulty. I have seen your translation of The Hill Wife but have too little Spanish to judge from it for myself how fortunate I am in my translator. I am told however by a good friend whom I trust that you have caught the spirit of the poem and done me something more than justice. Of course I am very grateful.

I hardly see why I should have the five dollars for what is your work as it stands. To plant a tree with for you to find growing when you come to America? Why shouldn't you have kept the money to plant a tree with yourself for us to find growing when we come to Spain as we have been long planning to do for our children and mean to do the minute the world subsides to peaceful prices. Well the great thing is that you are planting *North of Boston* for me over there. I suppose I must plant you the tree in requital, though I think it ought to wait till we settle down where we know we are going to live the rest of our lives.

Sometime will you give me the pleasure of setting An Old Man's Winter Night and perhaps The Gum Gatherer in your language? An Old Man's Winter Night is my favorite among them all in all three of the books.

And will you understand and forgive my long delay and believe me,

Gratefully yours,

Robert Frost

The friendly correspondence led to a meeting arranged by my mother. While there appears to be no record of their conversation, Juan Ramón wrote Frost to thank him for the inscription—the last seven lines of "The Wood-Pile," a poem he much admired—in his edition of the *Collected Poems*. After meeting Frost, he wrote, "Fue ver y tocar el tronco, de los ricos frutos que en todas las estaciones de muchos años hemos gozado con todos nuestros sentidos" (was to see and to touch the trunk of the rich fruits that in all the seasons of many years we have enjoyed with all our senses). In turn, my mother and her father sent Zenobia and Juan Ramón a signed copy of his new book, *A Masque of Reason*. Commenting at one of his readings on the broadening effect of humor—not found, he observed, in more noble creatures—Frost would recall the Spanish poet: "You get these people with a kind of high, saintly, passionate way of taking life. I saw a Spaniard like that. ... [H]e's reckoned a very great poet in Spain. ... Very handsome, dark person and understanding English well, and nothing but a sustained gloom, perfectly sustained—pale, pale features, black hair, very striking."

The fact that the Mexican poet Octavio Paz made his way on foot up to RF's cabin near Bread Loaf to visit the aging poet attests to Frost's growing reputation in the Spanish-speaking world. Paz later published his notes on their interview during which they exchanged ideas on aesthetic concerns: on the creative process, how to read and reread a poem, the need for solitude, the importance of philosophic humor. Paz compared the harsh Mexican terrain with the summer verdure of Vermont and noted the importance of landscape in their verse. The interview concluded where RF's life in poetry began—with his first poem. Recounting the genesis of "La Noche Triste," he asked Paz whether he had read Prescott's *History and Conquest of Mexico*. Paz replied: "Era una de las lecturas favoritas de mi abuelo. De modo que lo leí casi niño. Me gustaría volver a leerlo." (It was one of my grandfather's favorite books, so I read it when I was a child. I would like to read it again.) Paz and Frost met only once, and they did not correspond.

While it is very difficult to gauge the degree of familiarity with Frost's poems in the Spanish language—and RF warns us that poetry is what is lost in translation—the evidence suggests a growing appreciation of his work in Spain and Central and South America, an appreciation that can only increase with the publication of entire volumes of his verse, the universal appeal of American literature and the English language, and the technological advances in communication.

Honorary Degrees in England and Ireland

I was fortunate to be with my grandfather for several milestones in his final years. As I mentioned, after graduating from Radcliffe College, I returned to Washington, D.C., staying until I landed a secretarial position with the U.S. Operations Mission in Spain. While I was still in Madrid, my grandfather was invited to England to receive honorary degrees at Cambridge, Oxford, and Durham Universities in England and National University in Dublin, becoming only the third American—after Henry Wadsworth Longfellow and James Russell Lowell—to receive honors from both Oxford and Cambridge in the same year. Taking leave from my job, I flew to London on June 1, 1957; RF had arrived a few days earlier, together with Lawrance Thompson, his biographer.

Since returning to America in 1915, and, in 1928, spending a few weeks in England and France with his wife, Elinor, and daughter Marjorie, RF had not been back to Britain. On this occasion, he was invited by the Department of State's American Specialists Program, after a discussion about whether a man of his advanced years could endure the rigors of such a trip. Harold E. Howland at State explains the purpose of the mission:

It was our belief that we needed someone, not in politics, not in government, but rather from "our people," who was loved and respected by both England and America, to remind the British people of our mutual aspirations and hope. Mr. Frost's greatness as a poet was discovered in England even before our country recognized his abilities. . . .

So we called on Mr. Frost and discussed with him our desire for him to go, but also our especial concern over his age and his well-being. I shall never forget his words: "I was re-reading recently the life of Voltaire. You will recall that Voltaire, in 1778, left the serenity of his village residence in Ferney, Switzerland to again appear with the crowds of Paris. It was a strenuous visit and he died on that trip.

His age then was, as is mine now, 82. Nevertheless, if my country believes I can be of any use in reminding the British people of our own warm affection and strong friendship, why, of course, I'll go. I don't want to be an unguided missile, however; don't spare me. Tell me where you want me to go and when. I'll be ready."

That he was ready, and that he was successful, may be attested to by the abundant acclaim, honors, and tributes he received throughout the British Isles.

Personal highlights were the meeting with W. H. Auden and E. M. Forster while at Oxford. Back in London, RF and I accompanied the then poet laureate, C. Day-Lewis, to Hyde Park to watch the sheep dog trials with border collies like our Gillie herding the sheep into corrals on whistled commands from their shepherds.

At Oxford University, we listened to the Oration delivered in Latin to "one who has loved his Virgil from his schooldays onwards." In his brief talk, RF jokingly referred to his own education as "by degrees"—"degradation." The Brits loved the dry humor. On the drive back to London, accompanied by reporters from *Life* magazine and by me as the only family member, we called on the now nearly blind Jack Haines (his botanist friend of the poets in Gloucestershire), who was living with his son Robin in Cheltenham. Left alone for the night, the two old men reminisced about their time together in 1914 with Edward Thomas, Eleanor Farjeon, and his wife, Dorothy, all gone now. "We are not as sentimental about anything as we used to be unless it is friendship," RF told Haines as the trials of a long life were coming to an end: "I shall have less to say," RF's English poem about trees had proclaimed, "but I shall be gone."

The next day the official party stopped at the Old Nailshop at the Greenway, where W. W. Gibson and his wife had resided in 1914. In his book *Dymock Down the Ages*, the Reverend J. E. Gethyn Jones describes the memory-charged moment as RF entered the Nailshop: "Slowly he entered the 'Golden Room' where, in the distant past, he had held the silent circle spellbound. Within that room, the central meeting place of their fellowship, Frost was strangely silent. Did the shades speak to him? Did a laughing voice echo across land and sea from the Aegean Isle where Brooke's body rests? Did Frost hear again the measured phrase of Thomas from the Vimy Ridge [Arras]? In his imagination were they all there, those whom he knew so well and loved so dear? Who knows?" Moving on, our small caravan stopped across from Little Iddens, the laborer's cottage where the Frosts had lived in the months before the declaration of war in August 1914.

RF hesitated to enter the home where Elinor had once held sway. Reverend Jones commented on the poet's change of fortune since those days:

"Elinor and the children had been with him when first he came. In 1957 a grown up granddaughter stood by his side, but the older generation had passed within the 'veil.'" The *Life* photographer captured the American poet as he stood in the field of young green oats—Little Iddens in the distance behind him—his hand covering his eyes in ache of memory. Here in this place he and Elinor and their four children had experienced the joy of poetry in motion—in Nature as in their natures. Here he and Edward had known the "easy hours" of talks-walking and friendship. And he had savored, for the first time, overwhelmingly favorable reviews of his poems in *A Boy's Will* and *North of Boston*. The cares of a lifetime weighed heavily on him now, but the resolve, hope, and expectations from those early years gave way to the demands of the heart. As I look now at my grandfather's picture from that day together, I can hear his measured voice recite the lines from his "Wild Grapes": "The mind—is not the heart. / . . . / but nothing tells me / That I need to learn to let go with the heart." An emotional moment, of course, but RF approached the poor, cramped cottage quietly, touching the low box hedge and water pump by the kitchen door, remarking that they were there "when we were here." Making his way up the narrow staircase and through the upstairs rooms, he was relaxed with the current occupants, chatting with their young son. Out one window, he could catch a glimpse of May Hill.

Back in London, before and after my arrival, there were numerous social functions in honor of the poet: he was entertained by Amy Smith Pantin, the daughter of J. C. Smith of Edinburgh; he visited with Jessy Mair, now married to Lord William Beveridge, and their daughter, Lucy, at the House of Lords. RF had met T. S. Eliot for the first time in 1928; on this trip, he dined with the Eliots at their home; we both were invited to dinner at the English-Speaking Union, where the two poets offered each other a cordial toast. He had tea at the Westbury with Mrs. Lascelles (Catherine) Abercrombie and Mrs. Ralph Abercrombie, her daughter-in-law.

RF caught only a glimpse of Helen Thomas and her daughter, Myfanwy. Elinor Frost and her husband had been dismayed by Helen Thomas's two volumes of memoirs—*As It Was* and *World Without End*—which, they believed, included intimacies about their marriage Edward would have wanted kept private. When the Frosts, with Marjorie in tow, returned to England in 1928, they met with Helen and her children; forthrightly, they told Helen how they felt.

Contrary to some accounts, there was no formal break or bitterness in these developments. According to correspondence between Helen and her friend Eleanor Farjeon, on the one hand, and the Frosts, on the other, while in London in June 1957, Helen and Eleanor attended RF's London appearance. Arrangements were made for RF to visit the Thomas family in Helen's home in Lambourn. But just trying to keep up with as many as three social functions daily and travel to highly taxing events at the various universities had proved overwhelming. Suffering from a debilitating cold and exhaustion, RF was unable to drive the three hours to Lambourn, and efforts to meet with Helen's son, Merfyn, were also unsuccessful.

Because she lived nearby, Eleanor Farjeon was able to meet alone with Robert at her home at Perrins Walk (Hampstead). Eleanor was another of the strong women authors and poets underappreciated by her literary critics, in part, I believe, because women like her and my mother found an easy readership with books for children. Eleanor was a close friend to Helen and Edward Thomas, and an important confidante to Edward as he moved, with RF's urging, to write verse for the first time.

On this occasion, Eleanor invited me to go with her to see Shakespeare's *Antony and Cleopatra* at the Old Vic. Later, she presented me with a copy of her lavishly illustrated *Kings and Queens,* a collection of witty biographical poems put together by Eleanor and her brother Herbert, which she inscribed: "To [Lesley] Lee with love from Eleanor Farjeon in memory of our evening at the Old Vic here are more Kings than even Shakespeare wrote of, and as much of English History as anybody needs to know. June 10th 1957." For RF, she inscribed a copy of Edward Thomas's first volume of poems (published in London in 1917 under the pseudonym Edward Eastaway, it was the first book ever dedicated to Robert Frost): "To Robert from Eleanor June 1957 (October 1917).

Seeming to understand the problems of illness and logistics that my grandfather encountered on this exhausting trip, as well as the overriding momentousness of the occasion, Eleanor Farjeon concluded her account of her final meeting with the poet (at her hayloft on Whit Monday): "We did not meet again, and we did not write. The friendship that stretched from the day I met Robert Frost in 1914 to the day he died in 1963, remains as unbroken as in those forty-two years of silence. We do not lose our friends when they die; we only lose sight of them."

Robert Frost's Eighty-Fifth Birthday and Lionel Trilling

Another milestone in my grandfather's final years was the occasion of his eighty-fifth birthday, March 26, 1959, to be celebrated with a distinguished group of friends and family—myself included—at the Waldorf Astoria Hotel in New York. Invited to make remarks, the critic Lionel Trilling, a latecomer to the work of the poet, offered this assessment: "The universe that he conceives is a terrifying universe.... Read 'Neither Out Far Nor In Deep,' which often seems to me the most perfect poem of our time, and see if you are warmed by anything in it except the energy with which emptiness is perceived." He seemed to want us to believe he had independently discovered the dark poems, the dark places in a number of RF's poems and in his expression of the dark side of life with which most of us were long familiar. RF *was* startled by the assessment, but on reconsideration wrote a reassuring note to Trilling, who had been scolded in the press for his "intemperate" remarks: "Not distressed at all. Just a little taken aback or thrown back on myself by being so closely examined so close by.... You weren't there to sing "Happy Birthday, dear Robert," and I don't mind being made controversial. No sweeter music can come to my ears than the clash of arms over my dead body when I am down" (June 18, 1959). He especially liked the "clash of arms" when pursued at a high level of perception and sensibility; less so, certainly, when critics and others presented unreasoned, unsubstantiated, often mean-spirited attacks—or out of a crude sense of humor—where the poet had no opportunity to respond. I think of Jeffery Meyers's crude and error-filled biography; the "monster myth" that Helen Vendler helped generate (and from which she seems now to have moved away); or the latest reinvention in Joyce Carol Oates's short story "Lovely, Dark, Deep," in which a young writer at Bread Loaf interviews the aging poet in his cabin, portraying him as a perverted fat idiot. Yet, I find in my files a long essay by Ms. Oates from the *American Poetry Review* (November–December 1999) entitled "First Loves: From 'Jabberwocky' to 'After Apple-Picking'" in which she states that "After Apple-Picking" is a "hypnotic, haunting poem." Her praise of this poem extends to the positive influence of RF on her life as a poet, in its free choice of subject matter as an American and made worthy because of the seriousness and subtlety of his expression. She concludes with praise of Parini's "excellent" biography. What to make of all this back and forth? Very little, I imagine.

In truth, as RF wrote, "it takes a lot of in and outdoor schooling to understand my kind of fooling." Let me repeat: the man *was* the poet, his poems the central expression of the man—complex and varied but understandable. As he liked to say: "I am a teacher, and I like to be understood."

Robert Frost and Politics

RF had come to enjoy the intrigue and excitement of the seat of power in the nation's capital, something Elinor Frost would have shunned. In fact, RF had been caught up in politics since his father was elected delegate to the Democratic National Convention in Cincinnati (1880), which nominated General Winfield S. Hancock for president, losing to the Republican nominee, James A. Garfield. Although depressed by the Democratic loss, RF's father supported General William S. Rosecrans in his successful bid for Congress; he took his son, Robert, with him during campaign events in San Francisco. In 1884, Robert worked enthusiastically in his father's campaign to become the city's tax collector, a closely contested loss that deepened his father's depression, leading up to his death from consumption the following year.

When asked in later years what political party he belonged to, RF would respond: "You can tell if you read my books, *all* my books. I have been a Democrat all my life but I haven't been happy since 1898," thus covering, I imagine, the two terms of Grover Cleveland. Despite frequent nominations, the Nobel Prize committee seemed to look askance at RF's maverick politics. Perhaps they resented RF's proposed contribution to a United Nations sculpture: "Nature, within her inmost self divides/to trouble man with having to take sides." He also mixed it up in politics by taking an activist role, in 1957, in freeing Ezra Pound from St. Elizabeth's Hospital, where he had been held since he was returned in a cage from Italy at the end of the war and charged with treason for his pro-Mussolini broadcasts. His commitment to St. Elizabeth's had allowed Pound to avoid a trial.

RF had been dismayed when Pound received the prestigious Bollingen Award while still under indictment at St. Elizabeth's. (He would be pleased to learn, just before he died in 1963, that *he* had finally received the award.) Although RF had stayed away from Ezra since 1914, he joined others in seeking Pound's release in recognition of his extraordinary contribution as a poet to poetry. A number of noted literary figures—besides RF, there was T. S. Eliot, Ernest Hemingway, and Archibald MacLeish—prepared a joint petition, asserting that such a worthy and influential poet should not spend the rest of his life at St. Elizabeth's. The petition was presented to the courts in Washington, and, in 1959, with a push from RF, who was well connected at the Supreme Court, the effort was successful. Ezra was sent back to Italy for good, where he was welcomed by the two women who had cared for him over many years—Elizabeth Shakespeare and Olga Rudge.

In 1958, RF was named Consultant in Poetry to the Library of Congress; after two years, he was retained as Consultant in the Humanities. The designation poet laureate was added to the title of later poets, starting with Robert Penn Warren. While the American version of the British poet laureate is freed of any obligation to write dedicatory verses or for particular state occasions, the American honor cannot boast the type of recognition given to the post in England. Nevertheless, the appointment gave my grandfather a pulpit of sorts in Washington, where he could develop his ideas on the need for government support of the humanities—hoping it might remain more "aesthetic" than "cultural" or too "departmental." RF could give interviews, talks, TV appearances, opportunities he had learned to enjoy with his sharp wit and humor. Elinor Frost would have shrunk from these public performances, but my grandfather just wanted to have a good time for those final years, hamming it up with the press and his by now large audiences.

Robert Frost and President Kennedy: The Inauguration and Russia

RF enjoyed, as well, taking an active part in the debate over the issue of regional superiority. In his relations with Ezra Pound, Harriet Monroe, Amy Lowell, and others, RF defended the people of New England north of Boston and outside of academia. The humor, the tragedy, the strength of character—all were found in New England, he had argued. And he would be named poet laureate of Vermont and receive many honors throughout New England.

When John F. Kennedy and his family came onto the political scene, RF jumped again into the debate over region by prophesying the nomination of then Senator Jack Kennedy for president, proving what he believed to be the durability of New England and its national influence—always adding a caveat, his wish that Jack be more Boston Irish than Harvard elitist. Jack and Stewart Udall, RF's former student and President Kennedy's choice for secretary of the interior, were charmed by the endorsement. Jackie, who loved the poetry and the man, invited RF to the White House. At the urging of Udall, the president persuaded the aging poet to present a poem, "The Gift Outright," at his inauguration in January 1961. He also convinced RF to compose a poem for the occasion, a request the poet would normally have rejected, preferring to reach back "on the shelf," he would say, to previously composed verses.

The result was a somewhat disappointing congratulatory ode, "For John F. Kennedy His Inauguration/Gift Outright of 'The Gift Outright'/With Some Preliminary History in Rhyme." Due to the extreme winter weather at the time of the inauguration that prevented the poet from seeing the script and finding less than helpful LBJ's frantic attempts to shield the flimsy, elite-typed sheet of paper with his hat, RF was forced to abandon the effort. In horrified suspense, I sat with family members in a front row far below the podium, all of us freezing.

At the time of the inaugural events I was an assistant professor of Spanish at Sweet Briar College, located about two hours by car south of the District. In anticipation of JFK's inauguration, I had purchased a simple long dress in nearby Lynchburg. The afternoon before the inaugural, I climbed into my Volkswagen Beetle (brought home from Spain) and headed north. Within a mile on the icy road, I knew I was in trouble. Stopping in the small town of Amherst, Virginia, I put chains on the car and kept going. The windshield wipers froze; the road became increasingly invisible in what had turned out to be a full-scale blizzard. To help guide my lonely progress toward Washington, I gauged the shoulders from the many abandoned cars and jackknifed trucks along the route. Once I had parked in the District near Dupont Circle, the battery went dead.

Years later, I sat before a live recording of the inaugural event played for me at the JFK Library in Boston. I was struck by how long RF had struggled to read the recently composed poem and was amazed once more at the power of his voice as he recited from memory "The Gift Outright," the words overriding both the numbing cold and wind and the acute embarrassment of the moment. As part of the dedication, RF had changed the last line—for the occasion only, as he had explained beforehand to the president—from "such as she was, such as she *would* become" to "such as she *will* become."

Following the inaugural ceremony, still combating the icy mess brought on by the storm in the streets of the capital, we as family joined RF at one of the balls held citywide that evening. The poet was depressed, faulting his inability to read the dedicatory poem as a personal failure. Chilled and exhausted, those of us still standing called it an evening.

On RF's eighty-eighth birthday—March 26, 1962—President Kennedy presented the Congressional Gold Medal to the poet in the Fish Room of the White House, noting the unusual bipartisan action of Congress in voting the medal in 1960 and congratulating the poet on the release of *In the Clearing,* his final book of verse.

In late August, the aging poet would enjoy something of a last hurrah, accepting another invitation from the president, this time to travel to the Soviet Union as part of a cultural exchange program sponsored by the State Department. Accompanied by Stewart Udall, Franklin D. Reeve (a Russian scholar at Wesleyan University and father of the actor Christopher Reeve), and Frederick B. Adams (director of the Morgan Library), RF flew to Moscow, where he gave public readings in Leningrad and Moscow, mixing freely with such noted Russian poets as Anna Akhmatova, Yevgeny Yevtushenko, Andrei Voznesensky, and Andrei Tvardovsky.

From Moscow, the group traveled to Gagra to visit Premier Nikita Khrushchev at his Black Sea retreat. Arriving exhausted and ill, RF was unable to proceed to the premier's dacha. His concerned host sent his personal physician to check on the ailing poet; she soon arranged the one-on-one exchange at the poet's bedside, Professor Reeve serving as interpreter.

Flying back to Kennedy Airport, the party arrived at night to a bevy of reporters greeting him on the tarmac; the exhausted eighty-eight-year-old was quoted in a headline in the press: "Frost Says Khrushchev Sees U.S. as Too Liberal to Defend Itself." RF later apologized for the apparent misquote, expressing an opinion the premier may well have held (when he sent missiles to Cuba) but that he had not spoken. President Kennedy—although both he and Jackie remained great admirers of the poet—was reported to have been angered by the press accounts; RF never heard from him again, not even a formal get-well message during the month the poet lingered in hospital (although he did receive one from Jack's brother). Fortunately, the president's underlying admiration would surface during his prepared remarks at the dedication of the Robert Frost Library at Amherst College the following October.

Udall and his interviewers recount fruitless efforts by Udall to convince JFK to forgive RF for his mistake. RF sent the president a two-word congratulation for the successful outcome of the Cuban Missile Crisis—"Great Going"—but the chill lasted through the lengthy final illness of the poet. We know, from Kay Morrison's book and correspondence, that RF was deeply hurt by Kennedy's lack of any acknowledgment upon his return from Russia.

The Death of Robert Frost

During those final weeks in hospital, I believe my grandfather knew the end was near. He received visitors, retained a sharp mind, and continued to banter cheerfully with those around him. Kay and her daughter, Anne, spent long hours at his bedside, taking dictation for letters he was unable to write out. Mother kept a distance from her father; after visiting him on one occasion, she reported to those too far away to visit how RF had wasted away, unable to eat. These two strong personalities had gone through troubled times, and both had struggled to keep more dependent and unwell family members protected and nourished. From a woman's perspective, Mother would have wanted *her* mother to have had a different, less anguished life. But it was a different time and an unusual situation: Elinor Frost had craved a "life that goes rather poetically," as her husband stated, but physically the trials she and her husband were to endure were far more than she could have anticipated.

And yet my mother and her father had come to an understanding, to enjoy a sense of peace and mutual love and respect. In her get-well letter to her father, she said, "I think of you as 'Robert Coeur de Lion.'" We have her father's encouraging response—dictated on January 12, 1963, from his hospital bed:

Dear Lesley: You're something of a Lesley de Lion yourself. I am not hard to touch but I'd rather be taken for brave than anything else. A little hard and stern in judgment, perhaps, but always touched by the heroic. You have passed muster. So has Prescott. You have both found a way to make shift. You can't know how much I have counted on you in family matters. It is no time yet to defer a little to others in my future affairs but I have deferred not a little in my thoughts to the strength I find in you and Prescott and [Lesley] Lee, and very very affectionately to K. Morrison and Anne Morrison Gentry, who are with me taking this dictation in the hospital, and to Al Edwards in all his powerful friendship. I trust my word can bind you all together as long as my name as a poet lasts. I am too emotional for my state. Life has been a long trial yet I mean to see more of it. We all liked your poems [*Going on Two*]. It must add to your confidence that you have found a way with the young. RF

Upon his death seventeen days later, Alfred C. Edwards, former head of Holt, Rinehart and Winston and a close friend, was designated the sole executor and trustee of the poet's estate, for which he declined remuneration. Al was a loving, loyal, and lovable man.

I traveled back to Cambridge from Texas upon learning of my grandfather's death on January 29 at Peter Bent Brigham Hospital in Boston. It was an emotional time, with tension between my mother and Kay Morrison, and the difficult private memorial service we attended in the Appleton Chapel at Harvard Yard on January 31. At Amherst College, a memorial service had been conducted for Elinor Frost upon her death in 1938; a public service was held for RF in the same Johnson Chapel on February 17.

A decision was made to celebrate the poet during the groundbreaking of the college's Robert Frost Library. On October 26, 1963, President Kennedy flew on Air Force One with Arthur Schlesinger to Amherst College, where he received an honorary degree in what would be his last trip to Massachusetts. He then delivered a moving eulogy in the deceased poet's memory. Few at the time knew of their estrangement over the Khrushchev quote. Press accounts suggest that the president had rejected Ted Sorensen's speech for the occasion as "thin and stale." Instead, Kennedy's remarks that day were more personal. He came to pay tribute to a friend, reminding us of the importance of the arts in the life of a great nation and the importance of one artist in particular:

> For Robert Frost was one of the granite figures of our time in America. He was supremely two things: an artist and an American. A nation reveals itself not only by the men it produces but also by the men it honors, the men it remembers. . . . The men who create power make an indispensable contribution to the nation's greatness, but the men who question power make a contribution just as indispensable, especially when that questioning is disinterested, for they determine whether we use power or power uses us. . . . "I have been," he wrote, "one acquainted with the night." And because he knew the midnight as well as the high noon, because he understood the ordeal as well as the triumph of the human spirit, he gave his age strength with which to overcome despair. . . . [I]t is hardly an accident that Robert Frost coupled poetry and power, for he saw poetry as the means of saving power from itself. When power leads man towards arrogance, poetry reminds him of his limitations. When power narrows the areas of man's concern, poetry reminds him of the richness and diversity of his existence. When power corrupts, poetry cleanses.

It was a remarkable speech, and one of the last JFK would give us. I like to think that Jackie Bouvier, who adored RF and treasured mementos from the inauguration, had had a hand in her husband's tribute.

You may wonder why I do not have a personal account of this event. When my grandfather died, he left his Cambridge house and its contents to my mother, the property in Ripton to Middlebury College, and his manuscripts to Kay. It was generally understood that RF's personal library, left behind in Cambridge, would go to the new Robert Frost Library at Amherst College. The Cambridge house was quickly sold, and the books were boxed and sent to the college.

Mother had remarried in 1952 a widowed retiree from the Foreign Service, Joseph W. Ballantine, who served as head of the Far Eastern Division under Secretary of State Cordell Hull and had completed a distinguished career in China and Japan. After several years at Coromandel, in Silver Spring, and a time at the home RF had helped them build on his property in South Miami, the couple settled on East Tenth Street in Manhattan, where Joe taught at the New School for Social Research. Until shortly before her death in 1983, East Tenth Street was Mother's home, Joe having passed away in 1973.

As a graduate of Amherst College, Joe received an invitation to the groundbreaking ceremony; his wife, my mother, did not. As far as I know, no one in the Frost family was included. Mother's reaction to this dismissive behavior was understandable. She asked Amherst to return the personal library to her, and, over a period of years, she donated the books to New York University, where a relative, John Frost, served as librarian and where she could enjoy their proximity. Putting all of this behind me, I have visited Amherst College several times, the last when our Frost Symposium met there with former Special Collections librarian John Lancaster.

"Education by Poetry": Escuela de la Tahona

Once my grandfather was gone from the scene, I realized that Mother had already envisioned the next adventure in the "education-by-poetry" saga: her own school in Spain in which the whole family could participate. And not just any school! Imagine moving to the foothills of the Guadarrama Mountains, one chain of many along the Iberian Peninsula, and locating an eighteenth-century palace, the summer home of kings, surrounded by a historic town in which the one-time *tahona*—or gristmill and bakery that serviced the palace—would become the school, the Escuela de la Tahona. Here is how I once described the encompassing Castilian plain:

THE PLAIN OF OLD CASTILE: ON THE ROAD TO PEDRAZA

There were more shades of brown than there were trees,
And those few, scattered clumps of trees
    That could be found
    On the plains around
Were lofty, turpentine pines:
Sentinels grouped in long, straight lines,

The bark cut back to open veins
    For the bucket, which
    Would catch the pitch
Like sap that from the maple flows,
In springtime, with the melting snows.

Beneath the trees, a few lone cones,
    In the sandy loam,
    To be taken home
For the rich aroma they could provide
On a winter's eve, at the fire's side.

And out beyond the shade of pines,
    The fields of wheat
    Dried out by heat,

Their stalks of yellow and ochre shimmering
Like the rippling splash of gold fish swimming.

And off in the distance, red clay hills.
   Where peasants toil
   To till the soil,
Dressed in the habitual garb of mourning
Far from their village that August morning.

And a sliver of cloud stood against the sky
   Like a silver lance
   In the blue expanse,
Its shadow slicing across the plain,
Its grey reflection a wavering chain,

As when a knight from chivalric times
   Rode forth to smite
   From castle's height
The roving armies of lambs and sheep*
That raise the dusty dreams of sleep.

Our nostalgia was intensified
   By a lone stork's cry;
   Left behind to die
In the abandoned nest of a single tower,
It tolled for us the passing hour.

And the sunflowers watched us going past,
   Faces curiously turning,
   Their dark eyes yearning
To ask us what had brought us there,
Seekers of pure art and pure air.

*An allusion to *Don Quijote de la Mancha*, 1.18, "Adventure of the Sheep"

During the summer of 1963, Mother was in Spain with her granddaughter, Marcia Wilber (my sister's eldest daughter), looking for a summer home near but not in Madrid, where she could visit with her many friends from earlier years. What she found, in Old Castile, near the provincial capital Segovia, was part of the summer palace of the Bourbon kings of Spain. Known as *la tahona*, it was located close to the town's gilded wrought-iron entry gate. The property initially belonged to the Patrimonio (state); over time such royal sites were acquired by private owners. By the 1960s, the historic buildings of the *tahona* were occupied by the Quiroga family. Once purchased, the buildings presented themselves to my mother as a perfect location for a school.

The history of the gristmill and the surrounding town was part of its attraction, putting into context what was to be our family's next big adventure. In 1700, upon the death of Charles II, the last of the Hapsburg kings, Louis XIV of France, who would prevail in the subsequent War of Spanish Succession, sent his seventeen-year-old grandson to Spain to serve as Philip V (1700–1746), the first of the Bourbon kings. Philip was twice married. The fourteen-year-old María Luisa de Savoy produced a male heir before her early death in 1714. (When Philip abdicated in 1724, naming his son, Luis, as his successor, he was forced to return to power upon the child's sudden death from smallpox in the same year.)

Upon the death of his first wife, Philip soon married Isabel de Farnesi, who dominated the court and her weak and vacillating husband, returning the Crown to its territorial ambitions in Italy. We can see her Italian influence in the buildings and furnishing of the royal palace and gardens of what is today La Granja de San Ildefonso.

Drawn to the foothills of the Guadarrama Mountains just north of Madrid, where he hunted wild boar and other game, Philip V chose the area near Segovia for his summer palace because it was cool, wooded, free from Madrid's congestion and pollution, yet centrally located. The royal couple developed the classical gardens and fountains of the palace—often referred to as a "little Versailles"—importing much of the artwork and sculpture seen there today. The town of La Granja gradually grew up around the palace and came to include official residences and a glass factory that is the source of many of the chandeliers in the royal palaces of eighteenth-century Europe and today an impressive glass museum. At least two movies—*Patton* and *The Three Musketeers*—used the palace as a set. La Granja is but six miles from Segovia, a provincial capital noted for its Roman aqueduct, more than twenty Romanesque churches, a castle straight out of Neuschwanstein or its Disneyland successor, an impressive late Gothic cathedral, and as the home of two poets, San Juan de la Cruz and Antonio Machado.

Mother undertook this adventure as she had many others before and after. There were few legal papers, other than proof of purchase of the *tahona* and all its furnishings from the property's last owner, Antonia Quiroga. Ms. Quiroga had taught crafts there to Smith and Middlebury students under the aegis of the International Institute for Girls in Spain; the Institute helped provide the teachers necessary to launch our new program. Under her directorship, my mother hoped to help young American women learn foreign languages and immerse themselves in the attractions of a foreign culture. As was true at both the Frost School in Washington and the Maddox House at Rockford College, it was Mother's vision, energy, and charm that carried the program forward, guaranteeing its success, assuring that all the young women who participated were grateful and enthusiastic about their experience, returning whenever possible and keeping in touch as they scattered across the United States in later years.

The program was opened to girls, many of them friends of my sister's daughters, ages roughly fifteen to eighteen—the years leading up to college; the total number varied from year to year, but the aim was for around fifteen girls. The length of the program, at first offered for two months, July and August, was, in later years, reduced to a month or six weeks: the program itself changed very little over the years. There was an emphasis on reading—using their school summer reading lists and access to the small library at the Escuela. As you might imagine, Mother talked to the girls a great deal about American poetry and read from her father's poems. Often, a student would be attracted to the school simply because of the family connection. Others were exposed to poetry for the first time. We taught both Spanish and French languages and Spanish civilization. My husband and I taught classes and organized the many field trips, and I oversaw the kitchen and evening activities.

One of the school's graduates wrote an essay for her school's paper she entitled "Fiesta en España," noting that "the schedules consisted of three classes a day, four times a week." She described a course in Spanish conversation concerning such topics as NATO, economics, music, the arts; another in Spanish grammar and vocabulary; the third, a Spanish civilization class covering the Moslem occupation, Cervantes, or the castles in Spain, about which the students had to write. "To some," she added, "this may seem like a lot of work to do during the summer, but the atmosphere was perfect for this type of program," allowing for a family atmosphere and individual attention.

Besides frequent trips down the road to Segovia, the City of Monuments, we led one-day excursions, often twice a week with picnics, to such historic sites as El Escorial, Avila, Salamanca, Pedraza, Turégano, Cuellar, and Coca. Once in Madrid, we would include—besides the beautiful plazas, the Retiro park, and time for shopping and eating—the Prado museum, enjoying the extraordinary painters of the Golden Age and their followers. It was here that Mother was inspired to write her "Ballad of the Three Painters":

El Greco's reds and blues
  Velázquez's browns and golds
And Goya's lights and shades
  Are what the eye beholds.

El Greco's love of God
  Velázquez's of the Man
And Goya's of Mankind
  Is how it all began.

But Mankind trusts not Man
  And neither trust in God
It took these men of Faith
  To make the three tripod.

On Prado's walls are hung
  Their symbols still sublime
While outside rage the wars
  Of hatred, lust and crime.

Back home, I shared with my grandfather the excitement of studying the history of a people through its art, architecture, and literature. The excursions gave me a glimpse of the many layers of civilization: the Celtic Iberians; the early sea peoples, such as the Carthaginians; the Romans, so pervasive throughout Spain with their indestructible monuments. I never tire of walking in Segovia under the first-century Roman aqueduct; built with calipers without mortar, a balletic balancing act, it has withstood the onslaught of technology, noise, and the pollution carried by trucks under its arches.

Mother arranged in Segovia for a series of lectures to be given to our students by the well-known Spanish artist Joaquín Turcios Vaquero, whose father, the noted architect and painter Joaquín Turcios Palacios, and his Cuban wife were close friends of my mother's. We would go as a group to their studio home, overlooking the plain rising beside the Veracruz (Knights Templar) church, and sit on the floor in their beautifully furnished studio and balcony. The young Joaquín, casually dressed in loafers, soon had the girls—and me, for that matter—swooning more over the beauty of the man than over the art treasures he described.

In La Granja, the students enjoyed the informal living, often meeting up with the town's *chicos* for hiking up to the palace gardens and lake or just sitting in one of the many cafés. We always had at least one native speaker, and both my husband and I were able to teach the academic offerings. Stan was especially talented in guiding the girls around the historic landmarks.

The staff worked with me each year to purchase staple goods and organize the three-meals-a-day menu. When I first arrived at the Escuela, a very elderly woman named Eleuteria was the cook, a very important position. When she left, we were fortunate in discovering Petra Torquemada, the mother of our bus driver with a name famous in the Spanish Inquisition. She was an extraordinary woman who cooked and took care of us until we closed the school. But she was much more than that: she had an infectious zest for life; she could recite classic Spanish drama (usually Lope de Vega); and she had genuine affection for my mother and me. I remember visiting her in the state nursing home outside Segovia not long before her death well into her nineties; I was amazed at her dignity and strength.

The four buildings of the Escuela provided bedrooms for the students. There was a large dining area with long, marble tables, where we ate all our meals when called by a bell hanging from the balcony. Downstairs in the main building were a large fireplace, comfortable chairs, and bookcases. In the school compound, entered by a large, antique wooden door, we had both an upper and a lower patio. To help us with the shrubs, flowers, and small trees—watering and grafting—we called upon one of the palace gardeners, Francisco, to come in summer and cultivate the roses, phlox, and geraniums; we even had a pear tree and a small fountain with goldfish. In the lower patio we used an enormous millstone as a table around which we spent many happy hours discussing both local and world events.

When my children were small and traveled with us to Spain, they loved to help Petra water the geraniums and feed the fish and help Francisco find snails in the garden; they spent hours in the street with a young woman named Mari Cruz who later settled in La Granja with her husband and children. As our children grew older, they, too, became students. Melanie, the youngest, attended the St. Louis University program in Madrid as a college freshman; there she fell in love with Isidoro Reverte Alarcón, her future husband.

In the early years of the program, Generalísimo Francisco Franco, victor in the bloody three-year Civil War (1936–39), seldom visited La Granja, which had sided with the Republicans during the war. When he did come, he would enter on a back road—no helicopters in those days—and make his way to the lake high up in the palace gardens. There, his men would take his boat out of the boathouse, having stocked the water with trout from the adjacent nursery, and the caudillo would enjoy a day's fishing.

During his regime, Franco celebrated the date of his uprising on the Canary Islands on July 18, 1936, with a national holiday. Each year he would throw a diplomatic reception at the La Granja palace, including the luminaries of the diplomatic corps in Madrid. In preparation for the annual gala, electricity and water would be cut periodically in town as the palace grounds were lit and the flowerbeds tidied in advance. On the day in question, high-end limos made their way through the small town at great speed with windows drawn. The girls, excited by so much commotion, would seek out the U.S. embassy car and leave a note for the ambassador. Of course, no one from the town was invited, and the restoration of utilities was welcomed as soon as the caravan left town without so much as a salute to its citizens.

One year we took the girls in our bus over to Cuellar for the running of the bulls, mercifully absent from the fiestas in La Granja in those years. The local boys followed in separate transportation, meeting our group in the streets to await the bulls. Each time the crowd anticipated the arrival of the animals, a cry of "Vienen los toros" (the bulls are coming) filled the air, and everyone ran. It happened over and over; when the bulls finally came boring down on the crowd, most of the girls escaped. But Beth (I think that was her name) just stood there paralyzed. The bull lifted her in the air like a Raggedy Ann and dropped her unceremoniously before rushing on his way. The ambulance and medical crew were at the ready, but Beth picked herself up with no more than a few bruises, including a black eye. Her parents, whom Mother quickly notified by phone, took the news calmly, having another child with a broken leg from skiing.

In the final years before I sold the *tahona* and purchased a duplex just up the street, we were more flexible in accepting a mixed group for the summer program. I realized that once Mother could no longer run the program, and I was committed to my full-time employment in the States, I would probably have to sell the property and move on.

Once Mother's health failed, following the death of Joe Ballantine, my stepfather, in 1973, and following a diagnosis for Parkinson's disease that ultimately led to my mother's death in 1983, I continued the summer program in the Escuela until 1988. The school had been Mother's creation, and her spirit of adventure and imagination continued to sustain the program those final summers. It would be Mother's last adventure—an inspired showing of Spanish art, history, and the power of poetry in our lives. We as participants since the early 1960s had come to share a love of the place: long walks in the palace gardens, through the town of La Granja and into its surrounding mountain scenery; sketching the Versaillesesque fountains, trees, and flowers; or just breathing the mountain air while sitting in one of the many cafes or relaxed around the millstone table in the patio. The flexibility and adaptability of the school program was part of its fun. I believe almost every member of the extended Frost family had visited and come to appreciate the wonder of Mother's undertaking. Mother and I had experienced this part of my journey together, with its mutual enrichment in the arts, and in literature, all encouraged by being part of the Frost family. And then it was time to go.

Afterword

I have touched upon some of the themes and concerns that have filled the years with my grandfather, personally until 1963, in memory and scholarship since. The emphasis has been on the poetry itself, the close interaction of family and friends serving as catalyst—many of them strong, independent women. In my grandfather's search for recognition as a poet, the thread that runs throughout is a love of family, books, and literature: not only education by poetry and library collections but also art and aesthetics—exploratory, haphazard reading as a way of life. These themes will suggest, I hope, a navigable bridge between the memoir of memory and autobiography and the dry precision of the academic treatise, between what RF called the cavalier knowledge of the poet "in the wild free ways of wit and art," and the scholar's "conscientious thoroughness along projected lines of logic."

Despite family setbacks that included frequent illness and premature deaths, my grandfather's spirit and strength prevailed. He left behind for his children and grandchildren an inspiring message: act intuitively on limited knowledge; good does not exist without evil; poetry tempered by humor is a power that controls extremes; poetry, in all matters, provides a "temporary stay against confusion" and a spiritual lifting above the brim "toward Heaven." This high calling reaches us through his poems and asks of us a will to believe in risking the spiritual in the material. For some this will mean establishing a relationship with God. Above all, the power of poetry!

Part of my interest and energies in recent years have focused on the historical sites associated with my grandfather and his family. A little more than twenty years ago, several Frost scholars—the late Peter J. Stanlis and others—met over lunch at one of those seemingly endless annual meetings of what I believe was the American Literature Association, held that year in Baltimore. I was at home, close to retirement from the professional staff of the AAUP, when the phone rang. My colleagues in Frost wanted, and certainly I wanted, to arrange to meet periodically for a day in a location where we could converse without papers, media attention, or audience. There would be no minutes or summary report.

And so it began. We gathered that first year (1994) in the barn of the Derry Farm in New Hampshire—now the reception and exhibition area of the New Hampshire historical site, restored to its 1900–1911 appearance and opened to the public in 1977. We sat in a circle in small chairs and talked. Then, on that beautiful September day, we tramped around the orchard and wooded areas of the property, later developed as a nature walk by the caretakers and board. I had insisted, as the nominal secretary (with a small "s"), that we include not only interested scholars of Robert Frost but related enthusiasts. In particular, we started the custom, of which I am most proud, of including by invitation the curators of Frost collections, some of whom have stayed with us over the years.

Many of the places where we were hosted do have outstanding Frost collections in their libraries: Dartmouth and Amherst Colleges, the University of Virginia (where we have met three times!), Middlebury College, Harvard University, the University of Michigan, and the Jones Library in Amherst. UVA was favored in part because of the Frost family's closeness to C. Waller Barrett and his wife, Cornelia, and to Joan St. Crane and, later, Michael Plunkett, at the Special Collections Library. Besides Derry, we were able to meet in other places directly connected to the poet: Bread Loaf; Lawrence; the Stone House in Shaftsbury; and the Frost Place in Franconia. Twice—at Winthrop University and Bread Loaf (an offshoot of Middlebury College)—we tucked our group into a larger conference on Frost; and sometimes, as at Georgetown and Vanderbilt Universities, Agnes Scott College—where the poet visited some twenty-six times—and the University of Richmond, there were less celebrated associations. I know my grandfather would have approved, although he would have wanted to join us and to take a prominent part in the lively discussion. By meeting informally each year, we have facilitated Frost studies by finding old ways to be new and by providing and reactivating the old ties, both organizational and personal.

These gatherings of Frost scholars and others bring me back to the historic underpinnings of our goal, the ongoing examination and appreciation of the poet and his work: the Robert Frost Society and *Robert Frost Review;* the publication of biographies and critical studies and reviews; contributions of Frost materials to libraries' special collections; helping to raise awareness of poetry in schools and colleges, with a special emphasis on the high schools.

Those of us in Frost studies have learned to appreciate over the years the fine work done by the Robert Frost Society, whose current secretary, Jonathan Barron, edits the *Robert Frost Review.* Going over the Society's papers brought back memories of the fledgling Society and the efforts of Kathryn Harris, Richard Calhoun, Peter Van Egmond, and others to sustain the membership and a newsletter, facilitating an ongoing affiliation with the Modern Language Association. In 1991, Earl J. Wilcox (Winthrop University) edited the first issue of the *Robert Frost Review*. I have remained a member of the Executive Committee of the Society and the Advisory Board of the *Review*. We have renewed efforts to attract not only published Frost scholars but also those associated with Frost studies in less professional ways.

In the realm of biography, we are witnessing further progress in achieving a more balanced assessment of my grandfather's life and work. You can imagine how pleased I was to read Jay Parini's *Robert Frost: A Life:* at last, I thought, Lawrance Thompson's harsh, one-dimensional judgment has been laid to rest; a corner has been turned in the rehabilitation of the man behind the poetry! What so often perplexes the Frost biographer is the many-faceted nature of a man's public and private persona, the complexity and contradictions inherent, I believe, in the life of a dedicated poet, especially one who reached celebrity status. Excepting Jeffrey Meyers, the Frost biographers since Thompson—such as Richard Poirier, William Pritchard, John Walsh, Jay Parini, and Mark Richardson—correctly stress the centrality of the poetry and the remarkable humor, personal courage, and devotion to family and friends throughout a long lifetime.

I suspect that until there is a closing of the gap between the Frost scholars in academia and his admirers and fans in the larger public, there can be no comprehensive assessment of the man or his myth. And perhaps that is how it should be. Literary tastes change; biographical methodology is in flux, and the sensibilities and moral priorities often are confused at best. It is right that attention be drawn to RF's darker side, in his personality as in his work: we know he often blamed himself for personal tragedies beyond his control, was a man of many moods as reflected in his verse. But in the process we must not lose sight of Frost the love poet, the man for whom the "play for mortal stakes" used humor to convey the deepest sentiments, and whose craftsmanship stands unchallenged. In 1959, as mentioned earlier, RF wrote Trilling: "No sweeter music can come to my ears than the clash of arms over my dead body when I am down." He was right, and it is good that he was right. With the appearance of new Frost studies—together with the *Notebooks* and volume 1 of the *Letters*—that in themselves raise other perplexing or interesting questions, the need for further research and comment seems endless.

As the only family member to be deeply immersed in Frost studies, I have spent the past years since retirement from the AAUP in not only writing but speaking to the larger public about my grandfather: as a professor of Spanish literature and history, and as a member of the professional staff of AAUP, I had limited time for my Frost studies, but I found those years helpful in acquiring a general appreciation of higher education and the skills I would need as a speaker. I accepted invitations to make presentations on RF at a variety of institutions of higher learning, at poetry societies, libraries, and English classes. It amazes me that there are so many people hungry for good poetry, many of whom have only a superficial understanding of any poet, while others have loved RF's poetry since childhood.

I continue to find opportunities to teach Spanish literature and history, and for a time held teaching positions at Shenandoah and George Mason Universities. More recently, I have changed my focus to a number of adult programs in my area. I have developed four courses on the poetry of Robert Frost: a general survey of his life and work entitled simply "The Poetry of Robert Frost"; the others are "Robert Frost, Storyteller" (treating primarily the narrative verse); "Robert Frost, Love Poet" (reading poems reflecting various types of love: love of country; friendship; love of labor; love of nature; and, of course, romantic love); and "Robert Frost, Philosopher" (discussing poems that show an understanding of such thinkers as Emerson, William James, Bergson, Swedenborg, and Darwin)—the hardest course I ever taught! These adult programs also accept several offerings in Spanish literature (in translation): "Cervantes and the *Don Quijote*"; "Golden Age Drama"; and a course on the plays of Federico García Lorca. Combining the two academic interests, I was invited to Texas A&M University in Laredo to give a course on RF and the South American poets (Borges, Neruda, Gabriela Mistral, and Paz). It was very hot, but some of the students, passing what were then more peaceful border crossings from Mexico, took me across the bridge in the opposite direction, where I enjoyed delicious fajitas with my Dos Equis.

◆ ◆ ◆

Location, RF tells us, does not determine the strength of the Muse in producing poetry; inspiration must come from within. Yes, but the years the Frost family spent on the Derry Farm gave the poet the unstructured lifestyle he needed, as he said, "like a doctor's prescription." It follows that the Derry Farm and the other historic sites mentioned in the context of RF's life still have the power to awaken the imagination to reflect and meditate upon his legacy: San Francisco; Lawrence; Derry; two homes in England

(Beaconsfield and Dymock); the Frost Place (Franconia); the Stone House (Shaftsbury, Vermont); the Homer Noble Farm and RF's cabin (Middlebury and Ripton); 35 Brewster Street (Cambridge); and Pencil Pines (South Miami).

In San Francisco, RF's birthplace and early childhood, numerous associations can be found: a memorial plaque with several RF poems etched around its base, located centrally at the terminal roundabout for the trolley; up the steep hill, in Grace Cathedral, a magnificent stained-glass window (at the left front of the basilica in the apse) with its full-length image of RF representing the Humanities; and in the small Swedenborgian church, an inscribed Frost family Bible listing my grandfather's birth and christening.

Although RF spent the first years of his life in San Francisco, he found his poetic voice in the North of Boston region. In spite of financial constraints—inevitable wherever or whenever poetry is concerned—these historic landmarks continue to reach out to the young, to future adults.

Lawrence, Massachusetts, where the Frost family settled following the death of RF's father in 1885, is today an economically depressed mill town. At the time of the city's industrial growth, RF's grandfather, William Prescott Frost Sr., held a managerial position in the mills. Robert, Jeanie, and RF's future wife, Elinor, graduated with honors from Lawrence High School.

The high school as RF knew it no longer stands, but the town is proud of the poet's accomplishments. Not only were his poems being published in the *Lawrence High School Bulletin*, on which he served as editor, but he was active in sports and on the debating team; he was named class poet and co-valedictorian of his graduating class with Elinor. Through his family, RF made valuable contacts in Lawrence, such as the Reverend Wolcott at the Presbyterian Church and his future in-laws. The family burial plot is in Lawrence and was used by RF until after his wife's death.

The site is enhanced by the work of the Robert Frost Foundation and its dedicated volunteers: Gary Keating, and, more recently, Mark Schorr. With limited resources, the Foundation has organized an annual Robert Frost Festival, celebrated the naming of the Robert Frost Elementary School, attended by the poet himself, and reached out to children in a number of Frost-related activities both in the schools and in the library. Held the fourth Saturday of each October since 1997, the festival celebrates the poet in his hometown, about which RF wrote: "My year and a half of the district school, and my four years in the Lawrence High School were the heart of my education. They suited me perfectly." Before leaving Lawrence, living on Tremont Street, RF would receive word of the publication of his poem "My Butterfly: An Elegy."

RF's grandfather purchased the Derry Farm house and acreage for $1,800 at the turn of the century, hoping that farming would cure his grandson of his literary ambitions. Having assumed full ownership in 1911, RF sold the property to cover expenses for the family of six to live in England. In the 1960s, not long after RF's death, Stewart Udall—who served as U.S. secretary of the interior from 1961 to 1969—with my mother's full support, successfully persuaded the State of New Hampshire to acquire the property in Derry and to ensure that the National Park Service assigned it Historic Landmark status. When, in 1974, the New Hampshire legislature appropriated thirty thousand dollars for the restoration of the farm, the house and grounds were in disrepair. With the added support of several state governors and other state representatives, the Derry Farm was restored and formally dedicated in an outdoor ceremony on May 22, 1977.

Over the years leading up to the dedication, my mother served as the chief consultant to assist in the authentic restoration of the turn-of-the-century farm. Although only a few original pieces have survived—such as the Morris chair taken to and returned from England, my grandmother's dishes, and a few of the kitchen items—Mother was able to recall a remarkable number of details, including the pattern and color of the wallpaper, the sleeping arrangements, and the furnishings for the all-important front parlor and kitchen. The barn has been wonderfully preserved and is used as an exhibition area and space for informal talks.

Days before the dedication, the area of the Homestead had been inundated by the filming crews from the TV program *Old Friends and New*, directed by the late Fred Rogers. Touring the house together with my mother, Mr. Rogers was kindness itself, drawing my mother out to reveal many interesting details not known to any of us. In the parlor, she talked about the Morris chair and rustic lapboard used in Derry, in England, and back in Franconia.

In the kitchen, a favorite place for family gatherings at fireside, Mother explained to Mr. Rogers how her father, in discussing her daily journals, "never told me how to change my work. He only pointed out which parts he thought were good and I had to figure out the rest." This helps me understand why, when I examined the facsimile reproduction of her journals in *New Hampshire's Child*, there were no correction marks; her mother had taught the subjects of spelling and grammar in a separate class. In the barn, Mother pointed to the large hooks in the beams from which ropes for shimmying were suspended.

The coverage of Mr. Rogers's visit, carried in the May 22, 1977, *New Hampshire Sunday News*, includes a photo of Mr. Rogers placing a friendly arm around my mother's shoulders. For years, the resulting documentary was shown in the exhibition area of the barn.

At the dedication itself, my mother—despite her age and the onset of Parkinson's—stood on the front porch and read from her Derry journals and reminisced with obvious emotion about her early childhood on the farm:

> The farm was enough of a world to take journeys upon. A child (who else but myself) could take the long long path down to the lower pasture, eating the seeds of sweet fern as she went, to bring the cow home at almost dark; could ride beside the driver (who else but Papa) on the high narrow seat of the horse-drawn hay rake and be permitted to press the peddle that releases the hay at the windrows . . . ; could ride beside another driver (who else but Mama) with reins wound tight around her hands, trying her best to hold Eunice-the-horse in control as she swept the little sleigh (with bells) out of the Church stables in Derry Depot.

A journey, indeed! *Her* journey and now mine. Only over time did I come to realize the significance for my mother of this culminating event, the restoration and opening to the public of what had been for her a fairyland shared with a loving family, what her Mama and Papa likened to "sheer morning gladness at the brim."

At the event there were the usual remarks from many dignitaries: John Sloan Dickey, president of Dartmouth College; New Hampshire governor Meldrim Thomson Jr.; Frederick A. Tompkins, chairman, Derry Board of Trustees; David F. Hales, under secretary of the interior; the Honorable Richard F. Upton, president, New Hampshire Historical Society. Music was provided by the Pinkerton Academy Band. It was a memorable occasion for all of us in attendance that warm spring day, looking out over what had been the productive orchards of my grandfather's farm, the stone walls and Hyla Brook at the back of the property, soon to be turned into a nature walk for visitors.

Rick Holmes, a local historian in Derry, is completing a book on the Derry years of Robert Frost, based on archival information from Pinkerton Academy and the Derry Farm. One story that Rick has shared with me was written up in the *Friends of the Robert Frost Farm Newsletter* (Summer 2013), and it reinforces my faith in my mother's sharp memory of the Derry years. It seems Mother had informed the farm management that there was a telephone in the house during her family's time there and that her father used to eavesdrop on the telephone's party line so he could practice the short, crisp speech patterns and cadence of the New Hampshire farmer.

When Rick was unable to verify Mother's assertion, the reference to a phone was removed from the tour script. But then Rick discovered on eBay a copy of the 1907 telephone directory with a listing for Robert L. Frost, Derry, confirming that Lesley Frost Ballantine *was* right after all. At the end of the bidding, Rick (with help from others) won the auction, paying $398. He learned that there were 133 phones in Derry for a population of five thousand residents. RF's number was 33-4; on his party line there were eight other subscribers, each with a unique ring sequence; RF's was four short rings. The telephone directory is now on display at the Robert Frost Farm. I am sure there are many more stories to tell.

Every year, Professor David Watters (University of New Hampshire) runs a Youth Poet Program that offers New Hampshire fourth-grade students in public and private schools the opportunity to express their feelings about New Hampshire in a poem, taking the students to the Derry Farm, the State Historic Site on Route 28. I am especially indebted to Professor Watters (now a state senator) and other members of the Board of Trustees: Hannah Martin, Wilbur F. LaPage, Laura Burnham, the late Joseph William Pepperrell Frost, the late Jane and John Pillsbury, Robert K. and Doris Frost, Natale Brown, the late Maxine Kumin, and Claire Tiernan, just a few of those I have had the pleasure of working with following my mother's death in 1983, representing the many volunteers who have assumed responsibility for the restoration, management, and preservation of the homestead.

The Summer Literary Series, in which I have participated several times, still flourishes, as does the Hyla Brook Reading Series. In 2007, there was a big flurry over the decision to cut down the ancient sugar maple tree that stood outside RF's room on the farm. Chunks of the wood were distributed among several sculptors, including David Flood of Ipswich. A number of bowls were also made and shared with relatives. It was noted that RF's father-in-law, Edwin White, had left the ministry of the Universalist Church to devote himself to wood carving: "A relative of mine," RF wrote a friend, "left the agony of forced preaching in the pulpit of the Universalist Church for the comfort of turning wood. . . . He had been at it forty years and was still learning every day. A number of his fingers had been stubbed. . . . He inhaled more wood dust than I could have stood."

More recently, in 1993, a close friend, Dorothy Hatch, made a contribution in my mother's name to help the Garden Committee plant flowers around the house. Later, the Board of Trustees worked with local children in planting a vegetable garden based on RF's poem "A Girl's Garden." And, in 2012, I learned of the establishment of the Natale and J. Wilcox Brown

Endowment Fund, honoring two devoted trustees of the Robert Frost Homestead Foundation.

My sister, Elinor, my cousin Robin Fraser Hudnut, and I were appointed honorary trustees of the Derry Farm. My daughter Deborah Lee Zimic and I established a Lesley Frost Endowment, approved by the Board of Trustees and administered by Peter S. Gaucher, treasurer of the Friends of the Robert Frost Farm:

> The Lesley Frost Endowment is a fitting tribute to the person whose unsur-
> passed efforts to preserve the details of Frost's years on the Derry Farm
> have provided humanity with valuable insight into the life and times of the
> struggling poet during the most critical period of his literary development.
> Through her composition notebooks, an integral part of the Frost children's
> home-schooling lessons, Lesley offers the reader a rare and intimate glimpse
> into this family's unique history from 1905 to 1909.

Lesley Frost wholeheartedly shared her parents' fondness for the Derry Farm and supervised the restoration of the homestead and surrounding grounds in accordance with her childhood memories.

Although England gave RF an important boost as a poet, with publication of his first two volumes of verse, the Frost family, in renting several houses, never considered them home. The Bungalow in Beaconsfield, recently demolished, and Little Iddens in Gloucestershire (greatly gentrified but still standing) are more important historically in RF's biography than in the shaping of his verse. Keeping its memory alive, Frost aficionados in Beaconsfield conducted ceremonial events, including a dramatic program on the English Years of RF, to celebrate the one hundredth anniversary of his residency there; Linda Hart, Sean Street, and Jeff Cooper with others formed the Friends of the Dymock Poets, dedicated to Lascelles Abercrombie, Rupert Brook, John Drinkwater, Robert Frost, Wilfrid Gibson, Edward Thomas and their friends. Besides publishing both a newsletter and a journal, it organizes an annual program with speakers and a walk in the Gloucestershire countryside.

Until last year, I had not been inside the Frost Place in Franconia, New Hampshire. I had driven by when it was closed to visitors and greatly admired my grandfather's sense of location and view. Over the years, the restoration of the Frost Place has been hampered by a lack of funds. However, beginning in the mid-1970s, the effort resulted in what we have today. A number of poets, including Donald Hall and Richard Wilbur, have given their generous support. Open to the public spring, summer, and fall, it boasts the Center for Poetry and the Arts and a museum. The former executive director, the late Donald Sheehan, a classical scholar who taught at Dartmouth College, served for twenty-five years, offering a number of seminars and conferences at the Frost Place; the current director is Maudell Driskell. Each summer the director chooses a poet who, as part of the Frost Place Poet-in-Residence program, has the opportunity to write new poems and give poetry readings in the old timbered barn.

The Stone House, having been sold out of the Frost family following the death of Carol Frost in 1940, knew several owners before two women, Carole Thompson and Lea Newman, undertook the restorative efforts we see today, serving as president and vice president of what would become the Robert Frost Stone House Museum. Carole had retired to Vermont after thirty years with Reynolds Aluminum. She says she was "surprised to find a literary adventure with Robert Frost waiting in Bennington." It all started, she explains, with the formation of a small Frost discussion group; 1999 was the year of RF's 125th birthday, and, after putting up a small exhibit, she made contact with the current owner of the property.

Starting out with "no board, no organization, and no money," by March 2000, Carole's enterprise had been incorporated as the Friends of Robert Frost, written bylaws, and applied for tax-exempt status. The following year they signed contracts to buy the house and began the seemingly hopeless chore of raising enough money to execute the contract. With a one-hundred-thousand-dollar grant from the Vermont Housing Conservation Board and a two-hundred-thousand-dollar mortgage, the museum was able to operate: it was fully operational by 2003, and the mortgage was paid off in four-and-a-half years.

The primary activity at the Stone House is to operate the museum May through October. As part of the educational mission to raise the general public's awareness of and appreciation for RF's poetry, the museum supports a "Sunday Afternoons with Robert Frost" series organized by Vice President Lea Newman. Talks take place in the little red barn on the grounds of the museum, and the public is invited free of charge. Besides a number of poets—Richard Wilbur, Robert Pinsky, the late Galway Kinnell, the late Grace Paley, Sydney Lee, the late Franklin Reeve—as well as Frost scholars, I have participated twice.

The museum offers tours with trained docents to local schools. And, throughout the seasons, Carole and Lea concern themselves with historic preservation. They soon created a small orchard, in which one of the original snow apple trees, standing behind the Stone House and referred to as the "Heritage Tree," has propagated cuttings on two occasions (2008 and 2010). As a gift from the Friends of Robert Frost, I received two of the grafted cuttings of the "Robert Frost Snow Apple," both blooming in my backyard in Virginia.

We know Robert and Elinor loved to stay at their home at the nearby Gully, and we, as children, enjoyed the freedom and beauty of the farmland. Today, after being massively renovated by Norman Lear and Kenneth Noland, it is unlikely to be restored as a Frost home.

The Homer Noble Farm, mentioned earlier, was another place we visited, staying in the large farmhouse below RF's cabin. My daughter Deborah and I secured the key to the cabin, now the property of Middlebury College. We noticed how well kept the property was and were sorry to see the barn no longer there. Later, I learned that some intoxicated students had vandalized the farmhouse, used by the college for visiting dignitaries, smashing and burning furniture on a winter's eve. Jay Parini, one of Middlebury's distinguished professors and a biographer of Robert Frost, was recruited to educate the out-of-control youngsters in the value of a historic site such as the Ripton cabin and farmhouse.

Through his close ties with Stewart Udall during the Kennedy administration, RF purchased an additional ninety acres in Ripton in the hope of executing a land swap with the Forestry Service. Udall had been trying, since the early 1960s, to develop the Ripton area as part of the National Park Service, a move by the Interior Department that was strenuously opposed by fewer than two hundred local residents, by the state administration, and by congressional opponents in Washington. Wilderness preservation was not popular in Vermont, and RF said he was relieved that the land deal with the government had collapsed.

Soon after my grandfather's death, another effort was made by Udall and Senator Aiken, among others, to establish the Robert Frost National Historic Site at Ripton, forming part of the National Park Service, an effort once more opposed in Vermont. Finally, in 1966, the Morrisons sold the Frost homestead to Middlebury College for thirty-five thousand dollars, with the agreement that the Morrisons be allowed to reside in and manage the property for the next ten years. In 1969 Congress authorized the Department of the Interior to recognize the cabin and grounds as a National Historic Landmark; the town announced an "Annual Day with Robert Frost"; and the state designated the sixteen miles of Route 125 between East Middlebury and Hancock as "Robert Frost Memorial Drive." In 1976, the National Forest Service opened an interpretive hiking trail in Ripton with RF's poems posted along its length. Udall had to be pleased that, although government acquisition had not been achieved, he had contributed in many ways to the "indestructibility and immortality of Robert

Frost."

Those of us visiting the Bread Loaf Writers' Conference, still a going concern, are aware of the history of the conference as it relates to Robert Frost. Jay Parini and the late Peter J. Stanlis are among those who have brought greater understanding to the association of poet and conference: the richness of intellect and excitement a poet of RF's stature can bring and brought to Bread Loaf as a participant and as a magnet to other, younger talent. It is satisfying to look online today and see photos of current participants in the Bread Loaf program enjoying the property in Ripton, sitting below the cabin and at the Homer Noble Farm itself.

Although several homes maintained in Amherst, Massachusetts, prior to Elinor's death, the last on Sunset Avenue, as well as Pencil Pines, in South Miami, are no longer associated with the poet, they are recalled as important earlier homes. After Elinor's death, the Pencil Pines cottages became RF's home as a winter-months refuge, developed with the help of Hervey Allen. The builder in South Miami, with detailed written instructions from the poet in Cambridge, was the late Ralph Baldwin Lamb, who, according to his daughter, Ada M. Clark, was engaged by RF in 1941 to build the two cottages, prefabricated in New England and assembled on the five-acre clearing on SW Fifty-Third Avenue and named Pencil Pines by the poet. When both men met in Miami, after going over the plans, the two would sit for hours just talking, Mr. Lamb coming home late for dinner aglow from having shared great thoughts as equals.

◆ ◆ ◆

My journey with my grandfather has been a personal one, greatly enriching both *my* life and that of family members. For me it is a tribute to the perseverance of the poet's genius and to the power of poetry for those who surrounded him, many of us women. Yet, as I draw this account to a close, with its passing back and forth between those accounts drawn from memory and those retrieved from research, and while I realize that the two approaches are, in many ways, inseparable, I must hasten to warn my readers of the obvious conclusion: that the man and the poet are one.

My take, shared with you here, is mine alone; each of you will have the pleasure of experiencing a different journey or simply a single impact. For me, the journey began as a young child, with its sensations varying at each step along the way, and leading me to a more integrated and coherent appreciation of what my grandparents and the courageous supporters of his genius had lived and passed on to the future. I like to believe that the love of books, the heightened appreciation of poetry and art, and the excitement these gifts provide us daily have blessed your homes, as well.

As I cannot take it with me—and neither can you—join me in holding close the aesthetic power and beauty of the verses this poet and others have entrusted to our memories for as long as we have a hold on this planet.

Acknowledgments

Published sources for the book are drawn primarily from my own published articles, listed below, as well as the Derry journals of my mother, Lesley Frost, published as *New Hampshire's Child* (1969). These works, together with the standard research volumes related to my grandfather, Robert Frost, are acknowledged here, as they were in my earlier biographical study, *Robert Frost: An Adventure in Poetry, 1900–1918*.

Because this is a memoir, I have avoided endnotes and other scholarly distractions from the freer style of personal recollection even where it includes academic research, which by itself is fully annotated elsewhere. Lesley Frost left behind an extensive record of her life; her papers are housed in the University of New Hampshire Library, where they are accessible to scholars. Other papers, such as the surviving issues I inherited of the *Bouquet*, can be found in the Special Collections of the University of Virginia; others are found at Dartmouth College as elsewhere scattered around the country. Of particular interest to me in this account of my journey with my grandfather were my mother's unpublished notes, letters, poems, press clippings, and photographs, from which I have drawn extensively, as well as, of course, my own memories. The poems by various poets she quotes during her adventures recounted here come from her notes.

In the preparation of this book, I have expressed my gratitude to many—too many to list here—librarians of Frost collections at the many colleges and universities associated with the poet and his family, as well as colleagues in Frost studies: Mark Richardson, above all, for his prompt and knowledgeable help. I also wish to thank the editorial staff of the University of Virginia Press, especially Susan Murray, for her excellent copyediting from the snows of Maine. And personal friends—in particular, Saundra Maley, Eleanor Hegginbotham, Jean Aloe, and my co-copyeditor, Deborah Zimic—for their encouragement and expertise in the daunting process of editing.

Finally, none of this portrayal of my grandfather, mother, and other family members could have been undertaken or pursued without the feeling of love, concern, and encouragement I received from my own loved ones: my children and grandchildren. I know they and others like them will help keep the poetry alive in their memories and dreams.

I have received written permission from Henry Holt & Co. to include the quotations from my grandfather's work. Below, I have listed my articles on the poet from which I have written permission to quote:

"Between Poets: Robert Frost and Harriet Monroe." special Frost issue, *South Carolina Review* 19 (Summer 1987): 2–15.

"A Decade of 'Stirring Times': Robert Frost and Amy Lowell." *New England Quarterly* 59, no. 4 (December 1986): 508–22.

"The Derry Years of Robert Frost." In *Robert Frost in Context,* edited by Mark Richardson, 263–70. New York: Cambridge University Press, 2014.

The Frost Family's Adventure in Poetry: Sheer Morning Gladness at the Brim. Columbia: University of Missouri Press, 1994. Reprinted in paperback by Transaction Publishers with a new title, *Robert Frost: An Adventure in Poetry, 1900–1918,* and a new introduction by the author.

Introduction to *As Told to a Child: Stories from the Derry Notebooks,* by Robert Frost. Cheltenham, U.K.: Cyder Press, 2000.

"A Poet's Daughter at Sea, 'The Wander Bird.'" *Sea History,* no. 129 (Winter 2009–10): 10–15.

Review of *Homage to Robert Frost,* by Jospeh Brodsky, Seamus Heaney, and Derek Walcott. *Robert Frost Review* (Fall 1997): 88–92.

Review of *Robert Frost and Jerusalem: The Hidden Scenario,* by Sholom J. Kahn. *Robert Frost Review* (Fall 1998): 110.

Review of *Now All Roads Lead to France: The Final Years of Edward Thomas,* by Matthew Hollis. *Robert Frost Review,* no. 21 (Fall 2011): 86–99. An abridged version of this review appeared in the *Friends of the Dymock Poets Newsletter,* Summer 2012, 8–9.

Robert Frost: An Adventure in Poetry, 1900–1918. Brunswick, NJ: Transaction, 2004. This is a paperback edition of *The Frost Family's Adventure in Poetry* (1994); please see above.

"Robert Frost and Helen Thomas Revisited." *Dartmouth College Library Bulletin,* n.s., 32, no. 1 (November 1991): 10–17.

"Robert Frost and the Child: *Mother Goose* and "The Imagination Thing.'" *Dymock Poets and Friends,* no. 2 (2003): 1–11; *Massachusetts Review* (Summer 2004): 256–68.

"Robert Frost and the Majesty of Stones upon Stones." *Journal of Modern Literature* 9, no. 1 (1981/82): 3–26.

"Robert Frost and Susan Hayes Ward." *Massachusetts Review* 26, nos. 2 and 3 (Summer–Autumn 1985): 341–50.

"Robert Frost at Harvard: 'Imperfectly Academic.'" *Harvard Magazine,* March–April 1984, 51–56.

"Robert Frost in Spanish Translation." *Robert Frost Review* (Fall 1999): 1–14.

"Some Comments and a Question." Response to *Robert Frost Speaking on Campus: Excerpts from His Talks, 1949–1962*, edited by Edward Connery Lathem. *Robert Frost Review* (Fall 2009): 68–70.

Selected Bibliography

Brodsky, Joseph, Seamus Heaney, and Derek Walcott. *Homage to Robert Frost.* New York: Farrar, Straus and Giroux, 1996.

Burnshaw, Stanley. *Robert Frost Himself.* New York: George Braziller, 1986.

Cook, Reginald. *The Dimensions of Robert Frost.* New York: Rinehart, 1958.

———. *Robert Frost: A Living Voice.* Amherst: University of Massachusetts Press, 1974.

Cox, Sidney. *A Swinger of Birches: A Portrait of Robert Frost.* Introduction by Robert Frost. New York: New York University Press, 1957.

Francis, Lesley Lee. *Robert Frost: An Adventure in Poetry, 1900–1918.* New Brunswick, NJ: Transaction, 2004. Originally published as *The Frost Family's Adventure in Poetry.* Columbia: University of Missouri Press, 1994.

Francis, Robert. *A Time to Talk.* Amherst: University of Massachusetts Press, 1972.

Frost, Lesley. "Certain Intensities." *Ball State University Forum* 15, no. 3 (Summer 1974): 3–8.

———, ed. *Come Christmas.* New York: Coward-McCann, 1929.

———. *Digging Down to China.* Illustrations by Robin Hudnut. New York: Devin Adair, 1968.

———. *Going on Two.* With drawings by Robin Hudnut. Old Greenwich, CT: Devin-Adair, 1973.

———. "The Knapsack of the Open Book." *Publisher's Weekly,* July 7, 1928.

———. *Murder at Large.* New York: Coward-McCann, 1932.

———. *New Hampshire's Child: The Derry Journals of Lesley Frost.* Edited by Arnold Grade and Lawrance Thompson. Albany: State University of New York Press, 1969.

———. *Not Really.* Introduction by Louis Untermeyer, with illustrations by James Reid. New York: Coward-McCann, 1939.

———. "Our Family Christmas." *Redbook Magazine* 122, no. 9 (December 1963): 45, 97–98.

———. *Really Not Really.* Illustrations by Barbara Remington. New York: Channel Press, 1962.

———. "Robert Frost Remembered." *American Way* 7, no. 2 (March 1974): 12–17.

——. "Somewhat Atavistic." *Ball State University Forum* 11, no. 1 (Winter 1970): 3–6.

Frost, Robert. *As Told to a Child: Stories from Derry Notebook.* Edited by the Cyder Press, with an introduction by Lesley Lee Francis and illustrations from the *Bouquet.* Gloucestershire, U.K.: Cyder Press, 2000.

——. *Collected Poems, Prose, and Plays.* Edited by Richard Poirier and Mark Richardson. New York: Library of America, 1995.

——. *Family Letters of Robert and Elinor Frost.* Edited by Arnold Grade. Albany: State University of New York, 1972.

——. *The Letters of Robert Frost.* Vol. 1, *1886–1920.* Edited by Donald Sheehy, Mark Richardson, and Robert Faggen. Cambridge: Harvard University Press, 2014.

——. *The Letters of Robert Frost to Louis Untermeyer.* Edited by Louis Untermeyer. New York: Holt, Rinehart and Winston, 1963.

——. *The Notebooks of Robert Frost.* Edited by Robert Faggen. Cambridge: Harvard University Press, 2006.

——. *The Poetry of Robert Frost.* Edited by Edward C. Lathem. New York: Holt, Rinehart and Winston, 1969.

——. *The Selected Letters of Robert Frost.* Edited by Lawrance C. Thompson. New York: Holt, Rinehart and Winston, 1964.

——. *You Come Too.* Foreword by Noel Perrin. New York: Henry Holt, 2002.

——. *You Come Too: Favorite Poems for Young Readers.* Foreword by Hyde Cox, with wood engravings by Thomas W. Nason. New York: Henry Holt, 1916.

Lehmann, John. *Three Literary Friendships: Byron and Shelley, Rimbaud and Verlaine, and Robert Frost and Edward Thomas.* New York: Holt, Rinehart and Winston, 1983.

Mertins, Louis. *Robert Frost: Life and Walks-Talking.* Norman: University of Oklahoma Press, 1977.

Monroe, Harriet. *Poets and Their Art.* New York: Macmillan, 1926.

Morrison, Kathleen. *Robert Frost: A Pictorial Chronicle.* New York: Holt, Rinehart and Winston, 1974.

Parini, Jay. *Robert Frost: A Life.* New York: Henry Holt, 1999.

Poirier, Richard. *Robert Frost: The Work of Knowing.* New York: Oxford University Press, 1977.

Pritchard, William H. *Robert Frost: A Literary Life Reconsidered.* New York: Oxford University Press, 1984.

Reeve, F. D. *Robert Frost in Russia.* Boston: Little, Brown, 1964.

Richardson, Mark. *The Ordeal of Robert Frost.* Urbana: University of Illinois Press, 1997.

Mark Richardson, ed. *Robert Frost in Context*. New York: Cambridge University Press, 2014.

Sergeant, Elizabeth Shepley. *Robert Frost: The Trial by Existence*. New York: Holt, Rinehart and Winston, 1960.

Thompson, Lawrance. *Robert Frost: The Early Years, 1874–1915*. New York: Holt, Rinehart and Winston, 1966.

———. *Robert Frost: The Years of Triumph, 1915–1938*. New York: Holt, Rinehart and Winston, 1970.

Walsh, John Evangelist. *Into My Own: The English Years of Robert Frost*. New York: Grove Press, 1988.

Index

for and been granted permission to use the opening simile, "I think some-body's bow and arrow must have flown away together," a simile Edward later included in "Haymaking":

> While over them shrill shrieked in his fierce glee
> The swift with wings and tail as sharp and narrow
> As if the bow had flown off with the arrow.

RF was proud to echo his friends' assessment of his eldest daughter: "Lesley will hardly be one of the children much longer. She is as tall as her mother and reads a decent paragraph of Caesar off without looking up more than a couple of words. Sometimes too she does a paragraph of English writing I admire."

The road Mother chose—inspired by an early life of reading and writ-ing, she would explain—gave full expression to her boundless energy, leav-ing room for an early assumption of her role as family caretaker, especially where her mother and siblings were concerned. As the trajectory of her life evolved, she came to understand the dominant role her father and other poets would play in her public appearances and in her writings.

Having returned from England in 1915, she settled first in Franconia, New Hampshire, and then with her parents in Amherst, Massachusetts, where her father assumed a teaching position at Amherst College. In one year, she had completed her high school studies and was admitted as a freshman at Wellesley College for the fall semester of 1917.

Still very young, but mature for her years in the role she had assumed within the Frost family and in her writing, she managed to be a source of almost continual conflict at Wellesley. First, she found herself expelled from the court in the middle of a tennis match she was winning, and soon she was excluded from the tennis team altogether—without explanation. Papa wants Lesley to demand an explanation. And then matters get worse when her Latin teacher ridiculed her for having started Latin by reading it as literature, and for having shared her translations with other students; even worse, a French instructor marked her down for having composed a poem in French without first having studied prosody.

Letters that passed furiously—like texting today—between my mother and her parents in Amherst reveal how hard it was for RF and Elinor to stay out of their daughter's crises. RF wrote first to her and then to Professor Charles Lowell Young, a colleague in the Wellesley English Department (December 7, 1917). In his effort to intervene, he took to task both the Latin and French instructors, colorfully accusing them of stifling the spirit of a naturally excited student; but the spirit, he wrote Young, "will not be put off." He pointed out that just such a painful approach to learning he had experienced at Harvard—where his early poem "A Tuft of Flowers" received a "B" grade from his instructor; he shared with Young "four lines to the tune of Tararaboomdeay I once addressed to Sheffy [Alfred D. Sheffield] when I was a patient at Harvard:

> Perhaps you think I am going to wait
> Till I can write like a graduate
> Before I can write to my friends any more
> You prig stick, what do you take me for."

Years later Sheffield took the dig in good grace and asked to be forgiven his ignorance of young talent. While his message about the teaching of English, French, or Latin was a serious one, RF concluded his letter in a friendly appeal to an old friend: "But blast all this. What a father I am! I promise never to talk to you about my children again—any of them. That is if you will forgive my having talked this time and the last time and the time before that and so on back to the day on top of [Mt.] Lafayette. They are really not worth talking about. Lesley in particular is not. She is no good. You can tell her I said so." Let no one take the last quote literally—he was a poet, after all! Although it was true that, as the eldest and by far the most adventuresome of the Frost family's children, my mother never stopped worrying her parents, they soon realized that RF's well-intentioned meddling in the daily drama only made matters worse.

It would be my mother's rather fiercely independent lifestyle that defined the rest of her life and the extraordinary adventures it led to as my sister, Elinor, and I were growing up. And it was her imagination and particular sense of poetry as it guided the life that she shared with us and that I want to share with you.

Once again on her own, Mother sought ways to satisfy her passion for airplanes and flying and to express her hatred of Germany. With no money for flying lessons, she decided to find work in a Curtis airplane propeller factory in Marblehead, Massachusetts. Having picked up some last-minute tutoring in wood carving from a family friend who carved wooden toys, she was able to secure a drafting job at the factory, a job generally not open to women, and thereby raise her salary to fifteen dollars weekly, enough to cover her food and lodging nearby, working from seven in the morning to six at night, through to the signing of the Armistice. Her parents became increasingly worried upon learning that factory workers alongside her were succumbing to the lethal "Spanish flu" of 1918: Elinor Frost had become seriously ill, her husband less so.

The next two academic years, ones Mother would enjoy both academically and athletically, were spent at Barnard College in New York City. One puzzle for me—and for her later in life—is why she did not complete her studies at Barnard. She had transferred to Barnard from Wellesley for the spring semester of 1919, continuing her studies through the 1919–20 academic year as a junior in the class of '21 before joining her parents in Ann Arbor, where her father had accepted a teaching appointment. Yes, it was true that finances were a constant worry and also true that her father took a rather cavalier approach to any formal education, but Mother was a talented student and excelled at Barnard. The failure to complete the undergraduate degree would haunt her the rest of her life.

At Barnard she found herself challenged not only academically but also socially, culturally, and athletically. From the beginning, although she studied hard and suffered as any undergraduate over examinations and grades, her activities outside the classroom filled her letters home. And there were *many* letters, addressed sometimes to "Papa," sometimes to "Mama," or simply to "Everyone."

Residing her first year in Furnald Hall, she moved to Brooke Hall her second year. Through her father, she was able to spend valuable time with a number of literary friends and their families: Louis Untermeyer, Padraic Colum, James Chapin, Ridgely Torrence, Harriet Vaughn Moody (often visiting New York City from her home in Chicago). On one occasion, Harriet took her to the Ridgely Torrence Garrick Theater. After watching a performance of the Spanish play *Bonds of Interest* (*Los intereses creados*), she was taken backstage to meet what she called a "rottenly" behaved Edna St. Vincent Millay. She praised productions by the Shakespearean actors Walter Hampden in *Hamlet* and John Barrymore in *Richard III,* returning to several more performances for the thrill. She made passing reference in her letters home to the numerous luncheons and dinners spent with these and others associated with her father.

For a time, her sister Irma came to New York to study art at the Art Students League; while Mother accepted responsibility for her sister, they lived in two different worlds. Mother tried to keep her father out of her affairs at Barnard, but it seemed that everywhere she turned, RF and his relationship to her were noted. Louis Untermeyer embarrassed her, making her life at college more difficult, by praising as superior her poem "Pan," one of a number of student entries in a competition, in front of the actual winner and in front of her. Louis later apologized. When RF came to town, he often stayed in the apartment of the publisher Alfred Harcourt, but, here as well, the Frost family's perennial shortness of funds restricted his visits.

To her parents' dismay, Mother soon began dating men—in particular, Donald Schlesinger (spelled Slesinger at the time}, and, more seriously, Carroll Hollister, an accomplished pianist—and hanging out with a left-leaning group of students at museums, the theater, and many concerts.

In one adventure, she and Donald Schlesinger decided to "raid" the Columbia University publication *Columbia Literary Monthly* and take charge of the editorship. The literary magazine, a student monthly, had never admitted women to its editorial staff. Surprisingly, after considerable comment by the administration, the Student Council gave Mother permission to serve as an associate editor. Writing home shortly after on the *Literary Monthly*'s letterhead, Mother explained the outcome: "The magazine is over, at least till next year. At the last moment we had a terrible quarrel with the college organizations (King's Crown and Student Government) about a Jew being Editor in Chief, which held us up so long that when we finally went to press the printer refused to print it in the time we gave him. [Virgil] Markham is appointed Editor for next year." According to the Columbia University Archives, the *Literary Monthly* was discontinued and replaced by the *Varsity*, which would publish its first issue (volume 1, no. 1) in December 1919. Lesley Frost is listed as a contributor: "During the war," the editors comment, "[Miss Lesley Frost] was employed in the manufacture of army aeroplanes, and after the armistice she returned to college, where she is a leader in athletics. Miss Frost is the daughter of Robert Frost, the noted New England poet." In this issue of *Varsity*, we find two poems by Lesley, "Blue Heron" and "The Awakening," about the god Pan, which, as mentioned, she had submitted earlier to a college competition. Virgil Markham, who lived in the shadow of his father, Edwin Markham, the poet laureate of Oregon known for his celebration of the downtrodden laborer in his poem "The Man with the Hoe," did, indeed, become editor in chief; there is no mention of Donald Schlesinger as a contributor or on the editorial staff.

Mother seemed to take unusual pride in her accomplishments as an athlete. Representing the class of '21, she entered and won frequent tennis matches; the Barnard College Athletic Association invited her to join the Barnard Varsity Base Ball squad, where she played a number of positions, including pitcher; she won the Torch Race and Hoop Race at the Greek Games, a Barnard tradition; at two different Field Days (May 1919 and October 1919), she excelled in individual events (second place in the 40-yard dash and first in the javelin, a college record of 68 feet 10 1/2 inches; only ten other American women had thrown farther), for which she received a gold medallion now in my possession: next to a Greek goddess, perhaps Athena,

"Allez à l'enfer," the third Brethren shouted hoarsely, shifting his rifle and aiming for Gabriel's head.

Go to hell. But he was already there.

"Tais-toi." With a sweep of his arm Gabriel threw the sword.

The blade deflected the shot meant for Gabriel's face and neatly decapitated the man. His body pitched forward as his head dropped and rolled out into the hall. The many descended in a blanket to drape the remains and to feast on them.

The many showed him one man carrying the other out of the house and to a waiting van. He could have sent them to batter the vehicle and devour the pair, but he could hear Benait's voice ringing in his memory.

Unlike you, I am no monster.

Now all you will know is darkness.

Then Nicola's voice, sharp and disapproving: *Is that what Jesus would do?*

He was no monster. He was lost, alone, and afraid. He no longer knew who he was or what he would do. Killing these men would not change that, or make him feel repaid for his suffering. It would only further horrify Nicola, who had shown him nothing but kindness and pleasure, who had risked her life twice now to save his.

Gabriel reined in the swarms and watched through them as the remaining Brethren escaped. As he did, the blood he had taken from the human hummed through him, healing the last of his wounds and investing him with new power.

He retrieved his sword and gripped the hilt in a hot fist as he searched the room. Moths fluttering around the flashlight Nicola had dropped, eagerly seeking the warmth promised by the light, came to him. He needed to find her at once and explain.

Take me to her.

Chapter 13

Gabriel followed the moths through the tangled, over-grown ruin of his *tresora*'s gardens and into the woods where he had spent so many peaceful hours over the last century. More moths came out of the trees, joining the ones he had taken from the house and adding their individual ommatidial vision until he could clearly see all around him.

He found Nicola's motorcycle by the smell of the exhaust and the bright orange glow of the still-warm engine. She had propped it between two trees and covered it with leafy branches stripped from young trees. Yet there was no sign of her anywhere near the bike.

Through the many's oval, compound eyes, Gabriel followed a trail of the very faintest reddish orange, some small, residual trail on the forest floor that Nicola's passage had left in its wake. It wound in an erratic trail around the trees, through brush with broken branches and over fallen logs.

Gabriel tracked her for several minutes before the moths at last homed in on the dark shape of a woman. Nicola sat curled up against the black, gnarled trunk of a massive oak. She should have been dark red, the color moths saw human forms, but her color was lighter and thinner, as pink and delicate as a blush.

"Nicola." He stopped a few feet away from her, and breathed in. "Dear God. You are hurt."

"I didn't . . . I'm not . . ." The shapes of her hands

moved from her face to the ground, and her color darkened from pink to rose. "I'm fine."

"I smell blood." Remembering the reddish orange trail, he went to her, ignoring her cringing and using the moths to see the shallow gash on her neck. "The men who broke in, they shot you."

"No. I got cut by a piece of plaster from a ricochet." She covered the wound with her hand. "Did you do that? That thing with the bugs? Make them come out of the ground and the walls and everything?"

"Yes, I did. It is my talent." He knelt before her. Shame for what he had done seemed a distant, untouchable thing, but he regretted terrifying her. "I was angry and I lost control of it. I am sorry that I frightened you."

"I thought you were pissed at me, that you . . ." She turned away and her voice thickened. "You need to find someone else to be your *tresora*, Gabriel. I'm not the right person. I can't do it anymore."

"I understand." The last remnant of his heart died in his chest, and he went down on his knees. "Will you be so kind as to perform one last service for me?"

"I'll take you wherever you want to go."

"I have only one destination in mind." He extended the sword to her. "It is very sharp. If you swing it in the same way you do your baseball bat, it should go through my neck in one pass."

She took in a quick breath. "Are you asking me to cut off your head with this sword?"

"I am."

"Really." Her voice sharpened. "And how do you feel about me shoving it up your ass?"

"Vlad the Impaler may have thought otherwise, but that will not end my life," he told her. "I killed one of the humans who came into the house. Think of it as an even exchange."

"I'm not cutting off your fucking head, Gabriel." She stood up. "Stupid. This is so stupid, all of it; it's so pointless. Don't add to it."

"I agree." He would have to persuade her. "My life has been destroyed by murderers and thieves and liars. My own sister among them, feeding them information, betraying our kind. My friends are dead or indifferent to me. You wish to leave me, and you should. I have intruded on your life long enough. I have no wish to continue living in such a world."

"I'm not listening to this." She walked around him, heading back toward her motorcycle.

Gabriel followed and caught up with her, stopping her. "I don't have the strength to do it myself, or I would." He held out the sword again. "Please do this one last thing for me. I beg you."

"No."

He gestured toward the ruin of his house. "You may take the money and the diamonds—"

"*No.*" She knocked the sword out of his hands. "I don't want your money, or your diamonds, or your sob story. Your life has sucked; okay, I get that. But you can't put this on me. I'm not cutting off your head. Go to Iraq. They love doing it over there. Just stand in the street and yell out that you're an American oil company executive. Or Jewish."

"I understand. I forget that you are human, that such things are abhorrent to you." He reached for the blade. "I will find another—"

"I don't *think* so." She threw his sword into the brush.

He felt his blood run cold. If she would not release him, then the torment would never end. "Have I not suffered enough? Is my humiliation not complete?"

"Run the part about your humiliation by me again."

She did not care for him, could not love him. He understood her reasons: The Brethren had reduced him to a blind, unfeeling ruin, and he had badly frightened her. He had pushed her too far. But he would not make her feel responsible. She would never carry the burden of guilt over him.

"You read the letter Dalente wrote," he said. "Angelica, my own sister, was the one who betrayed us. She put me and her husband and her own son into the hands of our enemies. She knew about this place, and sent them here to kill Dalente. How can I live with what she has done?"

"You didn't do it; she did. She has to answer for what she's done." She stepped closer to him and jabbed her finger into his chest. "Maybe you should quit whining and go find her. Stop her from hurting other people."

"I'm too tired." His shoulders sagged under the weight of his sorrow. "Tired unto death of this ugliness, this horror. It never ends. How much more pain and humiliation must I endure before I have earned my rest?" And how many lonely centuries more would he live without her?

This time her hand connected with his face, her palm shockingly hard as it struck his cheek.

"You shut up," she snarled. "Pain and humiliation, my ass. You keep talking like this and I'll clean your clock so hard you'll wish that you were *back* in the torture chamber."

"Nicola." Gabriel felt appalled by her threats.

"I mean it," she insisted. "I didn't save you to listen to your bitching and moaning and watch you kill yourself. I did it because . . . because if I can keep going, then so can you."

She did care for him. "Tell me how."

"Well, for one thing you can stop trying to be so goddamn noble about everything," she snapped. "The Renaissance days or whatever it was like when you were human? They're over. If you want to survive in *this* day and age, then you *have* to toughen up and be smart. You deal with the murderers, thieves, and liars. Yes, it's awful, but that's the way it is. The world's full of them. You have to think the way they do. For all you know, I could be one of them."

"I do not think I am strong enough." Gabriel could taste her tears, hear the swallowed sobs beneath her sharp words. That seemed far worse than the blow she had given him. "They didn't break my body, Nicola. They broke my heart."

"You're breaking mine now." Her voice trembled. "Don't you know that? I know you're blind, but can't you feel it, what's happening between us?"

Gabriel kept his hands at his sides. "What I feel is wrong."

"Giving up, that's wrong. I lost everything that mattered to me ten years ago, along with everyone I loved, and I haven't thrown in the towel yet. I've still got a heart, don't I? It works, most of the time. Jesus, I hit you. You're making me nuts. Come here." She put her arms around him and pulled him down so that their foreheads touched. "I'm not giving up on you. There's a reason we found each other. Let's find out what it is."

Hopelessness dragged at him. "I did not intend to make you angry."

"Guys never do." She slowly rolled her brow against his. "Look, we can be strong together, right? We're survivors, you and me."

"Survivors."

"Exactly. So the world fucked us over; who cares? It doesn't have to be all about that. We're free." She grabbed a handful of his shirt. "Once I find the Madonna and take care of that, we can go wherever we want. We can get away from the holy freaks and the Kyn. We can *live*. We're good together, aren't we?"

He was infecting her with his despair. She was healing him with her dignity. Which one of them would succeed?

"I think," he said, very slowly, "that of the two of us, you are the noble one."

"You're crazy." She brushed her mouth over his in one of her quick, startling kisses. "And you're shaking." She turned her head and drew his down to the wound in her neck. "Take it."

Her blood wet his lips, sweeter than any honey, more tempting than any wine. "I fed on one of the shooters."

"So don't take much." She pressed her slim body against his. "I like it. It felt good when you did it in the forest. I want to feel that way again."

Her embrace and her softness proved stronger than his self-disgust. He drank from the bleeding wound, tasting her, savoring her as he felt the violent coldness inside him retreat. Madness and sorrow evaporated, replaced by a grinding, demanding need for more of her flesh. That hunger became so intense that his cock swelled between them and pressed into her flat belly.

He put her at arm's length. "If you despise me as much as I do myself, you should go now."

"Not going to happen. We need each other." Her hands slipped under the edge of his shirt, and she rubbed herself subtly against the ridge of his penis. "Every time I'm near you, I don't know whether I should kiss you or jump on you. I couldn't help myself in the shower. You feel it too, don't you?"

He gave his heart to her in that moment. Loved her, a human woman, as he would never love another. And as he stooped to pick her up in his arms, he found that he didn't care.

"Hello. Blind man." Her arms went around his neck. "You're going to walk into a tree."

"I know where I am going." He carried her back to the oak where he had found her, and lowered her onto the bed of moss there.

Gabriel wanted to rip her clothing apart and feast on her body, and feared he might do just that if he fell back into the darkness. He reached out with his talent, dismissing the moths and summoning the quietest creatures in the forest, the patient watchers who formed and wove their hungry threads into silken traps.

"Do spiders frighten you?" he asked as he stretched out beside her.

"No, I . . ." She went still. "Uh, Gabriel?"

He followed the bridge of her nose with his finger, gliding over the curves of her lips and chin and sliding down the slope of her throat.

"Did you ask me that because there are about two hundred spiders hanging over us?"

He nuzzled her hair. "I want to see you," he murmured against her ear. "Through their eyes, I can." He sent for a

very specific forest dweller, calling them from their bur-
rows in the ground and under the tree bark.

"Does this seeing-through-them thing involve their
crawling on me?"

"No." He took her hands and stretched them out over
her head as he rolled on top of her. "I'm going to do that."

The spiders showed him the long lines of beetles
marching up the trunk of the oak tree, flashing green bio-
luminescent light from their abdomens until there was
enough to illuminate Nicola's face and body.

"Your eyes shoot laser beams, too?" she asked, looking
up.

"Fireflies," he told her, fascinated to see that she had a
sprinkling of freckles across the bridge of her nose. What
other parts of her were dusted with these little gold specks?
She shifted under him and tried to pull her hands free, but
he held her tight. "Be still."

"I can't." She lifted her hips, driving them into his.
"I've been wanting you all day. All my life. I don't want to
wait another second. Hurry up."

"Shhhh." He put his mouth on hers, opening her lips with
his tongue and tasting her with slow, deep strokes. He lifted
his head and breathed in her gasp. "You will have me."

Gabriel stripped off her T-shirt, taking her bra with it,
jerking open his own shirt so that he could feel her breasts
against his skin. He peeled her jeans down and off her legs,
inserting his hands between her knees to coax her thighs
apart. The pants she had borrowed from Jean Laguerre
were loose enough for him to shake off, but he couldn't
wait now, not smelling the delicious dampness of her exposed sex. He reached down to push them out of the way,
taking his cock and guiding it to her.

She felt plump and hot and meltingly sweet against the dry,
tight bulb of his penis head, sending a surge of answering wet-
ness through his shaft. It had been so long—too long—since
he had put himself in a woman's body that Gabriel feared he
would spill his seed before he fully penetrated her.

"Oh, my man."

Through the many he saw that she was looking down at their bodies, her eyes narrow and her bottom lip caught between her teeth. He watched her face as he worked in the head of his cock, finding the angle of her sheath and pushing in past muscles tight with nerves. Her arousal eased the way, but the rest of her body was as tightly wound as his.

"Take me as you did with your breasts, your mouth," he said, kissing her brow.

"No soap," she whispered. "No water."

He moved his hand to cup her sex. "Feel how wet you are?" His fingers made a vee around his cock, massaging her with her own moisture. "So soft and smooth."

Gabriel exposed her clit and tucked two fingers on either side of it, pressing and stroking the insides of her labia but not touching it. At the same time he sank deeper into her, making her take more of him, feeling her lower labia stretch around the thickest part of his shaft.

Nicola had caught her breath; now she seemed to forget how to release it. Her eyelids lowered and opened, and she stretched under him, arching and tightening until he impaled her fully, and then she uttered a moan that nearly sent him over the edge.

Not yet, not yet.

He recoiled, pulling out of her until only his head remained embedded in her, and then thrust back inside her with one long, smooth stroke, angling higher, catching the tiny bulge of her clit and dragging at it. Their body hair tangled and her hips rolled as she shuddered under him, not there yet but speeding toward it.

Gabriel wanted to tell her how lovely she was, how good she felt on him, but the words would not come. His balls had tightened as much as his throat. So he showed her with his fingers and mouth and penis, working her as sweetly and slowly as she clasped him, putting his mouth to her breasts and his teeth to her nipples, licking the drop of blood from her lip before giving her his tongue and kissing her as deeply as he was fucking her.

Nicola thrashed under him, trying to force him to thrust faster, but he held her down and buried himself inside, feeling the head of his cock nudging the mouth of her womb. It was agony not to move, but he brought his hand to her breast and cradled it, holding it up for his mouth. He held her like that until she trembled and whimpered, and then he put his *dents acérées* to her breast, grazing her skin with them before he sucked hard, and then drew back and drove his cock into her as deeply as he could, once, twice, three times.

Pleasure so sharp it might have been pain surged out of him and gushed inside her, mingling their fluids and wrenching cries from both of them. Then Gabriel pulled out and up, working the beating pulse of her clit against the base of his shaft until she came again, the contractions dragging his cock back inside her body and milking the last drops of semen from him.

Gabriel slipped from her and eased to her side, his hand still cradling her breast, his softening cock caught between her thighs.

An eternity later, Nicola's eyes slowly opened. "Damn. I could have had that."

He ran his hand through her curls. "You just did."

"I could have had that this *morning*." She tapped his shoulder with a limp-fisted mock punch. "You held out on me in the shower." She touched her breast where his fangs had grazed but not pierced her skin. "You can also bite me while you're having sex with me anytime you like. It was . . . I thought I was going to . . . Well." She sighed. "Damn."

A distant rumble of thunder made him send the spiders to do other work, and he used the fireflies to see Nicola. "What color is your hair?"

"Mud brown."

He kissed the part in her hair above her left brow. The hair close to her scalp was much lighter than the rest of it. "I meant, under the mud brown dye."

"White. I'm really a little old lady of sixty who's had two hundred face-lifts." She laughed.

Even her laughter made him hard. "You should pay your plastic surgeon triple his fee. His work is flawless."

"It won't help us much with the holy freaks." She sat up. "We should get out of here before those two come back with reinforcements."

"You brought your bike here; they will think we left the house. My watchers will alert us if anyone comes into the forest. I want to be with you." He pulled her back to him and lifted her left leg to ease inside her. "You make me feel alive again. Feel so much, so many things."

"You've been locked up for a couple of years." She curled her leg over his hip, stiffening for a moment and then relaxing into the rhythm of his movements. "I think we can do better than 'damn.'"

Gabriel buried himself in Nicola's eager young body, taking her as many ways as she could manage. She never turned him away. Each touch inched him away from thoughts of oblivion, until he could not imagine not being a part of her, moving in her, kissing her and holding her as she found her pleasure and brought him to his.

He kept her unaware of the thousands of spiders above them, some serving as his eyes, the rest weaving a tent of protective silk around them. When he drifted off into the nightlands, he felt a contentment he had never before experienced.

In the nightlands Gabriel found Nicola standing over him, naked, a stiletto in her hand. It did not alarm him. Nothing about her could. Still content, he watched her use the knife to cut her way out of the tent of webs.

Where was she going? Afraid of alarming her, he sent his watchers after her.

The spiders skittered through the forest, catching up with Nicola in Dalente's neglected garden, where she was drawing water from the old well.

"Okay." She flicked out the stiletto and stared at it.

"He's gorgeous and sweet and sets my body on fire. I let him fuck my brains out because we both needed it. He needs someone to take care of him. Just because I'm falling for him doesn't mean I get the job."

She used the blade to cut up a shirt, and then soaked the pieces in the bucket of water before pouring a bottle of dark, watery fluid over them. Gabriel directed his spiders to climb up the sides of the well so that he could better see her face.

"I don't need a blind boyfriend. He doesn't need my shit. I'll just take him to the others and get him safe and forget about him." She sniffed and rubbed the back of her hand against her nose. "It's the only way."

Nicola was talking herself out of caring for him, something that after the events of the night he could well understand. Still, that she would abandon him so ruthlessly tore at him, until the many moved to where they could look upon her countenance.

The wet marks on her face ran from eyes to chin. She was weeping.

Unaware that she was being watched, Nicola put the soaked strips of fabric on the edge of the well, turned the bucket over to dump out the water, and then propped her leg on the bottom of it.

"If you love something, you have to let it go." The blade flashed as she brought it down, stabbing herself in the back of the leg. "So let him go, Nick; let him be free or you'll fuck up his life too."

Nicola. He almost sent the many to her, to wrench the stiletto out of her hand.

"It'll be for the best. He'll be happy. I'll get over it." She worked the knife from side to side. "Maybe in a couple hundred years."

A dark, deformed slug dropped with a bloody *splat* into a patch of chickweed, and she grabbed the soaked fabric, pressing a wad of it to the back of her leg—

"Nicola."

Gabriel woke with a lurch, turning at once to grope with his hands. He found her curled up beside him, her head pillowed on her hand, and ran his fingers over her. No gunshot wounds marred her bare legs, although he checked over every centimeter of her skin twice.

It had been his imagination, a fantasy that had played out in his head. But if it had been only that, then why had he been blind? In all of his dreams, he could see perfectly.

His hand strayed up to her face and felt the cool, damp remnants of tears.

Sometimes dreams are just reality turned inside out.

Gabriel lay back, pulling her to him and holding her against his pounding heart.

Although Michael Cyprien had been to Dublin countless times over the centuries, the lack of skyscrapers and two- and three-story buildings in the city allowed him to recall the place as it had been before the age of steel and concrete. Dublin was still something of a squat, overgrown village divided in half by the river Liffey, with its back against the pewter sea.

There were changes, radical and subtle. Perhaps the most lasting was the Irish resentment of British colonialism. Dublin displayed it very subtly, as with the street signs written in English and Gaelic, as if to remind visitors that the inhabitants had had their own language, even if no one spoke it anymore. Yet the Irish wanted respectability, and tried to project it with the many buildings prefixed with tall, white Grecian columns.

As Richard's people monitored all of the best hotels in the city, Michael had directed Phillipe to book them in a small, somewhat dismal bed-and-breakfast on Dublin's working-class northside. The proprietor, a widow whose wardrobe seemed to consist only of long-skirted black crepe de chine dresses, warned them that she had gone along with the city's ban on smoking in pubs and restaurants, and would eject them the minute she smelled tobacco or caught anyone lighting up in their rooms. To Michael's displeasure, the innkeeper proved to be one of the rare humans who had a natural resistance to *l'attrait*. It had been a relief to leave the place and take Leary down to the local pub for a meal.

"So you've just come up from London, then?" the dark, wiry bartender asked Cyprien as he handed him a glass of wine.

"Yesterday." Michael looked over at Phillipe and Marcella, who had taken a table in the corner of the pub and were watching the doors. Between them, Leary sat slowly masticating his way through a plate of corned beef and cabbage.

"Lovely cities the Brits have, don't they? Five or six thousand pubs in London alone. Can't build a proper beer in any of them, but you're in Ireland now, lad." The bartender patted his arm. "You're safe."

Michael remembered the last time he had tasted Irish beer. In that era it had been dark, rough, and almost chewable—not very different from this brew. "Thank you."

A couple of men dressed in overalls and smelling of fish came in, drawing the bartender down to the other end of the bar and giving Cyprien a moment to think.

On the journey to Ireland, Marcella had told him that sending Phillipe and Leary into Dundellan was too dangerous. She didn't believe his seneschal could make a convincing pretense of being yet another drug addict Leary had brought from the streets, or that Leary could be trusted at all. She disdained what she called old siege tactics and wanted to use more modern methods to gain entry to Dundellan.

Cyprien had disagreed. The guards would recognize all of the Kyn, if not by sight then by smell, and the only way to penetrate the castle's defenses was with humans.

Michael was not worried about getting caught—he had every intention of confronting Richard—but like Marcella, he worried about Leary. The man had sat in the very back of the passenger van, his hands and ankles bound to prevent him from making another attempt to escape, but leaving London had not disturbed him. When told they were going to Ireland, Leary had smiled and even giggled.

"Seigneur."

Michael turned to look into haunted dark eyes. "What is it?"

"I am leaving for the village now," Marcella told him. "I would speak to you privately before I go."

He glanced over at Phillipe, who nodded before speaking in a low voice to Leary. Cyprien paid for their drinks before he followed Marcella out of the pub.

"This plan is not sound," she told him as they walked down the street of old brick buildings and brightly colored doors. "Richard holds the advantage. Leary cannot be trusted. We are only three. If you mean to besiege Dundellan, let us return to America and raise a proper army."

"This is not the fourteenth century," he reminded her. "I cannot invade England."

"Very well. There is one thing more I would say to you." She led him around a corner and onto a street of furniture stores. "I did not speak of this when I agreed to serve as your second because it was not my place. Phillipe will not tell you because he is your man."

He lifted his brows. "No one wishes to talk to me?"

"Not in your present mood, my lord." Her mouth twisted. "We are all very fond of our heads."

"I vow not to touch a hair on your head. There." He spread his hands. "Say what you will."

"The bond a Kyn lord shares with his *sygkenis* is for life, but yours and Alexandra's is particularly strong," she said carefully. "Testing such a bond results in serious consequences, as I well know."

Michael frowned. "You have never belonged to a Kyn lord."

"My brother Arnaud lost his *sygkenis* during the Revolution," Cella said, her voice falling to a whisper. "Madness and sorrow nearly destroyed his life. It is why we came to America. To escape all of the things that reminded him of his loss."

Michael remembered how Thierry Durand had also lost his mind after believing that his wife had been tortured to death. "You think I will go insane?"

She shook her head. "I fear that you will be made the victim of your feelings for Alexandra."

Michael fought back a surge of anger. "The separation will soon be ended."

"The strain of being apart from Alexandra is affecting your ability to make rational decisions now. You are becoming more and more reckless. Such as your decision to bring Leary with us." She halted in front of a mattress and bedding shop that promised, NO MORE BACK PAIN OR YOUR MONEY BACK! on the advertisement posters plastered in the windows. "There is something very wrong with this man. Have you not heard him muttering to himself?"

"I have heard him muttering." It was all the man seemed to do. "His prayers appear to comfort him."

"He is not praying," Cella said sharply. "He whispers filth under his breath. He is obsessed with some woman, and plans to do great harm to her. What if he means to harm your *sygkenis*?"

"I have taken away his fear of the Kyn," Michael said. "He has no reason to hurt Alexandra, but if he tries, Phillipe will be there to protect her."

"I hope you are correct." She flagged down a taxi. "I will be waiting in the village. God be with you, seigneur."

Cyprien kissed her cheeks and helped her into the cab, standing and watching as the taxi headed out toward the northbound beltway. His temper had become quicker to flare since leaving the States, but they were all on edge.

A hand touched his arm. "Master."

"Take Leary to gather his quota," Michael told Phillipe. "As soon as he collects them, we leave for Dundellan."

Chapter 14

The captain of Tremayne's guard, Korvel, had just finished cleaning the wounds on John's neck when Alexandra and another guard came into the castle infirmary. Or, rather, John's sister strode in with the guard chasing after her.

"Doctor, you are not permitted in this part of the castle," the guard said in a strange, pleading tone. "If you would—"

Alexandra turned and punched the man in the face, knocking him across the room. He hit the floor and sat there rubbing his jaw and looking more like a crushed schoolboy than a wounded man.

"Hey, John," his sister said as she came to him. "Korvel, take Stefan and get out of here."

John knew that tone. "I'm all right, Alex. She didn't take enough to hurt me. It just left me with a headache."

"I'm the goddamn doctor; I'll decide what condition you're in." She pulled up the edge of the taped dressing. "That bitch. Another centimeter over and she'd have punctured your carotid." She eyed the captain. "Do I have to belt you, too?"

"You lied to me," Korvel said with matching chilly courtesy. "You broke out of your chamber and intruded on Lady Elizabeth's privacy."

"Oh, yeah?" Alex's expression darkened. "Lady Elizabeth was *feeding* on my brother. In *front* of me. I'm not thinking privacy's a big priority in her life."

The captain's brows lowered. "I will not trust you out of my sight again."

"Like you did before. Did you irrigate these wounds with antiseptic?" When Korvel nodded, she taped the dressing back into place and spoke to John. "I didn't know it was you under the mask at first."

"That guard over there"—John nodded at Stefan, who was finally getting to his feet—"he did something that made me unable to move."

"Stefan's talent is to paralyze humans," Korvel said.

Alexandra took out a penlight and checked his eyes. "When did the headache start?"

"I don't know. That woman—Elizabeth—hypnotized me to make me frightened, I think. It gave me some kind of vertigo, too. I was afraid that I'd throw up with the gag on." John squinted. "The light's not helping, Alex."

"Nauseated, photosensitive, and generally disoriented. Headache bad?" When he nodded, she glared at Korvel before adding, "I wouldn't have let her do that to you."

"You live on blood, don't you?" he couldn't help asking. "If it comes from me or another human, what difference does it make?"

"She didn't need your blood. She was doing it to mess with my head. I don't bite people, either." She pressed her hand to his cheek for a moment. "You're still my brother, John. Jesus."

"Doctor, you must leave here now," Korvel demanded, "before the high lord discovers your presence."

Alexandra gave John an expected hug, and murmured, "They've got you on candid camera, bro." When she straightened, she nodded toward the mirror across from his bed.

"Wait." John rose and took his sister's hand. "Have they been treating you well?"

"Not counting the threats and scaring me, yeah, they have." She stared up at him. "The castle isn't so bad. It's just like the mansion in my favorite Nancy Drew book."

The Hidden Staircase. John remembered the novel because Alex had demanded he read it to her over and over. In the story, the girl detective investigated a mansion haunted not by ghosts, but by a fugitive using secret passageways to try to scare off the elderly owner. Alex had spent months tapping the Kellers' walls in hopes of finding a secret passage. "Is it."

"We will go now." Korvel took her by the arm and escorted her out, locking the door behind him.

Orson Leary watched the scarred-faced man, Phillipe, as he drove the van from the pub into the city. Now that he was back in Ireland, he felt happier than ever. His savior had destroyed all the old fears, and now he could attend to the women properly.

He felt impatient with his escort, however. The man plodded along as if he and Orson had all the time in the world. "Do we go to see the high lord? His castle is in the country."

"We will collect the humans first," Phillipe said. "Where do you take them?"

"A special place," Leary said, feeling more cheerful. Once he collected his quota, they would go to the demon king, and he would be able to complete the work. "Turn left there."

Leary directed Phillipe to Meath Street, and from there to a darkened laneway where cars cruised slowly.

All along the street, clusters of two and three young men moved from the shadows of the shops and businesses to make quick exchanges with the drivers of the cars. Other thin and hungry-looking youths wove their way down the walks, going from cluster to cluster. As people came together on the street, they spoke briefly and traded small twists of cellophane and tinfoil for rolls of money.

Leary had once despised coming here—frightened of the disease and despair, always fearing he would be caught in the act—but no more. These weaklings, for whom he had sometimes felt pity, were nothing to him now. He didn't fear infection or contamination. He feared nothing. *This last time, and then I will be free of them as well as her.*

A shriek drew Leary's gaze to a thickset man who backhanded a young girl away from him. She tumbled into the street, where she got up on her knees and promptly vomited all over herself. The sight gladdened him, for if he was taken in this battle, surely others would carry on his good works.

Phillipe parked the van on a side street. "What is this place?"

"Needle Paradise," he said, watching the girl collapse on top of her own puke. "It's where they sell most of the heroin and crack in the city."

"You are to collect humans, not drugs."

"I always come here to make up my quota," Leary told him. "No one cares what happens to the addicts. They're easily persuaded."

Phillipe shut off the engine. "Make this quick, Father."

Leary climbed out of the van and walked out of the alley. A lone skeletal figure standing by the corner darted a look at him. From the way the young man was shivering, he was in need. Leary gestured with a folded fifty between his fingers. When the junkie stepped into the light to reach for it, Leary saw open sores on his arms and the yellow mark of jaundice on his face. He snatched the bill back just as the dirty fingers snatched at it.

"Wot d'ya want, then?"

"A quick one." Leary swept a hand toward Phillipe and the parked van.

"Both of ya?"

Leary shook his head. "Just me."

The junkie hunched his shoulders and trudged down the alley to the back of the van.

Leary opened the doors and gave the young man a nudge. "Inside."

"Wot's tha' smell?"

Honeysuckle sweetness wafted out of the back of the van. "Come, *mon ami*," Phillipe said, reaching out to touch the addict's neck. "You look in need of a rest."

Leary caught the junkie as he crumpled. "What's wrong with him?" Usually he had to drug or beat the humans he collected.

"I put him to sleep." Phillipe took the young man and put him on the floor of the van. "Bring the rest of them here, to me. I will do the same to them."

The Brethren interrogator found four more young men who were willing to sell themselves, and a lone dealer interested in making a buy, and led them all into the alley to Phillipe, who sent each one into a deep, sound slumber. Leary felt very happy with the arrangement, until he saw her at the end of the block.

"This is enough," Phillipe said. "We will leave this place."

"I've got to take a piss," Leary told the vampire. "Then we'll go."

The fair-haired girl stood with her hips against the back of a rusted-out MINI. She looked older than the other addicts, her skin as pale as milk. Grease spots and food stains spattered the front of the polyester uniform she wore, and as Leary drew closer, he smelled oily potatoes and fried fish.

It was a clever disguise, of course. The bitch would not lower herself to serve others.

Leary didn't want to speak to her—she didn't deserve such kind attention—but this was too public a place to do what was needed.

"Evening, miss," he said as he stopped a few feet from the MINI. Pretending to be fooled by her ruse would keep her from suspecting that he'd recognized her. "All by yourself, then?"

The girl stabbed the air with her middle finger. "Piss off."

"I don't mean to bother you," Leary protested with a phony, genial heartiness. "I'm looking for someone to share what I've got."

"I'm waiting for me boyfriend," she said, checking her cheap wristwatch. "He sees you here, he'll rip off your arm and crack your skull with it."

She sounded so real, but then, she always did.

"Getting a bit late." Leary glanced around. "Maybe he's not coming. You have something if he doesn't show up?"

"He wouldn't . . . Ah, fuck it." She wrapped her arms around her middle. "How much then?"

"No charge but the pleasure of your company." And that soft, flabby throat between his hands.

"You sods all want something," the girl said bitterly. "What is it then? A knobber in the backseat once I'm cranked, is that it? Or you take me back to your crib so your mates can have turns?"

Leary shook his head. "I like to see a bird get off, but I don't have to. You watch my back; I watch yours." He showed her two twists of heroin that he'd taken off the dealer. "A snort's better than a needle; you know that. Dirty needles'll kill you."

"Yeah. Got me friend Jamie just last winter." The sight of the drugs made her eyes shine. "Yeah, yeah, okay. But me first."

She was going through with it to the end. She probably thought to take him once he'd snorted the heroin. The stupid bitch.

"I'm a gentleman," he told her, gesturing toward the MINI. "We'll do it right here."

She took out a set of keys, and then stopped abruptly. "You're like that Percy in *Silence of the Lambs*, aren't you?" She started to back away. "You're not cutting me up like clothes—"

"Shut up." Leary caught her by the hair in midstep, ramming her face into the side of the MINI, breaking her nose and stunning her. "You think I don't know who you are?" When she sagged, he dragged her around the car and down into the shadows of the alley.

Rats squealed and disappeared into the nearest cranny. Leary hoisted the girl under his arm, clamping her to his side as he looked for anyone sleeping rough in the alley. He needed a dark place where the shadows ran deep, where no one walked and no one looked—

"By doze," she said, spitting blood out and twisting in the circle of his arm. "By doze, hugh broke it."

"Quiet." Leary pulled his elbow in tight and stepped into a narrow space behind a row of rubbish cans. "You talk too much." He dropped her onto the ground, pinning her wrists under his shoes. "You always talked too much." Blood roared in his ears as he checked the front and back of the alley for anyone she might command to stop him. "No one can hear you now."

Leary had to kneel in filth as he straddled her, but it seemed only fitting. The alley sullied his trouser legs as much as her neck contaminated his hands.

"This won't kill you," he told the girl as he cut off her air, and ignored her fingers clawing at his sleeves. Her pretense didn't fool him. "I know it won't. There are too many of you. But you'll not use this body for your evil anymore."

He had almost choked the life out of her when honeysuckle filled the alley, and a hand snatched him up and held him over the coughing, thrashing girl.

"What have you done to her?" Phillipe demanded.

Paralyzed, Leary could only look down at his dangling feet and the one he should have killed. He had not been cautious enough. He had failed. If he had been able to move, he would have torn Phillipe's heart from his chest with his bare hand.

Now was not the time to attack. He had to be more cunning. "I don't know," he blubbered through forced tears. "She wanted money. She threatened to kill me."

Phillipe put him down, although Leary still could not

move. The vampire reached for the girl, but she crawled backward, shaking her head and covering her bruised throat with one hand. She didn't seem to be able to speak.

"You cannot attack people like this," Phillipe told him. "Do you understand?"

You must fear me.

You must not fear the Kyn.

Take them.

You will not harm them.

Kill the women.

You cannot attack.

Something tore inside Leary's head. "The master said to take them and I obeyed."

Phillipe grabbed him by the throat, and for a moment Leary thought the young vampire might snap his neck. "We are done here."

Leary thought he would go into the dark place where it was safe, and never come back, but then all the voices came together into one. He feared, but he did not have to fear. He took, but he did not have to be taken. He killed, but he was not to be killed.

The one voice kindly explained everything to Leary as his body began walking on its own toward the front of the alley.

There was so much to do, but for tonight his work was done.

A soft blue-and-rose glow lured Gabriel from his rest, filling his eyes with the hazy colors of a sunset sky. He reached for Nicola, but found only soft moss and leaves under his hand.

It wasn't until he automatically blinked and experienced a momentary return of the blackness that he realized that the colors he saw in his mind were not coming through the shared vision of the many, but from his own eyes.

It cannot be. Benait blinded me months ago.

Gabriel stood, turning and seeing the blue-and-rose blur

turn to brown and green. He could not make out shapes, but the colors of the forest were there, just as he remembered them. He brought up his hand in front of his face, added the mottled green paleness of his own flesh to his vision.

Unconvinced, he covered his eyes with one hand, shadowing them. The light dimmed, and the blurred colors appeared only through the separations of his fingers. As he stared, the blurring sharpened a single degree.

His ruined eyes were healing.

"Nicola." Aware that the Brethren may have returned to the house, he didn't shout. "Nicola, where are you?" He had to tell her. He had to see, even in a blur, her face.

The only answer he received was the calls of songbirds.

Gabriel stepped out of the cobwebbed tent and halted just outside, shocked anew. In his dream Nicola had used a stiletto to cut her way out, and he had just stepped through that opening.

He nearly panicked, until he remembered waking near dawn and checking her legs. She had not been injured. She was not hurt, and he was healing. No more would he have to rely on the many to be his eyes. He could be free of them and look upon the world once more, a whole man.

I could go to Ireland and watch the look on the high lord's face when I present myself to him. I can see if Richard knew that I was left to rot in the hands of the Brethren.

Gabriel couldn't summon the cold anger he had felt for so long toward the Kyn. Benait had lied to him; that much was obvious from Dalente's letters. Had Richard believed him dead, he would have had no reason to continue searching for him. He would never know what had happened until he spoke to the high lord himself.

He had to know the extent of Angelica's betrayal, too. If his sister had to be brought to justice, he would be the one to do it.

Restless now, Gabriel turned and breathed in deeply.

Making love to Nicola had drenched him with her scent; he could track her in his sleep. He bent down and found her trail leading away from the tent and toward the house.

Why did she go up there?

Using his blurred vision and his memories of the forest allowed him to follow her scent path, but it veered away toward the back of the house rather than the front. Weeds had nearly overgrown the irregular sheets of slate Dalente had placed as a walkway through the garden, but Gabriel remembered the way it curled through the flower beds. Nicola had followed it, too, up to the old well by his *tresora*'s toolshed.

Gabriel smelled blood, and saw a pile of white and red left by the base of the well stones. He reached down and picked up a handful of torn, damp T-shirt fabric. He pressed his face against it to be sure, but he knew from his dream the blood on it was Nicola's.

A dream that had not been a dream at all.

He found her leather jacket left draped on the edge of the well by the bucket pulley. He ran his hands over it, feeling again the bulges in the lining. Yesterday he had not disturbed them, but now he found the folded seams that opened them and slowly went through the contents of each.

Nicola carried several rolls of euros, rail passes or tickets of some sort, and a folded book of traveler's checks, but no coins or wallet. One small, hard plastic case contained a dozen slim, bent metal instruments Gabriel guessed were lock picks. He also found a canister of spray lubricant, a pair of folding binoculars, and a long, flat piece of metal that he had seen on television as something car thieves employed. From the last pocket he pulled a bundle of identification cards, passports, and work visas.

Nowhere did Gabriel find the film, lenses, or any other camera accessories he had expected.

It was not photography or random accident that had brought her to the château. Nicola carried too many specific tools for him to believe that anymore. It seemed that she was the human thief that his interrogators in Paris had spoken of—the thief whom the Brethren had been trying to trap by using him as bait.

Why did she deceive me?

Gabriel carefully returned the items he had examined precisely where he had found them, and put the jacket and the bloodied fabric back where Nicola had left them. He turned and silently followed his own path to the spider-silk tent.

What else has she stolen?

Now that he knew this about her, some things made more sense. Why she dyed her hair: to alter her appearance; she likely did it regularly. Why she traveled by motorcycle: to have the means to get away quickly; a motorcycle could weave in and out of traffic and go places off-road where cars could not.

But what did she steal? Did she take relics and antiques from these churches and chapels she had claimed to be photographing?

Why had she kept this from him?

I would not tell a stranger that I was a thief, he admitted to himself. *But after yesterday and last night, are we still strangers?*

The enormity of his discovery would have bothered him more if she had been lying to him for a long period of time, but in truth they had known each other for only three days. Enough time to become lovers, but not to establish trust. Perhaps she was ashamed of what she did, and sought to conceal it from him for that reason.

Or she is up at the house this minute, taking the money and the diamonds that Dalente left hidden for me.

Gabriel found that he didn't care if she did take them for herself. Nicola had saved his life, but more important, she had salvaged his soul. She could have anything she wished for that.

In her own way, she had tried to warn him. *You deal*

*with the murderers, thieves, and liars. . . . The world's full
of them. . . . You have to think the way they do. . . . For all
you know, I could be one of them.*

Something touched his neck. "If I were a holy freak,
you'd be a dead vampire."

"Fortunately for me you are not." He caught Nicola's
hand and brought it to his lips. "I missed you."

"Well, I had to do some recon and get some supplies."
She placed a cold, thick plastic bag in his hands. "Some
breakfast."

"Blood?" He could see that it was from the dark red
smear of color, but decided to keep silent about his returning vision. If she could keep secrets, then so could he—at
least until he had some better idea of what she stole, and
why.

"Blood and more blood," she said, placing a small, box-
shaped object next to him. "This is a cooler with six more
units. It's fresh from the blood bank at the city hospital."

"How did you get it?" Had she stolen this as well? "A
hospital would not sell bagged blood to you."

"I sort of borrowed it," she said. "It's okay; it's type O,
and I made sure they had plenty in stock. They won't
miss it."

Was that how she thought of what she did? As borrowing? How did so generous and kind a woman become a
thief? None of it made sense to Gabriel.

"I picked up some extra bungee cords so I can strap the
cooler to the bike." She sorted through a bag. "Got jeans,
T-shirts, and some decent shoes. You're about a size nine,
right?" She moved closer. "Aren't you hungry?"

"I am." Hungry, and puzzled, and not sure of what to
do. "Where did you get the clothes?"

"From a men's sportswear shop in town; where else? I
picked out some long-sleeved tracksuits. They'll cover
everything, but they're cotton, so you won't sweat to
death." She brought his hand to a shirt. "See? Nice and
soft. I got them in solid colors: dark green, blue, and

black." Her voice went uncertain. "I didn't know what to do about underwear."

The Brethren had denied him the dignity of clothing. That she would care about such a small detail touched him deeply. "It doesn't matter. I am not accustomed to wearing it anymore."

"Well, I got three pairs of cotton boxers in case, you know, you decide you want to. I couldn't picture you in briefs." She tapped the bag in his lap. "Go on; drink up. We have to catch a train."

"A train."

"First-class sleeper compartment," she added. "I picked up some rail passes. They run the *Occitan* to the coast now."

She couldn't have stolen train tickets—could she? "I thought we would take your motorcycle."

"Well, I'm not leaving it behind." The blur of her face appeared in front of him, and he had to remember to keep his gaze fixed. "I remove the front wheel and crate it at the station as cargo. The train's good for staying out of sight while we travel during the day, and I think we need to get out of France."

That much he agreed with. "Where are we going?"

"The train takes us all the way to Calais," she said. "I'll put the bike back together there, and then it's twenty minutes through the Eurotunnel to Dover. From Dover, it's a couple of hours to my place."

She had done this before, obviously. "You are taking me home with you?"

"Unless you'd rather go somewhere else, yeah." She bent forward and kissed him. "That okay?"

"Very much so." Gabriel set aside the bag of blood and pulled her into his arms. "There is someone I should see in London first, to find out what has happened since my imprisonment. Will you take me to him before we go to your home?"

"Sure." She linked her hands around his neck. "Is

everything okay? You seem kind of out of it this morning."
Her voice softened. "I guess you've had nothing but one
rude shock after another."

  "I will, as you say, handle it." Gabriel held her close. He
would be lost without her now. "Only stay with me,
Nicola."

"The high lord wishes a progress report," he reminded her.

Of course he did. "Tell the royal pain in my ass that I'm not going to get anything done if he keeps sending you in here every five minutes."

"I have not bothered you every five minutes."

She sighed and jotted down her counts. "You want me to start clocking you, Captain?" She swiveled her chair around and saw his expression. "Look, this is a process. Processes take time. Testing can't be rushed, because it screws up the tests. And I'm working on stuff I haven't done since I was an intern and read about it in the textbooks. When I have something more definite than the number of weird blood cells currently running around in Richard's veins, you'll be the first to know."

"His condition grows worse." His voice rasped on the words.

"It's not going to get better on its own." Alex felt as tired as Korvel sounded, and focused on his pale, drawn features. "You look like you could use a transfusion or three. Has Elizabeth been tapping you?"

"No." That surprised him. "The lady only uses humans. I am well."

"My ass." She went over and checked his pulse. His skin felt cold and stiff to the touch, a sure sign of Kyn dehydration. His fresh-baked-pound-cake scent had also grown noticeably weaker. "Just out of curiosity, how long has it been since you've fed?"

"I do not know. Some days now." He frowned as if he couldn't remember. "My duties have occupied me."

Alex noticed a slash mark on his neck, a recent injury that had healed on the surface but that she'd bet good money was still knitting beneath the dermis.

"I can't give you a Tylenol for this, Korvel. If you don't feed, you don't heal. Wine by itself doesn't count. The pathogen needs a blood chaser, and it will take it out on you if you don't give it . . ." She stepped back. "Holy shit."

Chapter 15

The door to the lab opened and closed again. A certain tall, blond Kyn cleared his throat.

Alex didn't stop working, and sent a wish to the medical research fairy to open a bottomless pit inside the lab door.

"The high lord wishes to know what progress you have made," Korvel said from behind Alex.

If the captain of Richard's guards interrupted her one more time, Alex decided, she was going to beat him to death with her coagulyzer. A girl just couldn't rely on the medical research fairy anymore.

"I'm four more blood tests and one partial extrapolated blood absorption simulation ahead of where I was yesterday," she told him. "Half of one comparative screen farther than I was an hour ago. No farther along than ten minutes ago." She paused and stared at her watch. "Why, look, I'm still not any farther along."

"I meant, have you any reports prepared?"

"Not a one. I hate reports, and I really hate typing. How's my brother?"

"I have posted new guards, and instructed them to alert me if Lady Elizabeth sends for John," Korvel said. "Your brother tells me that his migraine has improved, but he would like aspirin."

"Aspirin promotes bleeding, and his neck injury hasn't healed yet. He stays on the Tylenol. Just don't let him drink any wine." She didn't look up from the scope. "What else?"

Korvel's eyebrows rose. "I cannot eat shit, Doctor. Blessed or otherwise."

"No, that's not what I mean. It's something Lucan said to me in Florida. You are what you eat. You are . . . Tylenol . . . and the wine mixed in . . . holy shit." She went to the computer and pulled up the profile on Richard's blood count. She heard Korvel retreating. "Hold it, Captain. I need a sample of your blood. Grab a stool and roll up your right sleeve."

Alex grabbed a copper-tipped syringe from the supply cabinet and brought it over to Richard's seneschal, who had bared his arm. She tied a strip of rubber above his elbow and tightened it.

"How will my blood aid you? I am not a changeling."

"You're normal, for Kyn, and you're as old as Richard, and you've hung with him for seven centuries, and he infected you. This is going to sting." She plunged the needle into one of the raised veins under his skin and drew a sample. As soon as she withdrew the needle, the hole stopped bleeding but did not immediately close. "You really haven't fed in a while."

He averted his gaze. "I have had no desire to feed."

That definitely wasn't normal. And why was the captain suddenly acting like a shy kid? "Anyway, depressed as it presently is, the pathogen in your blood should be identical to the one Richard had before he contaminated his."

"Contaminated?"

"You are what you eat, Korvel. Richard hasn't been eating humans." She transferred a few drops of Korvel's blood onto a test strip and fed it into the analyzer, running a second profile. "Hold on to your helm, big guy. Last time I did this, I found out a human with diabetes was actually a repressed vampire."

The efficient equipment conducted the tests and created a blood profile for Korvel, which Alex transferred to the computer and put up next to Richard's aberrant profile.

"Same cell counts, different DNA. Now watch; this is cool." She ran the absorption simulation she had been working on with Richard's blood. "Richard's DNA mutated, creating an extra, distinct set of chromosomes that should have dusted him the minute it happened, but didn't. Since our chromosomes determine what we look like, I blamed the extra set for his physical changes and altered physiology. Thing I couldn't figure out was why the DNA mutated. As far as I can tell, Richard wasn't exposed to any toxin, radioactive material, or other substance responsible for the mutation."

The captain peered at the computer screen. "What has that to do with my blood?"

"Human blood cells die almost immediately after they're removed from the body. Kyn's remain alive and active for three weeks. Now watch this." She ran the simulation of introducing human red blood cells into Richard's blood sample. "See how the pathogenic cells try to absorb these red blood cells, and then spit them out? It's almost the same type of toxic reaction that happens in the human liver when someone ingests wine with Tylenol. Richard can't digest whole human blood anymore."

"We know this, lady," Korvel said gently.

"Wait, there's more." She changed the simulation parameters. "I'm going to feed a little rodent blood into your sample. Watch what happens."

The same violent reaction occurred as Korvel's pathogen rejected the animal blood cells.

"I cannot feed on rats any more than I can eat shit," the captain said. "I also know this."

"But wait; there's more." Alex mentally crossed her fingers as she mixed equal portions of rat and human blood cells, and fed them first to Korvel's blood sample, and then to Richard's. A few of the cells in each sample were rejected, but the majority were absorbed. "I knew it, I knew it, I knew it. This is a fifty-fifty mix; half human blood, half rat. See? It's not discriminating as much this time."

He shrugged. "All Kyn can tolerate small amounts of animal blood."

"Yes, but this test proves that you could handle more if you drank it mixed in with human blood," she told him, running the simulation a second time. "The same way you can drink wine as long as it's mixed with human blood. Korvel, the pathogen needs blood. It lives on it. It's willing to tolerate even absorb foreign cells and substances as long as it gets its fix. If it doesn't, it's forced to adapt. Ergo, extra set of chromosomes and unpleasant physical mutation."

Korvel seemed dazed now. "I do not understand."

"I thought it was about physical changes. I'm an idiot. This all starts at the cellular level." She tried to think of how to put it in layman's terms. "Richard was forced to live on animal blood for years. To survive, the pathogen created a new set of DNA to process the foreign cells and attract the new blood supply. It changed Richard so that he would attract it. Like any evolving organism, it's simply been adapting itself according to its environment. If it adapts once, it'll definitely adapt again."

Korvel looked stunned. "You mean, this can be reversed?"

Alex remembered Elizabeth's threat. She'd have to cure Richard on the condition that he have John returned to the States first. Then Elizabeth couldn't do anything to him.

"We deny the new DNA what it wants, absolutely." Alex realized that a cure was also her ticket out of Dundellan, and felt like kissing the computer, the captain, and every rat in the castle. "It shouldn't take that long, either— Richard still has Kyn DNA lying dormant in his cells."

"Do I indeed."

Alex stopped feeling so great and stooped to pick up the plump tabby that had strolled in with Richard. "Hey, kitty," she said, stroking the affectionate feline. "Look what you dragged in here."

"Korvel, leave us."

"Yes, my lord." The captain walked to the door, turned back, gave Alex what she could classify only as a dire warning look, and left.

"My wife tells me that you called on her in her apartments," Richard said as he went to the lab door and locked it. "I do not recall giving you permission to do so."

"I don't recall asking permission." Alex shut down the simulation. She could tell Richard that his wife had threatened to kill John if Alex made any progress, but she doubted he would believe her. Elizabeth was his wife, the home team; Alex was the unwilling, uncooperative captive. "What can I do for you?"

"According to my captain, I killed the last of the humans we keep as blood suppliers. I cannot recall doing so, but I have lost most of the last two days." He removed his mask, revealing his distorted face and the thick layer of hair and long, bunched whiskers that had grown in.

With the hair in place, Alex finally understood what Richard had been feeding on. She looked down at the tabby, and ran her thumb through the fur around its neck, feeling a number of puncture wounds. "It's the cats. You're feeding on the cats."

Alex recalled all of the cats running around the castle. There were dozens, and half of the females were pregnant. He probably encouraged them to breed to provide him with a steady supply. And she was going to puke if she kept thinking about it.

"When the Brethren held me prisoner in Rome," Richard said, "they refused to let me feed. I endured the deprivation as long as possible, but in time it became apparent that I had to feed on something or wither away. My choices were limited to the rats that infested the catacombs, or the stray cats I assumed had wandered in from the city streets to feed on them."

"I'd have picked the cats," she admitted.

"Their bodies contained a greater quantity of blood, so I had to feed less often." He bared his pointed, feline teeth in a grotesque smile. "It wasn't until after some years of feeding on them that I discovered the Brethren had deliberately put both types of animals into the Kyn cell block."

"Jesus. Why?"

"They wished to see how feeding on animal blood would affect us." His pupils expanded to black diamonds as he limped toward her. "I expect there was some hope of soul saving or reformation involved initially. Then it seemed to become some form of entertainment for them."

"And hell for you." Despite everything she felt about the high lord, Alex experienced a small twinge of sympathy. "Nothing but cat blood ever since, right?"

"Not entirely," Richard told her. "I have never told anyone this, but I have managed to control my condition by also drinking a little human blood each day."

That supported her theory, and may have explained why Richard's Kyn DNA had remained dormant instead of being replaced by the feline-adapted DNA. "How little?"

"A teaspoon in every feeding, or a single swallow from a human. Any more than that makes me violently ill."

"Who do you get the blood from? Éliane," Alex guessed, remembering the *tresora*'s penchant for high-necked blouses.

"Providing me with sex and blood are part of her duties." He made it sound like secretarial work.

That clinched it. "You know, you're a total jerk with women, but we'll save that chat for another time. I have an idea, if you want to hear it."

He leaned against her dissection table. "Tell me."

Alex explained why she believed the blood of stray cats Richard was forced to live on had caused the Kyn pathogen to alter his DNA, the reason behind his physical mutations. "I think I can reverse it, too. You'll have to stop feeding on feline blood."

"Do you propose to starve me, as they did?"

"No." Alex checked the refrigeration unit, but saw her human blood supply bin was empty. She couldn't remember using the last unit, but she had been wrapped up in her research. "I want to inject you with a serum. It'll be human blood mixed with a small amount of feline blood. If that works, I'll add some Kyn tranquilizer to the next batch."

"Why must you tranquilize me?"

"I'm pretty sure this is going to make you feel sick, so the tranquilizer will slow down your body processes and help keep your reaction to a minimum. The presence of the feline blood should force the pathogen to digest the human blood cells. We'll have to take it slow, but by decreasing the amount of feline blood with each dose, I think we'll wake up your Kyn DNA and put the changeling process in remission."

He looked at her for a long, silent moment. "By doing this, you will save me."

She didn't want his gratitude, or the credit for what she was about to do. "You saved yourself, Richard. If you hadn't ingested human blood daily, you would never have held on to your humanity, such as it is, for as long as you have." She hit the intercom. "Korvel, I need a unit of human blood, please."

One of Richard's servants delivered the bag of blood and, after giving the high lord a frightened look, hurried out of the lab.

"How many humans did you slaughter this time?" Alex asked as she prepared the serum.

"I cannot say." He bared his arm for her and watched as she injected him. "What does it matter?"

"Humans are our friends. We like humans. And if we kill all the humans, we don't have any dinner." She withdrew the syringe and sighed. "I hate being a vampire. It's really freaking out my brother. Have I mentioned that?"

Richard got up quickly from the stool and turned his back on her. "I can feel it moving in my veins."

"It might make you puke." She looked around for an empty container. "Just relax and let it happen."

"Let it happen." His voice dropped to a low growl. "I am done with letting it happen. It should not have happened. Not to me. I am king."

The anger startled Alex. "Richard? Look at me."

He looked. His pupils had shrunk down to slivers, and his fangs shot out of his mouth, three times longer than Alex had ever seen them.

"Right, this is not working." She grabbed the bag of blood, but it was marked as human, type A. She took a sip from it and immediately spit it out. "Goddamn it, this isn't human blood. What the *hell* is going on?"

"You think to poison me." Richard whipped out his arm, sending a row of beakers and a microscope crashing to the floor. "I am king. I will never die."

"Then let's go for calming down the king," Alex said softly, not moving. "Someone gave me the wrong bag, Richard. That's what's making you nuts. Hang on, and I'll—"

"Bitch." He picked up the edge of a table and turned it over. Her computer exploded in a fountain of sparks, and the cracked console of the analyzer began spitting out sample strips. The high lord tore out of his cloak and dropped onto all fours, where his twisted body assumed a new, powerful configuration.

Alex backed away, turning to run.

From behind Richard leaped at her, latching onto her back with his curved claws and dragging her to the floor. His hot breath burned the back of her neck as he held her head down with one paw and began ripping at the back of her lab coat with the other.

"Richard." Alex could feel his erect cock jabbing at the seat of her trousers. Something sticking out from the side of his shaft penetrated her clothing like sharp thorns, and she remembered an article she had read about male cats having barbed organs.

She'd tear out her own throat before she let him put that inside her.

Alex screamed, throwing her head back and smashing it into Richard's teeth. He roared, digging his claws deep into her shoulder and ripping at her flesh. She tried to throw him off, but he had her pinned too well.

"My lord," a cool voice said. "Forgive me."

Alex felt Richard stiffen and fall over, and scrambled out from under his weight. A pressure dart planted in the center of his back wiggled back and forth.

"Doctor." Éliane put aside the tranquilizer gun and helped Alex to her feet. "You are badly injured."

"No shit. I think I owe you a huge apology." She looked over the *tresora*'s shoulder to see Korvel and Stefan rush in. "I think someone gave me pure feline blood instead of human. It made him do this."

"Who?" Éliane demanded.

"Lady Elizabeth," Alex said. "She wishes him dead."

"You have no proof," the captain said.

"She told me that she'd kill my brother if I found a cure for Richard," Alex said, groaning as she tried to feel how badly the high lord had ripped up her back. "Does that work for you?"

"Why did you not tell me?" Korvel demanded.

"Like you'd have believed me." She was dripping blood all over Richard, and saw his lacerated lips heal under the crimson splashes. "Wait a minute." She dropped down and wiped her blood from his face with her sleeve. All the hair around his mouth came with it, and the split in his upper lip disappeared. "Pick up that microscope and see if it's still working." Through the shrinking tunnel of her vision, she groped for a box of slides Richard had knocked to the floor.

"You are hurt." Korvel reached for her.

"I'll heal. Take him out of here . . . and get me some human blood. . . ." She saw Éliane's hands appear in front of her, and sighed as she fainted into them.

*   *   *

Nick led Gabriel past the curious eyes of the travelers in the crowded, six-berth couchette compartments and through the back of the car. "I think it's up here."

Few tourists bought tickets for the *Occitan*'s expensive first class, preferring the cheaper reclining seats in second class. The younger travelers gravitated toward the partying, college-dorm atmosphere of the shared couchettes. But Nick didn't mind paying double the fare plus the extra supplement charge so that they could have one of the lower, two-berth rooms. Gabriel needed privacy as much as she did, and that always came with a price tag.

She found their compartment nestled in the back of the very first car, which, aside from two well-dressed businessmen, seemed deserted. "Here we go." She steered Gabriel in through the narrow door.

He stood still. "I confess, I have never slept on a train."

"You need to get around more." She took his hands and used them to show him the room by touch. "There's a sofa here, and two bunk beds up top, near the ceiling. The bedding isn't the greatest, and you'll probably have to curl up, but they're pretty comfy. Soap, towels, washbasin. The bathroom is at the other end of the car."

"Is there a place you can dine?" he asked. "You've not had anything to eat."

"I grabbed something while you were sleeping back at the inn," she told him. "I can get something from the attendant when he comes around later." She checked the compartment locks before stowing their bags in the tiny corner cabinet. "This door has a security latch on it that can't be opened from the outside, even by the train attendants. We'll keep that locked." She went to the window and looked out at the station platform. She hadn't seen anyone suspicious, but she wouldn't relax until she got Gabriel out of France. "I don't think anyone was on the lookout for us."

He came up behind her, reached out, and with uncanny

precision pulled down the window shade. "I think we are safe here. All we have to do is occupy ourselves until the train reaches Calais."

Nick leaned back against him, letting the heat of his body melt the tension out of her muscles. "What have you got in mind?"

He guided her over to the small sofa and pulled her down next to him. "We should talk."

"About what?" She tugged down the zipper on the front of his jacket and slipped her hand inside.

He promptly took it out and raised it to his lips, brushing a kiss across her knuckles. "You."

"Not much to tell." Nick shifted closer.

"I want to know more about you," Gabriel said as he put an arm around her. "You said that you've been alone for ten years. You lost your family when you were only sixteen?"

"Yeah." Nick needed to change the subject. "I don't like talking about that, okay?"

He nodded. "Then tell me about the Golden Madonna. I have some knowledge of art; perhaps I know of it."

Nick started to get up, but he held her in place. "Gabriel, you couldn't possibly . . . It's all tied up with bad stuff that happened a long time ago. I just need to find it. That's all."

"But what is it, Nicola? A painting? A triptych?"

"No." She sighed. "The Madonna was this statue that my stepdad found buried under our house. The original owners built it on top of a bunch of old ruins. After this bad rain, Malcolm—my stepdad—found the edge of a wall in the garden. It ran under the house, so he started digging in the cellar to see how far it went. I think my mom was worried about the stability of the foundation or something."

"What did he find?"

"Well, a lot of old Norman stuff from when they came over and kicked Saxon butt. They built an outpost on top of a Saxon keep they burned down. The Saxons made that from parts of this really old Roman fortress. It was all in layers and stuff. Malcolm took pictures of everything he found and then covered it back up."

Gabriel frowned. "Why?"

"He didn't like messing with things. He was afraid of archeologists finding out about the site, too. He thought they were glorified looters." How silly that seemed now, considering what had happened. "The only thing Mal ever brought up from the cellar was the Madonna." She blinked back hot tears. "I don't know why, but it fascinated him. He tried to find out where it came from and who made it."

He rubbed his hand up and down her arm. "What did it look like, this Madonna?"

"I only saw it once; Malcolm kept it locked up." She described the statue, and added, "It didn't do any good."

"Someone stole this statue from your home?"

"Yes, and I want it back. I've been searching for it ever since." She bolted off the sofa. "I think I am hungry. I'll go get something to eat and be back in a few minutes."

Gabriel came after her, putting his hand over hers and making her close the door. "Did the thief kill your parents, Nicola?"

"I told you—"

He whirled her around. "Does the murderer have the Madonna?"

"Yes. So the Madonna could be returned to her shrine. Only I don't know where her shrine is." Was that her voice, so thin and cold? "So I'm looking through all of them. Any chapel, church, or holy place I can get into, I search. I'll find her someday." She shoved at him. "Satisfied? Or do you want to hear how they were tortured before they were killed?"

"Your parents were tortured?"

"My stepdad wouldn't give up the Madonna. Not until he . . ." She refused to sob. "Hey, we could compare notes, see if it was worse than what the holy freaks did to you."

"That is why you've been releasing the Kyn." The compartment filled with the scent of evergreen as Gabriel moved toward her. "What is done to us is the same thing that happened to your parents."

Revulsion filled her. "No. It's not the same. They weren't . . . You don't understand." She covered her face with her hands. "Please, Gabriel, I can't talk about them anymore. Please stop asking me questions."

"Forgive me." He bent down and kissed the tears from her face. "I only want to understand better what has happened to you." His breath warmed her cold lips. "You can trust me, Nicola. I swear it."

If only he knew. "I trust you as much as I can, Gabriel." Nick burrowed against him, needing his warmth as much as she needed air to breathe. "Come to bed with me."

Gabriel held her at arm's length. "But I have upset you, and made you weep."

She brought his hand to her heart. "Start kissing here, where it hurts."

A short time later Nick was breathless, half-undressed, and wedged between Gabriel and the sofa. She watched him expertly tug her jeans and panties down the length of her legs. "There are two perfectly good beds in here, you know."

He tossed her clothes out of his way. "Both of us will not fit on one berth. So unless you wish to gaze at me from afar—"

"Floor's good." Nick took the cushions from the sofa and pushed them together into a makeshift mattress. "I kind of miss the spiders, though."

He sat up, went still for a minute, and then grinned. "There are several dozen living in this car. Shall I summon them?"

"Don't you dare." Laughing, she tackled him. "I love you, but the bug thing is really . . . not so . . . great." Had she just blurted that out? She had. No wonder he looked as if he'd turned to stone, and acted as if she'd sucker punched him. "It's the dreams. You know how women are. We get emotional about stuff like that."

"Not you, *ma mie*." He pulled her down until only a whisper separated their lips. "Tell me again."

"It's not—"

"Tell me again." Gabriel rolled over, tucking her under him. "Tell me when I'm inside you."

"Gabriel." She wound her legs around his hips, offering herself to him. He pushed into her, hard and fast, almost knocking the breath out of her. "I love you."

Alexandra woke up naked and lying facedown on an uncomfortable pallet. Someone with very gentle hands was washing the wounds on her back, but whatever they were using didn't irritate or sting but soothed. For a few minutes she simply enjoyed the relief.

"I'd like the recipe for whatever you're putting on me," she said at last.

"Water boiled with willow bark and valerian," Korvel told her, "left to cool."

"Sounds herbal. You sure you boiled it?" Alex craned her neck to see the captain in only a pair of trousers, sitting on a three-legged wooden stool by the bed. Barely healed claw marks slashed across his chest in four placcs. "Did you lock him up?"

"My master is sleeping."

"That's not what I asked you, Korvel."

"Dr. Keller, I cannot *lock up* the high lord of the Darkyn." He rose, picked up the stool, and moved it closer to her upper body. "Be still. I am not finished."

Alex laid her cheek on her folded hands and studied Korvel's face. In the firelight, like now, he seemed more ordinary than movie-star handsome, but there was something compelling about him. "What's your talent?"

He didn't answer, but squeezed out a soaked cloth over her back, letting the warm liquid pour over her wounds.

"I can read the minds of killers," she offered. "Is yours worse than mine?"

"Kyn do not trade tales about talent." He pulled up the

sheet covering her legs and hips and tucked it around her. "It is undignified."

"So it's worse than mine."

He almost smiled. "Does anything discourage you?"

"The Bush administration, our foreign policy, and Alison getting kicked off *Project Runway*," she told him. "So on a scale from one to ten, how bad is your talent?"

"It has never failed me." Korvel got to his feet. "Even when I wish that it would."

Under the grim all-business, fight-to-the-death warrior facade was, Alex suspected, a very nice man. Why else would he be playing her nurse?

"I'd help you, but intelligent design screwed up our arm-to-back motor skills." She tested her shoulders, moving them and wincing. "He really did a number on me, huh?"

He nodded. "You do not heal like us."

"When I'm not being held hostage, I actually heal pretty fast. Being here has slowed me down on a couple of levels." She frowned as a clear image of herself being beaten with a copper pipe passed through her mind. "Quit thinking about killing me."

"I do not wish to *kill* you."

She didn't like the way he said it, at least until she breathed in. "You know, when you get pissed off or upset, you smell like vanilla pound cake."

"Larkspur," he said, coming over and looking down at her face. "When I go to wash at dawn, I can sometimes smell lavender on my clothes. From you."

"That's nice. Makes me feel all warm and fuzzy." Too warm, too fuzzy. "And a bit like a skunk."

"You do not smell like one."

Alex was staring at his mouth, but she didn't know quite why. Then she did, all in a rush, as soon as her breasts tightened and something very neglected and sulky stirred between her legs.

Which brought home some facts: She was naked, alone

with Korvel, and in his bed. In a very small room with no real ventilation. "I have to get out of here."

"Yes." Korvel didn't move. "Unfortunately, so do I. It is not your doing, Doctor."

Pornography popped into her head, starring the captain of the guard and herself. "You know what I'm thinking?"

"My talent put the thoughts in your mind." He flashed his fangs as he spoke. "No human woman can resist me. Neither, I fear, can you."

"You can make any woman want to . . . *fuck*." She pushed herself up with her arms. "Give me my clothes." She remembered Richard had torn them from her. "Give me *some* clothes. And turn off your talent. This minute."

He brought a light robe to her and went to stand by the fireplace, averting his gaze. "I apologize. I have always controlled myself before this."

Alex wanted his hands on her breasts. His tongue in her mouth. His cock in her pussy. "Try harder."

"I am not seducing you," he pointed out. "However much I wish to at this moment."

Alex felt herself go wet. "Yeah. No. Christ, I am out of here." She went to the door, startled by how sore she was and how slowly she was moving, and stopped there. "Thank you for patching me up, Captain."

"I am at your service, my lady."

"God, don't ever say that to me again." She opened the door and hobbled out.

Chapter 16

Although some Brits returning from the Continent grumbled incessantly about it, Nick never minded riding at the back of the Eurotunnel shuttle. The shuttle company put bikers in the back for safety reasons, but all Nick cared about was that they let her book and pay for her ticket online, and the thirty-five-minute trip from Calais to Folkstone meant that she and Gabriel didn't even have to get off the bike. Besides, the most interesting passengers on the trip were always the bikers.

Making the channel crossing today were mostly weekend solo bikers, but one German couple on a wicked blackand-silver Triumph Tiger outfitted for transcon touring parked next to her and exchanged admiring looks. Knowing Gabriel couldn't see it, Nick described the couple's bike to him.

"You sound as another woman would when she describes a diamond necklace," he teased.

"I can't ride a necklace," she told him. "That bike I could take around the world. In a heartbeat."

"BMW GS?" the German man asked her.

Nick seesawed her hand, making the man's wife giggle. Her German was nonexistent, so she pointed to the different parts of the bike she'd rebuilt and named the make of the new parts. She then pointed to the reinforced molded luggage containers fastened to the custom rack at the back of the Triumph, and fluttered her hand over her heart.

Gabriel unexpectedly said something in very precise,

rapid German to the couple, who responded enthusiastically. When he had finished, he said to Nick, "I told them that you admired their motorcycle. They are envious of your ingenuity with your engine refittings."

"*Danke,*" she said to the couple. At least she could say that much. She glanced back at Gabriel. "I should take you with me every time I cross over. You could be my interpreter."

"I have never traveled through the Channel Tunnel," Gabriel said. "I suppose it was the thought of being under so much water."

"We're forty-five meters down. We could swim, but it takes a whole day and my bike would rust to pieces." She leaned back against him and enjoyed the way his arms came up around her waist to pull her closer. "I was really bummed to hear that the company that built this had to file for bankruptcy over the summer. I'd hate it if they have to shut it down; it's the fastest way to get from France to England and back again."

He kissed the side of her neck. "You are impatient about everything."

"You didn't think so on the train from Toulouse," she reminded him.

Nick wasn't quite sure how to classify what Gabriel did to her. He had sex with her, of course. That was the clinical way of looking at it. Over the last couple of days they had gone at it like bunnies. But he also made love to her, the way the heroes did in chick movies. And then he took her, too, as dominantly and erotically as some of the Emma Holly novels she'd read.

"That trip should have taken much longer," Gabriel insisted. "They drove the train too fast, and then you rushed us through the station."

Nick thought about the Interpol bulletin she'd seen when they'd passed through the station at Calais. Whoever had given them the description of her had told the artist that she was a boy, but despite that it was a fairly accurate

sketch of her face on it. The list of properties she'd bur-
glarized didn't include the ones where she'd found Kyn
and released them, so the holy freaks were definitely involved.

She couldn't tell Gabriel she was being chased by Interpol any more than she could explain about her parents;
he'd want to know all the details. She also wondered if the
same bulletins were being posted around London, and how
she would feel if he found out she was a thief—and a liar.

He won't find out. He can't see me or them.

Nick knew she might be able to keep the truth from
Gabriel because he was blind, but that wouldn't keep the
authorities away. They could see her just fine, and with Father Claudio and the men from the house in Toulouse helping them, they'd soon change the description on the
bulletin from a boy to a girl.

As the shuttle stopped at Folkstone station and the vehicles were driven off, Nick's nerves got the better of her. She
wasn't sure she could even do this. "How long do you think
this meeting with your friend in the city is going to take?"

"Only an hour at the most."

Not much time for her. "Can he get you in touch with
your friends? I mean, the ones who are Kyn?"

"Croft serves the suzerain of London. He can put me in
contact with any Kyn in the world." Gabriel tugged at a
piece of her hair. "Why do you ask?"

"Just curious." She saw a customs officer and two police constables approaching the rear of the shuttle, led by
an elderly man walking with a familiar-looking cane.
"Gabriel, we might not make that meeting."

His arms tightened around her. "What is it?"

"Father Claudio is here. They're checking each shuttle
deck." She saw Claudio pointing at her and Gabriel, and
the two constables picked up their pace. "Fuck me; he just
made us." She turned, checking the clearance in front and
behind the bike before kicking up the center stand. "Strap
on the helmet and hold on to me."

The German couple on the beautiful Triumph both looked back as Nick started her engine, and the husband glanced from Nick to the approaching constables and frowned. His wife whispered something in his ear, and he winked at Nick before he rolled his bike forward. The Triumph's bulk blocked the side entry and gave Nick enough clearance to go around him.

No matter what country they came from, in an emergency bikers were always happy to give you a hand.

"Whatever you do," Nick shouted over the sound of her revving engine to Gabriel, "don't let go of me."

As she released the parking brake and shot forward, a fluttering cloud filled the deck, causing the passengers to shriek. Nick drove through the swarm of moths, nosing the bike around the vehicles in front of her and speeding up and out of the tunnel station.

Gabriel's moths provided enough of a distraction to get them safely out of Folkstone, but Nick didn't stop until they were miles away. She pulled off the road to shake off some moths still clinging to her shirt, and make sure Gabriel wasn't too freaked out by what she had done.

"We're good," she told him as she helped him remove the helmet. The sunlight irritated his eyes, so she handed him her spare pair of shades. "You all right?"

"I am wishing I had killed that old man," he muttered, stroking one hand over her head. "It would have saved us much grief."

"We got away. What's a little grief, huh?" She hugged him, which turned into a kiss, which threatened to end up with the two of them rolling around the grass in the ditch. "Whoa. Save that for later, and tell me how to get to this guy Croft's shop."

Nick followed Gabriel's directions into the business district of London, and ended up in front of an old rare bookshop.

" 'Mr. Pickard's Emporium of Literature'?" she read

from the ornate sign painted in white across the spotless window. "Sounds like the captain from that second *Star Trek* series."

"My name is not Jean-Luc, young woman," a crisp, cultured voice informed her. It belonged to the man stepping out of the shop. "I am, regrettably, equally as bald and stuffy. I say, is that vampire on the back of your motorbike bothering you?"

Nick grinned. "Not really."

"Count yourself fortunate." He made an elegant sweep of his hand toward the sun. "Daylight does not make them turn to ash, but they become bloody damn infants, whinging on about irritated eyes and sluggish limbs and so forth."

Gabriel climbed off the motorcycle and embraced the short, thin bald man.

"Croft, it has been too long since I've listened to your insults." Gabriel kissed both of his cheeks before turning toward Nick. "This is Nicola Jefferson. Nicola, although he would have you think otherwise, this is my very good friend Croft Pickard."

Pickard clasped Nick's hand between his before urging them into the shop. "Come inside before some religious zealot has at you with a pike or something."

Nick knew from the moment she stepped under the glass door's tinkling bell that she had entered someplace special. The aroma of old paper and aged leather tickled her nose, but so did another scent; something like mint and chocolate.

Croft's shop, she decided, had the perfect name. Elegantly carved, freestanding bookcases held shelf after shelf of antique books. Most were bound in leather and still showed their titles stamped in faded gilt on the spines. Some were displayed open under round glass domes, like cakes, while others were bound in sets of three and four with cream and gold silk ribbons.

Precious, beautiful things had to be kept safe. This more than anything decided things for Nick.

One sparkling crystal dish offered wrapped Swiss chocolates for the customers, and a live mint plant sprouted in one corner of the desk from a brass urn. Nick bent over to breathe in its fragrance. Mint and chocolate, two things she had genuinely missed.

"I hate to say it, but of all the Kyn I have expected to walk through that door," Croft said as he closed the blinds and locked the front door, "you never made the list."

"The Kyn believe I'm dead."

"They sent the word out on you more than a year ago. We had a very nice memorial service over at the club." Croft switched on an electric teakettle. "I know you can't stomach the stuff, but your charming escort appears in very great need of a cup of tea."

That was her cue.

"I can't stay." Nick stuffed her hands in her jacket pockets and forced a smile. "I have some things to do. Gabriel, I'll be back in an hour to pick you up."

Croft stopped spooning tea leaves into the ceramic pot in his hand. "You don't have to leave, surely."

"You guys need some time to chat. By the way, they blinded him," she said, nodding toward Gabriel, "so don't let him wander out into traffic, okay?"

"Heavens, no." The bookshop owner looked horrified. "Completely blind?"

"Yeah." Nick kissed Gabriel on the cheek, keeping it casual. "See you."

She left the shop before he could say another word or she could change her mind. Because she wasn't coming back in an hour, and would never see him again, she didn't look back.

Gabriel was a gentleman. She was a thief. They had no future together.

If Nick stayed with him, she would risk leading the holy freaks to him. She'd rather never see him again than know she had helped put him back in some bricked-up room to die.

She didn't owe Gabriel anything, either. On the contrary.

Nick felt a little better as she climbed onto the bike. She'd done right by him; no one could say that she hadn't. She'd taken care of him, gotten him to his friend, and now she could take off and know he'd be all right. Being blind, he couldn't help her find the Golden Madonna. He'd only slow her down. He belonged with better people, people like Croft. All she'd do was get him arrested. The holy freaks knew how to use the cops to get what they wanted; they were experts at it.

Gabriel deserved better. He'd get back together with the Kyn, and she could go on with her life. She'd pack up her stuff at the farm and move north. She liked Scotland; maybe she'd try spending the winter in the Highlands. Once the cops lost interest she'd make some other changes and start fresh on her search for the Madonna in the spring.

She got as far as Hyde Park before she had to pull into a parking space and jump off the bike. Her chest heaved with the pain of breathing in cold, damp English air. This was going to kill her, leaving him like this, without knowing, without a word. Would he ever forgive her?

The Kyn had abandoned him, his sister had betrayed him, and now she was dumping him. He'd been lost for so long, just like her. How would he feel when he realized she wasn't coming back for him?

He'll hate you forever.

Oh, God. What was she doing?

"I'll go back." She checked her watch and saw she still had ten minutes before he would expect her to return. "I'll ride by one time and look in the window and make sure he's okay. But after that I have to head out of town and forget about him."

Well, she'd head out of town, anyway.

Nick turned around and drove back toward Croft's shop. She couldn't ride by, she realized; Gabriel would hear the bike. She'd have to find a spot by the corner and take a look from there.

One look and that's all. Nick knew that if she did any more than look, she'd never be able to leave him.

The south corner of the intersection nearest Croft's shop had a phone box that gave her some cover while allowing her to see the front of the shop. Croft had rolled up the blinds in the big front window, probably so he could watch for her.

But she wasn't going back.

Nick eyed the telephone. Maybe she would call and tell Croft she was taking off and leaving Gabriel with him. Just so he knew and didn't wait there for her for hours or think something had happened to her. Croft wouldn't hate her for it. Not if she told him how much she loved Gabriel, and how dangerous she was to him.

This is why you don't get involved with anyone, she told herself viciously. *Because you don't know how to walk away.*

A book hit the inside of the shop window and slid down it to knock over Croft's artful front display. Nick frowned and reached into her jacket, taking out her binoculars. Through them she clearly saw three strange men standing inside the front of the shop. Two of them were holding Croft by the arms. The third had Gabriel by the front of his shirt.

The Kyn couldn't have gotten there that fast.

As she watched, the man holding Gabriel punched him in the face.

Rage exploded inside her. "Oh, *fuck* this."

Nick pulled down her visor, grabbed her bat from the back of the bike, and rounded the corner, cutting off a Jag and darting between a delivery van and a cab. She jumped the curb, scattering shoppers as she sped toward the front of the bookshop. At the last moment she locked up the brakes and let the bike skid sideways, slamming the rear tire into the display window.

Glass smashed and rained down on her as she put the bike in park and jumped off, using the bat to knock out the last jagged section of glass before climbing into the shop.

"Hey, asshole."

The man who had punched Gabriel stared at her in shock. He had a gun tucked in his belt.

"Yeah, you." She swung the bat at his head, and knocked him back into a collection of Victorian poetry. "Home run."

The other two rushed at her, guns in their hands, but she shoved the bat into the belly of one and clipped the other in the jaw with the grip. Both tottered backward, but not far enough to miss her second and third swings.

She saw that Croft was braced against his desk but unhurt. "Sorry about the window."

"My dear girl," he breathed. "Do not apologize." He hurried over and collected the guns the two men had dropped and the one still tucked in the belt of the third. "Guns are illegal in this country," he told the groaning men. "So is pummeling innocent vampires."

Nick went to Gabriel. "Let's get out of here." She took his arm and dragged him through the window.

A small group of startled Londoners had begun gathering, but they backed away as she helped Gabriel onto the bike and swung onto the seat.

"We'll get you, Seran," a man shouted, and Nick saw that one of the men inside the shop had gotten to his feet. "Every Brethren in England is hunting you and your thief bitch now. You can't hide forever—"

Croft stepped up behind him and slammed a large volume on the back of his head. The man collapsed in a heap.

"My apologies, dear boy," he called out to them. "It seems I've been compromised. If you need to reach me, you'll have to contact Geoff. So sorry you couldn't stay for tea, my dear."

"Next time." Nick looked down to see Gabriel's hands on her waist, and took off.

Michael left Phillipe and Leary with the van and took a horse from a nearby stable to ride along the boundaries of Dundellan.

Riding around Richard's stronghold should have calmed Michael, for it had been months since he had indulged his love of horseback riding and solitude. But Marcella's predictions had come true. Over the last days his temper had worn down his will, and not an hour passed that he did not feel as if his skin would crawl off his body. Often now he thought if he spent another day without her, he would go mad. In his head Michael understood it was the bond he shared with Alexandra, and the price of it, but in his heart all that mattered was to be with her again.

We are here. I will take back what is mine.

Michael led the horse out of the shadows, risking being spotted by the castle guard, but unable to resist looking up at the light shining from one of the narrow windows in the east stone tower. He had no way to know if Alexandra was being kept in that room or, as Leary suggested, had been locked away deep in the bowels of Dundellan.

A measure of calmness came to him as he focused his thoughts on her, the memory of her face, the smell of her skin. *Soon,* mon amour. *I will be with you again, very soon.*

Once Michael finished scouting the property, he put together the signs that all was not well at Dundellan. Richard had twice the usual amount of men patrolling, but they kept to the castle itself and did not stray out onto the surrounding acres. The neglected condition of the land indicated his household staff had possibly been locked in, dismissed, or perhaps killed. He suspected that as the high lord's mind deteriorated, his Kyn guards might begin quietly abandoning him. Perhaps, hearing of Lucan's attempt to assassinate him, they already had.

Michael met Phillipe back at the van. Inside, Leary sat watching the castle while the addicts they had taken from Dublin, made docile by Phillipe's compulsion over them, looked at nothing at all.

"The patrols are riding no more than two hundred yards out from the castle," he told his seneschal. "Six Kyn guard the delivery entrances at the west and north sides. The windows have been secured but the fences are falling apart. Nothing stands in our way."

"I called Marcella from the mobile," Phillipe said. "She has been monitoring the patrols, and says that Richard's men are carrying standard weapons as well as copper."

Armed to kill both humans and Kyn. "He's expecting someone other than us."

Phillipe brought a small case out of the back, which he placed on the hood of the van. He opened it and produced what appeared to be a Young Fine Gael campaign button and put it on his lapel.

"This is a radio transceiver," he told Cyprien. "It will pick up and transmit my voice and any others within twenty feet of me."

Cyprien fitted the earpiece. "When you are inside, find Alexandra and help her out through one of the second-floor windows, there," Michael told him, pointing to the least guarded area of the castle. "Whatever happens, do not engage Richard."

His seneschal nodded. "You will wait here for us."

"No." Michael stripped off his jacket, revealing the body armor and weapons beneath it. "I am challenging Richard."

"As a diversion?" Phillipe touched his arm. "Master, there is surely another way."

Michael shook his head. "To defeat him, I must kill him and take his throne."

Leary rolled down the passenger window. "It's time to go in now," he said, looking anxious. "They're waiting for us."

Nick rode through the night, stopping only for petrol as she headed north. She spoke little and seemed distant. Gabriel didn't disturb her, sensing that she had withdrawn into herself again. He was only grateful that she had returned to Croft's shop when she had. The Brethren who had cornered him there had fully intended to take him back to France and Benait.

He also didn't know how to tell her that he was no longer blind. Seeing her disable three men with nothing more than a baseball bat had left him speechless as well. She had moved like a trained warrior, with no hesitation and utter ruthlessness.

Whatever she was hiding from him, it had a great deal to do with the way she fought.

After several hours, Nick turned off the main roadway and took a series of country roads toward a farming community. Gabriel's vision, always better in the dark, expanded to take in the hedgerows and slumbering sheep herds. She went down a long drive and came to a stop in what appeared to be an old farmhouse.

She tugged off her helmet and tucked it under her arm as she climbed off the bike. "This is my place."

From the stones and portions of ancient walls scattered to the right and left of the farmhouse, her place appeared to be built within the ruins of a far older structure.

"Come on." She took his arm, reminding Gabriel that she still thought he was blind. "Don't worry. My house is in better shape than yours."

Nicola guided him to the door, which she pushed open with her hand.

"You do not secure your property?" he asked.

"I don't live in the house." She led him through an empty kitchen and to a padlocked door, for which she took a key from the heel of her boot. "I live under it."

Gabriel put his hand on Nick's shoulder and climbed down a long incline of stone steps through a cellar and into a sublevel basement that was equally bare.

"I wish you could see this. Stay here." She went to one of the bare walls, tapped it in three places, and pushed. The entire wall made a low scraping sound as it swung out, revolving on hidden bearings. "My stepdad meant to fill in this part with dirt, but he died before he could get to it." She came back and took his hand in hers. "It's okay. It's perfectly safe."

She thought he was afraid of her secret underground dwelling, when he was nearly shaking with anger. "Why do you live down here? Why not live in the house?"

"I have to travel a lot," she said. "I rent out the pastures to neighbors and they watch the house, but they think I live in America and visit only once or twice a year. If I lived upstairs, they'd expect me to go to church and hang out at the horse club and be part of the community. It's more private for me this way."

She wanted him to admire this hole in the ground; to her it was a home. "Then please show me the way."

Nicola tucked her arm through his and steered him through the opening in the revolving wall.

"My stepdad thought this might be where the commander of the fortress hid his wife and kids when they were attacked," she said as they walked down a narrow corridor. "A lot of the Brits didn't like the Romans coming here and taking over, while the Romans brought their families and tried to live normal lives, so I guess this was their version of a bomb shelter. Evidently the Saxons never found it."

She walked him through a room so dazzling that he stumbled, and she stopped. "Hey, you okay?"

"A brief dizziness. Give me a moment." He needed a week, a month, a year, for he could not believe his eyes.

The room was filled with Templar gold. Gabriel recognized the crosses and chalices, for he had pressed his lips to them and drunk the blood of Christ from them during his human life. A stack of ivory tablets, sculptured with figures and animals from the Scriptures that had been gilded with fine gold leaf, sat neatly atop an eagle lectern of bronze; boxes in which the Templars had kept the gold and silver coins of pilgrims visiting the Holy Land had been stacked like milk crates.

It was Aladdin's cave, come to life.

In the corner Gabriel glimpsed one of the few traveling altars his brothers had brought back intact from the Holy

Land stand, its polished ash-and-black marble still gleaming, the embellishments showing the martyrdom of Saint Paul, and the image of the Trinity in silver gilt. It had vanished in Paris on Black Friday, when the pope had ordered all of the Templars to be arrested, and it had been rumored to have been destroyed in the flames of a temple burned by its own retreating warrior-priests. And yet here it was, almost as it had been seven hundred years before, when he had knelt and prayed before it.

"Your head clear yet?"

He had to leave the room. "Yes." Blinded now by the sight of the treasures the Kyn had thought plundered and looted and lost forever, Gabriel took her hand and let her take him into the next room.

He expected to see more grandeur, but she brought him into what appeared to be a simple, whitewashed root cellar that had been converted to basic living quarters. A modest dresser and bed were the only furnishings; a plain wooden cross hung on the wall over the bed.

"Where are we now?" he asked her.

"This is where I live and keep my stuff stashed," she said, "until I can sell it."

"Sell it?"

"I steal things, Gabriel. Old things from churches and chapels, like the one where I found you. Sometimes I've taken them off the bodies of the dead people I find hidden away, like you were." She sat down on the bed and folded her hands in her lap.

"I don't understand."

"I started doing it in England ten years ago, when I began looking for the Madonna. I went through every chapel, church, and shrine in the country looking for her. I found other things and took them to sell. I moved on to Scotland and Ireland, and now I'm working in France. It's how I make a living."

"So you never took photographs."

"No. I lied to you. I'm a thief." She said each word

flatly, without emotion. "I'm a very good thief. In fact, I'm one of the best in Europe. Maybe the world."

What she was telling him and the treasures in the next room did not match. "Do you ever keep anything for yourself?"

"Are you kidding?" She laughed. "I can't afford to be a collector. Everything I make off the stuff I take goes to cover my expenses."

Living in a hole in the ground, traveling by motorcycle, what expenses could she have? "What about the Golden Madonna? Do you intend to sell her after you find her?"

"No." Her face darkened. "I'll bury her with her owner."

He went over to the bed and sat down beside her. "You sound tired. Lie with me."

Nick stared at him. "I just told you I'm a thief, Gabriel. I'm wanted by every cop and Interpol agent in Europe. I've committed hundreds of crimes."

"We have spent more time making love than sleeping these past few days," he said. "Even the greatest thief in Europe must occasionally rest."

Her curls bounced as she shook her head. "Sometimes I think you are crazy."

He pulled her down to the mattress and turned her, tucking her back against him. "For now, I would like to sleep with you in my arms."

Gabriel held Nick and listened to her breathing even out as she fell asleep. Only when he was sure she would not wake did he rise and slip back out to the treasure room to inspect its contents. It took an hour of opening boxes and inspecting relics, but by his calculations, Nick had somehow amassed a collection of artifacts to rival that of any world museum.

She had not been exaggerating when she had claimed to be one of the best thieves in Europe. There were a dozen kings' ransoms here if one only counted the value of the gold. Add to it the irreplaceable historical value of the objects and Gabriel suspected the woman who had saved him might be worth millions.

What was very odd was that all of the artifacts, precious icons, and symbols, as well as the pilgrim coins, appeared to belong to the Templars before they became Kyn.

Why hadn't she sold them off? A single box of coins alone would fetch an inordinate amount of money at auction. Why would she lie about keeping them? Did it have something to do with the man who had killed her parents and stolen the Golden Madonna?

Gabriel found the cross his father had given to the Temple master when Gabriel had taken his vows, a simple piece with only a few emeralds; almost paltry compared to some of the other families' contributions. He had been so proud the day his father had given so much.

Gabriel pressed the cross between his hands, and for the first time in years offered a prayer: *God in heaven, help us.*

Chapter 17

"So this is the best you could do?" the Kyn guard demanded of Leary as he looked over Phillipe and the addicts from Dublin. "The high lord expected a dozen or more. He will be very displeased."

Leary's mouth drooped. "I did my best, as I always do."

"Tell that to him with the mood he's in, and he'll tear you to ribbons." The guard seemed agitated. "Still, not my head. Come on, this way."

Phillipe had taken position at the very back of the group. When the guard led them around a corner, the seneschal stepped back and waited until their footsteps faded down the hall. After he listened and heard no sounds, he walked quickly in the opposite direction toward the door Leary had said would take him down to the dungeons.

A human guard stopped him at that door. Phillipe remembered to keep a vacant-eyed look as the guard asked, "They send you for the leech, lad?"

He nodded slowly.

"Go on with you, then." The guard stepped aside.

He climbed down the stairs and passed a number of archaic-looking chambers before coming to a closed door with a glass window. Through it he saw Alexandra and Éliane Selvais working at a table. He tried the door, which was unlocked, and slipped inside.

"Not yet, Korvel," Alexandra said, adding a measure of dark liquid to a beaker of blood.

Phillipe felt such relief at seeing her whole and well that

he could only lean back against the door. "I am not Korvel."

The beaker dropped out of Alexandra's hand, and she whirled around. "Phil? Oh, my God. What are you doing here? How . . . ?" She flew across the room and flung herself into his arms. As soon as he embraced her, she stiffened and hissed. "Ow. Careful. I still have some claw marks back there."

"Claw marks." He tried to look down her collar but saw only the edge of a bandage. "What did you get into a fight with this time?"

Her spiral curls bounced around her face. "I'll tell you all about it on the way home." She hugged him again. "How on earth did you get inside the castle?"

"Carefully." Phillipe held on to her but looked at Éliane. She didn't seem surprised to see him. "Are you ready to come home?"

"Is the pope an ex-Nazi? Phil, it's so good to see you. I can't tell you how scared I've been." Alex stepped back. "But I can't go yet."

"Master, I have found her," Phillipe said over the transmitter. "She is well." He put his hands on her shoulders. "We must leave, Alexandra. At once."

"You don't understand. I have to finish preparing this serum." She nodded toward a row of vials. "It could be a cure for Richard Tremayne's condition."

Confusion made him grope for the correct words in English. "You mean to cure Tremayne?"

She lifted her shoulders and gave him a rueful smile. "I took an oath that says I can't kill him."

Phillipe heard Cyprien's voice over his earpiece say, "Let me speak to her."

"This is a transmitter. The master can hear anything you say." He removed the earpiece and gently placed it in her ear.

"It took you long enough," she said to the button, and cupped her hand over her ear. "No, don't start telling me how much you love me; you'll make Phil jealous again. Listen up, seigneur, because we have serious problems in here."

Phillipe kept an eye on Éliane as Alexandra related to Michael what had happened since Richard had brought her to Dundellan. To that she added, "You have to get John out of here first. He's the one in danger; I have Phil running interference for me, and I'm immortal." She listened for a moment to whatever Cyprien was saying to her. "Right. I don't care. Get John out of here."

The Frenchwoman came over, but stopped when Phillipe moved to block the door. "I have no intention of sounding an alarm."

"I have no intention of killing you," he told her. "Let us not litter the road to hell with either."

"There's something else," Alexandra was saying. "You know how I tune in on killers. . . . Well, Lady Elizabeth has been broadcasting all day. She's found out that I have a treatment, maybe a cure, and she's planning to force Richard to complete his change before I can give it to him. Éliane and I are going to take care of her as soon as I get this serum made. We'll keep the guards busy, too, so Phil can get John out to you. I love you, too, babe. I have missed you so much. I hope you've been taking your vitamins. Yeah." She glanced at Phillipe. "We're embarrassing your seneschal. Quit it. And get going." She removed the earpiece and handed it to Phillipe. "Here's the new plan."

"Father Orson Leary, my lord," the servant announced him.

Leary went into the library, for once eager to see Richard Tremayne. The Darkyn King sat behind his desk, as always, although he had not covered his face, which now appeared as beastly as any hell-spawned demon's. For the first time Leary looked, unflinching and unafraid, directly into his satanic eyes. He could even feel pity for him now.

Being freed of all fear was a wondrous thing.

"They forced me to come here, my lord," Leary said. "The Frenchman and his scarred servant."

"Cyprien," Richard muttered.

"Yes, lord." He bowed his head. "They kidnapped me and forced me to do terrible things. They made me disguise the scarred man and bring him into your stronghold. Cyprien is outside, waiting for a signal to attack. I fear you are in great danger."

"You will stay here." Richard slowly rose and limped to the door.

Leary went over to the wall, where Richard kept a collection of bladed weapons. He found the two-handed sword quite tempting, but was not sure if he could even lift such a blade, much less wield it against the vile one. He helped himself instead to a number of daggers, tucking them inside his clothes, where they would not be seen. Then, after listening at the door, he walked out and crossed to the opposite wing.

It was time to find her.

"I know the rooms where Keller is being kept," he heard a woman say. "We can bring him out this way."

Leary knew the time for his true work had come at last. There would be no more pain, no more Legion. She would never torment him another night.

And there she was, walking with another, her radiance muted by the ugly clothes she wore. She had disguised herself again, as she had in the alley.

He drew one of the daggers he had stolen from the high lord's library and kept his footsteps silent as he came up behind them. It wouldn't do to fail now, not when he was so close.

So close.

So very close.

Close enough.

"Thy name is Legion!" Leary shouted as he buried the dagger in her back. "To hell with you!"

She turned, showing him the face of innocence, the face that made him scream in terror and stagger back, waving his arms to make it stop, make the vision leave him, now, before the worms came, and Leary wheeled around, knocking aside the small dark woman who caught the bitch goddess in her arms and shouted for help and called the demon Éliane.

That was not her name. Her name was Legion. She had told him so.

Leary ran and ran, but none of the doors would open for him, and he was caught, trapped, driven into the dark place where there was only one door that swung open, and the frozen flames of hell glittered all around.

"Father in heaven."

He fell forward, caught by soft, tender hands, shushed by a sweet voice. And when he dared open his eyes, he looked into those of the one he had been sent to kill, the one of whom all the others were but pale copies.

"Orson," she said, her little pink tongue peeping out from between sharp, white teeth. "I have been waiting for you."

Nick had never walked around inside a really good antique shop. Like jewelry stores and chick boutiques, they were not comfort zones for her. Also, the people who worked in them viewed girls in leather jackets with the same enthusiasm they usually afforded SpongeBob SquarePants.

Shame, because this place was nice. A real showcase location, with wide, asymmetrical aisles swirling around little islands of furniture and display cases of jewelry and old silver. Framed paintings of different sizes hung in neat rows across the golden oak walls, and a truckload of crystal and stained-glass chandeliers dangled from the high paneled ceilings.

Nick might have to live underground, like a garden mole, but she could still appreciate the finer things most people could never afford.

Gabriel probably had stuff like this at his place before the holy freaks stole it. She bent over to inspect a five-strand pearl choker that had been strung about the same time the *Titanic* sank. *It's what he's used to.*

Nick felt odd, and straightened to look around the shop. She'd had the forest dream so often that she'd come to expect it, not something like this. She didn't care about old, pricey junk. She had plenty of it stashed in her place, but it had never done anything for her. She'd tried to sell it a dozen times, but every time, almost at the last minute before she packed it up and took it to her fence, something stopped her. The special things, the treasures she kept in the room next to hers, they weren't hers, but she had to keep them. Watch over them.

Sometimes Nick wondered if she had lost her marbles ten years ago and just never realized it.

She saw an old book sitting on a table. It had a silver symbol on the blue fabric cover, a shape that resembled a fat 69. *Yin and yang?* In dreams, a person wasn't supposed to be able to read; the letters got all jumbled. She eased the cover open, and flipped, but the gilt-edged pages were all blank.

No story. She closed the book. *What kind of book has no story in it?* Maybe it was a photo album of some kind. *Or am I supposed to write the story?* She chuckled. She was no writer.

Nick moved on to the next display, a traditional ornate tea service, and checked her reflection in the polished tray. The solid silver informed her that her dye had worn off again and her hair was back to two shades of blond darker than white. She really needed a shampoo and cut. Maybe she'd go black this time. She was tired of mud brown.

I like you this way.

She looked toward the voice and saw the Green Man sitting behind a waist-high cherry-wood keyhole desk where he was using a soft cloth to wipe dust from some fussy statuette.

"What do you know?" she asked. "You have pine needles for hair."

True. He shook out the cloth, draping it over the piece.
Do you truly love him, Nicola?

He was talking about Gabriel. "I do. But I can't. I'm not
good enough for him."

*You were good enough to find him, and save him, and to
tell him the truth.* He came around the counter and walked
toward her. Mottled green burn scars covered his body, and
as her gaze shifted up she saw blond-streaked brown hair
instead of pine needles, and Gabriel's green eyes fixed on
her. *It's time. You know what you have to do now.*

"I can't."

*The shadows around the truth are what keep you apart.
Tell him.* One of his/Gabriel's hands lifted toward a chan-
delier that was a hanging waterfall of prismatic crystal.
Show him. Trust in my love.

Dimensions changed. The high ceilings began to drop,
and the aisles narrowed. Either Nick had begun a very be-
lated growth spurt, or Antique World was starting to
shrink.

At least now she knew it was a dream, and she could
wake up. And she tried to, but the nightlands wouldn't let
her go.

I cannot live in the dark anymore. He spoke so low that
she could barely hear him now. *Bring me into the light. Be
with me in it. Let me see you as you are.*

"You're—he's—blind. I can't." Nick swiveled, looking
for an exit. There wasn't any. A porcelain pitcher and basin
bumped into her hip, fell over, and smashed. If she stayed
here, she was going to end up a sardine. "How do I get out
of here?"

You know the way.

Nick ducked to keep her skull from ramming into the
roof, and then something cracked the shop in half and split
it open like an eggshell. The whole place fell away from
her as she sat up, alone in bed.

258 *Lynn Viehl*

them with a careless touch. They began landing on her hands and arms, fairy creatures of every color in the rainbow, covering her with their wings.

The butterflies flew off as Gabriel came to stand beside her. "Don't be afraid of me, Nicola. I love you."

"I'm not afraid." She stared down at the ground. "I'm a thief and I'm a liar, the things you hate the most, but I'm not a coward."

"I'm not blind anymore," Gabriel murmured, turning her toward him. "I can see your face now. I can look into your eyes. I know what you feel, because I feel the same for you. There's no need to keep hiding behind more lies."

She wiped the tears from her face with the back of her hand. "I don't know how to be any other way."

"Tell me the rest of it."

"There's not much more to tell." She turned around, hugging herself with her arms. "My parents were murdered here ten years ago. I buried the bodies and went away for a while. When I came back, I made everyone think that they had moved to America." She wandered away from the blank space in the garden.

Gabriel came with her and put his arm around her. "You found the Templar treasures while you were looking for the Madonna."

She nodded. "I'm good at finding things. Everything but her."

He brushed the hair back from her brow. "These objects that you have collected, they all belonged to Templars who rose to become Darkyn."

"I didn't know that. They just . . . felt different. Like things that needed to be guarded. I only wanted the Madonna. If I don't find her, my parents will never be at peace." She sagged against him, exhausted, drained of everything but sorrow.

Gabriel lifted her into his arms. "You have more courage and honor in your heart than any woman I have known. I will help you find the Madonna; I promise."

"Gabriel?"

Nick rolled out of bed and crossed the room, stopping in the doorway. Gabriel was sitting on the floor with her lantern, holding one of the old books in his hands.

He glanced up at her, and she saw that the strange green glow had vanished from his eyes. As she shifted her weight, his eyes followed her movements.

Blind eyes didn't move like that.

"You can see." He nodded, and a crushing, unseen weight she hadn't known she'd been carrying fell away. It was replaced almost at once by one twice as heavy. "When did this happen?"

"My eyes began healing the night we first made love." He closed the book and reverently set it aside before standing and looking down at her. "Your hair is white."

"I told you it was." She touched it before she ducked her head. "I'm sorry."

"Why did you lie to me about keeping all these things?" He gestured around him. "Did you fear that I would steal them from you?"

"No. I just . . . couldn't. It's hard to explain." She tried to think of reasonable excuses, but her brain wasn't working anymore. "I'm sorry."

"I want to know the truth about you." He started walking toward her.

That was what the Green Man hadn't understood in the dream, what he had been trying to warn her of. But she couldn't tell him, couldn't tell anyone. With a sob she ran around him, dodging his hands and rushing out through the opening in the wall.

Nick didn't know where she was running to, but her feet did. They took her up through the house and out into her mother's rose garden. There she found herself standing over two patches of ground, carefully tended pools of delicate green grass. As the tears spilled down her face, hundreds of butterflies swirled up out of the surrounding flowers and hedges. Nick stood still, unwilling to hurt

Nick looked up at him. "What about you and the Kyn?"

"Croft told me many things," he said. "I must go to Ireland and speak with the high lord. I must settle matters regarding my sister."

"I was thinking of moving to Scotland for the winter," Nick said. "Maybe we could go see this lord guy on the way, tell him about all the stuff I have here. I really don't want it. What do you think?"

"Tomorrow." Gabriel turned and carried her back to the house.

Chapter 18

"The doctor injected you with this new serum she has created," Korvel told Richard. "It has counteracted what the feline blood did. I am told that Lady Elizabeth made the switch."

"I will deal with my wife later." Richard noticed the weapons missing from his collection. "You must go and find Orson Leary. Quickly."

Korvel hesitated. "I do not wish to leave you to face Cyprien alone."

"If he can get in, I will remind him that I have what he wants. Michael will not jeopardize her safety to take personal revenge." Richard gestured impatiently. "Go. I will collect our hostages."

Richard did not find Alexandra in the lab, but nearly ran into her as their paths collided at the entrance to the dungeons. She was carrying an unconscious Éliane over her shoulder. Richard saw the dagger left in his *tresora*'s back—his dagger—and his claws extended.

"Who did this?"

"Some crazy-looking man." Alex carried her burden downstairs to the lab.

Richard received a second shock when he saw Phillipe waiting at the lab entrance.

"Has someone killed *all* of my guards?" he asked no one in particular.

"I don't have time for one of your tantrums, Richard.

Shut up or get out." Alex kicked open the door to the lab.
"I'll need help with Éliane, Phillipe."

"Do you mean to leave me?" Richard asked.

"I mean to stop this woman from bleeding to death."
Alex put the unconscious Frenchwoman on the exam table,
facedown, and used a scalpel to cut through the back of her
jacket and blouse. "He missed the spinal cord. Thank you,
Jesus, thank you. Phillipe, get me a suture kit out of the
supply cabinet."

"What does it look like?" the seneschal asked as he
walked over to the cabinet.

"A plastic package that says 'suture kit' on the front."
One slim hand reached up to train the overhead light on the
dagger hilt protruding from Éliane's left upper back.
"Blondie, you are so freaking lucky, I can't believe this."
She grabbed some gauze pads and piled them around the
wound before jerking out the dagger. Crimson blood
spilled out from under the gauze. "Hurry up, Phil."

As Richard watched the emergency surgery, Alex began
to talk. "Your wife is the crazy one around here. She
switched feline blood for the human blood I needed. It was
as if she knew it would make you lose control."

"I regret what happened," he told her. "I cannot remember it."

"Like you can't remember killing half your servants,
and all the zombies the other day." Alex put on a face mask
and gloves and began to work on Éliane's back. "It's aw-
fully convenient how your blackouts coincide with killings
that you can't remember committing, don't you think?"

"What are you trying to say, Doctor?"

"I think your wife killed them and made it look as if you
did it. The blackouts she could have controlled by making
sure you got some Kyn tranquilizer mixed in with pure feline blood right before they happened." She discarded a
bloodied instrument. "She might even be using her talent
on humans that you've already bespelled. Korvel told me

she always sees every human before they are presented to you. Stefan is her favorite guard, too."

"How would that affect the humans?"

"One talent is enough for any human. Being subjected to the pressure of two or more, on the other hand, might just be enough to turn them catatonic."

Richard brooded over what she had said until Alex finished dressing the newly sutured wound and pulled down her mask. "That's it. She's out of danger."

Korvel came down to the lab to report that Leary was nowhere to be found, and Richard ordered him to send guards out of the castle bearing the white flag to invite Michael inside.

"Before you negotiate things with my love," Alex said, coming over with a syringe, "take another hit of the serum."

Richard studied the needle, the contents of which looked like blood but might be anything. "Do you not trust me to control myself?"

"No, I don't," she said, uncapping the needle. "Sleeve up. Now."

The injection did not kill Richard, but made him feel calmer and more collected than he had in months. He left Korvel to guard the women and returned to his library to prepare to receive Cyprien. Perhaps it meant nothing, but for the first time in nearly a century he felt some hope.

Éliane had left several handwritten messages on his desk, which he would have ignored had he not spotted the name. Gabriel Seran, one of the best men Richard had ever known, who had died under Brethren torture and interrogation.

Richard felt the loss of Gabriel most keenly. He had been a superb hunter, an intelligent soldier, and possibly the best tracker among the Kyn. Seran had also been one of the gentlest of the immortal souls in Richard's charge. He had sent Lucan to Dublin specifically to free Gabriel Seran, but by that time the Brethren had killed him. They sent several sickening photographs of Gabriel's severed head and mutilated body.

He picked up the message and read it. The paper drifted out of his distorted hand and rocked through the air until it landed noiselessly beside the desk.

"My lord," Stefan said as he escorted Michael in. His protégé stood dressed in full black body armor and carried two sheathed swords. "Seigneur Cyprien."

Richard rose and inclined his head. Michael did not bow in return. "Leave us, Stefan."

As soon as the guard departed, Michael drew both swords and held them crossed in front of him with the blades down. "I challenge you."

"I refuse. I abdicate to you." Richard sat back down.

Michael said nothing for a full minute. "You think to jest with me, my lord?"

"I think to hand my people over to the one man I know who can rule them." The injection Alexandra had given him had begun to make him feel sluggish, and the news about Gabriel—that he lived—drove twin spikes of amazement and dread through his chest. "I am in the end throes of this thing. Your *sygkenis*, who is a remarkable woman, has done her best. It has not worked, and I believe that I am too far gone to be retrieved. Your last task as my seigneur will be to take my head."

"I did not come here to execute you."

"Now who is jesting?" Richard covered a cough. "You have always been my only choice for my successor. I doubt you will have an easy time of it, but your head was always cooler than mine, even before—"

"I came here for my woman."

"So you shall have her." Another spate of coughing nearly stole his voice. "And the kingship as well."

"I don't want it."

"Neither did I," Richard assured him in a hoarse whisper. "To lead the Kyn, you must serve the Kyn. Remember that."

"What is wrong with you? You have never surrendered. Not even when they dragged you naked through the streets of London."

"I received a message from one of Geoffrey's men in London. He called to say that Gabriel Seran is free, that the Brethren are pursuing him, and that Gabriel and his female companion, a young human, left London this morning on a flight to Dublin."

"The man is mistaken. Gabriel is dead. You yourself have the photographs."

"I believe, as Alexandra would put it, someone has been jerking me off for the last two years." He wanted to rub his face, but his talons made that impossible now. "I know this human, Pickard. He is completely reliable. If he says that he saw Gabriel, then he did. I imagine that Gabriel is coming here to find out why we abandoned him."

"We thought he was dead."

"They knew he was special to me. For two years they tortured him." Richard slammed his fist onto the desk, making everything on it jump six inches into the air. "May their souls rot within sight of the gates of heaven."

Something that had nothing to do with his lungs made him double over and shake uncontrollably. He would have said good-bye to his successor, but Richard could no longer move, or speak, or breathe.

Michael sheathed his swords and went to the door. "Guard! The high lord is ill; get help."

He went over to where Richard had fallen and rolled him onto his side. The convulsions slowed to a stop, but he could not rouse the high lord back to consciousness. When heavy footsteps marched in, he looked up impatiently. "Come; he is very ill."

A petite figure swept in around the guards. Lady Elizabeth, dressed in her favorite shade of peach, looked down at Cyprien and Richard and tapped her cheek with one finger.

"Is he dead yet?"

Cyprien rose. "He will be, if you don't summon help."

"I think not." Elizabeth turned to the guards. "Take this murderer and his leech and confine them to a dungeon cell."

Cyprien came around the desk but didn't draw his swords or fight the guards. "Is this how you repay Richard for keeping you as wife all these years?"

Elizabeth tilted her head. "Wife? To that?" She laughed. "I will miss your notions of romantic love. Frenchmen were always so much better at it." She snapped her fan. "Take him, and drag that body out to the compost heap."

Stefan came forward and looked over the desk, then next to it, and then under it.

"Well?"

"My lady, he is not here."

"Of course he is, you idiot," Elizabeth said as she came around the desk. "He's right over . . . Where is he?"

Michael saw that Richard's body had indeed vanished, and began to laugh as the guards marched him out of the room.

Gabriel and Nick took a flight to Dublin, but once in the city rented a motorbike to take them the rest of the way to the village of Bardow.

"I should have ridden my bike up here," Nick pronounced once she had checked it over. "The rear drive on this one is total crap, and the driveshaft and the valves are almost shot. We'll be lucky if we don't end up walking to see the king."

"Then we will walk." Gabriel lifted her up and put her on the bike. "We can spend a few nights in the woods."

She grinned. "Oh, so you never want to get there."

Much to Nick's disappointment, the rented bike ran fine and got them to Bardow just before sunset.

"Pretty place," Nick said, admiring the quaint cottages and thatched rooftops. Her gaze was drawn to a priest nailing crosses to the front door of a Catholic church. "Very, ah, religious."

The priest turned and began shouting at people passing down the street. "Lock your doors and windows! The beautiful ones are here, the harbingers of evil, the vampires, and they crave your blood!"

"They can have me son," one farmer called back. "For free. I'll even deliver."

As the priest continued ranting, more villagers stopped to listen. Most laughed, and one man offered to buy the priest a pint. A pair of older women crossed themselves and hurried on their way.

"Our Brethren will come to save us," the priest called out. "But you must be on your guard. Keep your children home and stay out of the pubs. The vampires are hunting you like sheep straying from the fold."

No Irishman gave up his after-work pint at the pub, so the few who had been listening to the old man shook their heads and strolled away.

"Sounds like the holy freaks have been spreading the bad word," Nick muttered.

Gabriel scanned the surrounding homes and shops. "We should perhaps keep out of sight until dark."

Nick eyed the priest, who had taken out another cross and was nailing it in place. "Amen."

As they walked away from the village's main street, a tall, dark woman came out of a doorway and stood in front of them.

Nick smelled flowers and stepped up to her. "Call the priest; I think I found one."

"*Qui êtes-vous?*" She peered. "Gabriel Seran? *C'est toi?*"

"Marcella Evareaux. *Oui, c'est moi.*" He caught the gorgeous woman as she flung herself at him and embraced her with the joy of a long-lost lover reunited.

An outrageously large spike of jealousy kept Nick nailed to the sidelines, quietly watching. The two chatted in a strange dialect of French she'd never heard before, so she made out only bits and pieces of the conversation. Her resentment built and then ebbed as she saw tears in the female vampire's eyes. She seemed completely rattled yet genuinely delighted to see Gabriel.

"This is my companion, Nicola Jefferson." Gabriel was introducing her to Marcella. "She brought me out of France, and again rescued me in London."

"Mademoiselle." The woman actually curtsied to Nick. "You have done us a great service by saving Gabriel. The Kyn are deeply in your debt." Marcella turned to Gabriel. "You have come at a difficult time. I assume that Croft told you that Lucan liberated the Durands, and that your sister was killed in America?"

It was time for Nick to get lost.

"I'm going to take a ride around the farms," she told Gabriel. Over both their protests, she added, "I can't follow your French when you talk that fast, and I'd like to get the lay of the land. You and Marcella can catch up while I'm gone." She could also follow this feeling in her gut, which had been growing bigger and stronger ever since they'd come to the village.

"We can speak in English." Gabriel looked torn. "You will come back?"

Nick nodded; no way was she going through trying to dump him again. But while Gabriel was occupied, she could track whatever was setting off her internal radar. "Try not to get detained, captured, questioned, or crucified while I'm gone."

Phillipe and John dragged Richard's body through the hidden passage and into the now-deserted part of the castle where Richard had been keeping John Keller locked up. "You found these passages on your own?"

"Alexandra hinted at them." John checked Richard's neck. "I can't feel a pulse."

"It does not mean he is dead. When Kyn suffer serious injuries, our hearts stop beating for a time." Phillipe lifted

Richard into a wide armoire and nestled him in behind the hanging gowns, arranging the long skirts over him so that he wouldn't be seen. "You should stay here."

John shook his head. "I overheard the guards talking in the corridor. Lady Elizabeth had Alexandra and Cyprien thrown into the dungeon."

"She will be busy taking control of the humans," Phillipe said. "That will give us time to do the same with the guards."

"Won't they be loyal to her?"

The seneschal offered a grim smile. "Not after I tell them she has been slowly poisoning their king."

Alexandra hit the stone floor, rolled, and landed in a pile of moldy, rotting straw. Most of the dim light from the torches outside disappeared as the heavy door slammed shut and someone bolted it from the outside.

"Welcome to the dungeon." She spit out a piece of straw and struggled to her feet, rubbing her hip. It didn't feel broken, which only made her more pissed off. "I swear, Phil had better bust me out of here soon or I'll . . ." She stopped as she sniffed the air.

"Do you wish to leave me so soon?"

That was it. She'd finally lost her mind. Or . . . "Who's there?"

A soft blanket of roses rolled around her, weaving with the bright lavender that answered it. Alex didn't know whether to laugh or cry. She started to do a little of both.

"I imagined this so many times," Michael Cyprien said as he knelt down before her. "Every hour, every minute at times. Never once did I think it would happen in such a place." He took her grimy hand and pressed it to his lips. "I have missed you, my lady."

"Michael." She couldn't get past his name. "Michael."

He started to stand at the same moment her knees gave out. They came together, two souls filling the broken, empty spaces forced between them.

"Oh, God." Alex kissed every inch of his beloved face, drinking in the taste and smell and feel of him until she thought she really would go mad. She began babbling like a lunatic. "I missed you. I love you. Why did you take so long to get here? I missed you."

A face blocked out the small shaft of light coming from the cell window, and a man laughed.

"Save it for the mistress," the guard shouted. "She likes a good show."

Alex stiffened. "An audience. Terrific."

Michael held her close as he gave the door a murderous look before his expression softened. "Elizabeth has taken control of the castle. Richard has vanished, but he may be dead or dying."

Business as usual. "We're up to our ears, then."

He nodded and stroked his hand over her curls. "It is my fault. I might have planned this rescue somewhat better than I did."

"We'll find a way out. We always do." She couldn't get close enough to him. She wanted to rip off the stupid clothes keeping her skin from touching his. "My head's not exactly on straight yet. I know what I'd like to do to you, but not with that guard or Lady Liz watching. Still, I need to . . ." She didn't know what she needed.

He yanked at the collar of his shirt, baring his throat.

"That?" Even with her fangs fully extended and aching for him, to feed directly from his body seemed as intimate as fucking him. Then there was her need. "What if I drink too much?"

"You won't." He cradled the back of her head with his hand and urged her forward. "Take me, Alexandra."

She kissed the smooth skin first, choosing the place where his blood pulsed strongest. Her mouth opened as his fingers entwined with hers. Her fangs slid into him, deep and sure, as if she had taken him like this a thousand times, and then his lifeblood flowed into her, hot and sweet and silky. The world became a river of warm, honeyed rose petals.

Michael's voice reached through the pleasure, adding to it, changing it. "Come back to me, *mon amour.*"

Somehow Alex wrenched her mouth from him, panting, shuddering as she ripped open the front of her shirt. She didn't have to urge him to her; his mouth found the inside of her breast, one of his favorite spots to kiss and nuzzle when they made love. When she felt his teeth, she arched up against his mouth, making him penetrate her as deeply as she had taken him. He sucked at her with a soft, dreamy sigh, and then lifted his head and looked into her wet eyes.

"I love you, Alexandra."

Chapter 19

Korvel intercepted a human female coming toward Dundellan on a rather noisy motorcycle. She stopped when he held up one hand and shut off the bike.

"You are trespassing." He walked up to her and nearly stumbled when he picked up the scent of evergreen from her skin.

"Watch your step." She took off the black helmet she was wearing, revealing a very young face and a headful of blond curls. "You're a vampire, right?"

"No." Korvel reached out to touch her, but she glided out of range.

"No, I don't think so." She glanced at the castle. "I need to talk to the vampire who lives in there. Is that you?" When he said nothing, she sighed. "Okay, can you get me in to see him?"

"There are no such things as vampires." He took another swipe at her, trying to make the skin contact he needed to use his talent. Once he had her panting after him, he'd find out how she had gotten Gabriel Seran's scent all over her.

"Forget it; I'll just go up and knock." She pushed the bike off the road and left it under a tree.

Frustrated by his inability to touch her, Korvel caught up with her and blocked her path. "I won't hurt you, miss." He looked into her eyes and shed more scent, but it seemed to have no effect on her.

"You're very cute, but I don't screw complete strangers.

Most of the time." She sidestepped him. "So you can turn off the charm."

"You cannot go inside the castle," he told her.

"Trouble in Camelot?" She heard his men shouting and tilted her head. "Thanks for the heads-up. Now can I go in and talk to the high lord?"

She had to be a *tresora*. "I am sorry; I do not mean to frighten you." He breathed in the deep, faintly sweet scent clinging to her. "Who do you serve?"

The girl lifted her chin. "I don't serve anyone, but if it counts, I'm sleeping with Gabriel Seran."

Korvel could hardly think straight. "He truly is alive?"

"He truly is." She smiled. "Do you know him?"

"He was—is—a great friend to my master."

"Gabriel's down in the village, talking to some super-model vampire." She sounded oddly resigned. "Now can I go in there? There's something in this place I really need to find."

Nick thought the big blond vampire was about to have a nervous breakdown, he was so agitated. The scent rolling off him made her feel as if she were locked in a French bakery.

"What's your name?" she asked as she looked up over the edge of the ditch and watched for men on horseback.

"Korvel."

"I'm Nick."

The patrol of four huge-looking armed soldiers passed, and as soon as they had ridden out of sight, the vampire grabbed her hand. "They'll be back in two minutes. We must hurry."

Nick ran with him across to the side entry, pausing here and there to take refuge behind a tree trunk. Korvel opened the door with an impressive show of one-armed Kyn strength, almost wrenching it off its three bolts as they ducked inside.

The interior of this castle, Nick discovered, was particularly cold. It was also as silent as a church. She imagined the place where they were standing had once been a kitchen.

Korvel lifted a finger to his lips and pointed toward an open passage on the other side of the room. "We go through there," he told her in a barely audible whisper, "and down into the dungeons."

"Is that where the king is?"

"It's where my friends are. We have to free them." He picked up a couple of dark-colored swords from where they had been left on the counter. "Can you use one of these?"

Nick nodded. It was slightly bigger than her stiletto. It worked on the same principal.

The vampire led Nick through the corridor, where they met another vampire, this one with a scar running down his face.

"Who are you?" he asked, sniffing her.

"Nick. You?"

"Phillipe," he answered. "You smell like Gabriel Seran."

"Not now," Korvel said, and gestured for them to move down a set of stone steps.

Nick went first, and stepped into what looked to her like a set from one of Vincent Price's old movies. Flaming torches blazed from sconces on the brick walls, while dull copper chains and various nasty-looking apparatuses hung from huge iron rings and suspension bars.

"New guests?"

Nick froze in midstep. A group of dazed-looking humans seemed to appear out of nowhere, and formed a circle around her, Korvel, and Phillipe. They said nothing, but began hitting and scratching at them and kicking their legs and knees. The thin faces were blank, but the eyes were filled with terror.

"Ah, you're here for the tour." Behind them, a fair-haired woman in a bright silk gown appeared. "Welcome to our stronghold."

Nick stopped thinking, shoving three zombie-eyed humans out of her way as she brought her sword up and used it to stab the smiling woman in the shoulder. The blond woman didn't scream, but looked very annoyed.

"Ungrateful little girl." She clasped her shoulder and glared at the humans, who converged and pulled the sword from Nick's hand. "I invite you into my home, and this is how you repay my hospitality?"

Nick saw Korvel attack two of the guards, while Phillipe seemed to be trying to touch as many of the zombies as he could. With each touch the human minions stopped clawing and kicking, and turned toward the woman. Nick struggled wildly against the four that had her by the arms now.

"Elizabeth."

The zombies' eyes suddenly cleared, and their voices rose with very normal-sounding terror and panic as they tried to find a way out of the dungeon's center. It was during the confusion that someone grabbed Nick from behind, clamping a hand over her mouth and dragging her out of the room.

When Nicola did not return within the promised hour, Gabriel questioned a few of the villagers coming in from the fields and discovered from their sightings that she had ridden out to Dundellan.

"You don't have to track her on foot." Marcella brought him to the town stable and removed two white mares from their stalls. "I will ride with you."

Gabriel was more concerned about Nicola, especially when they arrived at the castle and saw it sitting open and unguarded.

"Richard must be dead," he said, "for he would never allow his stronghold to be found so vulnerable."

They tethered the horses to a tree and without invitation walked through the front entry of Dundellan. Gabriel picked up Nick's scent almost immediately. He followed it to the basement access door. "They are all down there."

Marcella nodded. "I smell them, too."

The first person Gabriel saw as he walked down into Richard Tremayne's dungeons was the high lord himself.

"Gabriel." The man was Richard, and a much more human-looking Richard than Gabriel remembered in the past. "You *are* alive."

"My lord." He made his bow. "My traveling companion came here. I have come to collect her."

"She has disappeared, as have my wife and a Brethren interrogator." Richard raised his voice over the cries of the newly awakened addicts. "Calm yourselves."

Phillipe handed Marcella a bunch of keys. "The seigneur and his *sygkenis* are locked in one of these cells."

"I do not need keys," she told him, and placed a hand on the steel locking mechanism on one cell's barred door. Something inside the lock rattled, and Marcella pulled the door open. At the same time, two muffled voices called out. "I hear them. Down here." She led Phillipe down the row of cells.

Gabriel heard his name being called frantically but from some distance away. "Nicola?" He projected his talent, summoning every insect in the castle and sharing their knowledge of the place. The beetles led him back upstairs and into the west wing of the castle. The termites led him to the locked door of a secured, sealed chamber. Behind it, he could hear Nick screaming.

Come to me.

Gabriel's command thundered through the halls of Dundellan, drawing every insect within its cold stone walls. He reached farther, out into the fields for the ants and bees and spiders, and into the woods for the crickets and moths and wasps. He brought together the many that were one mind, one house, one soul, and one spirit, and they poured in through every window in the castle, the winged ones carrying those that could not fly, streaming through the castle in a single column, past the cringing humans and Darkyn and into the west wing, becoming a living battering ram against the door that separated Gabriel from Nicola.

The door exploded inward.

Gabriel stepped into the stream of the many, moving with them into the glittering room made of amber. Richard's wife huddled in one corner, her arms over her head. Leary was jerking his arm up and down, up and down over another woman. Gabriel saw the bloodied knife in his hand and with a guttural roar brought the column of the many down on Leary's arm, severing it cleanly from his body at the shoulder.

Nicola dropped to the floor, her body covered in blood.

The priest tottered around, his left hand grasping the empty socket of his right arm, and smiled at Gabriel. "Their name is Legion," he choked out. "And you are many."

The column descended on Leary and dragged him, writhing within their suffocating mass, out of the room.

Chapter 20

Gabriel carefully slid one arm beneath Nick's lax shoulders and lifted her into his arms. Blood pulsed from dozens of stab wounds in her chest, stomach, and arms. The mad priest had slashed her face, and there were matching wounds on her hands. Bruised eyelids covered her eyes, blood staining the fine lashes. Her blond curls spilled over his arm.

"Nicola." She had saved him, protected him, and now when she had needed him most . . . "No."

She did not stir, and as her breathing faltered the bleeding of her wounds slowed.

Gabriel carried her to a velvet settee as Alexandra and the others slowly came into the amber room. Nicola could not survive such damage to her human body; he knew that. Yet she was young, and strong, and there was still time.

There had to be time.

"Is there a doctor here?" He dropped down with her in his lap, unable to release her, and held her like a child.

"Yeah, me. I'm Alexandra," the woman said, coming to his side.

A breath escaped Nicola's lips but did not return.

"Alexandra." He looked up, desperate. "She is not breathing. Please. Show me what to do."

Cyprien's *sygkenis* pressed her fingertips to Nick's wrist, and then carefully lowered her hand.

"Gabriel," she said very gently, "there's nothing you can do for her now. She's gone. I'm so sorry."

He looked down at Nicola's lacerated face. "You cannot

leave me again. I waited for you. I lived for you. I have only just found you."

Someone—Cyprien, perhaps—touched his shoulder. He ignored it, unable to move, unwilling to release her fragile mortal form. There was no reason to do so. He had nothing left, nothing for which to live.

The touch changed, and Gabriel finally looked up. The blazing colors of the glorious room around him faded from his senses. It seemed right that everything had dulled to a meaningless blur of dull, ugly gray. She had gone and taken his last hope of happiness with her.

He would not allow her to go into the darkness without him. Wherever she was, that was where he had to go. "Kill me."

Michael shook his head.

"Give me a blade, then."

Alexandra made a strange sound, and Michael's gaze shifted to her.

"Not yet, my friend." Cyprien nodded toward Nick.

Gabriel looked down at his beloved's ruined face. The wounds slashed across it were shrinking, the edges pulling together, the raw exposed tissues vanishing.

"So," Alex murmured, fascinated. "That diagnosis sucked."

Watching her heal, Gabriel blanked his mind, until he saw his hand carefully pull aside her jacket, exposing the torn front of her T-shirt. The stab wounds in her chest had also closed and were disappearing.

"She's Kyn." He stared across at Alexandra. "How can this be?"

She shook her head. "Wasn't anything I did this time." She rolled up her sleeve. "But I think I can help her now." She bit her wrist and pressed the wound to Nick's lips.

The younger woman opened her mouth as soon as Alex's blood touched it. She drank and swallowed, and a rosy flush tinted her pale skin under the drying blood on her face.

"That should about do it," Alex said, taking her bloody wrist away.

Nick opened her eyes and pushed out of Gabriel's arms. She staggered as she got to her feet, then found her balance and moved away from him, Alex, and the other Kyn. As soon as she tasted blood on her lips, she rubbed the back of her hand across them.

"She is Darkyn," Marcella said, and breathed in. "But she smells human."

Nick pulled down the shreds of her T-shirt, and then noticed that she was the center of attention. "Stop doing that. Stop looking at me." She pressed a hand to her face, as if to cover what was happening to it.

"Kind of hard to do that," Alex said, "after the show you just gave us. Honey, exactly how long have you been Kyn?"

"I'm not Kyn. I'm not like you. Any of you." Her voice rose to a shout. "I'm human. Do you hear me? *I'm still human.*"

"Okay, you're still human," Alex said reasonably as she got to her feet. "We'll just pretend we never saw you heal from fatal stab wounds and major blood loss in ten seconds flat."

Gabriel tried to go to Nicola, but she backed away from him, and he went still with shock a second time.

"Why didn't you tell me?" he asked.

"Tell you what? I drink blood, I heal fast, and I can't die. There, I told you." She bent down and picked up Leary's gore-smeared knife. "Now get out of my way."

Nick didn't wait for him to move, but went around him. She went past Richard and Michael, past Korvel and Phillipe, and halted in front of one of the niches, taking the small statue of the Virgin Mary from it before moving on to stand in front of Elizabeth. Richard's wife drew back, turning her head away, but Marcella grabbed her and made her face Nick.

"You remember me," Nick said softly. She held up the statue. "And this. Don't you?"

Elizabeth looked down her nose at her. "The statue is mine, but alas, I fear that we have never met."

"Alas, you're a fucking liar." Nick tucked the knife under Elizabeth's chin, pressing it into the soft flesh of her throat. "It was in Hartfordshire, ten years ago. Little dairy farm outside Grandale. You remember. You came to visit my parents one night in June. You came to ask my stepdad about the Golden Madonna. You said it belonged to you."

Elizabeth's expression turned to boredom. "I do not trifle with dairy farmers, and I know nothing about any Madonna. That statue is of the Virgin Mary, and it has been in my possession for over sixty years. Now, would you remove the knife from my neck? I—" She gasped as the sharp blade cut deeper. "Richard, she is deranged. Stop her. Kill her."

"You already did, you bitch." Nick leaned in. "You killed me after you butchered my parents. For this." She shoved the statue in Elizabeth's face.

Gabriel came to stand beside her. "Elizabeth attacked you and your family?"

"She tortured my parents and murdered them. She made me watch while she did it. She made me dig the grave in my mother's rose garden and drag the bodies out to it." Nick smiled. "Only she took too much blood from them, and got a little drunk on it."

Gabriel felt her cold rage building into something worse, but waited, determined to know everything that had resulted in this miracle.

"What else happened, Nick?" Alex asked.

"I got away from her and grabbed my stepdad's shovel," Nick said. "I tried to take her head off with it. It hurt her, but it didn't stop her. Nothing did. She tore open my throat and took a shower in my blood. Then she threw me in the grave. Right on top of my mother's body."

Elizabeth chuckled. "Now I know you are deranged. I would never do such a barbaric thing."

Nick snapped out her arm, and the statue of the Golden

Madonna went flying across the room. It shattered against one of the amber panels and rained in small pieces all over the floor.

Elizabeth's eyes bulged. "How dare you!"

Nick glanced over at Richard. "She your wife?" When he nodded, she said, "She has a scar on her ass. It's dark pink and shaped like a triangle. On the left cheek. Am I right?"

"Yes." Richard regarded Elizabeth. "How does the girl know this?"

Elizabeth shrugged. "Someone told her."

"She doesn't like getting blood on her fancy clothes," Nick told Richard. "She strips down before she does people."

"If I had killed you," Elizabeth said with exaggerated patience, "then why do you still live? My dear, if you wish to deceive us into believing that you are human, not Kyn, then you must invent a better story than this."

"I don't think it's a story, Liz," Alex said. "Nick, when she attacked you, was she wounded?"

"I hit her in the face with a goddamned shovel," Nick said. "What do you think?"

Alex nodded. "I think that, unlike your parents, she nearly drained you dry. You didn't die, Nick, because while she was doing that, she bled on you. She infected you."

"Whatever." Nick didn't seem interested in how she had become Kyn.

"But you don't have *dents acérées*," Gabriel said. "I would have felt them when I kissed you. You cannot possess *l'attrait*, or I would know you by scent. We all would."

"Oh, I have the goods." Nick glanced at him, and the sharp-sweet scent of juniper suddenly colored the air. It was so much like Gabriel's own scent that it stunned him. She smiled, baring fangs that quickly retracted. "I just don't flaunt them. And I can make them go away whenever I want." The echoing scent abruptly vanished.

"She protects herself and lures humans by passing as one of them," Cyprien said. "An interesting talent."

"I'm not one of you," Nick insisted. "I can walk around in daylight. I don't bite people when I can get bagged blood from hospitals. I sure as hell don't butcher them."

"We do not harm humans," Gabriel said.

"Really." She stared into Elizabeth's face. "Then what do you call what she does?"

"If what you say is true, and you have simply mistaken me for the Kyn who took you, you should be grateful," Elizabeth said. "The woman who attacked you compensated you with the gift of immortal life."

"Vampire King?" Nick said softly as she shifted her grip on the blade. "Say good-bye to the wife."

"Wait." Gabriel put his hand over hers so that they both held the knife.

Nick shook her head. "I'm doing it. I've been looking for this sick cunt for ten years. It'll be easier than how my parents died, but she deserves it."

"If this is what you must do," Gabriel said, "then she will die by my hand as well."

Nick didn't say anything, and the blade didn't move deeper into Elizabeth's neck.

"Miss Jefferson, before you cut off my wife's head," Richard said quietly, "I would ask a favor of you. Permit me to punish my wife for her crimes against you and your family."

"So she can live and do it again? Make more like me? Let me think." Nick looked at him. *"No."*

"I will see to it that Elizabeth never has contact with another human for as long as she lives. We live quite a long time, even when we can no longer feed." The high lord's voice remained low and level. "I swear this to you."

"Don't be a fool, Richard," his wife snapped. "She cannot prove any part of her ridiculous story. I've done nothing wrong. She's been sent here by your enemies; can't you see that? I would not be surprised if Cyprien had a hand in this. He turned that leech; he must have the ability to create new Kyn. Kill her and put an end to this."

Nick saw the fear in Elizabeth's wide eyes, and heard it in her sharp voice. "You can really keep her away from humans forever?"

"He can," Gabriel confirmed.

"My husband would never harm me," Elizabeth said, smiling. "He'll do nothing, and you'll be cheated of your revenge."

"You'd rather have me cut off your head than let him deal with you?" Nick didn't wait for an answer, but pulled the knife away. "She's all yours, Your Kingship." She dropped the blade and turned to Gabriel.

He wanted to take her into his arms. He was afraid to touch her. "All this time, and I never guessed."

"I'm just as good at hiding things as I am at finding them." Her eyes scanned the faces around them. "I can't be a part of this, Gabriel. I love you, but . . . I'm sorry." She strode out of the Amber Room.

Gabriel took a moment to disperse the last of the many before he spoke to Michael. "I must go with her."

Cyprien nodded. "Will we see you again?"

"I cannot say." Gabriel could think only of her.

Richard came to him. His eyes, once so alien, were becoming human. "They sent photographs of your body, decapitated, and your head thrust on the spikes of a church gate in Rome. Had I known you still lived, I would never have called off the search."

Doctored photographs. That was all it had taken to convince the high lord of his death.

"There is this computer program called Photoshop, my lord," Gabriel said softly. "You should become acquainted with it. Now I must take my leave of you."

"I will not compel you to live under Kyn rule, not after what has happened to you both," the high lord said. "But know that in this place, you will always have an ally." He performed a bow of deep respect.

Gabriel put his hand on Richard's shoulder for a moment, and then hurried out into the corridor.

Nick was adjusting something on the back wheel of the rental bike and cursing under her breath when Gabriel reached her. "Piece of cheap, run-down Dublin trash."

"We should have brought your bike," he said, stopping a few feet away.

She didn't look at him and said nothing.

"You are not leaving here without me," he continued. "I would have no way to get back to the farm."

"I told you, I can't be a part of this." Nicola stood and wiped her hands on a piece of her shirt. "I'm not like them. I don't want to be like them. You . . . you're like them. You need them. They have mansions and libraries and Mozart. I have a bike and a farm and Nickelback."

"Is Nickelback an American band?"

"Canadian." She stuck her wrench back in her tool kit. "Gabriel, don't try. You know? I'm a peasant. I'm okay with that. You're a nobleman. You need someone like that French chick in the village. I mean, she was hot."

"Marcella is like a sister to me."

She brought up her hands and let them fall. "Okay, so, there are other vampire ladies out there."

"I don't want them. I don't love them." He stepped up to her. "I love you." He took her hands in his. "You went through the change alone. That's never happened to a Kyn before you." As she opened her mouth, he touched her cheek. "It's just a word. But when you came to me, you were seeking something, weren't you?"

"Dreams. I fell in love with a guy from my dreams. It turned out to be you."

"You were looking for me."

"I was *looking* for that fucking bitch in there who killed my parents." Her expression softened. "Yeah, and you. But you're not all green, and you don't have pine needles for hair, and you smell like Christmas."

"I am free of the Kyn." He frowned. "I am homeless and almost penniless as well." He caressed her shoulder. "Perhaps I only want you for your money."

"*Gabriel.*"

"Or I could want you for your body. And your mouth." He kissed it. "And your eyes. And your hair. And your smile." He rested his hand over her left breast. "And your heart."

Their eyes met. Gabriel saw hers warm slowly, timidly, as if she wanted to give him time to change his mind and leave her.

"I will never leave you."

"Fine." She stepped back and handed him the helmet. "Get on. I want to dump this bike as soon as we get to Dublin. You think the vampire king is good for a new Triumph Tiger?"

He waited for her to climb on in front of him, and wrapped his arms around her waist as she kicked up the center stand and took off down the road.

"I think eventually Gabriel and Nicola will come back to the Kyn," Michael Cyprien said. "They need time to be together, and to bond."

"From what I saw in front of the castle yesterday, they need a hotel room." Alexandra lifted her hair off the back of her neck. "Speaking of which . . ."

"I will not detain you." Richard looked down at his hand, which appeared half-human, half-feline. "Dr. Keller—"

"You're covered. I made up the next round of treatments and showed Korvel how to prepare more serum. If you can't trust him, you can't trust anyone." With a decided thump, she placed a small vial case on his desk. "I thought you might like to lock this batch up yourself."

That she had anticipated his request did not surprise him, but that she would grant it did. She had no allegiance to him.

"Will you ever forgive me?" he asked her.

"No." She met his gaze. "But I'm still your doctor. Call me if your symptoms change, you marry another psychotic bitch, or something else goes wrong."

She did care what happened to him. Richard thought of using that, then saw Cyprien's expression and decided against it. "Your generosity humbles me."

"Enjoy the novelty of the experience." She glanced at Michael. "I'll go wait in the car now." She left without looking back.

"That mouth." Richard breathed in a trace of lavender. "I will miss it."

"I will have her call you weekly, if you like. She loves to bend a sympathetic ear." Michael looked at the portrait on the wall behind Richard's desk. "What will you do with Elizabeth?"

"I will keep my promise to Nicola."

His surrogate son gave him a long, measuring look. "I will leave you to it." He executed a respectful bow. "*Adieu, my lord.*"

"*Adieu*, seigneur."

After Michael departed, Richard took Alexandra's advice and carefully placed the alteration treatments in his safe. She had warned him that the rate of transformation could be slow, and consequently that his change back to human form might take months, even years, but he had all the time in the world.

Time had always been Richard's enemy. Now it would serve as his wife's executioner.

Richard left his study and walked over to the west wing. There he found Stefan hard at work with one of the recovering addicts now employed by Richard, filling in the spaces. He waited until there remained but one stone to mortar into place, and then called a halt to the work.

"Go," he told them. "I will do the rest."

Stefan nodded and took the new man's arm. The junkie gave the high lord a quick, uncertain look before leaving with his guard.

Richard inspected the mortar work to assure it was sound and made of the special mixture he had obtained from an old Dublin masonry yard that guaranteed it to last for five centuries or more.

He looked in through the last gap in the stone. The glorious Amber Room remained perfectly intact, except for the addition of some copper manacles welded around a large wooden cross, to which Elizabeth had been attached. She had first been dressed in her finest gown, her hair brushed so that it fell around her face in a cascade of gleaming curls.

Since she was facing eternity imprisoned in the Amber Room, Richard had felt his wife should look her best.

Elizabeth turned her head and saw his eyes looking in at her, and twisted against the copper chains binding her limbs to the wooden cross. The copper band that had been welded over the lower half of her face allowed her to make only outraged sounds in her throat.

In the center of the world's most beautiful room, Orson Leary's remains had been carefully arranged on Elizabeth's velvet settee directly in front of the cross. Beside him was a small pile of broken amber.

Satisfied that his orders had been carried out to the letter, and that his wife would spend whatever remained of her life facing her final victim and watching him rot more quickly than she did, Richard picked up the last stone, applied a generous amount of mortar, and slid it into place.

Please read on for

an excerpt from Lynn Viehl's

EVERMORE
A Novel of the Darkyn

Coming soon from Signet Eclipse

Jayr watched the couples dancing the branle, but only heard the ensemble's music as if she sat somewhere far removed from the ball. The events of the evening seemed to please the guests of the realm, something that should have gratified her. It was her duty to attend to them and the thousand unseen details that ensured their pleasure. Yet here she sat, doing nothing at all. This unwelcome awareness had made her as useless as a moonstruck girl caught between the two cruelest of heart torments, doubt and hope.

It mattered not. Soon, Jayr knew, her wits would return and drag her back to her senses. Soon she would shrug off this appalling paralysis and get on with seeing to her master's guests. Soon—

Byrne's hand came to rest on her shoulder, half on the velvet yoke of her tunic, half on the bare curve of her throat. He leaned over to murmur, "Rob fancies himself a danseur this night."

Locksley might have been performing a string of triple *tours en l'air* and Jayr would have missed them, so absorbed was she by the weight and feel of her master's touch. His soft breath set fire to her cheek; the warmth of his nearness reduced her to ashes. The world dwindled to nothing but Byrne. She felt the length of his arm pressing across her back, and could it be . . . yes, there, the absent stroke of his thumb against her neck. He was petting her.

An idle caress. It means nothing.

Jayr smelled tansy entwined with heather and swallowed against the ache at the back of her throat. Locksley. Byrne had said something about his dancing. "The suzerain has much skill on the floor," she said.

"How can you tell?" He shifted his palm, causing his calluses to delicately chafe the edge of her collarbone. "Have you danced with him?"

"No, my lord. I have not had that privilege." Thank Christ, the ensemble had nearly finished the set. As the branle came to its elegant end, Jayr forced herself from her seat. "I should check on the bloodwine."

Byrne stood, catching her around the waist and turning her toward the politely applauding couples. She expected him to point out some flaw, some error to be corrected, but his hand urged her forward, through the spiral of tables and to the very edge of the dance floor.

Jayr heard muttered Arabic and low snickering, and felt Nottingham's Saracens staring at her. Ridicule's whip straightened her shoulders, and kept panic at bay, even when her master drew her toward him. He stepped back, and then something happened that froze her in place again.

Aedan mac Byrne made a brief but perfect révérence to her.

It had to be a mistake. The suzerain of the realm never showed such regard to his seneschal, his third blade, the eyes at his back. Such a man made révérence only to his lady, whose silk and lace swathed her soft limbs, and whose long, perfumed curls framed her delicate features.

Jayr could not be seen as a lady. She was not even wearing a gown.

"My lord?" Perhaps he made a clever jest. A moment of mockery to amuse the assembly. That had to be it. No wonder the heathens were entertained.

A lord paramount never bowed to his lowly servant.

Byrne said nothing, only taking up her hands in his. He arranged her arms in counterpoint to his before nodding to the leader of the ensemble. They began to play one of

Strauss's pieces, one Jayr should have been able to name,
had her voice and her brains still functioned. Her master
turned her again as he guided her out among the whirling
couples and into what had long ago been a vigorous and
rather silly provincial dance.

He was dancing with her—waltzing, with her.

Jayr could not ask her master if he had gone mad. Moving her feet in the whirling patterns of the dance demanded
much of her concentration, and the rest seemed fixed on
the lacing at the neck of his shirt. She also suspected that
if anyone might lose their wits on this night, it would be
her.

"My lord," she finally forced out, "I am honored, but
perhaps you could exchange me for a more appropriate
partner. Lord de Troyes seems rather ill-matched with his
lady, and I would—"

"Jayr?" He spun her down the length of his arm and
back to his body.

She braced herself against his chest to keep a respectful
space between them. "My lord?"

Byrne seized one of her errant hands and worked his
fingers through hers, locking them together. His arm
pulled her in until their bodies brushed. "Shut up and
dance with me."

"Yes, my lord."

Jayr found no comfort in silence or the waltz. She bus-
ied herself with counting steps and avoiding eyes. It
seemed as if every lord and lady on the floor was gaping at
them. And why should they not? The suzerain of the
Realm held his seneschal in his arms. Among the Kyn,
such a thing had never happened.

Jayr cursed herself for not listening to Alexandra and
donning more feminine attire. She might have looked less
the skinny boy in a gown, and the skirts would have en-
forced a respectable boundary between their bodies. As it
was, his person met hers in the most unseemly places: the
flat of her belly, the small of her back, the front of her

thighs. Little wonder that the waltz had often been condemned in the past as insidious and improper. The intimacy of it, of the constant press of his body to hers, quickly became unbearably erotic.

Behind the torture, a very small part of Jayr hoped that the waltz would never end.

As the music swelled to a giddy madness, Jayr glanced up to see her master's face darken, and followed his gaze. Alexandra, resplendent in an ivory lace gown, laughed as Cyprien lifted her off her feet and kissed her while they still twirled among the other couples.

What would it be like, Jayr thought, to have such love that you did not care who saw you express it? "The seigneur seems blessed in his choice of women," she said before she remembered that she was supposed to be holding her tongue.

Byrne changed direction, leading her through a tangle of couples and into the shadowy end of the floor, far from the sharp ears of those watching from the tables. When a burst of laughter drew the attention of the assembly, Jayr found herself being marched from the floor and around the corner to the empty corridor that led outside to the gardens and herbarium.

"I thank you for the dance, my lord." Jayr stepped out of his hold and straightened her sleeves. "It was most pleasant."

Byrne's broad back blocked out the moonlight streaming through the long, narrow panes of pale blue glass. His scent changed, growing heated and dark. When he put his hand to her throat, Jayr flinched.

"Pleasant, you say?" he asked, his voice dangerously soft.

"I meant enjoyable," she quickly added, feeling his fingers tighten. "Quite enjoyable. You are most accomplished, my lord."

"Pleasant." He walked her backward. "Enjoyable."

She felt cold stone against her shoulders. "I regret that I am not more adept myself. I rarely dance." He had her pinned now, body to body. She averted her face. "My lord, I should return and see to your guests."

"And Rob?" Byrne thrust his hand into her hair, his fingers curling against her scalp. "You will see to him? You will dance with him?"

She glanced up, confused. "Of course. I am happy to see to Suzerain Locksley's desires."

"He makes you happy. Unlike me."

Byrne's scent had fogged her thoughts; surely she had not heard him correctly. "My lord, it is not for you to make me happy."

"Is it not?" He lifted her in the same way Cyprien had Alexandra, sliding her up the stone wall until their eyes were level. "Did I not make you, Jayr?" His gaze moved from her eyes to her mouth. "Did you not swear your oath to me? Do you not belong to me, body and blood?"

Jayr felt drunk on his scent and touch, so much that she lost the last shred of her composure and shuddered uncontrollably against him as she told him the truth. "I am yours, my lord. Do with me what you will."

Byrne bent his head to hers, his long garnet hair spilling against her cheek as his lips touched hers. The contact made her jerk with shock, but he held her in place, his mouth slanting over hers as he deepened the kiss with his teeth and tongue.

Jayr had dreamed of this moment and what she might feel, but those paltry fantasies had not prepared her for how Byrne would take her mouth. He took and bit and thrust, reveling in the claiming, allowing her no retreat. The heat and scent of his passion smashed over her, reducing her to a clinging, moaning wreck writhing between his arms. In desperation she seized his shoulders, clutching at them as she fought her body's shameful response. His body became an oak, as still and unmovable, to which she had been chained. And there, pressing hard between her thighs—thrusting against her crotch—the heavy, stunning weight of his erection.

The ferocious hunger of his mouth eased away. "Mother of God." Byrne sounded as astounded as she felt. "What am I doing to you?" He carefully lowered her until she stood on her own again.

"You kissed me." She saw the pain and regret in his eyes, and cold, clammy horror crawled along her spine. She made her bruised mouth form a smile. "Needs are like cherished guests, my lord. At times they may be inconvenient, but one should never allow them to go unattended for too long."

"You are right." He looked disgusted now. "Jayr—"

"Your guests are waiting. Excuse me, my lord." She made her bow and ran.